For my
very loyal friend,
Jean FRANCE, of many
years who is an impor
true character in the
All good thoughts—

Los Angeles 2008

MW00944343

CLOSE ENCOUNTERS OF THE WORST KIND

Phillip Lambro

CLOSE ENCOUNTERS OF THE WORST KIND is an unconventional and startlingly truthful autobiographical memoir by the distinguished American composer-conductor Phillip Lambro. It includes little known highly personal and candid recollections and recounting of witty evocative situations and stories which Phillip Lambro has personally experienced during his interesting and varied life with an unbelievable diverse cast of famous personages ranging from Salvador Dali, Frank Sinatra, Jack Benny, Huntington Hartford, Howard Hughes, and Roman Polanski; to John F. Kennedy, Sylvia Plath, Harold Lloyd, Richard Nixon, Jack Nicholson, Alfred Hitchcock, Steven Spielberg, Antonio Carlos Jobim, and many more.

TABLE OF CONTENTS

DALI IN LAMBROVISION

I encountered Salvador Dali accidentally through his wife Gala at a social gathering which Huntington Hartford gave in New York City in his trilevel penthouse mansion at One Beekman Place around 1962. I had been acquainted with Huntington Hartford and used to play tennis with him occasionally indoors at the posh paneled River Club.

Hartford was interested in a painting by Ilja Jefimovitch Repin (a Russian impressionist Rembrandt) entrusted to me by a Swiss associate entitled *Reception At The Court Of The Czar* an oil on canvas authenticated, signed and dated 1894 which we kept in a New York City bank vault. Ilja Jefimovitch Repin, in my opinion, is probably one of the most underrated impressionist painters of all time. With the exception of the painting *The Cossaks Write The Sultan A Letter Of Rejection* which is hanging in the Louvre in Paris, the majority of Repin's paintings are in Russia at the Museum in Moscow. The whole East Wing of The Moscow Museum Of Art was transformed into a special Repin Museum where most of his drawings, oils, pictures and sketches are housed. Had Repin's work been allowed to leave Russia, he would have had a name as significant as Renoir in the West. I had not been familiar with Repin's work, but when I saw this painting I was unusually affected; it was just magnificent. As a painter Repin's work is every bit as gratifying as the celebrated French impressionists. However, with exceptionally few of his paintings outside of Russia (in the International Art Market) there isn't the active sales trading for Repin which would cause escalating prices, interest and publicity in his work. I think probably there are fewer than fifty of anything Repin ever sketched or painted outside of the former Soviet Union.

Huntington Hartford was attracted to this painting and that is how we became acquainted. Subsequently when he found out that I played tennis he invited me a few times to the ultra exclusive River Club on the East Side which had an excellent indoor Har-Tru clay court and an indoor swimming pool.

Afterward, Hartford asked me to several of his parties and at this particular one a strange looking woman (who reminded me of a female Rasputin) came up to within about five feet and pointed her finger directly at me and said, in the company of other people whom I assumed were her friends, "This young man very great artist. He has face of great artist. You are artist, no?"

I said, "Well, I'm a composer, conductor, pianist; I guess I'm an artist. Who are you?"

She said, "I Gala." At first, I did not grasp who Gala was the way she spoke with her gentle thick accent. Of course, I had heard of and had seen Gala in Dali paintings, but I did not associate her immediately with Dali until

1

she said, "I want you meet my husband, Dali. You know, Dali? No..?"

I said, "Oh yes, I'm a great admirer of his fantastic paintings. He's one of my favorite artists."

So Salvador Dali was in the next room and I met him. And after we conversed during the passage of the evening, he eventually offered me his telephone number.

Dali used to invite me to Knoedler's Art Gallery to view some of his paintings which he had shipped from his studio and home in Port Lligat, Spain where he lived mainly in the summer. He told me that his paintings were always rolled up into a large tube suspended in air by two wires and shipped in the hold of a transoceanic vessel as he did not want anything touching his canvases.

Dali also advised me that he never painted in the United States. In fact, an amusing incident occurred a few social gatherings later. I was speaking with Dali about the possibility of composing a symphonic work after one of his paintings. He initially liked the idea. I tried, unsuccessfully, to get someone to commission me to do the work for The Philadelphia Orchestra (which had performed my music) and I was envisaging a major orchestral piece based upon Dali's exceedingly large surrealist painting entitled *The Battle Of Tetuan* which measured 10 feet by 12 and 1/2 feet which Huntington Hartford had commissioned for his museum. I wanted to put *The Battle Of Tetuan* painting above The Philadelphia Orchestra as I conducted the world premiere. Dali originally thought that that was a great idea, because you could hear the music and you could see the picture; but subsequently he became fearful that the orchestral sound vibrations might affect the painting's pigment.

And so there I was discussing *The Battle Of Tetuan* with Dali when this conspicuous New York dilettante approached us and interrupted our dialogue by saying, "Oh, Salvador, how are you, my dear. You must come over and have dinner with us this week." Dali turned only his head ever so slightly to his right and said, "Madame, Dali never eat dinner," and then returned directly to the conversation we were having about *The Battle Of Tetuan*. (There was also this young natural looking blonde super model listening between us and responding to our colloquy by the name of Andrea Dromm; she was a rather popular photographer's print ideal and eventually became the girl in the TV airline commercial with a bathing suit lying on a tropical beach saying, "Is this any way to run an airline? You bet it is!") The affected dilettante endeavored to interject again, "Well, you must come over, Salvador, and have tea."

"Madame, Dali never drink tea," he said without looking at the socialite.

"Salvador, would you like to come over for brunch?" Then Dali turned in a disconcerted manner and said to the lady, "Madame, Dali never eat United States; only come United States sleep and make money."

With that, the dilettante left.

At that same aggregation, a young female socialite came over to us and started speaking rapidly with Dali who didn't seem to comprehend what the youthful lady was saying. As the presumptuous debutante kept repeating herself, she spoke faster and louder which caused Dali to back off from the girl. I said, "Miss, you don't have to yell; he's not deaf; he just doesn't understand you. Speak slower."

There were always an abundance of models in Huntington Hartford's life. At one time, he owned the Plaza Five Modeling Agency in Manhattan. These callow women attired in seductive dresses, were eleven feet tall, flat chested, with five pairs of eyelashes, exceptionally long fingernails, and thirteen inch up-swirled hair which looked like Brillo pirouettes. This is the type of paradigm Huntington Hartford seemed to relish. After I got to know him, I found out that Hartford definitely had an aversion to large busted women; which brings us to another entertaining incident which I concocted. Several bacchanals later (about January 1964 shortly after I conducted the recording of my first film score with the New York Philharmonic) Hartford invited me to a dinner party (which Dali also attended) given for Richard Nixon. At the time, I was actually friendlier with Hartford's twenty-two year old wife, Diane, who took a sincere interest in my career, because Huntington Hartford really knew little about music or the arts even though he financially sustained what certain people impressed upon him to support. He actually had no arts vision of his own, but thankfully he became moved by those who knew that Salvador Dali was a great painter; so Hartford sporadically invested $250,000, or so into one of Dali's canvases. Conversely, Hartford winnowed a million dollars into Show Magazine: The Magazine Of The Arts which I used to refer to in his presence as Shoe Magazine and truthfully told him that his magazine rarely had anything to do with what was actually going on in the arts.

Prior to the dinner party for Richard Nixon, Hartford asked me, "Are you going to bring a girl?"

"Yes." I said.

"Don't bring one too buxom," he said. Hartford wanted to remind me to escort a possible transfused mannequin candidate for his Plaza Five Modeling Agency.

By chance, I had met this damsel on Fifth Avenue who turned out to be a working Playboy bunny and who was insatiably curvaceous. I said to her, "Look, how would you like to go with me to an exclusive dinner party being given for Richard Nixon?"

3

She said, "You're not a spotter, are you?" I said, "What's a spotter?" She said "Oh, Hefner has these spotters and they say things like that to entice us to go out and we're not supposed to go out on dates with strangers, or we'll get fired." I said, "No, no, I'm not a spotter."

Well, as it turned out, this maiden, whose name was Lisa Aromi, was the sister-in-law of Life magazine photographer Paul Duckworth who had photographed me several weeks previously, and she nearly fell over when she found out that I knew him.

And so I said, "For the party, get into the tightest fitting gown that you can find with a real plunging neckline."

There were about forty guests which Richard Nixon was receiving prior to dinner.

I purposely made certain that we were the last ones in line with Lisa behind me. Hartford introduced me as a young, talented composer (I don't know how he knew since he had never heard any of my music) but anyway, he presented me as such after which I had a slight conversation with Richard Nixon about the fact that he played the piano and had composed some pieces. Nixon told me that he was a fellow member of ASCAP: American Society Of Composers Authors & Publishers. I said that I had heard him play one of his compositions on *The Tonight Show* and thought he performed his piano work rather well. And for a nonprofessional, he actually did. I think out of all the United States Presidents, what other problems Richard Nixon may have had, I know that he was a better pianist than Harry Truman.

I addressed Lisa to both Nixon and Hartford. Hartford's jaw dropped as he turned Bolshevik red, struggling to keep his lethargic composure because of his ostensible aversion to any female with sizable mammary glands.

I could tell that Richard Nixon was altogether struck by Lisa's dark eyed magnetic looks as he said, "I'm very pleased to meet you, Lisa; very pleased," peripherally examining her alluring cleavage.

The dinner party occurred at Hartford's One Beekman Place three floored twenty-two room penthouse where it was significantly apparent that you had to have committed a sin in society in order to be able to live there. These were inordinately large exclusive two and three level mansion homes within the framework of an apartment building. I believe one of the Rockefellers lived there as did a number of other super rich individuals.

About an hour later, I had the opportunity to chat a few moments privately with Richard Nixon. At that time, I was utterly surprised to find Nixon to be a personable, natural, intelligent, and totally relaxed individual because, in person, he bore little resemblance to his media image. When he appeared through the conduits of television, radio and the press, Richard Nixon's real personality somehow mutated into a rather washed out cardboard facsimile of the knowledgeable and interesting man I had met.

I asked Nixon if he had any intention of running for the Presidency once more. To my surprise, he told me that his only interest now was practicing law within his New York City firm and that he had no plan of ever running for Public Office again. Well, even though that was not to have been the case, Ladies and Gentlemen of the Jury, when Richard Nixon spoke to me, I absolutely believed him.

Hartford's living room overlooked the East River adjacent to the United Nations. One of his tall slender brunette Plaza Five Models was sitting at the end of the divan gazing vacuously out of the window into the moonlit night. I decided to sit down in the middle of the couch with Lisa, who was also a brunette, to my right.

Salvador Dali came up to me and said, "Good evening, composer." Dali would never say, "Hello, Phillip" or "Hello, Lambro." He would always refer to me as "Artist" or "Composer." He was wearing his customary dark dress jacket, flamboyant gold embroidered silk vest, striped formal trousers, black patent leather shoes, and with his mustache going up like two perpendicular fencing foils, he fervently held his exotic gold knobbed inlaid cane.

Dali stood in front of me. I was still sitting in the middle of the sofa, near the flattened Plaza Five Model with her thirteen inches of up-swept black hair and five pairs of eyelashes who continued to just stare vacantly into space with an extended cigarette holder. Lisa Aromi, my amply endowed brunette resumed smiling to my right as Dali, contemplating both females, said pointing to the Plaza Five Model, "Black veddy nice... Black veddy nice, I like paint." Then aiming his cane toward Lisa at the other end of the divan said, "Black also veddy nice, I like paint". Dali pondered both young ladies again (in reverse and forward) with Lisa widely beaming at Dali, and the Plaza Five Model deliberately ignoring him. Then Dali suddenly said to Lisa, with his arm extended, "Here, Dali let you hold cane; in five minutes make you veddy intelligent." So there was Lisa happily possessing Salvador Dali's cane, as Dali went off to converse with some of the other guests. Afterward, Dali returned and said to Lisa, "Now you veddy intelligent, please give Dali back cane."

Dali telephoned me a few times, and you would have to know it was he because (like Leopold Stokowski) he never announced himself over the telephone. In fact, Dali told me that Stokowski visited him once many years ago in Port Lligat, Spain uninvited and unannounced. He said, "Stokowski veddy fantastique with white gloves, double breasted pin stripe suit; marvelous... come Dali home Port Lligat and say nothing; in hallway, just lie down on Dali

Rhinoceros couch, fold arms like dead man and go to sleep."

Dali said, "You should see Stokowski sleep; sleep veddy beautiful, veddy fantastique, with arms crossed and white gloves; like dead."

And although I do not recall my ever mentioning Dali to Stokowski, I do recollect Dali mentioning this Stokowski episode to me.

Interestingly enough, Salvador Dali actually did not care very much about music. He never openly said so, but I could tell by observing him. On occasion, I used to see Dali in a Carnegie Hall box seat at usually one of the Hurok events. I particularly remember him one evening at Nathan Milstein's violin recital there where Milstein played one of the most illustrious concerts I have ever heard any violinist give. Milstein was in exceptional technical and musical form that evening as Dali was just daydreaming into space and obviously not receiving this brilliant display of virtuoso music making. On several other occasions I could sense that Salvador Dali was not triggered by music at all. His spheres of interest seemed totally occupied by the visual aspects of life; including human beings. In fact, when my commercial debut concert recording was released around 1972 (where I conducted *Ramiro Cortes Meditation for String Orchestra*, my *Structures for String Orchestra* and my *Music For Wind, Brass & Percussion*) I sent Dali a complimentary copy. All he talked about (I don't believe he ever played the disc) was the jacket cover art work which consisted of a five color separation photo of color chemicals exploding. Dali seemed to like the album cover as he would sometimes refer to me as "Oh yes, composer of explosion; composer explosion."

Dali would never refer to himself while speaking in the first person as "I" or "me", just Dali in the third person. One evening I was conversing with Dali over the telephone as he suddenly said, "Does composer love gold?" I paused a moment and said, "Yes, Composer likes gold."

"Ah, now Dali know you veddy great composer."

I said, "Why?" "

"Because gold, alchemy. You know alchemist? Alchemist veddy great artists Renaissance period. Veddy creative people. Therefore, gold...alchemy; alchemy...creation. Therefore, gold veddy good for creative spirit."

I think this was the main rationale for Salvador Dali's quenchless passion toward accumulating as much money as he could: because Dali perceived gold as fuel for his surrealistic creativity. Inwardly I did not wish to agree with Dali because it had always been quite apparent to me in our materialistic society that the concept of money as a medium of exchange had never really worked. If you don't understand or believe me, just examine the horrendous financial deficits of Russia and the United States not to mention other less fortunate countries and our accelerated and staggering world wide overpopulation and pollution. In reality, money and the concept of money is the result of an unenlightened and primitive exploitative society which has been unquestionably the monumental scientific, artistic, social and humanitarian impediment of mankind. The solution to money is quite simple: control the birth rate whereby two people may not have more than two children; thus equalling the death rate, and enabling us to erase the profit motive (eradicating ninety percent of valueless and detrimental items continually imposed upon society) resulting in a sociological order where advanced machines are at the service of men and women and where everyone may have the best of everything.

I remember Dali asking me about this new acquaintance of mine, Lester Avnet (the owner of Avnet Inc.) who had proudly shown me his collection of impressionist and contemporary paintings including Boudin oil panels and Giacometti statues and drawings which adorned his spacious offices in the Time-Life Building like posters and ash trays to the ambivalence of his secretaries, workers and executives.

Dali said of Lester Avnet, "Oh, collector. Dali love Collectors. Collector has lot of money? Has lot of gold?"

I said, "Oh yes, he's very wealthy. He owns Avnet Electronics."

"Bring to Dali preview."

Although Dali was attracted to all kinds of intriguing people, he was primarily interested in wealthy art collectors.

I did eventually introduce Lester Avnet to Dali, over the telephone, but Avnet revealed to me that the painting he would have liked to have had Dali create for him would have been where Dali painted one of his famous voluptuous nude female virgins with large breasts and buttocks. Avnet, I could tell, was referring to Dali's 1954 oil on canvas *Young Virgin Auto-Sodomized By Her Own Chastity* which is in the collection of Hugh Hefner, Playboy Enterprises, Los Angeles. However, Avnet feared that his wife would probably divorce him if he did that, so he said that he would have to forego any thoughts of commissioning a canvas from Dali.

I knew Salvador Dali fairly well from the end of 1962 through January 1964. And when I left New York City the end of January 1964 for Los Angeles and, largely due to the fact that I was rarely in New York City during the winter for more than a couple of days and never in Port Lligat, Spain during the summer, I did not see Dali again for quite a long time. Then in April of 1976, I had to spend a week in New York City on some futile concert management and music publishing contracts (which turned out similar to what poor Mozart went through with Hoffmeister; but unlike Mozart, I managed to get out of these agreements a year later) so, even though I was habitually occupied, I thought I should telephone Dali toward the last few days of my trip at the St. Regis Hotel (55th and Fifth Avenue) where he always stayed in New York City and see if he still remembered me.

If you're wondering why I waited until the end of my journey to telephone Dali, you must understand that to be a composer and concert musician (and even human being) in the designs of our present order, where everything is predicated upon "how much money will it make?" rather than "how functional or how truly invaluable is this?" has always hindered me from creating and accomplishing many of the inestimable entities I wish to contribute to this thing we call humanity. Consequently, like most genuine artists, I was busy with trying to convince people in the artistic validity of my ideas and projects rather than being allowed to do them. For example, I was endeavoring to form a major international music publishing corporation where all styles of exemplary music and quality educational music would be accepted without authors having to be subjugated to the political, financial and homosexual harassing maneuvers I had witnessed others go through while I was Assistant Director Of Publications at G. Schirmer. I was also trying to acquire a good concert manager for my guest conducting and I was attempting to interest CBS Records and other recording executives in allowing me to record some unique and unknown music. I was struggling to persuade certain people (through the aid of jet-set physician Dr. Louis Scarrone whom I had also met through Dali and Huntington Hartford) to investigate Dr. Wilburn Henry Ferguson's natural cancer therapeutic Amitosin (which shall be covered within my next book) where at a concentrated dosage level of 200 micromilliliters laboratory documentation exists to support that Amitosin totally prevents cancer cell proliferation. And, my Hollywood based film-scoring agent, Paul Kohner, was in New York City at that time to help with the promotional opening of his client's (Ingmar Bergman's) film *Face To Face* and he wanted me there to meet some people in the lobby of the Beekman Theater. I think I shook hands with Dino DeLaurentis who reminded me more of an Italian delicatessen owner than a motion picture producer; he eventually made my observation a reality about a decade later in Beverly Hills, California. Although, I had liked some of Bergman's earlier films, I wasn't particularly taken by this picture about conspicuously disturbed women; although I did appreciate the remarkable mechanical and technical aspects from the acting and directing, to the cinematography and lighting. Paul Kohner invited me after the premiere to a quiet, but animated dinner at the Hotel Pierre in the company of two delightful women and a man from the Swedish press, and actresses Bibi Andersson and Liv Ullman. I remember, in particular, that the quite formal waiter was giving me a difficult time with my order which prompted Paul Kohner to have his little fun by informing everyone with his mesmeric Austrian accent about my being "a Japanese Zen Macrobiotic and he eats all these strange little seaweeds and things," which caused a lot of Swedish and English inter-translation and bantering.

Bibi Andersson, who was sitting next to me, endeavored to tease me by asking, "How does it feel to be the only American among all these Swedes?"

I told her that after watching all the lunacy in *Face To Face* it felt reassuring to know that she and Ullman could have an ordinary good time.

"Oh," Andersson said, "we actresses only do those insane things for the cinema. We never do those things in real life."

Having watched these two ladies innumerable times in Swedish films over the years, one thing was entirely apparent that evening: they seemed quite different, indeed. Although, my estimation of Ullman lowered considerably several years later after I read an interview she gave to the Los Angeles Times where she was quoted as having offered to donate $250,000 of her personal savings to Robert Evans so he could finish one of his critical Celluloid disasters. In view of Ullman's tearful crusades to raise money for the starving children of the world, I thought that that exhibited rather ill judgment and poor taste on her part.

I rang up Dali that Saturday morning at the St. Regis Hotel and he came to the telephone in his low Baritone, "Ahh-looowwww."

He remembered me. "Ah, yes, yes; now Dali remember: composer explosion," he said. "Come and meet Dali."

"What time?" I asked.

"Seven o'clock, St. Regis lobby."

That evening I called his suite from the lobby and he came down about ten minutes later attired in Daliesque dark cape and suit jacket, rococo gold embroidered vest, striped formal trousers, patent leather shoes, and rapier cane.

I was dressed in a dark blue French suit, and I smiled, "Do you remember me?"

He looked at me for a long moment then said, "Now, Dali remember face veddy well. Dali remember."

I asked where Gala was and Dali informed me that she would be joining us shortly as he ushered me into the St. Regis dining room where about half a dozen people were waiting for him. Dali introduced me to everyone as "Composer fantastic, Lambro." I was a little startled because it was the first time I had ever heard Dali utter my name.

I sat down not too close to the table, and Dali seated himself next to me; about two feet away from the table, with his arms folded; his hands resting

9

on top of his perpendicular cane.

Dali and I were rather fascinated by a European gigolo in his mid-thirties sitting at the table smoking a cigarette quite affectedly with an overly cosmetic young New York female model companion snuggled close to him as the gigolo recounted his international exploits. He had on a handsomely tailored beige gabardine suit, and his olive skin and coal black hair were heavily greased. Evidently, Dali knew some of the wealthy women whom the gigolo was vocalizing about because the gigolo would say, "Ah, yes, Dali, she gave me this gold cigarette case and these diamond gold cuff-links I am wearing, and many other things." As the gigolo went on, I could not refrain from quietly laughing; especially as he was discussing the prices of each trinket and suit, and material conquests he had vanquished from all these prominent gentlewomen. I had never seen Dali so involved in a conversation before as he asked the gigolo some occasional questions; especially what the gigolo's consort that evening really thought about all of this.

"Oh, Dali," the gigolo said in his thick accent giving his model-companion a short kiss, "this is my real girl friend; she understands."

At that moment, Gala came in and joined us. She also remembered me.

Several other people subsequently arrived and after a few moments of inconsequential seven part contrapuntal chatter (I was trying to absorb everyone's conversation at once) Dali suggested that we leave. Now, you must understand, Ladies and Gentlemen of the Jury, I had not the slightest idea of where we were going, or what we were going to do, until we reached the front sidewalk of the St. Regis Hotel where I saw, to my astonishment, a convoy of black limousines with chauffeurs lined up like airport taxis. Dali told me that we were all departing to an Art Exhibit as he assigned everyone to a limousine directing us with his notorious cane. I was put in the rear of the limousine directly in front of the St. Regis entrance with the gigolo and his model girl friend. Seated up-front next to the chauffeur was a jovial middle aged slightly rotund receding American husband in a rather poorly tailored business suit with the most incongruous necktie imaginable. On the little rear seat facing me was his equally congenial furriered and emerald satined wife both of whom had unmistakable mid-west American accents and down-home vocabulary punctuated with occasional country aphorisms which endeared me to them. Of course I did not like riding in the limousine as I have always had an aversion to motoring in large passenger cars and Rolls Royces since people (who would not ordinarily pay any attention to you if you were wheeling in an average automobile) suddenly become curious as to who you are, what you might have, where you've been, and where you are going.

To the consternation of the gigolo and his quintessential girl friend, I asked the chauffeur to open the electronic glass partition of the limousine a little more so that we could all speak with our new friends from middle America. I found out that they were from Ohio; and since I had taken a commercial train ride once while in the military from Arkansas to Virginia, I brought out to them how much I had enjoyed seeing their state and spending a couple of days there. Of course, I had a lot of fun with the snobbish international jet-set gigolo and his vacant Revlon by asking them if they had ever been to Ohio, and doing everything naturally possible to bring them into the conversation. The gigolo looked at me incredulously from time to time as if to say, 'how could you, a well known concert musician, associate yourself with these bourgeois?'

Actually, I found our Ohioans more fun than the gigolo and his mannequin.

I knew there had to be a reason why these mid-westerners were there because if I knew one thing about Salvador Dali it was that everything he did, he did for a reason; whether personal, artistic, or material.

"Well, I declare," the lady from Ohio said to me. "You must come and visit us the next time you're in Ohio."

"I'd love to," I said.

I asked them if they liked Dali's paintings and they both responded excitedly (like happy youngsters) that Dali was their "favorite painter in the whole wide world" and matter-of-factly added that they had several of his "pictures" hanging in their home.

"Prints?" asked the gigolo sarcastically.

"Why, heck they'd better not be prints," exclaimed the jolly man from Ohio. "I paid an awful lot of money to Dali for those pictures."

The gigolo and his blonde paradigmatic immediately became interested in our familiars as I continued to smile broadly.

I found out later that our Ohioans were from Cleveland and had made a gigantic fortune in plastics. Their names were Reynolds and Eleanor Morse, and they owned the largest personal Salvador Dali collection in the world, and ultimately opened a Salvador Dali Museum.

Our limousine stopped, and I remembered getting out onto a narrow and dimly lit street with what looked like old brick warehouses on each side. 'What kind of a gallery is this?' I recalled thinking to myself. It loomed more like one of those London side streets where Jack-The-Ripper used to stalk his prey.

If my life depended on it, I don't think I could accurately tell you where it was; save to say, that I believe it was somewhere near Greenwich Village, but closer to the Soho District of New York City.

Our chauffeur did not know the exact address, but he managed to flag down the preceding limousine and the other driver directed us into a double doorway with a steep stairwell. Eventually, we came to a broad landing and then through a large entrance into a huge brightly lit reconverted factory room which I could see must have been used at the turn of the century to prematurely age hundreds of garment workers. But now it was an art gallery with ubiquitous green plants everywhere and even hanging from the ceiling trying to emulate The Hanging Gardens Of Babylon. There were all kinds of indirect track lighting, and from all the well dressed rank and file and fashion models who were there flashing champagne glasses as well as their lip-gloss smiles (there must have been over 250 people in attendance) I had been led to believe that this preview had been sponsored by Harper's Bazaar or one of those leading fashion magazines.

I was informed that the canvases on exhibit were the latest rage in the 1976 New York Art Market. The movement was called "Op-Art" and having sought out one of the artists represented, I found out that this specific technique usually involved the securing of a 35mm slide of common subject matter such as the inside of a Corvette engine or an old color photo of Marilyn Monroe, and by enlarging and charting it onto a particular canvas, the artist would then oil paint over the photographic blowup which was designed to give the paintings a neorealistic look.

Dali was slowly ambulating around looking at all the paintings, and after a while I went over to him as he stood in front of one picture contemplating it with deep concentration; pressing the head of his rococo cane against his lips.

"Composer, look at this." Dali said. "Do you like this painting?"

The medium sized canvas was of a summer beach scene with a bubble gum machine which had a little rust on the bottom rim taking up most of the lower right foreground, and in the background were people lying on the beach and a girl walking along the shore past a cabana under a sunny blue sky.

I said, "It's all right, but I'm not thrilled about any of this style of painting. They're using photography as a crutch for mechanics and technique."

"You are right," Dali said. "Well, painting not great; not veddy good; but rust on bubble gum machine fantastic." And so Dali asked the director of the gallery who was following Dali like a faithful puppy dog, "I want meet artist. Where is artist of this painting?"

The gallery workers scrambled around and after a couple of minutes found the artist; a pale, but sturdy young gentleman of medium height and thinning light brown hair; probably in his early thirties with a ruffled cotton shirt and worn blue jeans amid everyone else in their evening apparel. The artist seemed flabbergasted by the fact that out of all the painters represented here the great surrealist master Salvador Dali summoned him.

Dali said to the beaming young painter, "Are you artist of this painting?"

"Yes I am," said the young man.

"Dali like veddy much rust. Dali not like other part of painting, but rust, you are veddy great painter to do this rust. To do this rust, veddy difficult. This take terrific technique."

Dali encouraged the young artist to continue to paint and refine his systems. And the appreciative painter thanked Dali profusely.

I met a couple of models that evening whom I would have liked to have had an affair with; but since I was leaving within a couple of days, I just gave them my Los Angeles telephone numbers and told them to ring me up if they were ever on the West Coast. I never heard from any of them.

We stayed another forty-five minutes and it was getting to be about ten o'clock so we all decided to leave. I was surprised that Dali stayed as long as he did.

On the way back to the St. Regis Hotel I went with Dali and Gala in their limousine. I sat on the little back seat which folded out in front of Dali and Gala. I recall liking the sensation of riding in reverse because as we spoke I could peripherally see where we had been rather than where we were going. Gala asked me what I thought of the exhibit, and I advised her that I felt that most of these artists were basically commercial graphic designers instead of true painters because they were only painting over photographs, and that Op-Art (as far as I was concerned) was only a passing hallucination given too much attention by dilettante art traffickers.

As we sped along the East River, I informed Dali that I had been looking a long time for good quality large photo reproductions of his major paintings as I was disappointed in the manner which lithographs and etchings of his works were being reproduced because they did not reflect the faithful brilliance of his craftsmanship. I cited that I had always wanted a large photo reproduction of his *Christ Of Saint John Of The Cross* which is housed in the Glasgow Art Gallery and Museum, and the fact that people should be able to enjoy detailed photo facsimiles of his actual works rather than inferior lithographs or costly etchings of these paintings where the elements, color, draftsmanship, and perspective of his artistry is completely washed out. I told Dali that I only had found one drab photo duplicate of *Christ Of Saint John Of The Cross* in London and one that was less dull which I purchased in New York City and had framed. I said that I had also found a pretty good photo reproduction of The Last Supper so I suggested to him that he not allow these flimsy art merchandisers to water down his work and not sign anymore lithographs and etchings, but only sign genuine first rate five color separation photo reproductions of his originals. I further offered to introduce Dali to my good friends Phil and Steve Sugarman (owners of Printer's Inc. in North Hollywood, California) who in 1973 were assigned by the J. Paul Getty Museum to make large brilliant five color photo replications of the favorite paintings housed at the Getty Museum in Malibu, California which they sell reasonably to the public even to this day at their new location.

"Oh you know, Dali do not care," he sighed rather dejectedly; and did his breath smell. "Dealers come to Dali; pay Dali money and Dali sign."

"But you should care," I stressed. "You're one of the greatest painters this planet has ever produced. How many people can afford to go to the Glasgow Museum and see your original painting? But thousands can appreciate the work if you sign a superior color photo reproduction which shows everything in detail."

Yes, but Dali cannot control," he said. "Museum owns picture."

"But you have influence," I said. "You can control the reproductions which they come and ask you to sign. Tell these art dealers that you will only sign and approve faithful reproductions of your paintings."

Gala was agreeing with me, but Dali (although he was mildly interested in Phil and Steve Sugarman's process; especially when I mentioned the name of J. Paul Getty) I could tell was resigned to the enterprising seduction of money.

I did have Phil Sugarman write to Dali that summer in Port Lligat, Spain but Phil later advised me that he had never heard from him.

Even though I could see that Dali was in relatively good constitution for his age, macrobiotically speaking, I noticed that his condition was not especially positive and that serious illness lay ahead. His especially unpleasant breath made me change the subject to food.

"How are you eating, Dali?" I asked. "Are you eating enough natural grains and vegetables? You must take care of yourself," I said. "I think you may be consuming too much animal food. You still have much to accomplish and health is important."

Gala nodded in agreement; and Dali pursed his lips together and nodded from left to right as if to wonder how I knew what he had been eating. Because I do not believe that anyone ever saw Dali eat in public; even though he wanted his following to think that he ate the Shah Of Iran's personally fed Pheasants mixed with Quail Eggs, Caviar and Rhinoceros Milk.

The remainder of the conversation stayed upon the fact that I had missed them both all these years, but as a concert composer it was easier for me to struggle in California rather than New York City since everything was less expensive and I needed the yin and yang of Pacific vegetation. I also informed the Dalis that one day I hoped to visit them in Port Lligat. Unfortunately, with the vicissitudes of my musical and humanitarian goals I was never able to do so.

Earlier that evening I had asked Gala, "You know, I've known you for so many years, but you and Dali never speak Spanish. Why is that?" They either spoke a fractured English or French, but I never heard them speak Spanish. Gala disclosed that Dali had been agitated with the Spanish government over something she did not wish to elaborate upon, and even though they lived in Spain during the summers Dali did not choose to verbalize in Spanish unless it was absolutely imperative. However, the real reason I believe was that Gala (who had always reminded me of a female Rasputin) was indeed, as I was to discover later, of Russian birth and was more fluent in French and English rather than Spanish.

As soon as we returned to the front of the St. Regis Hotel, I went back to the other limousine to say goodbye to Reynolds and Eleanor Morse whom I actually relished meeting because they were so festive and unaffected.

Dali suddenly grabbed me by the arm, taking me off to the side, and said, "Come... you take ultraviolet home..."

At first I thought Dali wanted me to take home some sort of an ultraviolet radiation treatment. So I said, "I never take ultraviolet."

"Ultraviolet. You take ultraviolet home," he said again.

I said, "What? What ultraviolet?"

Dali took me by the arm toward one of the other limousines behind us and said, "Ultraviolet here."

And lo and behold there was this attractive brunette, who looked about thirty-eight, with strong blue eyes, and nice breasts posturing all alone in the back seat of the limousine dressed in a satin evening gown whom I had seen momentarily speaking with Dali at the crowded exhibit, and who had glanced at me and then seemed to have disappeared.

"This composer, Lambro...He take you home...You go with Ultraviolet," Dali said.

I was a bit astonished and bewildered because this Ultraviolet thing seemed quite comely and I was wondering what Dali and she were suggesting. Did he want me to sexually service her? I mean, he could have gotten the gigolo for that. But maybe since the gigolo was with his real girlfriend, Dali thought of me. All kinds of episodes were bolting through my brain at Daliesque speeds; especially, since I had to get up early the next morning and catch the train to Dix Hills and visit my old University of Miami buddy Nelson Case Jr.

and his family. Nelson and I had been low ranking members of the famous undefeated University of Miami Tennis Team 1953-1955; and he had been the producer of the first film I had ever scored (*Energy On The Move*) and since I had been the Best Man at his wedding, I could not very well come to New York and not see him. Plus Earl Price (at that time Head of CBS International Records) was a champion of my music and was to introduce me to Soprano Judith Blegen after her Carnegie Hall concert with the Johann Strauss Ensemble that following evening.

"I'm very pleased to meet you," I said to Ultraviolet. "But tomorrow, even though it's Sunday, I have to catch a train for Dix Hills very early in the morning and return in time for an appointment at Carnegie Hall. Can I see you again when I'm next in town?"

"Oh please," cooed Ultraviolet in her pronounced French accent. "I would like to talk with you. I promise not to keep you up too late."

Dali opened the limousine door. I had never seen him so persistent with anyone, let alone me. "You take Ultraviolet home for Dali," he said gently, but firmly pushing me toward the back seat. "You telephone Dali, Monday."

"Okay," I said to Ultraviolet. "if it's only for a few minutes."

As Dali opened the limousine door and was pushing me inside, I barely noticed (with her lengthy gown) that Ultraviolet (who was sitting close to the door) had this enormous white plaster cast on her extended right leg, and I had to use all my athletic capacity to avoid missing her as I went forward crouching down and lifting my legs. I should have annexed a special Olympic medal for the high low-hurdles with propulsion by Salvador Dali.

"Be careful of my leg," she pleaded.

"Don't worry, don't worry, I see it," I said.

Dali and Ultraviolet rattled off a few sentences in French as Dali went into the St. Regis, leaving me alone with this Ultraviolet, who was beginning to remind me of a poodle, as I wondered (along with the chauffeur) what was going to happen next.

"I must have some cheesecake," Ultraviolet suddenly said. "Let's go have some cheesecake."

"Cheesecake!" I exclaimed. "It's midnight and much too late to be eating cheesecake. And besides, cheesecake contains too much dairy and sugar; it will slow down the healing process of your broken leg."

"Don't remind me of my broken leg; it's ruining my career."

"What career is that..?"

"You do not know who I am; do you?"

"I've never seen you before tonight," I said. "But don't take that personally because other than Dali and Gala, I've never seen the rest of these people before tonight, either."

"You know Andy Warhol, don't you?"

"Not personally."

"You know who he is..."

"I saw some of his Madison Avenue graphics in the mid sixties," I said.

"Did you ever see any of his movies?"

"No; his graphic designs were enough; and beside since his pictures were void of any motion, how could he possibly do a motion picture?"

"I was the star of several of Warhol's films."

"I'm sorry, but I never saw them," I said.

"I want some cheesecake," she continued.

"Where would you like to go?" The young chauffeur, who spoke English with a German accent, asked me.

"Let's go to the Sixth Avenue Delicatessen," I said. "They might still be open; they used to have good cheesecake years ago."

"No," said Ultraviolet. "There's a place on, I believe, Second or Third Avenue that's still open which has fantastic cheesecake."

"Do you know the address?" I asked.

"Where would she like to go?" The chauffeur asked me again quite patiently.

"Driver," said Ultraviolet, "just go to Third Avenue and turn left and drive slowly for several blocks; I'll know it when I see it."

The limousine began gliding at a slow pace toward Third Avenue. As I reflected, I became rather entertained by this whole episode: here I am shoved by Salvador Dali into the back of a jet black limousine with a recycled Andy Warhol exotic, her broken right leg in a colossal white plaster cast, in search of cheesecake.

"What do you find so amusing?" Ultraviolet asked.

Not wanting to tell her my real cerebrations, I said, "Your name: I find your name very amusing."

"Why..? "

"Because you have a French accent. And I'm sure Ultraviolet is not your name; not your real name."

"Yes, it is my name."

"You mean to tell me that your mother and father, when you were born, named you Ultraviolet?"

"No, Ultraviolet is my stage name. The name Andy Warhol gave me. Oh, that man, I should sue him!"

"What for?" I asked.

"I broke this leg," she said, "in a stupid play I was doing for him. He's ruined my career."

"What's your real name?" I asked again.

"Why do you want to know my real name?"

"Because I don't feel Ultraviolet fits your personality. You seem to be more of a Jacqueline or Nicole; and besides, I don't wish to call you Ultraviolet."

"Well, you'll have to call me Ultraviolet."

"I won't get you any cheesecake unless you tell me your real name."

"I have my own money," she said indignantly.

"Fine," I said smiling. "When we get to where we're going, you can hobble out of the car with that Daliesque cane and get your own cheesecake."

Thinking the situation over and giving me a long sultry mischievous look, as only a French woman can, she said, "My real name is Isabelle...Isabelle Collin du Fresne."

"Now that's a name," I said. "If you had used your own name, you'd probably be so famous, that even I would know who you were."

"Driver, you're going too fast," she said. "It's someplace along here; to the right. Please go slower."

"He's going ten miles an hour as it is," I said. "If he goes any slower, he'll get a ticket for impeding the flow of traffic."

"Driver, slower please..." She said. "Oh, damn, I think the restaurant is on Second Avenue."

The patient chauffeur took us to Second Avenue where we finally found the restaurant. He jumped out quickly to open my door. "Please," I said, "you don't have to open my door; I can open the door. You just take it easy and sit behind the wheel."

"I'm paid to do this, Sir," the chauffeur said. "I'm instructed to always do it."

"Well, I'd rather you not do it because it causes too much attention," I said as about six or seven people stopped on the street and started staring at us and whispering to each other as they wondered who we were.

The restaurant had just closed and the proprietor told me through the glass door that they were out of cheesecake until tomorrow afternoon.

"Sorry, they're out of cheesecake," I said to Ultra Isabelle.

"I bet he had some," she said. "He just did not wish to open the door."

"Look," I said, "somebody's trying to tell you something. It's just not going to be your night for cheesecake. Monday, I'll have some macrobiotic strawberry tofu cheesecake made with barley malt sent to you."

"I know a restaurant where you can probably get some cheesecake," said the chauffeur.

"No, driver; please go down a few more blocks. There is another place

I know," she said.

"Why don't you listen to him," I said.

"No, no," she went on. "There's another place."

The chauffeur and I looked at one another in resignation, and he dutifully drove on.

"You probably think I'm crazy," she said.

"No; just a little insecure," I responded.

We found the other location which Ultra Isabelle was thinking about and it was closed. I convinced her to listen to the young German chauffeur and he took us to another place which, finally, had cheesecake.

As soon as we arrived in front of her building, which was on East 88th Street not far from Fifth Avenue, I was determined not to go up to her apartment since I had found her initial mystique wearing off after the cheesecake exertion she had put the poor chauffeur and me through; which I had mentally associated with an infiltration course I encountered dozens of times during my military training with the elite 39th Infantry in the Pike's Peak region of Colorado .

Isabelle, I could tell was intelligent, cultured and came from an obviously well bred family; but I could also see beneath the blush and mascara that here was a frustrated woman who had been looking for a prestigious identity for an insatiably long time.

I did everything I could to courteously say good night and go back to my hotel, but she asked, "Wouldn't you like to come up? I could make you some herb tea. I know you would not drink regular tea."

Immediately I thought to myself, 'Now look, Phillip, what the Hell are you going to do with this fading female Dorian Gray with a broken leg?'

"No," I said. Really, it's late; maybe some other time because I've had an extremely difficult week. I have to get up early; I'm returning to Los Angeles in a few days and then on my way to Europe and perhaps..."

"No, no, no, no," she said, "I want you to come up stairs."

"Well, look," I continued. You have a broken leg and I'm sure you need to rest it. Perhaps, Monday or Tuesday before I leave."

"Well, at least be gentleman enough to carry up the cheesecake," Isabelle snapped kind of losing her patience. "I have my broken leg, a cane and my purse. I can't carry this whole box of cheesecake."

The chauffeur looked at me through his rear view mirror. I could tell that he liked me through his faint smile.

"Okay," I said, "just for a little while."

I instructed the chauffeur not to wait for me as I would take a taxicab back to the Hotel.

Ultra Isabelle hobbled her way into the Lobby where the night watchman looked at us as if we were two porno stars. In a way, I was glad that I gave in because I wanted to see just what events lay in store for me since I wasn't really sure that Isabelle found me that fascinating; especially, since I had been so impassive about her.

The elevator was small and rather laggard. I could see from the dim light that Isabelle appeared somewhat weary, and frustrated. It was a look I had seen numerous times on the faces of financially troubled women.

The apartment was medium sized with many plants and appeared much smaller due to an abundance of tasteful antique furnishings. Isabelle told me to sit down and make myself comfortable while she made the herb tea.

"I don't suppose you want any cheesecake," she said half in jest.

"No, thank you," I said playing with one of her two cats which immediately came up to me and jumped onto my lap.

Isabelle was quite impressed about how her shy cat liked me, and over the fact that I selected and sat in her favorite chair. She began asking me a number of questions from why I chose to sit in that particular chair and my astrological sign, to when and where I first met Dali and Gala, and what kind of music I composed.

"Dali told me about you and that you're a famous musician; a great composer."

"Dali's very kind," I said. "I try to compose communicative and good music. It's a difficult profession."

"You look as if you're doing quite well," she said.

"I get by."

Isabelle then asked me if I would mind if she changed into her robe because she was becoming increasingly uncomfortable with her plaster cast and evening gown. I said that she should and, since it now was early morning, that I perhaps should call a taxi and leave.

"No, please stay a little while longer," she said as she went to change. "I have a young lady who boards with me here which helps with my expenses, and I'd appreciate your staying here until she comes. I'd like to get rid of her soon because she's rather untidy, but I need the money."

The apartment looked clean and neat to me in the muted light. But what could I say?

Another fifteen minutes, or so, went by with all kinds of interrogatories and responses; the central thread of which usually attached itself to career and money. I attempted to be delicately constructive and suggested that if Isabelle were having a difficult time endeavoring to acquire acting jobs in New York City, that she consider doing other forms of employment while pursuing her performing auditions. I told her that from my extensive familiarity of having scored ten motion pictures in ten years, and having come into contact with many actors and actresses, from the unquestionably famous to the beginning and struggling, that I personally felt it was not worth one's whole life for a cinematic, television or stage distortion. "And besides," I remember advising her, "unless you are doing acting on the level of an Annie Giradot, Katherine Hepburn, or Laurence Olivier, it would be exceedingly difficult for me to recommend that you continue. However, if you are really in earnest about acting, you won't pay any attention to what anybody says, anyway. If you find New York hopelessly not open to you, then you could try Hollywood. If that doesn't work then you should consider going to London for serious study and doing repertory; or going back to France."

"What about, Dali?" I asked. "Can't he help you?"

"He helps me sometimes," Isabelle said rather coyly. "I am doing some work for him; but you know how Dali is."

According to Isabelle, she was also dabbling as an art dealer, too, in an attempt to make money. And contacting certain Dali collectors for Dali, personally, as it seems at that time Dali was mounting a campaign to endeavor to buy back some of his works for his new Dali Museum in Spain.

About this time, her boarder came home; a nondescript rather plain American girl who seemed rational, but a trifle flighty. Isabelle introduced us and then the girl made herself a snack in the kitchen afterwhich she went to her bedroom.

Now, I could go home, I thought.

"Oh, please stay a little while longer," said Isabelle who was beginning to appear as if she needed a little ultraviolet herself.

"Look," I said. "You're intelligent enough to see that I'm a direct person. What do you want from me? You don't have to go through this myriad of situations to ask me something. "What's on your mind?"

"No, no," she said flapping her feathers, "it's not what you think. I ask you all these questions because I find you very interesting. I saw you at the gallery and I asked Dali about you. I wanted to meet you."

"Tell me what you want from me," I said quietly. "How can I help you?"

"I feel so embarrassed," she said.

"I'm going to leave," I said getting up.

"Alright, alright," Isabelle said. "Come into my bedroom. It's not what you think. I want to play something for you."

We went into her bedroom where, even though the enormous bed took up three-quarters of the chamber, she had a 15 ips reel to reel tape deck set upon her dresser.

"I have been considering a career as a singer," she said, "and I have been thinking up songs and having them put down. I made this album here in New York last year and I would like to get a recording company to release it. When Dali told me that you are a famous musician, I wanted to meet you and have you hear my recording."

And so Isabelle began playing these songs which had been well engineered with good professional sound reproduction. The raw quality of her untrained voice was not too bad considering that she did not know how to breathe properly, and the small pop band improvised arrangements accompanying her were adequate, too. But these verses were neither pop songs, rock tunes, middle of the road; and they certainly were not concert arias. Actually, they were quite boring. Although, her lyrics were interesting at times, there was no melodic distinction to the music. In fact, I wondered if Dali had put up the money for this exercise in musical futility since he wouldn't have known the difference between these songs, Cole Porter's, or Franz Schubert's. Later I found out through another source that our Ultraviolet Isabelle had been having discreet sexual encounters with Dali from time to time, and that he had been trying to assist her financially with her career attempts, but was tiring of the practice and that is why he was so assertive in my taking Isabelle home. Dali felt (since I had been a commercially recorded artist) that I could acquire an immediate recording contract for Ultraviolet Isabelle which would give her enough revenue to where Dali would eventually be relieved of further financial liabilities.

I told Isabelle what I thought quite candidly and as diplomatically as possible because I could see that she had the serious affliction in lack of musical talent coupled with the frustrated appetite to become celebrated. But she still wondered if I could be ministerial in gaining her a contract to release the album as it was; interest an A & R executive to convince a label to produce a new album; or have a record company sign her as an artist. I told her that even though my last film score (*Murph The Surf*) enjoyed the distinction of being the first "white" motion picture sound track album to be distributed by Motown Records, that if I sent these recordings to Motown on her behalf, I was certain that they would not listen to more than ten seconds and I seriously doubted that Isabelle would even get a reply or her tape returned. I suggested that perhaps she could use these songs as background music for Andy Warhol's next film, and then there might be a chance to attract some esoteric record label. She looked at me not knowing if I were in earnest or bantering.

As I was about to leave, Isabelle asked me for my California telephone number and address which I gave her; and she offered me hers. She also asked if I knew Paul Horn; and when I explained that he had played in my orchestra a couple of times, and had commissioned me to compose my *Parallelograms for Flute Quartet & Jazz Ensemble,* I thought she was going to have an orgasm right there in the doorway as she solicited me for his address. In order to finally retrieve myself, I promised as soon as I returned to California, that I would send it to her. I became excessively occupied and neglected to forward Paul Horn's address, and weeks later Isabelle telephoned me from New York and I gave it to her.

Isabelle wrote me a few letters during the next year which I politely answered, but that cheesecake and tape deck Odyssey was the last time I saw her and after about the third letter we lost contact with one another.

I remember asking Dali one afternoon as we were walking along Fifth Avenue, "Dali, please tell me in your honest opinion...I just want to know for myself...In your honest estimation (what you really think) who is the greatest painter of this century?"

"After Dali, Picasso." Dali answered immediately.

I also recall Dali asking me, "Composer; does composer ever compose greatest piece?"

"Well what do you mean?" I asked.

"Has composer written greatest work?"

"No," I said. "I'm just at the beginning of my career. I haven't written my greatest work, I'm sure."

Dali said, "Composer, never do greatest work. Dali never paint greatest painting."

I said, "Well, why? Don't you always strive to do your greatest work?"

"No...is never good; because if Dali do greatest painting, what else is there for the world? Nothing is left."

I thought that was an intriguing insight into Dali's artistic philosophy.

Just before I left New York City to live in Los Angeles January 1964, I telephoned Dali and he asked me if I would like to see his most recent work that afternoon which had just arrived from Port Lligat. I said, "Of course," and I met him at the St. Regis and we walked down Fifth Avenue to Knoedler's Art Gallery on 57th Street. A few of the art salespeople there made an inordinate fuss over Dali, and others who were trying to make an important sale of other painters' works with potential buyers did not pay too much attention to him.

Dali instructed me to wait for him at the center of the Knoedler Gallery until everything was ready. He went to the rear of Knoedler's and returned within about four minutes; escorting me into the large private viewing room in the back of the gallery.

I could have never imagined this painting. It was so powerfully executed.

It overwhelmed me. It was an oil on canvas 10 by 11 and 1/2 feet which he called *Galacidalacidesoxyribonucleicacid* also subtitled *Homage To Crick And Watson (the discoverers of DNA)* which Dali did on commission the summer of 1963 for the New England Merchants National Bank of Boston Massachusetts.

There was a 14th century Renaissance archetypical muscular male arm at the top of the canvas reaching down from the clouded heavens which Dali advised me "represents God and arm of God" and a transparent young Michelangelo influenced handsome nude dead man (comparable to a Pieta in the firmament) which Dali further disclosed was "Arm of God reaching down for dead man...take to heaven." There was Gala in the foreground; however, I had never seen such depth of field in any painting: it was as if you were sailing in the heavens and you could see five hundred miles into the Spanish plains in the distance with a winding river and all kinds of shafts of sunlight coming through the clouds. It was truly a fantastic surrealistic rendering.

I said, "Dali, what are these? Arabs here shooting each other?" Away from the centers of interest on the sizable canvas small Arab like people in desert dress with rifles pointed at each other's heads were drafted into a visually formulated subatomic quadrangle framework.

"This is molecular structure of desoxyribonucleic acid," Dali said. "Arabs shooting other Arabs."

I was thunderstruck by Dali's phenomenal technical and mechanical commands which allowed him to achieve an extraordinary vista with an immense depth of field. The shafts of sunlight streaming through the clouds over the pervasive Spanish wilderness in the distance remains vivid in my mind to this day. I remember closely examining the white swirling transparent clouds on the canvas and wondering in awe how Dali executed this.

"Dali," I said. "I don't see any brush strokes here. How did you do this?"

"Oh, Dali do with air-gun." He said.

I must have lingered there an hour just relishing that painting as Dali was quietly directing the track and indirect lighting of the viewing room with the workers. He also studied the work from many different angles; and I recall his leaving the room and returning with about a number two or three brush and some oils; minutely touching up a few places on the picture. I suggested to Dali that he be sure the tension of the canvas on the frame be as tight as possible and he checked that.

One of the salesmen came in with a couple of copies of a recently published book of Dali reproductions which Dali signed in front of me. Having been a student of graphology, I paid particular attention as to how Dali autographed the volumes. You might have thought the book was a fencing opponent as Dali set his balance and footwork over the table and stabbed the opening page of books with a black felt tipped pen which he used like a rapier, pausing an instant, then completing his Dali angular signature with dynamic speed and precision.

I once asked Dali what his first important success was here in the United States. He revealed to me that he needed money during one of his initial trips to New York City (which I understood was in the 1930's and humbly financed with a cash advance from his friend Picasso), so he reluctantly accepted a window designing assignment from one of the leading department stores.

"Composer, Dali do fantastic window department store with fur lined bathtub," he told me. "Jewels on rhinoceros and all kinds Dali fantastic hallucination mannequins. Window cause big publicity for Dali, but Dali veddy unhappy because Dali want real water in fur lined bathtub, but department store say no because water ruin expensive furs. Big argument between Dali and department store as Dali call press then go fill bathtub in window with water. Dali fight with department store and inside window Dali throw bathtub through plate glass window causing big crash on street. Police come; big publicity for Dali in newspapers next day. Dali become famous United States immediately."

When I first came to Los Angeles in 1964, I heard an amusing story from an art dealer in Beverly Hills who was acquainted with movie mogul Jack Warner who had commissioned Dali in advance to do a portrait of Jack Warner's new wife from several provided photographs. I understood, from what the art dealer told me, that the legally drawn contract stipulated that Jack Warner had to accept whatever conception and style Dali decided to paint of Mrs. Warner, to which Mr. Warner agreed. About six months later a rather small painting was delivered to Warner; really a beautiful portrait of his wife, but all around her head were the secondary portraits of all of Mrs. Warner's ex-husbands. The art dealer informed me that the Warners never hung the painting and kept it in a closet.

Around 1963, we were at a small party at Huntington Hartford's One Beekman Place triplex penthouse. I was having a good time speaking with some people in the living room and Dali was conversing with some other individuals adjacent to us. Suddenly I heard a small crashing sound. It seems that Dali who was trying to make a conversational point with his sweeping cane and arm, had accidentally hit the heavy crystal punch bowl which was resting along with some sandwiches and hor d'oeuvres on the oversized low coffee table in front of the couch causing a tidal wave of punch to spill over onto the coffee table. Unfortunately for Dali, Hartford's efficient Scotch Butler,

John, witnessed the whole incident. John had told me over the years that I was one of the few friends of Hartford's whom he genuinely liked because I wasn't pretentious with anyone and always dealt with him like a person rather than the butler; and he also saw how I often treated him with much more respect than I did with Huntington Hartford.

"Oh, Mr. Dali, how could you!" Calmly exclaimed John with his engaging Scotch brogue. "Look at what you've done."

Dali, I could see was rather rattled and stood there wide eyed and speechless. I had never seen Dali this way; it was quite amusing.

"Look at all the extra work you've made for me, Mr. Dali," John moaned. "Who's going to clean up this mess?"

"Don't touch it, John!" I exclaimed; over-acting a bit as I tried to save Dali as everyone in the room watched. "Don't you realize the historical accidental artistic implication of what Dali has just done?"

Now both Dali and John looked at me with astonished expressions as I took the pressurized can of whip cream and gave Dali's accidental tidal wave on the large coffee table a Jackson Pollock blast of my own; punctuating it with a few nuts, grapes and pieces of bread.

"What do you think of our joint work of art, Dali?" I asked as I threw a stirrer, green olive and cherry onto the mess; slicing it here and there with a skewer.

"Composition veddy good, Composer," Dali said as he outlined some of the mess with the point of his famous cane. "Veddy interesting."

John, the Butler, shaking his head at the both of us moaned, "Oh, Mr. Lambro..." then threw up his arms in sudden exasperation; but Dali thought John was going to hit him and so Dali quickly leaped back in fear clutching his cane close to his chest which was a hilarious sight in itself. Everyone was snickering and laughing, except John; he went to get the lady housekeeper to help him clean up the shambles. I followed John into the kitchen and offered to assist, which further endeared me to John, but he refused to let me help him clean up the shambles.

Incidentally, John was a keen admirer of Dali's paintings and he told me that he had "a great appreciation for Dali's draftsman like qualities."

Over the years, some people have thought that Salvador Dali must have taken mind expanding drugs such as LSD or Mescaline to achieve his surrealistic work, but I definitely do not believe that he ever did.

One Sunday afternoon I was taken to a gathering by art collector Mrs. Beatrice Glass to her friend's home in Manhattan late 1963 and I met Dali as he was leaving and introduced Beatrice and Dali to one another. As the three of us were speaking there on the sidewalk, a distinguished medical doctor psychiatrist friend of Beatrice Glass's had arrived for the social event in the company of a late middle aged woman whom I was to find out later was the mother of Maria Callas. Mrs. Callas excused herself because she was cold and wanted to go inside, and the doctor told her that he would be along shortly. The doctor began asking Beatrice a lot of questions about me and finding out that I was a composer, he then asked if I had ever taken any brain altering drugs to improve my composing. I looked at Dali and informed the psychiatrist, "we true artists don't need any synthetic means to expand our creative minds and consciousness; and personally I don't believe in drugs of any kind, not even aspirin."

The doctor then looked at Dali and said, "I've read where you take LSD and Mescaline."

"This is not true," Dali replied. "This is total fabrication. Dali never take LSD or Mescaline. Dali not need drugs to hallucinate. Dali hallucinate naturally."

Now, this was the closest I had ever witnessed Salvador Dali in becoming angry. And this is why I felt he was telling the truth. Of course, Dali would say things which were absolutely not genuine, from time to time, but these little and sometimes big canards were vocalized to create an illusory effect and he never became acrimonious when I pressured him into possibly denying an obvious misrepresentation.

"Are you sure you're both telling me the truth?" The doctor asked us.

I said nothing, but gave the physician a sarcastic look. Dali became animated and got into an active discussion with the psychiatrist disclaiming all those written stories about Dali's involvement with drugs.

"Dali never, never, never take drugs. Only stimulation come inside and outside mind," he said. "Yes, Dali sometime take fly's wings, or beautiful insect wings and put between two pieces of glass and hold up to light with Dali eyes and Dali look through. Yes; make Dali very high natural consciousness, but Dali never take drugs."

The last time I had any contact with Salvador Dali was around 1978. A Beverly Hills art dealer telephoned me one day as he had read that Dali was interested in buying back certain works of his own for his Museum in Spain. The art merchant had heard that I was friendly with Salvador Dali and could personally get him to come to the telephone. The dealer was representing a triptych panel which Dali had originally painted for cosmetic tycoon Helena Rubenstein that now belonged to some affluent client.

I advised the art dealer to come to my apartment and (since it was near springtime) I called Dali at the St. Regis in New York City. The merchant was extremely impressed when Dali eventually came to the telephone and spoke with me, because he had tried reaching Dali on his own to no avail.

I described to Dali what the dealer had revealed. I was under the impression that this was a three panel painting, but Dali said over the telephone, "Yes, Dali remember; but this work not really Dali."

"What do you mean?" I asked Dali glancing at the art dealer. "This is not your work? Is it a fake?"

"No, Dali do for Madame Rubenstein. Dali paint because Madame Rubenstein pay Dali a lot of money; but this not really Dali painting."

"I don't understand," I said. "Is this a three panel painting of yours, or what?"

"No, Composer; this Dali do advertisement for Madame Rubenstein one time three panel for models to change clothes behind and photograph. Dali not interested in this. Dali only do this for money. This like commercial art."

Now I understood. The Beverly Hills art dealer was trying to make a common three panel partition screen, behind which fashion models were photographed taking their clothes off and on and which Dali had painted onto, into three major works; but Dali was not the least bit concerned.

I did give the art merchant a thrill, by introducing him to Dali over the telephone and he told me excitedly several months later that Dali had responded to the dealer's letter to him with a hand written reply on the returned original document.

In April of 1983, I purchased a signed large hand colored engraving of *Corpus Hypercubicus* (generally referred to as *The Crucifixion*) on Japon paper which was printed in Paris early 1983 which meant that Dali would have had to sign all of the 200 Japon blank pieces of paper prior to that date. I was informed by international dealers that that was how reproductions of Dali's works were consummated: first the negotiations; then the contract and payment; and accordingly Dali would sign the blank pieces of paper before they were engraved, or lithographed. I never purchased a signed lithograph because I never liked the quality of reproduction. I reserved number 34 out of 200 of *The Crucifixion*; the original of which is on display at the Metropolitan Museum in New York City. I knew Dali was ill and had been in a fire and was slowly disintegrating into a withered condition. I also recognized that we would never see each other again in this extant dimension, so I thought it would be a pleasant remembrance to have a signed engraving hanging on my wall of one of Dali's great masterpieces.

As you must have surmised from my conversations with Dali, I have always had the strong conviction that every interested collector should have the opportunity of being allowed to possess an accurately reproduced large five color photo blow up of any Dali original masterpiece rather than the washed out engraved or lithographed realizations of the same works. Because, when all is said and done, it is the great and powerfully subtle mechanics, technique and draftsmanship which makes great paintings masterpieces; in much the same way these attributes translated into musical performance terms make Vladimir Horowitz, Vladimir Horowitz, or Jascha Heifetz, Jascha Heifetz. And if you use a system of reproduction which cannot capture the authentic and refined details of the very essence of what makes Dali Dali, or Rembrandt Rembrandt, or Sir Lawrence Alma-Tadema Sir Lawrence Alma-Tadema, then what's the point? It would be like recording or playing music with antiquated equipment when advanced recording equipment is available.

Whether one likes or dislikes Dali subject matter, one cannot deny that Salvador Dali, from the standpoint of painting mechanics, draftsmanship, perspective, and technique was perhaps the most distinguished painter of the 20th century; and one of the greatest painters of all time.

When The Crucifixion was delivered to me I thought the engraving was reasonably well done, as etchings go, but I questioned the signature; as it did not have the angularity and rapier sweep of what I recollected Dali's autograph to have been when I knew him. However, I had also seen such a disparate variety of Dali's subscriptions on his original oils that I felt (taking into consideration, graphologically speaking, that since the signature is one's personal photograph of oneself) that Dali's personal sign could have changed as dramatically as his physical health and appearance. The art dealer had sent me a recent press photo of Dali and I was shocked by the transformation; he barely looked anything like the Dali I had known. I also had noticed from old documents how much my own signature had changed over the years.

In 1984 I received a telephone call from another art dealer in Newport Beach, California who had discovered that I had been personally acquainted with Salvador Dali. He told me that he had one copy of a large H.C. (Museum Proof) of a Magui Publishers Inc. hand colored engraving of Dali's *The Last Supper* printed on Japon paper (only 25 H.C.'s had been printed); and he also had on Japon a Magui Publishers Inc. hand colored engraving of *Christ Of St. John Of The Cross* number 242 out of 450. Since I was so occupied with my music, it was two months and three or four telephone calls later before the art merchant could induce me to drive down from Los Angeles to Newport Beach.

I perused these engraved realizations which employed an ancient technique that had been refined by Rembrandt, but I still wondered why nobody bothered to just make exceptional photo reproductions of Dali's original masterpieces. Incidentally, the Dali signatures on both engravings looked authentic and were consistent to the way I had seen Dali sign his name in my presence.

The dealer invited me to lunch with two of his salesmen and asked me to relate to them a few of my most entertaining Dali personal experiences. The art merchant offered me both of these April 1982 editions (which meant that Dali had to have signed the blank paper in 1981 from which each engraving was struck) for $5,000 each. I laughed and told him that even though I was aware that the *Lincoln In Dalivision* reproduction was now fetching in some circles $42,000, and although I had been a friend of Dali's, to me, these hand colored etchings were not worth $5,000 apiece so I countered with a $1,500 offer which he promptly refused.

About six weeks later I received a call from the dealer's assistant informing me that his gallery had been robbed and they were in financial distress and, in a weak moment, I purchased both *The Last Supper* and *Christ Of St. John Of The Cross* for $2,500 each; even though I could hear Dali chiming in the back of my brain, 'Oh you know, Composer, this is not real Dali. Yes, Dali sign for money, but reproduction not real Dali.'

To which I responded telepathically, 'I know Dali, I know; but since the originals are housed in the Metropolitan, the Glasgow, and the National Gallery, I have to settle for these primitive etchings because you wouldn't listen to me when I advised you to only allow brilliant gigantic five color separation blow up photo copies of your original works.'

During 1988 the media focused attention to the reportedly vast amount of forged Dali lithographs and etchings (supposedly not actually signed by Dali himself) which, I understood prompted a series of law suits endeavoring to make it against the law for anyone to sell even their own legally purchased Dali's here in the United States. I decided to investigate the situation.

A dealer on Rodeo Drive in Beverly Hills where I saw some Dali lithographs gave me the name and phone number of a Mr. Albert Field in New York City who (although he markets his own collection and editions of signed Dali reproductions himself) is supposedly the Dali authenticity expert who advised me over the telephone that "the French Government has given me a sworn statement from Salvador Dali stating that Dali never signed anything after 1981."

"Well, Mr. Field," I replied. "Playboy Magazine during an interview also received confirmed testimony from Dali that he never ever had sex with anybody else except Gala; do you believe that too?"

In fact, I remember reading the Playboy interview and teasingly informed Dali that week, "For someone who never wants to have sex with anyone except Gala, you certainly pursue those cute young models, Dali."

Field went on to declare that the entire Magui Publishers Inc. Dali collection "is a fake and your etchings aren't worth a plug nickel because they were published in 1982."

Mr. Field may be to Dali lithography what Petrides was to Utrillo. At one time, if you owned an authentic Utrillo oil painting and you did not happen to have a signed Petrides authentication to go with it, it was assumed to be a fake. However, if you had a forged Utrillo with a Petrides certificate of validation (which you paid dearly for), it was considered genuine.

I attempted to make the point with Mr. Albert Field that since I knew Salvador Dali and had been with him several times when I saw him execute his signature (even though I questioned the authenticity of the autograph on my Crucifixion) I deemed that *The Last Supper* and *Christ Of St. John Of The Cross* signatures were bona fide.

"Well they're not," said Field. "You know, these forgers are quite clever."

"I mean, how can you say that Mr. Field without examining the signatures?" I asked. "Dali signed his works many different ways."

"I don't have to examine them," he said. "I have an affidavit from the French Government and that's good enough for me."

Mr. Field seemed to base his whole assertion upon the year 1981. What difference does the year make? Since I knew Dali, there were several things I absolutely understood to be indisputable about him: Salvador Dali did not care one iota about facsimiles of his works and rarely, if ever, saw the reproduction proofs since he only signed blank sheets of paper. Dali only cared passionately about his original paintings. For some inexplicable reason which I could never actually understand, Dali was obsessed with amassing abnormal amounts of money. For example, contrary to universal conviction, Salvador Dali was in reality a simple, tranquil apathetic Spanish individual. He only dressed and spoke flamboyantly and made those bizarre faces and gestures for the media to reinforce interest in his artistic pursuits and ultimately obtain higher fees. As he advised me several times, "Dali love gold," and "Dali love collectors."

As Dali got older he could not physically and mentally keep up with the demand for his originals. I had heard (similar to practices employed by even some of the great Renaissance masters) that Dali hired assistant artists to fill in the backgrounds and paint certain sub portions of his canvases according to his wants. I should like to ask Mr. Field if this invalidates Dali's work or signature on his original oils?

Also, like Ernest Hemingway, when Dali got ill and began needing more money for expert medical attention, I'm sure he found that signing his last name a few thousand times for millions of dollars was a way out of mounting expenses and the need for additional resources; which, in actuality, Dali did not really need since (unlike Hemingway) he had more than enough financial assets. Ernest Hemingway sold the screen rights to many of his novels and stories for comparatively little remuneration because Hemingway initially never needed a lot of money to live; until he got sick, and then he did everything conceivable to get as much cash for his writings as he possibly could in order to satisfy his burgeoning medical expenditures which probably contributed to Hemingway's ultimate and enfeebling decision to blow out his brains with a favorite shotgun. I am sure that Dali (as proud a person and whole artist that he was) in that slow debilitating state prior to his interminable lingering death would have also liked to have taken his own suffering life had he not been so infirmed and convoyed by financially exploitative sycophants.

I found Dali to be basically an honest person; even though his signature, graphologically speaking, indicated that he could be cruel. Although, I never once saw him do a truculent act; except, perhaps, force me to take Ultraviolet Isabelle home on that twilight cheesecake expedition.

But, Ladies and Gentlemen of the Jury, I have known for a long time that the general interest in fine art has basically been hypocritical and Salvador Dali unequivocally knew that as well. If we are to be honest, the media and most of the covetous art investors are more preoccupied in the cash value of Dali's signature on lithographs and etchings rather than in Dali's work itself.

This brings to mind a long telephone conversation which I once had with concert pianist Arthur Rubinstein in New York City when we were speaking about painting and painters and how often times the public is so blinded by whether the canvas is authentic or not that they fail to judge the picture for what it actually is.

"You know, my friend," said Rubinstein. "I purchased a painting by Renoir many years ago in France and the signature was not quite the same as Renoir usually signed his other paintings; but I must tell you that I liked that painting for what it was and hung it in my living room. Subsequently, some art experts were in my home and said that my painting wasn't a Renoir and definitely a fake. But, you know, I said to myself, there's something about this painting which speaks to me; and I don't care if it isn't a Renoir, I like it anyway for itself; and I enjoyed it. Several years later in Paris after one of my recitals, Renoir's daughter was introduced to me backstage and I asked her if she wouldn't mind coming to my home because I had a painting which I had purchased by her father and that there had been some controversy surrounding it and wondered if she could tell me anything about it. Well, my friend," Rubinstein went on, "Renoir's daughter came and she exclaimed, 'Yes, Maestro I remember this painting very well because he painted it in our home when I was a child.' That made me feel a little better," Rubinstein said, "to know that it was really a Renoir, but to tell you the truth, that painting gave me such pleasure when I looked at it, I really wouldn't have cared if she said that it wasn't a Renoir."

After my contact with Albert Field, I located the French owner of Magui Publishers Inc. right here in Beverly Hills, California by the name of Pierre Marcand.

I telephoned Pierre Marcand and informed him that I had known Salvador Dali personally and that I had purchased Magui editions of Dali's *The Last Supper* and *Christ Of Saint John Of The Cross* to go with my large engraving of *The Crucifixion* and about what Mr. Albert Field had said.

"I am not here to confront you, or to sue you," I assured Pierre Marcand. "I just want to know the truth. I bought these reproductions of Dali's masterworks because I love the original paintings and because I was fortunate enough to have known Dali. If you tell me that the signatures are false, I'll accept that. I just want to know the truth for myself. I am not here to cause trouble."

"Mr. Lambro," Pierre Marcand went on easily. "I'm aware of what Mr. Albert Field has been saying about me. All I can say to you is that I have here signed and notarized legal contracts and documents with Salvador Dali (and you are welcome to come up to my house and examine them; they are also in my attorney's office) and if these editions are not genuine, then I have paid over one million dollars for nothing."

One early evening a few weeks later, I drove to Pierre Marcand's white marbled home at the summit of the Trousdale area in Beverly Hills where we had a long and pleasant chat about Dali and where he showed me the documentation. I found Pierre Marcand, who is an artist himself, to be charming and cultured, and quite honest and direct.

Several weeks later, I again went to Pierre Marcand's residence where I had lunch and where he gave me supportive records concerning the legal rights, copyrights, and watermark dates of manufacture of the paper used in his reproductions. I feel, as I always have, that the Magui realizations of Dali's *The Last Supper* and *Christ Of St. John On The Cross* were actually signed by Dali during 1981 on blank sheets of paper before they were reproduced in March and April of 1982. I also believe that the International Multiples Ltd. edition of the other etching which I possess of Dali's *The Crucifixion* (while not a bad realization) might have been signed by Dali when he was infirmed, as his signature, which looks authentic, is rather weak.

But I appreciate looking at these three Dali masterpiece realizations; even though I know the market for Dali lithographs and etchings has wilted because of the controversy surrounding the question as to whether or not Salvador Dali actually signed his reproductions and whether or not these engravings were genuinely etched. Then too, as I have always maintained, I would thoroughly relish even more to be able to look at large exceptionally well reproduced five color blow up photographs of Dali originals. However, as I recall during my conversation with Albert Field when he maintained that all of my Dali etchings were worthless.

"How can you say they're worthless, Mr. Field?" I asked. "What about their artistic and aesthetic value?"

"Well, if you're speaking about aesthetics," he said, "that's something else."

"What else is there in art?" I asked.

From 1960 through 1964 I was Music Director & Consultant for the United Nations in New York City. I virtually fell into the part-time non-paying situation via my job as Assistant Director Of Publications with G. Schirmer from 1960 through the Leonard Bernstein Kaddish in the Autumn of 1963, afterwhich I resigned from Schirmer.

In 1960 I received a telephone call from Jeff Sparks, Communications Director for the United Nations, indicating that they were having difficulty in locating some music which they wanted to have performed by a prominent symphonic artist and could I help them formulate the music portion of their next Human Rights Day Concert.

We spoke at length over the telephone, and Jeff Sparks (who was to become one of my best friends) invited me to the United Nations for lunch that week. Jeff Sparks had been a well known Radio & TV announcer before he became Communications Director for the United Nations. In fact, he was the announcer for some of Morton Gould's popular symphonic musical shows during the Golden Age Of Radio.

Throughout my tenure at the United Nations we had two significant, but unpublicized programs each year: Human Rights Day, and Staff Day. The Human Rights Day was for both the delegates and some of the staff, but the Staff Day was wholly for the staff operatives. The Human Rights Day was in the form of a concert and was quite a ceremonial affair. The invitations would usually read, "The United Nations requests the pleasure of your company at the celebration of Human Rights Day on Tuesday the 10th of December 1963 at 8:30 pm in the General Assembly Hall." And, of course, everyone was required to use the Delegates' Entrance.

We would have, for example, Sir Laurence Olivier (who would donate his services and fly from London to New York at his own expense) open the program by reciting *The Declaration Of The Rights Of Man*. I remember on one of the Human Rights Day concerts we had Claudio Arrau play Beethoven's *Appassionata Sonata*. We also had Sir Michael Redgrave read *The Declaration*; and during an additional event Louis Jourdan narrated it both in French and English. One year I battled to have Richard Burton recite *The Declaration Of The Rights Of Man*, but I was overruled. The reason I was constantly being given alluded to Burton's off screen notoriety with screen actress Elizabeth Taylor. Personally, I did not see what his liaison with the stunning film personality had to do with Burton's great gifts as an actor and orator. "Look," I would say to Jeff Sparks and other UN executives, "Burton isn't doing anything vastly dissimilar from many of the delegates here at the UN; so why shouldn't we extend an invitation for him to narrate *The Declaration Of The Rights Of Man?*" I seriously regretted that we were never allowed to have Richard Burton because, in my estimation, he would have given a superior recitation.

I was specifically instructed in the procedural protocol as how to offer a celebrity an invitation to appear at either Human Rights Day or Staff Day. You must understand, no one ever was permitted to refuse an invitation from the Secretary General of the United Nations; it just wasn't done. To avoid this, we would have to make it apparent to the notable that if they happened to be given a proposal from the Secretary General, Mr. U Thant, to appear on Human Rights Day, or Staff Day, would they accept? If the answer was affirmative, then we would inform them that we would send a formal proffer on the condition that no refusals or cancellations would be acceptable.

One Human Rights Day concert we engaged Leontyne Price to sing a few operatic arias, and also on the same program were the Indrandi Dancers from India who performed colorfully.

It wasn't always that simple to formulate an International program because, especially for Human Rights Day, you had to attempt to engage representative artists from every part of the world. Many of the delegates from Africa would express their displeasure at our not having some of their native performers appear at these events which eventually led during the early 1960's to our importing from Africa the then unknown Miriam Makeba in what I believe was, perhaps, her very first appearance in the United States. She was accompanied only by several indigenous African musicians in ceremonial dress who sat on the carpeted floor of the General Assembly stage beating out rhythms on their talking drums and African metal Thumb Pianos. I was completely captivated by their splendid renderings of authentic African songs because it was so naturally aboriginal ànd well before Miriam Makeba's ultimate Americanization and commercialization.

Leontyne Price gave us some distress at the Human Rights Day concert where she appeared. She was specifically instructed as to United Nations protocol and informed that she would be picked up by a UN limousine, and upon arriving at the Delegates' Entrance, the attendant would open her limousine door after which she was advised to walk directly into the foyer of the Delegates' Entrance where she would be officially received by an Aide and ultimately introduced to the Secretary General during formal proceedings. Every Head Of State followed this procedure; it wasn't anything out of the ordinary. However, I never saw the usually poised Jeff Sparks so indignant. It seems Leontyne Price, at the last moment, refused to get out of the limousine; feeling that the Secretary General of the United Nations, U Thant, should come outside and escort Ms. Price into the UN interior. I nearly lost my balance when Jeff Sparks told me what was going on. Jeff finally ran out and spoke to Ms. Price (quite politely, but sternly) informing her that if she did not do what she had been instructed and previously had agreed upon doing, calmly and immediately, it would cast an irrevocable and lasting international negative aspersion upon both her personal character and her ability to cooperate professionally which might be reported in all the major newspapers around the world during the next few days. Prima Donna Price expeditiously got the message, and somewhat petulantly alighted from the car, but smilingly played her role. However, those few at the United Nations who knew what had just happened lost a great deal of respect for this talented soprano.

I first heard and saw Leontyne Price during the summer of 1958 at the wondrously preserved outdoor Roman Arena di Verona in Northern Italy where, relatively unknown, she gave a prodigious account of herself as Aida. I attended the opera with Lt. Caso, an Italian friend of mine during that time who had become an American citizen and Army officer, and who was about to be married to the Cinzano heiress. I sometimes wonder whatever happened to him; and certainly hope that he didn't end up living like a Cinzano awning or ashtray at some idle Northern Italian villa.

I particularly valued the United Nations Staff Day concerts because they were given for the tireless high-level staff workers who, at certain times, especially during Emergency Sessions, would labor up to three consecutive days with virtually little, or no sleep. A program would be given for them once a year that was the production envy of, and qualitatively completely beyond, any major theatrical or television variety show which you could possibly imagine. It was almost always completely void of any pre or post publicity because the UN did not wish to cheapen these unique events with prosaic reviews and press releases.

I delighted in helping put those Staff Day Concerts together and had the time of my life doing it.

I particularly enjoyed Staff Day 13 September 1963. We had arranged far in advance to have Frank Sinatra fly-in to the United Nations from California expressly for this event where he was a charming and outstanding Master Of Ceremonies as well as singer. Skitch Henderson accompanied

Frank Sinatra in several ballads. Henderson used to plant himself in my Schirmer office about ten times a year and want to tell my associate Harvey Rubenstein and myself endless show business stories to the consternation of our superior Hans Heinsheimer who always seemed to confuse Skitch Henderson with Mitch Miller (who never came to my office at all) although my cute cousin Gloria Lambert, I understand, was one of Miller's featured singers on his TV shows. Heinsheimer, walking by my office and seeing Skitch Henderson there, would invariably forget who he was and sometimes would ask me later in his pronounced Austrian accent, "Pheel, who ees that; Skeetch Mitch?"

My last teacher, Gyorgy Sandor, whom Frank Sinatra introduced as one of his favorite concert pianists, played some Chopin and Liszt. And as if this were not enough, we had Richard Rodgers accompanying singer Martha Wright in a medley of some of Rodgers' best songs; Gustavo Lopez, the classical guitarist and protege of Andres Segovia played several pieces; and Cora and Bil Baird brought their internationally famous Marionette Theatre to the floor of the General Assembly.

As you can observe, even though these programs were of a lighter nature, they practically covered the entire spectrum of musical and show business entertainment. Although the delegates were not formally invited to Staff Day, some of them did, on occasion, use their political influence and crash the event.

Shortly after Frank Sinatra was extended his official UN invitation to be Master Of Ceremonies for the 13 September 1963 Staff Day and he immediately accepted, the press reported that he was being investigated for some supposed improper business dealings surrounding an alleged interest in the Lake Tahoe Nevada Cal-Neva Lodge. As a result, the UN were more than a bit high-strung about this and they were seriously considering ways to delicately rescind the invitation.

I said, "Look, you've extended the invitation to the gentleman. You can't reverse it now on the basis of purported evidence; it just wouldn't be fair and it wouldn't look good."

Fortunately, by the preceding weeks of the Staff Day concert, the press coverage had all but vanished, as there were now new international mitigating issues with Vietnam and the Congo.

Jeff Sparks was fretting about the situation a couple of days before the event and said, "Phillip, we have to tell Mr. Sinatra that he is not to mention anything about the Congo or Vietnam in his monologues, or his investigation at the Cal-Neva Lodge in Lake Tahoe."

I reminded Jeff about a previous Staff Day, where we had one of my favorite iconoclasts, Alan King, and how Jeff had asked Alan King not to ridicule any of the public utilities or the Russians during his monologue. King brilliantly not only hurled satiric barbs at both the Telephone Company (with yours truly cheering him on) and the Russians, but Alan King's own wife received a few humorous cutting remarks as well.

I said to Jeff Sparks, "I think Frank Sinatra will be so excited about being Master Of Ceremonies and singing a few songs here on the floor of the General Assembly that it won't even enter his mind. I think it best we not mention it, Jeff."

"No, no, no. We can't take that chance; we have to mention it," said Jeff.

"Jeff, if I were you, I wouldn't mention to Mr. Sinatra the Congo, Vietnam, Lake Tahoe, or anything else because he's liable to turn it around and make one big joke out of it during his monologue."

"No, we'd better mention it."

"Well, you mention it," I said.

The early evening of the Staff Day we had a cocktail and hors d'oeuvres reception in the Delegates' Dining Room on the East Side of the General Assembly Building upon which Mr. Frank Sinatra and the other artists were introduced to me by Jeff Sparks. Sinatra arrived impeccably attired in evening dress and with an attractive young red haired lady (who had not been presented to me) in a beautiful emerald satin evening gown with a diamond tiara crowning her head.

Sinatra, I could tell, was elated to be at the UN and seemed to feel more at ease with me after Jeff Sparks informed him that I was a very talented symphonic composer and conductor. Sinatra was further surprised and pleased to learn that I was friendly with his close intimate of many years, composer and songwriter Alec Wilder. Alec used to come into the Schirmer offices and demand a financial accounting of his school chamber opera comedy Kittiwake Island. Wilder liked me because we both had the same parallel views of my Schirmer superior Hans Heinsheimer. Heinsheimer, in order to mollify Alec Wilder, would ask me to take him to lunch. "Pheel," Heinsheimer would plead with me. "Do something with this man; would you please?" We would make an appointment for a late lunch and then Wilder would invariably want me to take him to a bar where he could unwind his music business frustrations over several drinks. Since I really didn't drink, I would order a scotch and water and just let it sit there, listening to all kinds of interesting stories. Wilder had informed me of his great friendship (in their youth) with Frank Sinatra, and how he had acquainted Sinatra with good symphonic music and literature. "I wish to hell I could get Frank away from that terrible show business life he leads," I remember Wilder telling me. "I know he's not reading and studying as much as he was when we saw each other frequently." Wilder also revealed that even though he had hardly seen Sinatra the past few years, on a multitude of occasions Frank Sinatra saved his life financially by sending Wilder badly needed money to rescue himself.

"Do you happen to know where Alec is now?" Sinatra asked.

"I think he's in a motel in Key West, Florida." I said. "But I can find out for you."

"He telephoned my office in Hollywood last week, but he didn't leave a number." Sinatra said.

"You know how Alec likes trains," I said. "He's probably on a train bound for somewhere."

We both smiled because we knew Alec Wilder's incredible love and knowledge of trains. If you had to catch a train from Lake Okeechobee, Florida and wished to go to Cumbie, Texas I would have bet my life that Alec Wilder could have told you which trains to take and the times and connections you would have had to make in order to arrive there.

"I'm worried that he might be in trouble," Sinatra said. "So if you find out where he is, let me know."

Sinatra scribbled his name and office address on the back of an invitation envelope, "Here," he said. "Let me know when you find him."

I told Sinatra that I would wire him as soon as I located Alec, and additionally that I planned to move to Los Angeles and attempt to compose and conduct music for films. Sinatra said I should contact him after I arrived.

Sinatra wondered if I had been familiar with his recordings, and I informed him that even though I was a symphonic and concert composer I thoroughly appreciated good pop music and jazz. I proceeded to tell him that my favorite albums of his were *Swinging Lovers* which he did with Nelson Riddle, and a voiceless instrumental album entitled *Tone Poems of Colors* where Sinatra conducted the orchestra in short pieces based upon colors which he had commissioned from name Hollywood composers of the time.

"It's odd that you should like those two," Sinatra said, "because you have just mentioned my worst selling album *Colors* and my best selling album *Swinging Lovers.*"

"Well, that shows you what extreme tastes I have," I said.

"You know, Alec did one of the colors on the album," Sinatra reminded me.

"Alec told me that you like Mahler Symphonies."

"Yeah, Mahler's a gas," Sinatra said.

Just then my teacher Gyorgy Sandor, dressed in tails, came over and I introduced Sinatra and Gyorgy to each other.

After a few pleasantries, Gyorgy said to Sinatra, "I have a young son, Michael, who is a great fan of yours and I told him that we'll be performing on the same program, and he said that if I didn't bring him your autograph that he would be very upset."

Sinatra was amused over the fact that a celebrated concert pianist's young son was so affected in obtaining his autograph and obligingly wrote a warm inscription.

A UN security guard quietly approached me and said that a questionable looking man claiming to be Huntington Hartford was knocking at one of the locked glass side doors of the General Assembly Building next to the lawn informing the sentry that he had been invited to the cocktail party and Staff Day by Phillip Lambro, but had lost his invitation and did not have any identification to prove who he was.

"Mr. Lambro, he doesn't look right to me," said the guard.

"It's probably him," I sighed, excusing myself from both Sinatra and Sandor. "Where is he?"

The guard led me outside of the Delegates' Dining Room and over to the East Side of the General Assembly Building. Hartford had literally demanded that I get him an invitation in view of the fact (as he reminded me) that he had invited me to many of his dinner parties where I had met all the supposedly "beautiful people" including Salvador Dali and Richard Nixon. "But what about all the imbecilic infantiles you've also introduced me to?" I would jest with Hartford, as he would get indignant because he was basically shy and void of any subtle sense of humor.

After I arranged for Hartford's invitation, I specifically enumerated to him not to wear his usual rumpled gray flannel suit, but to come properly attired, at the very least, in a formal dark suit and to arrive via the Delegates' Entrance.

Well, there he was, Ladies and Gentlemen of the Jury, looking like a lost dog; standing patiently outside the thick, locked, and rarely used, side glass doors of the United Nations. I could not resist having some fun with both Hartford and the guard, so I said in an amazed natural way yelling through the glass door, "Who are you..?"

"Is this Mr. Hartford?" Asked the guard.

"What are you doing here?" I asked. "Where's your invitation?"

Hartford did not dare get irritable in front of the UN security guard.

"Come on, let me in," he said.

"Yes, that's him," I said to the sentry breaking into a smirk. "Let him in."

It took a while for the guard to open the doors because he didn't have the correct key and had to go to the main security office to acquire the right one.

"Sir," the guard said to Hartford. "You should never use this entrance; you should always come through the Delegates' Entrance."

It seems Hartford had used the Delegates' Entrance, but having walked not too far from his trilevel penthouse at One Beekman Place which is adjacent to the United Nations, and looking insignificantly unshaven in that Rumpelstiltskin gray flannel suit, and not having either his invitation or identification, the front security also would not admit him.

"Where's the invitation I got for you? And I told you to wear a dark suit," I said leniently.

"I know," said Hartford. "I just didn't have time to change and I couldn't find the invitation."

"It's a good thing I'm here; otherwise you probably would have been arrested."

The guard smiled at me, as Hartford was blandly nervous.

As I escorted Hartford into the Delegates' Dining Room, he loudly whispered into my ear, "I want you to promise that you'll introduce me to Frank Sinatra."

"No problem," I said. "We were having an interesting conversation before the security guard interrupted us with getting you in."

I first presented Hartford to an occupied Jeff Sparks who, although he was courteously succinct, I could tell was a bit dismayed by Hartford's drab appearance. Later on Jeff said to me, "With all his millions you'd think he'd be able to afford a decent suit."

Jeff was conversing with Gyorgy Sandor about the two compositions he was to perform: Chopin's *Grand Polonaise in G Major, Op. 22* without the *Andante Spianato*; followed by Franz Liszt's *Funerailles*. Jeff asked Sandor if he could announce the Liszt *Funerailles* as something else because a funeral march was absolutely prohibited at the UN. Sandor said that Liszt had also named the work *Harmonies poetiques et religieuses No. 7* so he could introduce the composition that way. This alternate title was acceptable.

I had left Hartford in a corner with an hors d'oeuvre and a beverage and returned to my conversation with Sinatra. After a minute I said, "Would you like to meet my friend Huntington Hartford?"

"Yes, I would," said Sinatra who seemed rather impressed. "I understand he's got some real estate in Los Angeles which might be for sale. I'd really like to talk with him about it."

It was one of the most humorous behavioral observations your humble court composer had ever witnessed. Here I am, as Huntington Hartford pretends that I'm dragging him away from his quagmire where he had been playing with an hors d'ouevre and his non-alcoholic drink, introducing Huntington Hartford to Frank Sinatra. After the introductions and initial pleasantries Sinatra was delicately trying to steer the conversation toward the world of commerce and big time real estate; however, Hartford was trying to guide the dialogue into the world of show business. Sinatra expressed to Hartford that he and a few other associates might be interested, if the price were right, in purchasing the Huntington Hartford Theater; now called the James A. Doolittle Theater on Vine Street near Hollywood Boulevard. Hartford had it built especially for his then wife aspiring actress Marjorie Steel whom he had met out on the prowl in a Hollywood nightclub with his movie star confidant Errol Flynn while she was working as a cigarette girl. Sinatra also seemed interested in procuring Hartford's large mountain Estate at the end of Fuller in Hollywood which had been the Huntington Hartford Artists Colony before a fire was to have destroyed the manor and dwellings a couple of years hence.

"I'm not so sure I want to sell it," Hartford smiled at Sinatra.

Jeff Sparks arrived as Sinatra and Hartford were continuing their chat. I could read his thoughts. "I have to tell him before he goes on," Jeff said to me. I just rolled my eyes and slightly shook my head to no avail.

"Excuse me Frank," said Jeff putting his arm around Sinatra's shoulder. "May I just have a brief word with you about your monologue?"

"Of course," said Sinatra as the two went off to the side.

I proceeded to introduce Hartford to Sandor. Then, as I was about to walk away, Sinatra's attractive young red haired lady in the emerald evening dress with the diamond tiara, necklace and earrings unexpectedly stood there in front of me.

"Good evening," I said. "Are you having a good time?"

"Yes, I am." she replied in a pronounced unusual British accent. "I was so excited to meet Mr. Thant."

"Are you from the United Kingdom?" I asked.

"I live in Hollywood. I'm a screen actress," she said. "Don't you know who I am?"

"I'm sorry," I said. "With my schedule, about all I see these days is

43

an occasional foreign film at the Carnegie Hall Cinema."

"What's your name?" I asked.

"Jill St. John," she replied in an even more Old Vic tone.

"I'm pleased to meet you," I said, "and I hope to see one of your films soon."

"What is your name?" She asked.

"Phillip Lambro," I said. "I assist in the musical formation of the programs here at the UN."

"Ohh," she cooed.

"Would you do me a great favor?" She asked.

"What would you like?"

"I'm just so impressed with Mr. Thant. Could you arrange for me to have my picture taken with him?"

"After the program," I said, "everyone will be photographed together and separately."

"You don't understand," she said. "I want to be photographed alone with the Secretary General."

I smiled at the lovely young lady. "I'll speak with Mr. Sparks and I'm sure he'll arrange for a shot of you and Mr. Thant off to the side after the conclusion of the program."

"Oh, thank you," she said.

The ceremonies were about to begin and we all filed into the General Assembly Hall. It was filled to capacity: even some of the Staff were sitting on the aisle steps and floor. For those who were unable to be seated in the General Assembly Hall, we arranged for closed-circuit TV on large screen projection in Conference Room 4.

I left everyone backstage and went to my desk seat in the General Assembly where I always liked to witness the finished program.

U Thant, as usual, came out and presented the Master Of Ceremonies in a brief introductory speech. However, this particular evening he was at his wittiest and in complete mastery of his subtle Burmese humor. Mr. Thant entered to a tumultuous applause and proceeded to summarize the year's progress for peace in a rather nebulous way praising the entire Staff for the wonderful support they had bestowed all year. "Ladies and gentlemen of the Staff," he concluded, "you have done such a brilliant job this year, as always, so this is our small way of thanking you for your efforts. This day is yours. And now it gives me great pleasure," U Thant went on, "to introduce to you your Master Of Ceremonies: one of humanity's great lifter of spirits; Mr. Frank Sinatra."

This was one of the most memorable double entendres I had ever heard. And if you had ever listened to U Thant speak, he did it within a completely mellifluous dry monotone.

There was a delayed ripple of laughter throughout the General Assembly Hall as Frank Sinatra, beaming, alighted from the wings to an equally thunderous applause. You could sense that he appreciated U Thant's humorous foreword. Sinatra looked remarkably well on stage; rested and tanned. And it was apparent that he was delighted to be there as he was eminently natural and polite.

After they both shook hands and Mr. Thant left the stage Sinatra said as he adjusted the microphone, "Mr. Secretary General, thank you very much. It's a great experience for me to be here on the floor of the General Assembly, this auspicious General Assembly. Especially in such troubled times as we have today in the Congo, Vietnam...and Lake Tahoe."

There was a louder ruffle of laughter followed by supportive applause and even a few whistles from the Staff. Jeff Sparks, who was sitting about twenty five yards away from me just hit his forehead with the palm of his hand, and as we looked at one another I silently mouthed, "I told you so."

Frank Sinatra's performing level was flawless. Toward the end of the concert as Sinatra was introducing classical guitarist Gustavo Lopez, an attendant came out and placed Lopez's tiny guitarist's foot stool and chair near an adjacent microphone; upon which, as the very short smiling Mexican guitarist began walking toward center stage (it was a comical sight), Sinatra slowly glanced down at the small foot stool and casually remarked, "That looks like a bench for one of my short Sicilian friends."

At the conclusion of the program Jeff Sparks arranged for all of the artists to be photographed with the Secretary General and I expressly asked Jeff to make sure that Jill St. John could also have a solo pose with Mr. Thant. Ordinarily, since she was not on the agenda, she would not have been afforded this opportunity. Sinatra had said to Jeff and myself, "You know, in all my years in show business, I've never asked for anyone's autograph, but it would be a privilege if you could arrange to have U Thant autograph one of the photos we took together and send it to me." Jill St. John came up to me again and asked if she could also have the Secretary General's autograph on her photo, too. I smiled and said that I'd see to it that Mr. Sparks would take care of her request.

There was a dance and reception afterward for the Staff on the Main Floor and Concourse with Meyer Davis and his Society Orchestra providing the music. I was on the carpeted mezzanine above the Concourse Main

Floor with Jeff Sparks; Nat Kalcheim (Head of the William Morris Agency); Hartford; Alfredo (an Argentinian friend of mine); Gyorgy Sandor; Diane Hartford (Huntington Hartford's young attractive wife) who telephoned me after the concert and I arranged for her to be admitted into the reception to the consternation of Hartford who had not wanted her there; and a few other friends of ours who were all unwinding with snacks and refreshments. My friend Alfredo was quite impressed with Gyrogy Sandor. "Not only is your teacher a great concert pianist," he said, "but he speaks Spanish like a native." Alfredo could not get over how Sandor (who had given hundreds of recitals all over Argentina) knew exactly all the little towns and provinces from where Alfredo had lived.

Later on I left with Sandor. As we walked through the General Assembly Hall and past the stage he asked me to sit down at the Steinway concert grand and play for him the opening measures of the Toccata for Piano which I had just begun to compose for him. I was pleased that he liked the quarter-tone sostenuto middle pedal effect which forms the nucleus of the whole piece. I was to complete this work a year and one-half later in Los Angeles.

During the 1962 Staff Day (the one with Alan King) I remember telephoning concert pianist Byron Janis on short notice and he agreed to appear. This was when Byron was at the height of his pianistic faculties.

He played a Schubert Impromptu and Prokofiev's Toccata in C Major, Op. 11. I recall Jeff Sparks asking me, "What is Byron Janis going to play?"

"I don't know," I replied. "He told me he hasn't made up his mind."

"Well, find out," Jeff Sparks implored.

Right up to Staff Day Byron kept telling me, "I just haven't made up my mind. I'll probably decide just as soon as I walk out to the piano."

I had asked Byron to play the Prokofiev Toccata as a particular favor to me, and I was quite surprised when he did.

You could do that with Staff Day concerts because the programs were made up entirely of photos and biographical data of each artist in order of appearance and they would announce the titles from the stage, or someone would broadcast what was to be performed over the inter-communications system. With Human Rights Day concerts, everything to be performed was printed on the program.

Out of all the concert pianists who had appeared at the UN, Byron Janis was Jeff Sparks' personal favorite. As a former radio and TV announcer and communications expert Jeff was particularly conscious of sound. He told me that he was amazed at Byron Janis' precision and clarity. This, of course was 1962, and Janis was at the apex of his buoyant technique.

On that same program Duke Ellington appeared and his Band furnished the music for the reception dance following the event. I'll never forget meeting Duke Ellington. As soon as I shook his hand, I noticed that I was shaking a cuff and a cuff-link. Duke Ellington's shirt cuffs came over his knuckles!

The last Staff Day I assisted (because I informed Jeff Sparks that I couldn't do it anymore as I was in Los Angeles and totally involved with my symphonic, concert and motion picture music career) was in 1965 where I was responsible for acquiring Jack Benny to commit to being the Master Of Ceremonies. I was not acquainted with Jack Benny, but I had known his close friend John Green (the songwriter of *Body And Soul* and *I Cover The Waterfront*) and John Green introduced me to Jack Benny.

Ladies and Gentlemen of the Jury, in all the five years I helped with those United Nations programs, getting Jack Benny to positively assure me that he would accept an invitation from the Secretary General and be Master Of Ceremonies for the 10 September 1965 Staff Day concert was perhaps the most delicately frustrating task I had ever encountered.

To understand this, you had to comprehend the authentic nature of Jack Benny's real personality compounded by his professional priorities in the twilight of his show business career.

At first, he was quite flattered and excited to be offered the invitation.

After several preliminary telephone conversations during May of 1965, I met with Jack Benny a few times at his office which was near the Friar's Club on little Santa Monica Boulevard in Beverly Hills. In that low keyed whining manner of his which I remembered listening to on the radio when I was seven years old, Jack Benny began to vacillate.

"Now, Phillip; I know it's the United Nations," he said, "and I know the United Nations is an important and worthwhile organization, but just who has appeared on these Staff Day programs?"

"Jack," I said, "we've had Frank Sinatra, Danny Kaye, Marian Anderson, Helen Hayes, Johnny Carson, Victor Borge, I mean it will be the crowning achievement of your show business career."

I could tell that even behind Jack Benny's deadpan exterior trademark, he was becoming more impressed with each name that I dropped.

"You know, I've done command performances in front of the Queen of England. How, would my performing at the United Nations compare with that?"

"No comparison at all," I said. "Without demeaning the Queen of England, performing at the United Nations is as if you're giving a command performance for all the heads of states and all the people of the world. Don't take my word for it, Jack; just ask Frank Sinatra. He told us it was the greatest thrill he'd ever had in his performing career."

Jack Benny wanted to see some copies of preceding Staff Day programs and he wanted me to send them to him, along with a covering letter, the following week at the Thunderbird Hotel in Las Vegas where he was scheduled to appear.

"Do you think I'd be able to play my violin?" Benny asked.

"Of course," I said not really certain if he were joking or serious. "I'm sure something could be arranged. You'll be Master Of Ceremonies. It's a variety show in concert and John Browning will be performing there, too."

"Oh, John Browning," Benny said getting more intrigued, "yes, a wonderful concert pianist. I met him at the Hollywood Bowl. Perhaps, John and I could do a little skit together and then I could play a short serious piece with him."

As I got to know Jack Benny during those succeeding months, it became evident that he really had been more attracted to the world of concert music and performing the violin all of his life rather than the adulation and fame he had achieved as a comedian. In fact, one time in his office I said, "Jack, you're such a serious minded person that you don't really remind me of a comedian at all."

"Well, you're right," he said. "I was never a comedian in the true sense. I was a violinist who failed. The violin to me was the most important thing in my whole life. I just happen to have fallen into comedy by not playing the violin very well. The only thing I excel in, in comedy, is my timing. I'm not funny at all," he went on, "it's my timing that makes people laugh. I'm really just a frustrated concert violinist who couldn't make it and went into comedy. I was never really a comedian; all I have is this gift for timing in the delivery of my lines and that makes people laugh. And I built a whole successful career out of that. The general public doesn't know how serious I am about my violin; they think it's all one big joke. I've practiced the violin a hundred times more than my comedy."

Additionally, I sensed that all those radio and TV situation comedy jokes and skits about Jack Benny being overly frugal and concerned with money (which made him notorious and which the general public thought were not true) were, in fact, rather accurate: Jack Benny, in actuality, was truly concerned about money.

I also noticed that he didn't wear a toupee when he was crouching down over a file cabinet looking for a symphony orchestra benefit program where he had appeared with violinist Isaac Stern which he wanted to impress me with. As a child I had remembered during his radio shows how he used to make fun of his toupee, and just then as I was standing over him, I noticed that (even though he had a receding hairline) Jack Benny had all of his own hair.

"Jack," I said, "you never really wore a toupee as you used to claim on your old shows. That's your own hair."

"Oh that was just one of my standing jokes on the old radio shows," he said.

After Jack Benny accepted the invitation, he telephoned me and said, "Phillip, I know that the United Nations does not pay any of the entertainers who perform there, but I have an opportunity to do this show at a theater in the round in San Francisco where I'll be making $25,000 dollars exactly the week when the Staff Day occurs. Now, you know, Phillip, $25,000 dollars is a lot of money and I still have a staff to pay and lot of ongoing expenses."

"Jack," I reminded him, "you did accept the Secretary General's invitation and you did give us your word."

"I know, I know," he went on as if he were doing one of his radio and TV shows; and, Ladies and Gentlemen of the Jury, at times, I felt like a combination of Rochester and Dennis Day. "Let me see what I can do," Jack Benny went on, "because I really don't want to lose this theater in the round date."

Since Jack Benny sensed my surprise and rather obvious, but polite, disenchantment over the fact that he would even consider doing the internationally unforgivable and cancel his United Nations appearance in favor of a sudden theatrical booking, he called me about twenty minutes later encouraging me that he actually did want to be Master Of Ceremonies at the United Nations Staff Day, but he still did not wish to lose the $25,000 dollar engagement which he had been offered. "I just spoke with the theater management," he said, "and I think we have a way out of this thing where I can do both. Now listen to this, Phillip: the theater management informed me that Judy Garland is doing her one woman show during the same season. So since I know Judy rather well,

I just telephoned her and left a message for her to call me right away because it's very urgent that I speak with her. Now, I'm going to tell Judy my predicament and see if she'd be willing to switch dates with me."

The next day Jack Benny phoned me somewhat proud of himself. "I can do the United Nations event, Phillip; there's no problem. I just spoke with Judy long distance and she's agreed to switch dates with me, so everything will be fine."

It's a good thing Jeff Sparks and I were separated by 2,468 miles and I was handling the arduous Jack Benny situation here on the West Coast because if Jeff had known what was truly going on, he would have had a heart attack.

Staff Day 1965 was doubly auspicious because it coincided with the United Nations 20th Anniversary. Jeff and I were on the telephone a few times each week considering other artists to complete the event.

Around the 10th of August 1965, Jack Benny was pressing me to let him know not only who else would be appearing with him; but he wanted me to inform him as far in advance as possible the program running order, and the biographical data of every artist. The reason for this he explained was so that he could prepare some interesting comedic material involving the other celebrities. I could see that everything Jack Benny did professionally, he did with a tremendous amount of preparation, and I admired him for that. Benny also wanted everything sent to him at Harrah's in State Line, Nevada where he was scheduled to appear for two weeks; however, he wanted the UN to duplicate everything and send it to me; just in case that he accidentally lost the documentation.

Since I had been responsible for John Browning, Jeff aligned the popular Italian tenor Sergio Franchi. I telephoned soprano Phyllis Curtin in New York City as I had been acquainted with her from my days at Schirmer. Jeff obtained humorist Yoel Sharr who was fluent in seven languages, and we both agreed that Lionel Hampton and his orchestra (along with the La Plata Sextet) should provide the music for the usual evening dance following the program.

Jack Benny called me in September, after he did the Staff Day, upon his return to Beverly Hills. "Phillip," he said, "I'm very sorry I was so much of a trouble-maker for you."

"Oh, no, you weren't." I said.

"Yes, I was. And it was because I could not imagine how exciting performing at the United Nations would be since I had never done anything like this in my life before."

"Did you enjoy doing the program?" I asked.

"It was the greatest experience in my show business life," he said. "It was wonderful. The feeling is unbelievable there on the stage of the United Nations General Assembly Hall. It's something you just cannot describe. The ambience there is unlike anywhere else I have ever performed. I got to play a serious piece with John Browning, who was absolutely marvelous, and then we did a funny little skit at the end of the program which everybody loved."

On my studio wall I have a commendation from Jeff Sparks and the United Nations which they gave me for helping with this particular occasion making Jack Benny's appearance possible.

We arranged to have the New York Philharmonic during one Human Rights Day where we had Karl Boehm conducting a Beethoven Symphony. I was responsible for influencing Jeff Sparks into engaging Sidney Poitier where Poitier became the first black man at the United Nations to read the *Declaration Of The Rights Of Man*. I would occasionally see Poitier (whom I had never been formally introduced to) at the Grocery Market in Hollywood during the mid sixties where I found him to be unsociable and rather snobbish; however, after he encountered me a few times at one of the Pennsylvania Life Insurance owner's sumptuous Tudor home where I on occasion played tennis during the mid seventies, Poitier tried then to be affable toward me; however, I courteously neglected him.

Laurence Olivier appeared two times on Human Rights Days and that was the only instance where anyone was ever asked again; with the exception of Staff Day, where Jeff Sparks had engaged Danny Kaye to perform twice. The official policy at the UN was never to have an artist appear more than once.

After Jack Benny performed at the United Nations, I did not maintain a relationship with him as with extreme financial pressures it was imperative (September of 1965) that I acquire another film score so that I could continue to compose concert music and learn orchestral scores for possible future guest conducting engagements. As it turned out, right after Staff Day, I had an interview with Joseph Gershenson (the Head Of Music at Universal Pictures) who was genuinely impressed with my ability and was influential in signing me to do the incidental music for their film *And Now Miguel*.

I was also working on my *Toccata for Piano* and my *Two Pictures for Solo Percussionist & Orchestra* at the time so I really did not have occasion to call Jack Benny and he did not telephone me. Besides, I believe that it was not too many years after this that he passed away.

I did communicate with Frank Sinatra early in 1964 upon my arrival here in Los Angeles and I was somewhat surprised when he did not return my call until a friend of mine showed me the morning edition of the Los Angeles Times. Frank Sinatra's son had just been kidnapped and was being held for a six figure ransom. So, clearly, it was not an opportune time; although his son was freed within several days and the notoriety quickly subsided. I actually waited a year and a half, early 1966, before I telephoned Sinatra's office again. It was directly after I had completed *And Now Miguel* and the newly sown MCA executives were going through a systematic Black Tower purge of Joseph Gershenson and other Universal Pictures executives. Sinatra's personal secretary said, "Yes, Mr. Sinatra does remember you and he'd like to know how he might help you because he's in the process of shooting a new film and he's extremely busy."

I explained to the secretary that at the UN Mr. Sinatra had suggested I contact him since I would be trying to secure motion pictures to score.

The following day, I received a telephone call from Sinatra's secretary informing me that Mr. Sinatra had spoken about me with then Vice President and Music Director of Warner Bros., Mr. Sonny Burke, and that I was to contact him for an interview. Sonny Burke was a jovial, pleasant and smoothly intelligent middle-aged fellow who I subsequently found out had written the music for one of my favorite songs, *Midnight Sun*, to words by Johnny Mercer. Although he was well educated and a good dance band arranger, record producer and popular songwriter, Sonny Burke did not really speak the language of advanced film scoring, or symphonic and contemporary music techniques. He was calm, polite and direct at our meeting.

"Frank remembers you and asked me to see what I can do for you."

I told him truthfully that I would like to do more film scores in order to sustain my concert music career. Sonny Burke felt that I had done quite well since I had scored two films in less than two years and like most pop musicians was impressed with my concert hall credentials. "Many guys have been out here for twenty years and haven't done two scores and all the things you've done," he said.

Just then an important telephone call came which Burke had to receive. As he was speaking, I glanced at the several galvanized 35mm film cans piled in the corner nearest my chair labeled *The Sand Castle*, Alec Wilder.

"I see that you've got a good little featurette there, *The Sand Castle*." I said after Sonny Burke finished his call.

"Have you seen it?" Asked Burke.

"I saw it in New York City a couple of years ago," I said. "I liked it. Alec Wilder did the music and he plays the fisherman in the film, too."

"Yeah, I don't know what we're going to do with it, but Alec sent it to Frank to see if we can get a sound track album out of it. But the film is too short and kind of off beat; an art-house type of film. I don't think we're going to put out an album."

We talked about film scoring agents. At that time, I was being represented by Howard Barnes (former producer of the New York Philharmonic CBS broadcasts) at Ashley Famous Agency (soon to be cloned into ICM) since Nat Kalcheim's nephew Sid Kalcheim (who had procured my first Hollywood film Embassy Pictures, *Git!*) had left the William Morris Agency disillusioned and went back to Law School. The William Morris Agency subsequently assigned me to their nervy, fast-talking agent, Sy Marsh. Although I liked Sy, who often made me laugh, I quickly became a bit disenchanted during our appointed meetings whereby as soon as his secretary escorted me into his office, Sy Marsh would vociferate while on three telephone lines, "Philly baby, just have a seat and I'll be with you in a minute, I have to take these important calls from Sammy Davis Jr. and Kim Novak." Then it was, "Sammy baby, you'll be pleased to know that I got you two weeks at The Sands in Las Vegas at great money, and I'm now trying to book you into the Copa and on Ed Sullivan." Sy Marsh would clatter along at unbelievable vocal speed. Then it was, "Hold on Sammy baby..." Then, "Kim baby, yes I saw you on TV baby, you looked great. You looked beautiful." Soon after, Sy Marsh, who was responsible for monetarily upgrading Sammy Davis Jr.'s career, left the William Morris Agency and formed Sy Marsh-Sammy Davis Jr. Enterprises. So I aligned myself with Howard Barnes who was flexible, knowledgeable and intelligent from the symphonic world to his most important client, Danny Kaye.

Sonny Burke said he had heard from Howard Barnes and had read the glowing reviews from Variety to the Saturday Review I had received for my music to *And Now Miguel* and felt that I should be in line for more assignments at Universal. I explained to Burke that Joseph Gershenson (who treated me as if I were his own son and had acquired the assignment for me over the initial objections of the film's producer, Robert Radnitz) had recently informed me that after thirty-five years he was losing his authority and position as a result of the absorbtion of Universal by MCA. I also found out that I had gotten the contract to *And Now Miguel* just a matter of weeks before Joe Gershenson had lost control. If it had been a few weeks later, I never would have been engaged for that film. I sensed something was amiss when I would visit Gershenson and notice that his three parking spaces suddenly had been reduced to one; and that his two assistants and two secretaries over a matter of four months had been lowered to one secretary; and how they had been moved into a smaller office. Afterward, I observed how MCA further inflicted, little by little, this humiliating Celluloid corporate Chinese torture in trying, systematically, to force Gershenson to resign. It seems that Joseph Gershenson (who a couple of years heretofore had part of his throat removed due to cancer) had a life's contract with Universal and could not be financially terminated. They had to pay him his substantial salary as long as he lived; even if he were to be dismissed. This was in 1966 and, ultimately after the new MCA suits took away all of Gershenson's powers, he departed the studio shortly thereafter; but I understand that Joseph Gershenson lived to be 84 and died in 1988. During 1966 MCA brought out a non-musician music publishing executive from New York City named Harry Garfield and installed him into the Black Tower as head of music. Joe Gershenson's secretary informed me that Gershenson had telephoned and wrote several memos to Garfield about how talented I was and that I should be given further major Universal films to score. Joe Gershenson who had initially sponsored Henry Mancini and Jerry Goldsmith during their commencement wanted me to be his third protege. He would emphatically instruct me to phone Harry Garfield (I really did not wish to), but out of consideration for Gershenson I did what he requested. I could not get an appointment to see Garfield and he would never return any of my calls.

Sonny Burke smiled. "Where will you be going after our meeting?" He asked.

"Home," I said.

"Will you be home in about an hour?"

"Yes; I should be."

"Good," smiled Burke. "As you're walking in the door, your telephone will be ringing and it'll be Harry Garfield on the other end of the line and he will give you an appointment."

"Are you kidding me?" I asked.

"No, I'm serious. When you get home the telephone will be ringing and it will be Harry Garfield."

Since I was financially in debt at the time, the only way I could support myself, or had any hope of preserving my concert music endeavors, was to acquire film scores. I began to view potential motion picture soundtracks as my fiscal stays of execution. Ladies and Gentlemen of the Jury, please believe me when I say that I was unequivocally not fascinated in having to go through all these political infiltration conduits in order to annex another Celluloid music assignment.

The conference ended and Sonny Burke said to me not to get discouraged. He took my biographical brochure and credit sheet stating that he would see what might be available at Warner Bros.

As I was driving back to my apartment, I really thought that Sonny Burke had been joking.

However, when I arrived home and opened the door, the telephone was ringing. It was Harry Garfield himself. He gave me an appointment that week. I arrived on time, but Garfield intentionally kept me waiting for over forty-five minutes even though (as his secretary informed me confidentially) that there were no other meetings taking place in his office. While I was patiently lingering, Garfield would walk in and out of his office giving his secretary obvious unessential commonplace instructions and functions while glancing me over in the process. He did this several times; once, asking me to bear with him as he was doing his best to convince me and his secretary how dreadfully occupied he was. Harry Garfield granted me a total of five agitated, but pacified abusive minutes; the first thirty seconds of which I rapidly got the message. It was like organized crime. He had been compelled to see me because of Frank Sinatra and Sonny Burke, even though he did not wish to; primarily because I was a protege of Joseph Gershenson's, the now banished Hollywood musical Godfather he was replacing. After I left Garfield's office, I went to see Joe Gershenson in another building for the last time. I thanked him for everything he had done and tried to do for me, but I told him that I knew I would never be asked to score another motion picture at Universal as long as Harry Garfield was there. This was one rare example where it was not beneficial to have had a recommendation from Frank Sinatra and his associate, and the former Head Of Music at Universal.

I became a close friend of Edward "Buzz" Barton (Huntington Hartford's son who was around my age) shortly after my arrival here in Hollywood. Buzz liked good music and literature, and was an excellent golfer. He was slight of build, looked a little like a distillation between Alan Ladd and James Dean, and was highly intelligent and quietly personable. Although he was living off of a multi-million dollar trust fund, he was not the least bit ostentatious. He was a member of the exclusive Beverly Hills private club The Daisy and he introduced me to all the unique hangouts from The Luau and The Whisky-A-Go-Go to Barney's Beanery and Cyrano's. One of the reasons I think Buzz liked me to accompany him on his afternoon and nocturnal prowls was usually the bizarre things I would sometimes say to attractive girls whom we were trying to meet. For example, during a particular occasion I asked this charming girl and her female confidant if they would like to take out a subscription to the International Tuba Journal and meet us later for dinner. To my absolute amazement, they joined us that evening for dinner.

One night during 1965, Buzz took me to the prominent Sunset Boulevard disco The Whisky-A-Go-Go when getting into and being seen at The Whisky-A-Go-Go was a social coup. Enrico Sarscini, the Life magazine photographer, whom I had met at Universal and had gotten to know on the set of Alfred Hitchcock's *Torn Curtain* motion picture had known that I was a concert composer and he was there doing a photo essay about The Whisky-A-Go-Go for Life. Enrico began rapidly shooting photographs of me there with his automatic machine-gun camera as I was being kissed by this risque girl whom I had just met two minutes earlier. I yelled over the loud disco music, "Enrico, if these pictures appear in Life magazine I'll sue you." Not that I personally cared, but having known the symphonic music world and the blue haired ladies who controlled most of it at that time, I did not think it would have done my future concert career any good if these images were to appear in Life.

So Buzz said to me rather excitedly, " Hey, there's Jill St. John over there."

There was this disheveled red-head in fried blue jeans and a tight fitting custom made white T-shirt bouncing to and fro in a small side booth sandwiched between two blond muscular and deeply tanned weight lifters.

I said, "Buzz, that's not Jill St. John because I met Jill St. John at the UN party we had with Frank Sinatra a couple of years ago."

"I'll bet you $20 dollars that's Jill St. John," Buzz said emphatically.

"I remember Jill St. John," I said, "and that's not Jill St. John."

Now I had encountered Jill St. John at the United Nations in a ramrod emerald evening gown with a diamond tiara, necklace and earrings coupled with affected United Kingdom speech. Here was this Californian red-head, teasing her drink, a little bit tripped out, moving her personality to the music in one of the side booths at the darkly lit smoke filled Whisky-A-Go-Go, during the height of it's mania with Johnny Rivers roaringly chanting *The Midnight Special* with his rock band from the small center stage and two tassled blonde Go-Go Girls flickering above him in twin plate glass cubicles bombarded by kaleidoscopic lighting.

That evening there were all kinds of illustrious personages in attendance. Baseball pitcher Sandy Koufax was there as was Italian film star Gina Lollobrigida. I particularly remember Lollobrigida because she accidentally stepped on my toe with her spiked high heel on the overly crowded dance floor as I was treading it with a captivating girl while Lollobrigida was rubbing her upper and lower intestines against a rather ambivalent but ubiquitously tanned George Hamilton. We all looked like sardines suffering from locomotor Ataxia on the crammed dance floor. Plus another inconsiderate young lady burned the handsome French suit I was wearing with her stupid cigarette.

Buzz said, "Well, how are we going to go up to her and prove it?" I said, "I could go up to her quite easily because she asked that I send her an autographed picture from U Thant."

I was so convinced that this wench was not Jill St. John that I eventually approached her and said, "Hi, I'm Phillip Lambro. Remember me from the United Nations?"

She said, "Oh, yeah. Hi. How are you?"

I said, "Did you get the pictures?"

"Oh, yeah...thanks a lot; you know, I got the pictures...Yeah, thanks a lot." Ladies and Gentlemen of the Jury, I could not believe it. It actually was Jill St. John. I immediately could see that at the UN she had been a much better actress than I had originally perceived her to be. I paid Buzz the twenty dollars.

Another intriguing thing happened to me at the United Nations. I was sending Schirmer music scores and one or two of my own works to Russia at the time and I would occasionally receive replies in Russian; so I would go to one of the Russian officials whom I knew in their office at the UN and he would quickly translate the letter.

It was kind of entertaining because the Russian fellow who used to translate my letters I would sometimes see at cocktail parties and he was rather a fun person to be around. One day I went into the Russian Delegates' office looking for him with a letter to be translated where several Russian staff members bluntly said without looking at me, "He is not here."

"Is he at lunch?" I asked.

They did not respond, so I said, "Well, I'll come back later." The Russian officials never said another word to me.

I was rather occupied the rest of the afternoon, but managed to return the next day. "He isn't here," they said again.

"Well, where is he?" I asked.

"We do not know."

Finally, I went to a few other United Nations officials and asked, "What's happened to him?" They said, "You didn't hear? He was asked to leave."

I said, "Why was he asked to leave?"

"He was a spy."

I said, "He was a spy? Really?" I thought I had known this fellow. We had gone out to lunch a few times and there he was in all probability a triple agent. Since he had had diplomatic immunity he was forced to return to Russia immediately.

Another amusing incident involved the painting by Ilja Jefimovitch Repin (the Russian impressionist) which had been entrusted to me by a Swiss associate who wanted to sell it entitled *Reception At The Court Of The Czar* an oil on canvas signed and dated 1894 (and authenticated) which we kept there in New York City in a bank vault. It was quite a remarkable painting.

Since there were so few of anything Repin ever sketched or painted outside of the Soviet Union, and since the majority of Repin's paintings are in Russia in the Museum there in Moscow, I thought the Soviets would, perhaps, be genuinely interested in purchasing the painting and returning it to its Russian birthplace.

I went to see one of the Russian delegates at the UN and informed him about the painting and how we would like to sell it. He put me in touch with another person in their Russian Embassy who made an appointment for me to see several Russian officials at the Amtorg Trading Commission a few days later on Madison Avenue.

As I was ushered into the offices of Amtorg, I suddenly felt, by the obvious formidable expressions of the several Russian administrators waiting for me, that I was going to be successful in negotiating the sale of the Repin.

As soon as I sat down, one of the executives asked me in his thick Russian inflection, "What kind of paint do you have?"

"Repin," I replied.

"What kind of paint is that?"

"It's an impressionist painting," I said. "It's very well known in Russia.

Immediately there was some Russian translation going on which I did not understand.

"Where can we see this paint?" The translating official asked.

"My associate and I have it in a bank vault here in New York,"

I said.

"In a bank vault..? Do you have a sample?"

"If you are really serious about the purchase," I said, "I can arrange to send you a color transparency and the supportive documentation."

"Are you ready to negotiate?" I asked.

"Yes," the Russian Amtorg officer said. "We are ready to negotiate if the price is fair and the quality is good. How many gallons can you supply us with?"

"Gallons!?" I politely exclaimed. "This is not paint. This is a famous Russian painting by Ilja Jefimovitch Repin one of your greatest impressionist painters. You should buy it for your museum."

I could not refrain from quietly chortling as more Russian paraphrasing went on. Now we were all laughing except for the Amtorg official who was doing the translating.

"Oh," he said, "we have no need for an Ilja Jefimovitch Repin painting; we have plenty of those. What we need in Russia now is paint; all kinds of paint."

Apropos that no one was ever extended an invitation from the Secretary General to appear at the United Nations if there was even the slightest indication of refusal, I must admit that there were two exceptions.

The artist or notable whom we wanted to appear would always have to give us assurances that he or she would not decline under any circumstance before a formal invitation was presented to them. There were two instances where well known celebrities had given us guarantees and at the last moment cancelled.

One was Sammy Davis Jr. (for a Staff Day) whom Jeff Sparks dealt with; and the other person was Anthony Quinn (for a Human Rights Day) whom I negotiated with. From what Jeff Sparks told me, Sammy Davis Jr.'s situation was simply a case of last minute fright. I feel that Davis actually wanted to be Master Of Ceremonies, but he was terrified of the monumental event. I did, eventually, meet Sammy Davis Jr. on a couple of fleeting occasions here in Hollywood during the middle to late 1960's, but I never spoke with him for more than a minute or two. Also, I don't believe I ever mentioned the UN incident to Sy Marsh (his agent-partner and my brief ex-agent) with whom I did have extended banterings.

Regarding Anthony Quinn, I had many telephone dialogues with him in New York City during 1963 regarding his scheduled appearance at the United Nations to recite *The Declaration Of The Rights Of Man*, although we never met in person. A few years later in Hollywood, when I had been friendly with actor-producer Tony Bill, Tony was making a film with Quinn at Warners and, as I recall, Tony briefly introduced us. Be that as it may, I had made it quite clear to Anthony Quinn that if he thought he could not appear at the UN because of the Broadway play he was scheduled to star in, or for any other reason, to let me know immediately and everything would be fine. I warned him not to accept the Secretary General's ceremonial invitation and then cancel. That would not be forgiven by the United Nations. Quinn gave me all kinds of assurances that he would be able to do it, and to send him the formal invitation. He specifically requested a copy of *The Declaration Of The Rights Of Man* which I forwarded to him; and I further informed Anthony Quinn that it would not be necessary for him to memorize *The Declaration* as he could just read it from the stage of the General Assembly.

We had several additional phone chats and spoke about a variety of subjects including art and painting, and his art collection. I also had several conversations with his then wife; an intelligent and cultured woman who I was apprised by an associate was the daughter of film mogul Cecil B. DeMille.

About a week before Human Rights Day, I received a call from Anthony Quinn's secretary at my Schirmer office informing me that Mr. Quinn was terribly sorry but he could not appear at the United Nations.

All the delegates and staff of the United Nations and their international associates world wide eventually learned of these breaches of promise by Sammy Davis Jr. and Anthony Quinn. Davis and Quinn never fathomed how much international respect they lost by the veritable nature of their slights.

Out of all the political leaders I saw and met at the UN, I was most affected by Madame Nehru of India. Jeff Sparks introduced me to her once at a cocktail party being given by some delegates late one afternoon. She had the most peaceful aura about her. Her eyes were notably deep and clear, and her skin had a rich color and purity to it. The thing which interested me most about Madame Nehru was her manner of speech and clarity of voice. Everyone was speaking rather loudly and there was so much chatter going on within many small groups that it was difficult to understand the person conversing next to you. I was about ten feet away from Madame Nehru who was voicing her opinion softly, but everyone could hear each word and understand her perfectly. That particular quality alone made a lasting impression upon me.

During this time, the United Nations was the most tranquil place I knew. I used to go there, on occasion, (even when I didn't have official work to do) and use part of Jeff Sparks office which he provided me with, just to clear my brain. I miss the particular quality and level of silence inherent in the Secretariat Building. Quietude has dissimilar characteristics of sound. You can hear stillness. That's why in motion picture production often times a sound engineer will put a recording machine in an empty room and just catalog an hour of silence. Sometimes I would do some composing in the Secretariat Building. And now and again I would just sit there and meditate; looking out over the East River before returning to my drab New York City living quarters.

One of the most amazing sights I ever experienced from the United Nations was during one late afternoon when I suddenly saw these huge life-like dinosaur brontosaur replicas being towed on two slim flat barges up the East River. An oil company, I believe, had commissioned these dinosaur brontosaur prototype replicas. There were two each on two separate barges which seemed so authentic I felt as if I had been frozen in time.

I looked out the window and thought at first that I might be hallucinating. Here was a flat barge coming up the East River with colossal dinosaurs on it. And then behind it, gigantic brontosaurs.

I alerted several UN staffers in adjacent offices and then called everyone I knew who lived along the East River to look out of their windows. It remains as one of the most amazing illusory sights I have ever witnessed.

THROUGH A GIGGLED LAUGH DARKLY

My earliest recollection of Sylvia Plath was when I was in the sixth grade at the Kingsbury School in Wellesley, Massachusetts. There was a new boy in our class, Warren Plath, who was around my age (Sylvia Plath was two grades ahead of us) and Warren Plath was assigned the seated desk directly behind me. He was a quiet, thin, sandy-haired boy with a calm exterior, but an inner nervousness. I undertook to speak with him a little at recess, and then at the end of that school day, he said to me, "My sister who's in Junior High now is going to meet me here. I have to wait for her; she's coming by for me on her bicycle."

That afternoon was the first time I met Sylvia Plath. She came to the rear of the Kingsbury School on her bicycle. She was about thirteen years old; tall and willowy with a broad white smile and ash blonde almost shoulder length hair with a small golden metal beret clasping her hair on the left side and every other strand in place. I was neat, but Sylvia Plath was immaculate in every respect. I don't recall the time of year it was, but it was after the semester had begun, because Warren did not begin the term with the rest of us. I remember the basket attached in front of the handle bars on Sylvia Plath's bicycle which neatly carried her books; and her brown loafer-moccasins, white bobbysocks, wool skirt with white blouse, and jacket. We didn't say too much to each other as I said goodbye to Warren. Warren later transferred from the Kingsbury School and I did not see him again until we both attended Alice L. Phillips Junior High School.

Afterward, on occasion I used to notice Sylvia Plath around town and we would acknowledge one another by saying, "Hello, how are you?" and all the other young peoples' salutations and goodbyes of the day.

The following year I went into the seventh grade at Wellesley's Alice L. Phillips Junior High School where I encountered Sylvia fairly often (because we were in the same art class) as she was in the ninth grade which was her last year at Alice L. Phillips. I also believe that Warren (whom I rarely had contact with) ultimately left the Phillips School for Exeter. But during this time, and especially in painting class, is where I first got to know Sylvia Plath.

When I advanced into the eighth grade, Sylvia went to the Gamaliel Bradford Senior High School which was the tenth, eleventh and twelfth grades. However, as soon as I got to the Bradford School (she was in her last year there) we were again in the same advanced art class together several times each week, so I once more began to understand her personality quite well from that environment; coupled with the fact that I used to see her drifting around Wellesley fairly often: either on her bicycle; walking home slowly, embracing her school books against her flush breasts, and looking down as she dilatorily shuffled through the Autumn leaves deep in thought; or as I remember her particularly infectious giggle-laugh with her friends having some fun and home made ice cream at either Bendslev's (the spacious pine paneled sandwich shop next to the colonial red brick Community Playhouse motion picture theater) or the Ice Cream Dairy directly across town.

Sylvia became interested in tennis during her senior year at Bradford, and since I was on the Tennis Team, I occasionally rallied with her at the Hunnewell Courts and tried to help her with her game. I had no other courses with Sylvia, simply because of our grade difference.

Our art class consisted of, roughly, fifteen students. Mr. Simone was the artist who was in charge and Miss Milner was the art supervisor who also attended classes. Miss Milner had been my art instructor since early grade school and she was also interested in concert music and was a Boston Symphony Orchestra subscriber. In fact, Miss Milner was the first person to acquaint me with pianist Aldo Ciccolini who had just made his debut with the Boston Symphony at that time. I was to eventually meet Ciccolini some years ago here at Ambassador Auditorium in Pasadena, California after one of his recitals. Miss Milner was an attractive woman in her late forties who wore designer opticals rather well. Mr. Simone was an energetic man of early middle age; short and lean, who looked of Spanish descent with swarthy rough skin, coal black hair and a thin moustache under his Roman nose and above his artist's smock.

Ladies and Gentlemen of the Jury, I can unequivocally state that nobody in this 1950 class shared my taste in contemporary art. And Sylvia Plath, quite frankly, thought I was crazy. I remember one day bringing into class a couple of Life Magazine pictorial articles devoted to a relatively unknown American painter by the name of Jackson Pollock. These illustrative essays showed Jackson Pollock dancing in rumpled jeans over his large canvases spread onto the floor of his East Hampton, New York studio with sticks and enamel house paint cans in hand; throwing, pirouetting, drooling and splattering the paints in a variety of powerfully wild and rhythmic arcs and patterns. In spite of the fact that I was sixteen, I was overpowered by the results of what I saw and I thought everyone would concur with my enthusiasm. Even though one of the iconographics made fun of Pollock and showed him with this rotund tavern owner in New York City where Pollock owed a few hundred dollars and couldn't pay his liquor bill (Pollock was a crude alcoholic even though Life Magazine did not recount him as such) and in order to efface that debt, Pollock gave the tavern owner a large action mural which he put behind all of the whiskey bottles and glasses. The tavern owner was quoted as saying that he seriously wondered if the painting was equal to the amount of the tab. We now know that if that tavern owner had kept it, the painting would probably fetch $22 million plus at auction. If Pollock were alive today that fact alone would be enough to sober him up rather expeditiously.

I was so immediately seized with the quality of Pollock's painting (the power, the depth, the organized complexity of happy accidents, the rhythm) that I brought it in to art class and my teachers, both Miss Milner and Mr. Simone, said that I was misguided; that Jackson Pollock would never achieve any significance in the art world; that he couldn't paint; and that what he was doing was not art at all.

I was so dismayed as the majority of the class laughed at me that I blurted out to my teachers and all, "You'll see... I hope you all live long enough to finally realize that Jackson Pollock is a great painter."

And Sylvia also giggled at me over her watercolor board saying, "Oh, Phillip, you're crazy!" In retrospect, that's kind of rich coming from eighteen year old Sylvia Plath.

I was the only one out of that whole class who felt that Jackson Pollock was an illustrious artist.

Ladies and Gentlemen of the Jury, I only bring this up to substantiate that Sylvia Plath, although she meteorically became quite a distinguished poetess toward the last few months of her life, and was a conventionally well read robot honor student, was also during her senior year at the Bradford School just an average artistically unenlightened regular Wellesley La-Dee-Da teenager.

Not in my wildest imagination did it ever occur to me at that time that in 1965 and 1966 I would compose *Two Pictures for Solo Percussionist & Orchestra* grounded upon two Jackson Pollock paintings, and that it would be premiered 14 October 1976 in a concert by the Rochester Philharmonic with John Beck as soloist and David Zinman, conducting; and that Herbert von Karajan would subsequently praise this work.

In many respects, my whole music career and life has been a series of unexpected surprises on an unforeseen path I knew I would travel. I knew the route I would choose, but I did not know the direction it would take me, and what exactly would happen along the way. I'm still on that road (in many respects my career and life has always been at a launching) and I am thankful that I still do not know, actually, what lies ahead. As I have learned from the Elohim Extraterrestrials, one cannot tell the future because one cannot travel in time; however, one can tell the future of a DNA biological entity, and all of humanity may be considered a biological entity with each of us as individual cells.

Two Pictures for Solo Percussionist & Orchestra was written at the 1963 request of Saul Goodman (the New York Philharmonic's virtuoso percussionist) after I had conducted the New York Philharmonic in a recording of my music. Saul Goodman, who played under every conductor there (from Toscanini and Bruno Walter to Bernstein and Pierre Boulez) was the only conducting coach and teacher I ever had. He put the stick in my hand and taught me what a great "band" like the 1963 New York Philharmonic expected from a conductor. Saul had conducted my *Dance Barbaro for Percussion* a number of times with his Juilliard Percussion Ensemble and had asked me on more than several occasions to compose a specific work for Solo Percussionist & Orchestra expressly for him which he could play with the New York Philharmonic. On an early January 1964 afternoon, I left Saul Goodman at Carnegie Hall after we had had lunch and then departed for an appointment with Maestro Leopold Stokowski who was going to conduct my *Miraflores for String Orchestra*. As I took off, Saul reminded me again about the composition. I told Saul that aurally it was very difficult to compose a composition for Solo Percussionist & Orchestra. Visually there's no problem; you just stick the percussionist out in front of the orchestra with his or her instruments where the piano or violin soloist normally is; but if one does not handle the orchestral fabrics correctly, you'll end up with what the majority of these other Solo Percussion & Orchestra works are, and that is an orchestral piece with a great deal of percussion, rather than an authentic Solo Percussion & Orchestra construction.

I had about thirty minutes before my engagement with Maestro Stokowski, so I decided to go into the Metropolitan Museum Of Art and see the recent acquisition of Rembrandt's *Aristotle With A Bust Of Homer* which at that time was the most expensive purchase in the history of art. There must have been two hundred people around the painting so I decided to go upstairs and see other works. As I turned into one room, there was this exceptionally large Jackson Pollock canvas which I had never seen before, but it instantaneously gave me the mechanical and technical orchestral accompaniment solutions for a Solo Percussionist & Orchestra work: as the Percussionist played what I would compose, I would use an action compositional accompaniment whereby I would throw my orchestral sounds and colors all around the canvas of my score so that the Solo Percussionist would "sound" through the orchestral fabric and not be absorbed by it. I was excited. Ideas rushed through my will at great speed.

"What's the name of this painting?" I asked the security guard standing nearby.

"The name's on that little plate over there at the end of the picture," he said.

I raced over. It was called *Autumn Rhythm* (1950).

So eventually, I selected *Number One* (1948) as the first movement and *Autumn Rhythm* as the second movement; and I composed *Two Pictures for Solo Percussionist & Orchestra* during 1965 and 1966. Unfortunately, when I completed the work, Saul Goodman had had a heart seizure and retired from the New York Philharmonic, but he was in the audience at Rochester when John Beck gave the world premiere and subsequent performance.

Sylvia Plath painted and liked painting in the customary puritanical sense and had some talent for watercolors and pastel chalks. Her paintings (we'd go into the woods sometimes during painting class) were usually landscapes and still lifes. She would spend four or five classes on a little watercolor of a jack-in-the-pulpit, a lady slipper, or a tree.

We both won prizes in the Ingersoll Awards. I sometimes would take the best large Grumbacher paper I could find and thumb tack the paper all around a large watercolor board and (as I did one day with Sylvia coming up and standing over me) submerge the whole board into the natural stream which went right across the grounds of the Bradford School quickly taking it out and applying Windsor Newton water color paints with large sable brushes as fast as I could; then I would let the paper dry for a day and rework these impressionistic forest scenes with smaller brushes of paint and India ink.

Sylvia asked, "What are you doing?" I said, "I'm sticking this whole board into the stream."

Well, she thought I was insane.

I used Windsor Newton water colors because they dried most brilliantly after I submerged the heavy watercolor paper into the stream for a few seconds. I would then take the board out and quickly do my forest scenes, or (depending upon the outcome of how the paper dried) forest fires, or backgrounds for other subjects such as city skylines. Sometimes I would go over the results with India ink, or not touch them at all. Or (if there was a happy accident) leave the entire picture alone with only minor additions and retouching.

Sylvia's watercolor works were usually small. She would paint meticulously with a number one, or two brush, and I'd say, "It's going to take you a year to finish that watercolor."

Sylvia won a prize for one of her delicate landscape watercolors which were actually quite good in their own benign stylistic format. I won two, and they were displayed at the Institute Of Contemporary Art in Boston, Massachusetts with about one hundred other winners. We went to see the exhibition of our paintings, and she looked at my work. Now, it would state on a card next to the painting, "Sylvia Plath, Gamaliel Bradford School, Wellesley, Massachusetts, (price)," if you wanted to sell the painting. So I put down for my large New York City skyline (which at that time I had only seen in photographs) $2,569.27, or something like that. Most of the kids put down $15 dollars or $5 dollars.

I'll never forget watching Sylvia going over and gaping twice at my prices. She said, "Are you crazy?" She would usually say that to me after I had done something rather daring for the time.

After her first suicide attempt she was the one who was really crazy, not Phillip Lambro.

At any rate, we saw a great deal of one another in that painting class.

Wilbury Crockett (English 21, 31, 41 Teacher and Sylvia's intellectual mentor) assigned me as Morning Devotionals Music Director which consisted, after someone recited a poem or short verse from the Bible over the loudspeaker system into each classroom, the recorded music which I would select and broadcast before the school day began. At this time, if you can imagine, I was sometimes chastised for playing anything beyond Bach's *Air On the G String*. I'd say, "Well, we can't just play Bach Chorales every morning." So I would put on commercially recorded performances of Vivaldi or Debussy; Rudolph Serkin playing a slow movement from a Beethoven Sonata; or Artur Rubinstein serving some short Chopin selections.

One day I played *Magda's Aria* from Gian Carlo Menotti's musical drama *The Consul*, which caused somewhat of an adverse reaction with certain teachers. I could not understand the cause celebre; it was as if I had put on something like *Musique Concrete*. Wilbury Crockett thought I had gone a little too far and when he saw me in the hallway he gave me one look over his eye glasses which needed no translation.

After things quieted down again, every once in a while I would insert another aria from *The Consul*.

I recall Sylvia seeking me out. I used to go into the auditorium during study period and practice my piano repertory and sometimes she would listen outside the stage door and ask me what I had been playing.

Following the *Magda's Aria* scandal, Sylvia came up to me somewhat excitedly and asked, "Phillip, what was that? I want to hear it again."

I had the vocal score and the original cast album, so I showed it to her and played the recordings for her a few times. Sylvia Plath was fascinated by *The Consul*. She seemed captivated by the whole story of how Magda Sorel, unable to solve the problems of her political environment, at the end of the last act, commits suicide by putting her head in the oven and turning on the gas. And as we have finally learned, that's how Sylvia relegated her own suicide in London during 1963.

I particularly recollect Sylvia's first suicide attempt because I was questioned by the Wellesley Police when she was missing and I thought I was going to go to the electric chair by circumstantial evidence in absentia. This was the summer of 1953. Sylvia had been going to Smith College and I believe she had won a fiction contest for writing which had been sponsored by Mademoiselle Magazine which required her and a group of other college girls to receive an all expenses paid work vacation at the Mademoiselle Magazine offices in New York City. Apropos Mademoiselle, I once suggested to Sylvia during art class in her Senior year at Bradford that perhaps she should give up thoughts about becoming a writer (since she was continually receiving rejection slips) and pursue a career as a fashion model.

"Look," I said, "you're tall and thin, and blonde. You'd be perfect as a fashion model; and think of all the money you could make which would give you entre to all the publishers in New York City that would eventually lead to getting all your little short stories printed; and then you could dabble in your watercolors on the side."

Sylvia gave me a nasty look as she rinsed out her brush.

During those Bradford years, Sylvia was writing a lot of short stories, essays and poems which would appear in our school newspaper The Bradford. I used to occasionally write a music column called *Face The Music*. I read her efforts. To me they weren't actually that interesting. But in the real world, she was getting a tract of rejection slips. In fact, in her senior yearbook (Sylvia used to bring these fat sandwiches to school) it alluded to her fat sandwiches which also paraphrased a popular Radio-TV cigarette commercial of the day which used to go "So round, so firm, so fully packed; so free and easy on the draw," and under her yearbook picture the caption read, "those sandwiches, so round, so firm, so fully packed" and, "Oh, those rejection slips!" Because Sylvia would send in these short stories, essays and poems to Mademoiselle, Harper's and all the other magazines at sea. Eventually, I believe she had one or two published after she went off to Smith College. Since I was playing on the Bradford tennis team and competing in a lot of tournaments during my senior year 1952 and that fateful 1953 summer, I did occasionally help Sylvia with her own tennis game if she happened to come by the Hunnewell Tennis Courts where I practiced when not practicing at Longwood Cricket Club in Brookline, or with my buddy Harrison Rowbotham III (a ranking Junior whom we called Robin) at the Waban Neighborhood Club, or the Wellesley College courts. I was extremely occupied after Bradford graduation in 1952 through the summer of 1953. Plus, I also had a forty hour a week job working in the mail room for an unrelenting firm in Wellesley's Babson Park owned by Roger Babson (who predicted the 1929 stock market crash) named Business Statistics in order to pay for my future education. It was adjacent to Babson Institute. During previous winter snow storms, when school would close, I earned excellent money by shoveling snow and during those summers I also made substantial cash by mowing some of the sumptuous lawns of Wellesley landscapes. In addition to tennis, there was my music and piano practice. I had made my piano debut earlier that year (1953) playing Chopin at Symphony Hall in Boston during The Pianist's Fair, and I was making audition recordings of Bach, Mozart and Chopin in order to decide where I was going to go to Music School. Since many of the highly regarded teachers had left Curtis, Juilliard and other name institutions for the University Of Miami in Florida (which surprised the hell out of me) I chose to go there before these pedagogues went off to infinity. And besides it was the furthest southern point in the United States to get away from the abrasive ignorance of my father.

Mr. Paul Murphy and his brother Jerome Murphy (owners of M. Steinert & Sons, The Home Of The Steinway, in Boston and a smaller store in Wellesley) helped my development immeasurably from my fourteenth year until I left Wellesley four years later by letting me exercise my fingers on all the great Steinway Concert Grands as all I had at home in our playroom was a dreadfully bad upright piano where several of the keys did not sound and some of the white keys had fallen off which sometimes would give my finger tips small wood splinters. To me, when I touched some of those wonderful Steinway Concert Grands it was like having sex with a beautiful girl. The charming blonde lady manager of the Wellesley store (Mrs. Gertrude Armstrong) let me practice on the best Steinways and attend to all of the commercial recordings in the listening rooms. I practically lived there.

As I progressed, around 16 years of age, and began studying in Boston, Paul Murphy allowed me to have the key to the Concert Grand Warehouse in the back alley of M. Steinert & Sons where I drilled hundreds of hours on the prestigious Steinway Concert Grands which were reserved for the likes of Horowitz, Rubinstein, Serkin and Kapell. In fact, one evening as I was locking-up to catch the B & W Bus back to Wellesley, I was somewhat startled by a bearded blind man who had been listening to me practice from inside the alley-way doors dressed in Biblical prophet's clothes who looked like a movie vision of Jesus Christ and who told me his name was Moon Dog. I helped him to where he wanted to go, but he immediately attracted quite a large crowd on Boylston Street in front of M. Steinert & Sons and I had to yell at the mob to protect Moon Dog and get him across the street into the safety of a large park known as The Boston Common. Some people actually thought Moon Dog was really Jesus Christ! It's a good thing M. Steinert & Sons was closed.

Ladies and Gentlemen of the Jury, the reason I'm telling you all of this is to give you an idea of the over activity in my teenage life; and that not only did I not have time for Sylvia Plath (unless we happened to be around one another), but I did not have time for anything or anyone outside of what or whom I needed to do or know to get a more advanced education in music; which I knew was imperative since I essentially had not begun music study until the late age of fourteen.

I had had a couple of attacks of paralysis (the last one when I was just about fourteen) which had been diagnosed as Rheumatic Fever. It was no fun. I was immediately dispensed to the hospitals in Boston. I thought my life was finished; but the Elohim Extraterrestrials must have been watching over me because all I ever had after those painful attacks was one slight heart murmur when the other kids on my floor had leaking heart valves and more. I'll never forget this one child (when I was staying for observation at The House Of The Good Samaritan) whom I would hobble about twenty feet to visit. His last name was Sullivan and he was around twelve. He never spoke or uttered a word to anyone; although, late at night I would sometimes hear Sullivan quietly crying. The nurses told me that he had had a number of leaking valves and that he had been in the hospital for three years. His parents had not visited him in two years; not even at Christmas time. Whoever went near his bed caused him to turn away.

"You're lucky your parents don't come and visit you," I'd say to him sitting on the chair next to his bed. "I'm really glad when my parents don't come. Everybody should not have parents," I'd go on in this manner trying to cheer him up and give him a new sociological perspective. "Parents interfere with our development," I'd go on, but Sullivan would just look away and never speak.

After I got out of the hospital, I had a tutor so I would not have to stay back a grade in school; that would have been far worse than death. I was so weak, I could not climb the stairs very well. It fatigued me just to walk from our front door down the walkway across our lawn to Windemere Road. In fact, when I did that, it was an event. Slowly, I got stronger and sturdier and when the next spring came (since my leg muscles were rather feeble) I began playing tennis; not only because it was a musical and rhythmical game, but I noticed that tennis players, virtually without exception, had strong healthy legs, and I usually felt better after playing. By the time I was a senior at Bradford, miraculously my leg muscles returned and developed enough to where I became very fast on the tennis court, but not that fast during the distance of seven mile cross country runs. I became interested in tennis primarily to strengthen and develop my legs, but after I became exposed to the game (like Schoenberg and Gershwin) I fell in love with tennis for its own unique qualities. However, since my music always took precedence, I never took tennis lessons or studied the game intelligently until I became friends with Alex Olmedo (the 1959 Wimbledon, Australian, and Davis Cup Champion) whom I studied with years later in California; and subsequently met great champions such as Pancho Segura, Pancho Gonzales, and Jack Kramer from whom I always received some valuable information pertaining to the mechanics of stroke production.

A teammate of mine from Bradford, Philip McCurdy who was a pretty good player, (he had ball-boyed in the U.S. National Doubles at Longwood) a talented pencil and ink artist, and an all around talkative intelligent young man, was sort of sweet on Sylvia Plath. However, in one of her biographical books, it intimated that they had had a love affair during this time. I'm sure (if anything) they just had had an exceptionally short accidental affair because at the time, Philip McCurdy was with me a great deal playing tennis, and he was going with another girl named Sue and interested in a third (who can blame him?) in addition to pursuing Sylvia. Of course, although I liked Sylvia very much as a person, individually I did not find her sexually attractive at all (I'm sure she felt the same way about me) and I often told Philip McCurdy, "She's never going to be romantically interested in you anyway; you're just out of High School and she's at Smith." So actually, the type of affair that McCurdy might have had was quite fleeting, and the following summer he wasn't even around Wellesley. Then too, they both had such intensely centripetal personalities which would have made a long term romance quite deflective.

After Sylvia's return from New York City, I saw her several times at the Hunnewell Tennis Courts. I could sense that she was quite introverted as she attempted to play; her mind was somewhere else. In fact, one of those days, I met and played tennis with composer Harold Shapero who had come to the courts from several towns away and I believe he told me that he was teaching music in Waltham. When I informed him that I wanted to be a composer and symphonic and concert musician, he said "You'd better marry a rich woman."

I could sense that Sylvia was frustrated about something, but she said that it was nothing and didn't wish to discuss it.

I was practicing tennis quite intensively for the Junior Davis Cup tournament which was about to take place on the beautiful grass courts of the Agawam Hunt Club in Providence, Rhode Island.

One particularly hot August day I was riding my bicycle past the Hunnewell Tennis Courts. It was over 100 degrees with 90% humidity; nobody was at the courts except Sylvia (in her white cotton field hockey blouse with navy blue shorts, white socks and tennis shoes) perspiring and knocking balls at the backboard like some demon possessed.

I had previously suggested that she practice a little on the backboard, but not too much because the ball is coming back at you twice as fast as it normally would if you were playing a regular game on the court. And it was quite obvious that the backboard and the elements were getting the best of Sylvia Plath even though she wasn't giving up in the least.

With her eyes sort of dazed, Sylvia said, "I'm going to get this game if it's the last thing I do. I'm going to learn it and I'm going to become a good tennis player."

"You'll get sun stroke and heat exhaustion, Sylvia. You shouldn't be playing on such a hot, humid day; and especially without a hat."

I said again, "How did things go in New York?" She still did not wish to talk about it. But I could sense something had affected her. I found out later that most of Sylvia's writings and ideas were rejected by the editorial woman to whom she was responsible at the magazine. Clearly they were not compatible when it came to the craft of creative writing which I'm sure thwarted Sylvia. I know how she must have felt, because I went through the same thing while I was Assistant Director Of Publications at G. Schirmer in New York City during my twenties. I think Sylvia also had had financial problems, too; which was rather hard to take living in Wellesley (one of the ten richest towns in the United States) although she had been given a full scholarship to Smith College.

After a while, Sylvia looked at me and grinned, "Yeah, I think you're right," she said. "It's too hot to play tennis." We both beamed then laughed. She took a drink from the water fountain and we left the Hunnewell Courts together with our bicycles walking up Washington Street a little way, but after that we parted and went in different directions.

I had quit my job that month (August 1953) at Business Statistics as I made plans to attend the University Of Miami School Of Music in Coral Gables, Florida the following month.

I went the next day with the New England Jr. Davis Cup team to the meticulously kept lush green grass courts of the Agawam Hunt Club in Providence, Rhode Island. (Previously we had played at the Newport Casino Club in Newport, Rhode Island.) I shared the same first class hotel room with my buddy Robin Rowbotham (whose father was a Vice President of the United States Tennis Association) and late that evening after we both had had a couple of bad losses, Robin kept waking me up itching and loudly complaining that the bed had bugs or crabs in it and that the blinking neon sign from the building across the street was bothering him through the drawn shade. I could not understand it because my bed was fine. However, since it was so hot and humid, I took one of the blankets and covered the window in an attempt to block out the flashing neon sign for Robin. Then Robin said it was too hot (we must have been up ten stories) and so he ripped the blanket off the window. Then he proceeded to throw the mattress pad out of the window.

"What the hell are you doing, Robin?" I asked. "Jesus Christ, we'll get into trouble with the Hotel."

"I don't give a damn," Robin said. "This bed is crawling with something."

This was so uncharacteristic of my tall, lanky, well bred teenage friend, so I immediately got up again, turned on the lights, and we started looking for microscopic bugs on the sheet and mattress.

"I don't see a thing, Robin. You must be imagining it," I said. "It's just the heat and our bad losses. Why don't you sleep on my bed?"

"No, no; that's okay," Robin said, "I'll just live with it."

"Come on, Robin, get some sleep. We have two tough matches tomorrow."

I fell asleep for about ten minutes and was awakened again by noises to see Robin in the dark bending and forcing his entire mattress through our window. There it went from about ten stories up at one a.m. in the morning.

"What the fuck did you do, Robin?" I exclaimed. "You'll kill somebody. Now you've done it; we're sure to be arrested."

"I don't give a shit," said Robin. "I'll just sleep on the springs."

After that, surprisingly, Robin went to sleep. I didn't sleep too well because I thought at any moment the police would be breaking down the door and handcuffing us both for murdering some pedestrian with a mattress.

The next morning we both went down into the lobby expecting the worse. I immediately went out onto the sidewalk. There was no mattress, or mattress cover to be seen anywhere. When we returned that evening there was a new mattress on Robin's bed and nobody at the front desk ever said a word. I could not believe it.

After the tournament I returned to Wellesley.

No sooner had I walked through the front door with my rackets and suitcase, my mother exclaimed, "The police were here! The police were here! What did you do?"

At first I thought Robin must have killed somebody with the mattress; but that was three days ago, and in Rhode Island.

I said, "I didn't do anything. What do you mean, what did I do? I haven't even been around." And my mother thought I had committed some heinous crime because the Wellesley police were at our front door looking for me earlier that day. They wouldn't tell my mother what it was about; only that they had wished to question me. I telephoned them and all they would say was that they wanted to see me in person immediately. I went to the station where this Wellesley police detective and his associates started interrogating me. The police detective's daughter had been in one of my classes at Bradford where a few years before, in the library, I had made an innocuous nasty remark to her after she had made some rather dumb statement after which she said that she was going to tell her daddy dearest policeman on me. The detective who, like his daughter, was rather arrogant never really liked me and I could not have cared one way or the other.

In the ninth grade during summer vacation I was chumming around with this only child, a son of wealthy parents, who had constructed an AM Radio transmitter (with the help of some extra cash) which we used to operate rather professionally for about three to six hours on selected days playing classical and popular music; running quiz shows with extremely difficult questions (such as "What was Ulysses S. Grant's grandmother's middle name) which nobody could answer so that we would not have to send the expensive gifts we had been offering. We also gave newscasts by reading from the Boston, New York, and Christian Science Monitor newspapers. We did this for over two years before the Federal Communications Commission finally caught the whereabouts of my friend's transmitter which was in the playroom basement of his parents large Tudor home in Wellesley with the antenna running up the chimney. It seems on certain damp or rainy days our little signal was carrying all the way from Wellesley, Massachusetts to New York State where our programs were being listened to with public interest, and sometimes interfering with major radio stations. Of course, as music director, I approved all the best recordings from the Boston Symphony and Horowitz, to Stan Kenton and Johnny Ray. However, in reality, this was a serious Federal Offense. Fortunately, I wasn't there when the FCC officials, who after two years eventually traced our signal, and confronted my friend's mother who was a relatively quiet thin blonde lady. I was informed that she nearly fainted when she found out what we had been doing.

After that, my friend, whose name was Tom, during the next summer vacation used to come and visit me occasionally after tennis practice at the Wellesley Tennis Club which leased the tennis courts on the campus of Wellesley College. One afternoon Tom approached me as I was having a delightful conversation with the distinguished British actor Nigel Bruce (whom you'll recall played Watson to Basil Rathbone's Sherlock Holmes in the movies) as Nigel Bruce was sunning himself in a white wicker chair on the grounds of the Wellesley College campus. I was to be introduced to Basil Rathbone years later by Jeff Sparks (my associate at the United Nations) and would frequently see Rathbone at concerts in Carnegie Hall from 1961 through 1963. Nigel Bruce was at Wellesley College doing a play with John Carradine whom I was also to meet years later (circa 1975) through my agents Paul and Walter Kohner. I noticed how badly John Carradine's hands had been deformed from arthritis when I met him in the Kohner Office and I enumerated to him how through the miracle of Japanese Zen Macrobiotics I had completely cured my own arthritic back, but he felt that nothing could remedy his arthritis so I could not help him as much as I wish to help anyone with any disease. Sitting next to Nigel Bruce on the grass was one of Carradine's children named David.

As we were leaving on our bicycles, my friend Tom told me that he knew where the Wellesley College campus radio station was and wanted me to go with him and investigate it since all the girls were on vacation for the most part. After the FCC incident, I suggested to Tom that he had better leave well enough alone. Then too, David Carradine wanted to accompany us. He was about twelve and we did not want him tagging along, but he began pestering us so we said that he could come with us only on the condition that he swear to secrecy and never tell anyone about our activities. He agreed so we took him with us. Tom turned on the Wellesley College campus radio station and started broadcasting; which, fortunately for us, only covered the immediate campus. I left after about ten minutes, but young David Carradine went squealing all over campus and I was the one who got blamed for turning on the station by the Wellesley police detective.

I never forgot David Carradine's name. During the middle 1970's while I was having lunch with film editor David Rawlins and his then wife Brooke Mills at the Old World Restaurant on Sunset Boulevard, David Rawlins reintroduced me to David Carradine (who had just walked in with a bunch of intimates) as the two Davids had just begun working together on a new television series entitled *Kung Fu.* Carradine, of course, did not recall me or my name, but I remembered his name; although I would never have recognized him physically because his delicate features and nature had changed so much. I was polite and cordial, but after he left the table, I told David Rawlins and Brooke Mills the story after which we all laughed and David Rawlins said, "Why that little squealing shit." David Rawlins was the main reason *Kung Fu* (although I rarely saw it) went to the top of the ratings. David Rawlins utilized many of the same brilliant editorial special effects technique for *Kung Fu* that he had also used for *Crypt Of The Living Dead* (the film for which I composed and conducted the music at MGM) giving a good scream to Dyan Cannon by pulling out her own and supplanting it with an authentic luminous Bette Davis shriek from one of her old pictures in the Warner Bros. library; and making David Carradine and others more effective in their performances by putting in sky and cloud formations which were never there; changing sound effects and reversing shots to give added force to basically weak dramatic situations. The producers kept promising David Rawlins segments to direct. Finally, after a few seasons and no directing assignments, David Rawlins quit. As soon as he did, the *Kung Fu* show lost its ratings and was eventually cancelled. I always felt that David Rawlins could have been one of the truly notable American Film Directors of all time if only he had been given an opportunity.

Shortly after twelve year old David Carradine informed on me for the Wellesley College campus radio station incident, my friend Tom and I broke into the Bradford School and made a raft of long distance telephone calls from the Principal's Office to important radio and television personalities located in New York City and Hollywood giving false names and publications and pretending to be interviewing them for major international articles. We both swore never to tell on each other regardless of what happened; even torture. The following September, I was summoned into the Principal's Office. There was that Wellesley police detective with the Principal. They both gave me the Third Degree. They said we had been seen and that my friend Tom (who was not present) had admitted to making all of the long distance telephone calls with me. I still remained silent. After ten minutes of interrogation they saw that I was not going to go back on my word of honor, so they brought in Tom who declared that he had revealed everything. I physically went after Tom and it took all of the police detective's strength to restrain me. I advised both the detective and the Principal that I did not like to lie, but I avoided telling the truth because I had given my word of honor not to reveal what we had done under any circumstance; and when I give my word, I do not ever want to break it. The Principal, I could tell, was more impressed with my code of honor than the detective, and I told them both that I would not be associating with Tom anymore. And, of course, I kept my word.

There I was now (eighteen years old) and again being given the Third Degree by my Wellesley police detective "friend" and some other officers whom I had never seen before.

They said, "Where's Sylvia Plath?" I said, "I don't know where Sylvia Plath is. I hardly ever see her."

They said, "We know you were with her."

I said, "I was not with her. I was in Providence, Rhode Island representing Massachusetts in Junior Davis Cup matches."

The detective continued to interrogate me because a little old lady, who had been walking along the aqueduct several days before, had seen Sylvia and disclosed to the police, "Oh, Sylvia Plath was at the Hunnewell Tennis Courts with the Lambro boy. They walked away together."

And that was the last time anyone had seen Sylvia.

They asked me a few more questions in the 1946 Hollywood Film Noir detective style and told me not to leave town.

"What do you mean not leave town?" I asked. "In several weeks I'm leaving for the University Of Miami in Coral Gables, Florida. I have to go to school. I left Sylvia that day; she was at the tennis courts; I helped her with her game a little; she was on her bicycle; she did not tell me where she was going; and that's the last time I saw her."

I had the feeling that they did not believe me, but at first I really didn't care until I began thinking about the whole situation lying awake in bed that evening and the following nightfalls.

It was around 25 August 1953 and search parties had been formed. There had been a headline in the Boston Globe with Sylvia's picture, "Beautiful Smith Girl Missing At Wellesley." I had heard that they were dragging Morse's Pond (where we all went swimming) and Lake Waban next to Wellesley College. I now began to think what if they were to find her murdered? "Oh, Sylvia Plath was at the Hunnewell Tennis Courts with the Lambro boy. They walked away together." I felt the possibility of being convicted on circumstantial evidence and electrocuted the way I had seen it depicted so many times growing up in the Film Noir movies at the Community Playhouse. My music career would be over. What career? All I had done at that point was make my debut playing some Chopin at The Pianist's Fair in Symphony Hall, Boston. I hadn't even composed one work, or conducted a Symphony Orchestra. I hadn't even begun my serious studies. That was it: I was finished before I ever began. I remember looking out the window from my bed. I had always loved the massive trees and summer foliage of Wellesley. To me trees were human and communicative and not inanimate objects. I meditated those evenings (as I often had ever since I was about five) trying to telepathically communicate with the superior group of beings I had had experiences with whom I knew existed who could come and take me off to their utopian planet where I could live out my existence in pursuit of contributory artistic intelligence and where everyone knew truth telepathically rather than, as we earth primitives have to do, waste time proving it.

Fortunately for me, they found Sylvia a few days later: from what I grasped, she had gone into the basement of her house and crawled up a pile of logs and rotted wood and placed herself behind a foundation wall of concrete cinder blocks where there was an earthen space where she sealed herself off with a piece of board. She had taken a blanket, a glass of water, and about forty sleeping pills. Anybody else who had ingested forty sleeping pills would have been an obituary, but I understood that Sylvia (during her descent into darkness) vomited during the following days she was right under the feet of her mother, grandmother, brother, and even a police bloodhound enrolled to sample her scents and sniff out her whereabouts.

I did not try and assist those who were looking for Sylvia because I thought they were going to find her dead, or not at all, and that I would eventually become the prime suspect; so I didn't want to have anything to do with the search, or investigation. You must appreciate one thing: nobody thought of suicide until Mrs. Plath found the missing bottle of sleeping pills. The initial feeling was that Sylvia ran away (because she had left a letter) and that perhaps she had met with foul play. The Sylvia Plath of that period was a smiling, ice cream loving, giggle-laughing, movie going, teaseable blonde co-ed. She had, as the majority of us had in Wellesley, a non-accented American speech (the New England accents sounded foreign to us) with a dairy smile, and was the last person you'd ever suspect who would have suicide on their mind. I mean, she would laugh even when I was fighting with her trying to retrieve my own paint brush in art class.

I understand that Sylvia's grandmother was in the basement and heard Sylvia moaning and called to Warren upstairs who telephoned the police, and an ambulance took her to the Newton Wellesley Hospital.

I was relieved.

I did not see or speak with Sylvia's mother, brother or grandmother. Actually, I never knew Sylvia's mother or grandmother; I only knew Sylvia and her brother Warren. And I hadn't seen Warren at all during this period. I never once went over to Sylvia's home; in fact, I don't believe I ever went by her house. Although over the years I used to see her, at times, walk by our home and sometimes sit on our stone wall. My mother seems to recall Sylvia stopping by our grounds now and then playing with my younger sister Holly for a few minutes at a time.

During this period I encountered Wilbury Crockett quite often on the street and he would inform me of Sylvia's progress. But you must also apprehend that in Wellesley, Massachusetts 1953 it was not socially acceptable to attempt suicide or have mental problems (even though in New York City and Hollywood concert pianist Oscar Levant was making a good deal of money out of his neuroses and psychoanalysts, and beginning to make it chic) and a great deal was being done to dilute the Sylvia Plath suicide attempt into a nervous breakdown.

I understood that Sylvia was in a "rest home," but I knew they were perhaps giving her electroshock treatments, and drugs; the same drugs as I was forced to take when I was paralyzed in the Peter Bent Brigham Hospital and The House Of The Good Samaritan. I remember being given (fourteen years of age) five aspirins an hour for the pain in my legs; and a pretty nurse who was a ballet student let me in on the fact that they had been "experimenting" on me with a new drug called cortisone, among other things. Most of the time I felt as if my brain was having an out of body experience. The attractive nurse also advised me confidentially (while doing her ballet exercises at the foot of my bed) that Judy Garland was in the next room from me suffering from -ha!- nervous exhaustion, which did not impress me at all (I never met Ms. Garland and had no desire to), as I was hoping to be released before the end of winter so I could meet pianist Claudio Arrau after his Symphony Hall recital, which I did, sitting next to a man during the concert who kept asking me to my consternation, "Is this guy any good?" and "What's he playing next?" who turned out to be band leader Spike Jones. Going to Arrau's Boston recital alone on the bus and trolley at that time (my first major trip after my illness) was for me like the ascent of K-2 in the Himalayas. After I escaped the hospitals and drugs, I threw away the prescribed medication because after that experience I felt that "Medical Science" metabolically was embarking upon the wrong road; the path of doctoring symptoms rather than getting to the root cause of an illness. It's like filling in a crack of a building and painting over it when the actual cause of the fissure is structural and in the shifting ground.

So, at eighteen years of age, I left Wellesley for the University Of Miami School Of Music in Coral Gables, Florida in search of a musical education and to find my fountain of youth.

Although I loved the physical beauty of Wellesley, I was glad to get away from its sociological and moral constraints; and quite frankly, I did not think of Sylvia Plath at all until I returned home that Christmas vacation and saw her coming out of Bendslev's Ice Cream Parlor (next to the Community Playhouse) and hopping the little one foot high white picket fence.

"Hi Sylvia," I remember saying to her as she turned around abruptly. "How've you been?"

"Oh, hi," she said half smiling and obviously in a hurry.

"Are you still in school?" I asked.

"Yes," she said, "I'm going back to Smith".

"That's nice," I said.

"I have to hurry," Sylvia said walking away. "I'll see you soon."

"I don't think you'll see me soon," I said a little louder. "I'm studying music in Florida and I doubt that I shall return for a very long time, if ever. I've sort of had it with Wellesley."

And that was the last time I ever saw Sylvia Plath.

I did read her novel *The Bell Jar* here in Los Angeles around 1967 or '68. I also purchased a copy of the British edition while I was living in London during 1974. I was impressed with Sylvia's literary style and rather proud of her improvement. Even though the fabric is autobiographical and some of the people are factual paradigms, I believe (in a sense) that these bona fide characters emerged from her particular psyche as personality distillations of how she wanted to perceive them.

For example, let's take authentic person Buddy Willard. Even though he lived in Wellesley, and I probably knew him by sight or name at that time, I don't remember him at all now. Be this as it may, character Buddy Willard in *The Bell Jar* is an amalgamation of several boys whom Sylvia had known from our area, or would liked to have known, rather than actual person Buddy Willard. Just as Esther was definitely a composite of what Sylvia Plath perceived herself to have been at the epoch she was writing about coupled with what she espied to have been her hypothetical other self; which, in the novelist's mechanical realm of deliberation, is no great mystery and actually quite prevalent, especially with first time authors. Sylvia Plath was to Esther and *The Bell Jar* what I suspect Sloan Wilson was to Tom Rath in *The Man In The Gray Flannel Suit*.

Sylvia's father had passed away when she was about ten and she had, I found out years later, this deep love-hate for her father after he had died. I don't recall Sylvia or Warren ever mentioning their father while I knew them. However, her mother owned a secretarial service of some sort in Brookline or Boston, and I only saw Mrs. Plath (out of all the years from the sixth grade to the twelfth grade) maybe four times. Mrs. Plath was an Austrian type of woman. Quite plain with straight blonde hair pulled back and braided into a circular bun. I never spoke with her at all, to my recollection.

I remember Sylvia Plath as always smiling, and sometimes joking or laughing in the hallways of the Bradford School. It was quite apparent that she wanted to be popular and well liked. One of her classmates would sometimes be stretching to put their books up onto the top shelf of their locker and occasionally Sylvia would come up from behind as if she were ice skating and give them one of those hockey player board checks with her rear end, or tickle them, or something like that and then run off to her next class giggling.

For the most part Sylvia and I got along well in art class. Although, I used to infrequently enjoy teasing her both in subtle and overt ways. Sporadically we would have these simple confrontations over paint or paint brushes.

Once I said, "This is my brush, go get your own brushes."

Another attractive girl in the class (Gail Murphy) came over to me and said, "That's my brush," and Gail tried to take the paint brush out of my hand and in the attempt stuck one of her fingernails into my left wrist, and I bled blue.

Gail exclaimed, "You're bleeding blue!"

Sylvia instantly became fascinated and came over saying, "Let me see." After observing my little trickle of blue blood, she quietly exclaimed rather incredulously, "Phillip, you're a blue blood." Eight years later while living in Italy, I found out that she was right: Lambro is a royal Italian name. And every time I signed my name in Italy, I received an abnormal amount of respect. There is a Lambro river in Milano and a via Lambro in Rome.

The types of music which Sylvia Plath liked were the favorite classical works and some of the popular song hits of the day. I used to notice her occasionally putting a coin into the juke box when she was with her friends having a sandwich or an ice cream. I know she liked Johnny Ray's hit recording *Cry* and *Little White Cloud That Cried*. Philip McCurdy amused us with his worthy endeavors attempting to impersonate Johnny Ray. Sylvia also had a genuine interest in concert music because she would sometimes rush into the Bradford office after I had played a disc of Chopin, Debussy, or Ravel during Morning Devotionals and would want to know what it was. She liked the Boston Symphony and other major symphony orchestras.

Sylvia Plath had an infectious half-giggle half-laugh which she coupled with a unique liquid manner of speech where the words almost sounded saturated as they came over her tongue. It was definitely feminine and quite unusual; and with no accent, no New England accent of any kind, because the teachers we had in Wellesley taught us to speak naturally. In early grade school I used to hear people from Brookline and Boston conversing, they lived about 28 miles outside of Wellesley, and I'd say to my mother, "Gee, they talk funny." Or I would hear John F. Kennedy who came back from World War II and was running for some political office, and I'd say, "He speaks differently." My mother would say, "Well yes dear, they're from Boston," as if they were from Mississippi or Louisiana.

Although Sylvia had an interesting and pleasing manner, she was also extroverted at times (she could talk you to death) and then at other times she became placidly introverted where she would hardly speak at all. For example, during art class sometimes I would glance at her as she painted and I could sense that she was lost in distant thoughts and not really concentrating; she seemed to be on automatic pilot and just going through the motions of painting.

I became aware of Sylvia Plath as a potentially arrived writer and poetess while working for G. Schirmer in New York City during 1962. One Sunday morning as I was reading the New York Times Book Review section, Alfred A. Knopf Publisher had taken out an advertisement for Sylvia's volume of poetry entitled *The Colossus*. I was genuinely happy for Sylvia, and although I was too busy to go and purchase the book, it then entered my mind that I should perhaps contact her, and ask her to write some powerfully original texts from which I might be able to parent a composition for Soprano & Orchestra. I did not like what was happening in our society and I wanted artistically biting texts which could speak out against the War in Vietnam; against prejudice; against over population; against exploitation and other injustices.

I eventually purchased the book and although I felt that the poems showed skill and craft, they seemed to lack the mastery and emotion I was looking for. However, I was still interested in contacting Sylvia and asked my mother during a telephone conversation with her in Wellesley to telephone Mrs. Plath and get Sylvia's address so that I could write to her and maybe influence her into furnishing me with some cutting prose poetry to wake up humanity which I could marry with my symphonic music. One thing led to another, and since I was so preoccupied with my music duties at Schirmer coupled with the fact that my mother obviously forgot because she never sent me Sylvia's address, I failed to communicate with Sylvia.

Another year danced by. It was early 1963, and for some strange reason (off and on) I began to think about Sylvia and my composition; but I had been so immersed with the opening of Lincoln Center, with setting up Leonard Bernstein's publishing company Amberson Music within the Schirmer framework, the never ending completion of Samuel Barber's Piano Concerto, and since every day at Schirmer was like the changing weather on Mt. Everest, I was reluctantly forced to put these personal creative thoughts aside.

During a late August 1963 afternoon in Manhattan, I left my office at Schirmer (609 Fifth Avenue at 49th Street) and went to have my hair cut. As I sat in the barber's chair, they gave me a copy of the August third The New Yorker and as if by some sensory vibration, I opened the magazine directly to pages twenty-eight and twenty-nine on which were seven poems by Sylvia Plath with the glaring foot notation after her name (1932-1963). At first, I was startled and didn't wish to accept it. And so with the barber's apron around me (the barber thought he had done something wrong) I said going to his telephone, "Listen, this is a friend of mine and I can't believe that she's dead." Through Leonard Bernstein, I had met his younger brother Burton who was working for The New Yorker in their Literary Department. So I called Burton Bernstein and said, "Burton, is this true? Sylvia was a childhood and teenage friend of mine; a school classmate. What happened to her?" He said, "I'm not too clear on it, but let me ask somebody in our poetry department. Can you hold on?"

"Yes," I said, hoping that there had been some mistake. I had recalled my concert pianist teacher Gyorgy Sandor once informing me how directly after World War II he had read his own erroneous and major obituary in a foreign newspaper complete with his picture and headline as he was about to resume his concert career.

Burton returned and said, "I just checked, and I'm afraid it's true: Plath definitely died late last winter." I said, "Well, how did she die?"

Burton said, "She'd been living in England. I'll try and find out for you."

Several telephone calls later in the week Burton Bernstein informed me that Sylvia had died of the influenza brought about by an extremely cold British winter.

I said, "Burton, what kind of nonsense is this? This is 1963, what twenty-nine year old dies from influenza anymore? Are you sure?" So a few months later, I managed to find out that Sylvia had committed suicide.

Several months previously, I had been speaking with my mother over the telephone in Wellesley, and she said (she had forgotten Sylvia's name), "Do you remember that blonde girl who used to come here; you used to walk home with?" And I said, "Which blonde girl?" She said, "You know, she used to sit on our stone wall and read, and sometimes she'd play with your sister, Holly." I could not think of Sylvia because there were other blonde girls who used to occasionally sit on the wall, too.

My mother said, "She died. It's so tragic, she was so young. You went to school with her. Oh, what was her name?"

I said, "Well, who is it? Find out who she was." And then now, it all dawned upon me; Sylvia was who my mother was endeavoring to recollect. I was rather downcast because as I read those poems (the barber let me have the magazine) I was thunderstruck with their powerful originality, their sheer genius and virtuosity, their rhythmic musicality; and what a notable improvement over *The Colossus*. As I walked along the streets of Manhattan back to my office I thought, 'Sylvia, you brilliant dumb bitch. Why did you have to kill yourself? I wanted to see you again and speak with you. We never really sat down and had a long conversation with each other in Wellesley. I got promoted. I'm an artist myself now, too. I had so much to tell you. I'm sure you had a lot to tell me. I could have encouraged you to write more great poetry which I could have used as texts for an important work for Soprano and Orchestra, if you hadn't died. We could have done a musical drama together, Sylvia. Now, what the hell are we going to do?'

So after Burton Bernstein, I was able to discover that Sylvia had been married to British poet Ted Hughes in the summer of 1957. At that time, I was in the military with the elite 39th Infantry at Fort Carson, Colorado and I definitely was not thinking about anything except surviving brutal waste-of-time war games up and around Pikes Peak. Then while I was in London on one of my music crusades, I was able to subsequently piece things together from the literary grapevine. Sylvia had had two children from 1960 to 1962 (a girl and a boy) after four years with Ted Hughes. Hughes began having an affair during the summer of 1962 with a young Canadian lady copywriter of Russian extraction who found themselves mutually attracted enough to embark on their somewhat disguised relationship right under Sylvia's nose. Remembering Sylvia's extreme independence and inner ego, it did not surprise me when I later discovered that Sylvia evicted her husband from their Devon cottage. But what did amaze me was that I heard Sylvia contemplated reconciliation, and I think she was somewhat stunned to learn that Hughes (who had taken a flat in Soho with his Canadian Russian girlfriend) really had no intention of returning home to Devon and conjugated life with Sylvia.

Also, it did not astonish me that Sylvia plunged into taking care of her two young children, doing all the difficult and muddy English countryside tasks, and keeping up disguises. The strange thing is that Sylvia's meteoric poems were flying off her kitchen table at the rate of, at least, one a day; and sometimes, two or three. Rare is the artist who amid adversity and anger can do their best work. Like tennis great Richard "Pancho" Gonzales. He was perhaps the only tennis player in the history of the game who (if you angered him) would play even that much better and win. The majority of athletes (and artists) who become acrimonious play worse and lose.

Eventually, Sylvia took a flat in London, where her idol Irish poet William Butler Yeats (1865-1939) had lived, since it was much too far to commute and quite frankly she had become a little disenchanted with rural domestic life. Then too, in London she could hire a girl quite easily to take care of her children while she sought to become a recognized writer. I understand that London represented optimism for Sylvia as a writer and poetess. She had been getting infrequent reading jobs at the BBC, even though in the main, nobody really cared about offering her a position or supporting her literary pursuits as, ironically, at this time she was just known as the wife of celebrity poet Ted Hughes, and still receiving rejection slips from her work.

They maintain it was the coldest winter in one hundred and fifty years. London was at a virtual standstill: snow bound and frozen for days at a time. Sylvia (which I found hard to believe) was now smoking and not eating. Published accounts stated that she had lost from her already lean frame another twenty pounds. The power outages left her apartment totally unheated for hours at a time, and her children came down with the flu. Doctors gave her tonic and pills in an attempt to regain her appetite and relieve her depression, but knowing what I do about Occidental Medicine, these drugs (like all pharmaceuticals) further exacerbated Sylvia's condition rather than alleviating it. Coupled with the financial failure of the initial printing of The Bell Jar (which she authored under her pen name of Victoria Lucas) and the mixed reviews it received must have further affected Sylvia's already weakened state of dejection.

Sylvia eventually came under the care of a Dr. Horder who sensing the further descent in her state of mental depression recommended a therapist and inscribed an official request which went astray to a wrong address.

According to published chronicles which I read in London, Sylvia (at about 6 a.m. on that overcast late February 1963 day) put some bread and butter with mugs of milk in the children's bedroom. She next returned to the kitchen and carefully sealed all the doors and windows with cloth and towels so that no leaks could escape to the sleeping children. Then like Magda Sorel in the last act of Gian Carlo Menotti's The Consul (which had so captivated Sylvia after I had exposed her to it during Morning Devotionals at the Bradford School 1950), Sylvia Plath Hughes, age twenty-nine, color of hair ashen blonde, color of eyes dazed, turned on the gas jets and rested her head upon the opened oven door.

She was discovered later that morning by a nurse who had had a scheduled appointment with Sylvia, and with the aid of workmen, the nurse broke into the flat.

It is my contention that if Sylvia Plath had been transported to a Japanese Zen Macrobiotic Monastery in Kyoto and learned the unique principles of a balanced diet of natural grains and vegetables and endeavored to live in harmony with her environment instead of fighting it, then she could have written poetry and novels with even greater authority. And if she had subscribed to the universal theory that it is not important who makes the beloved happy as long as the beloved be happy, yes, Sylvia Plath could have even gone on to more celebrated literary heights in a variety of different ways. Let us not (as a lot of feminists have done) condemn Ted Hughes. If Ted Hughes fell in love and wanted to be with that Canadian Russian girl (who, incidentally, I was informed ultimately committed suicide herself several years later) Sylvia should have been glad that someone else was making her beloved happy. Likewise, I understand that Sylvia had this sexual thing for Polish men, so she should have fulfilled this desire. Why not..? But how could she attract an interesting man during her metabolic breakdown? Depression is caused by an imbalance in the blood. How do we change the quality of our blood; one-tenth of which mutates every day? Through food and drink and how we live. If you do not eat (as Sylvia was doing) the body human simply feeds off itself and the blood is not renewed. Being realistic, Sylvia went into a distorted sick jealous rage of which the only good thing to come out of it was some of the most masterful prose poetry ever written in the English language. I was proud of her artistic results, but I was disappointed at how she achieved them.

Sylvia Plath's best work was the distillation of her own rather quick descent into self destruction. A greater artist is the one who can achieve the same results without bringing any harm to themselves, or those around them. In other words, if you are a William Shakespeare you don't go mad in order to create an Ophelia, or go out and kill a Desdemona in order to write *Othello*. Sylvia Plath was incapable of writing *Daddy* or *Lady Lazarus* apart from what happened in her life.

Who knows? Stravinsky never really achieved very much compositionally after *Firebird*, *Le Sacre*, *Petrouchka* and the *Violin Concerto*. But look at Bartok: he wrote his greatest compositions the last years of his life, and with a three year Leukemia fever. Fortunately, for all life in all universes, the only absolutes we have is that there aren't any.

Then too, poetess Anne Sexton (whom I never knew) who I understand also lived in Wellesley and knew Sylvia, correspondingly committed suicide, and relatively few care or are interested in either her work or her life.

It is quite evident that a combination of things caused Sylvia Plath to take her life. We know from medical reports that she wasn't eating and, since she was rather lanky to begin with, I personally think that Sylvia, perhaps, was approaching Anorexia. She began to smoke (smoking cuts off the oxygen to the blood supply and acts as a further depressant) and when I knew her, Sylvia used to detest tobacco and people who smoked; so we can deduce that she began embracing those things in her life which she abhorred. I imagine Sylvia (like most women) felt sexually unattractive after her husband left her for another woman; and with those rather unkind reviews, a literary failure as well.

Sylvia could not have written as incandescently those last months in her life as she did taking unbelievable poetic ventures (like a 1945 Bela Bartok rushing to finish his *Third Piano Concerto* from his death bed) had she not felt as my teacher Gyorgy Sandor (who premiered Bartok's *Third*) told me what Bartok said to him when Sandor had visited Bartok on his death bed. "I really don't mind dying," Bartok said, "but it's the fact that I regret not having left enough baggage behind." Sandor disclosed to me that "baggage" in Hungarian to Bartok referred to important musical works. So Sylvia, I'm absolutely certain, was dashing out these bantam masterpieces in her last ditch attempt to leave a little more "baggage" behind and quite possibly plant a lasting seed for herself in literature as slim as her output had been. However, it's not the aggregate which militates; for our most notable American symphonic composer, George Gershwin, rocketed the concert world with only seven major works.

Then too, all the elements were against Sylvia, and with the low blood sugar level she must have had with smoking, not eating, the tonics and drugs, death was now not something to be feared, but death was an intimate. Suicide was the only way she could grapple on to Ted Hughes. He would be forced to think about her every day of his life. One must understand that when a person commits suicide (with the possible historical exception of Field Marshal Erwin Rommel) they never once think that anything terrible is going to happen to them. On the contrary, if a person is terminally ill, suicide is a blessing because it ends the individual's suffering. And from the available data, it's quite apparent Sylvia Plath was mentally and physically suffering. Earth Humanity must learn that death is nothing, but suffering in our society should be considered intolerable and must be abolished.

Artistically and personally I'm not glad that Sylvia Plath killed herself because I wanted to see her and speak with her again. I would have liked to have seen her become the grand lady of poetry, literature and letters. However, humanistically, if she were mentally and physically suffering as much as I think she was, and life was just too painful for her and she definitely did not wish to live, then yes, society should be thankful that she took her own life and ended her agony.

I have on occasion wondered if I had been in London during that time, if I could have rescued her.

A 1962-63 Phillip Lambro would have tried to help Sylvia Plath, but he would not have known the root cause of her condition. He would have been doctoring the symptoms rather than the causes.

A 1966-67 Phillip Lambro who was being trained by the Japanese Zen Macrobiotics from Kyoto would have known the root causes by visual diagnosis and would have been able to rescue Sylvia Plath provided she wished to be saved. When in 1966 Phillip Lambro had sacroiliac arthritis and a form of Leukemia acquired as a side effect from the Omnipotent Medical Establishment's dispensation of Butazoladine and Prednisolone, he said to himself, "I'm too young to die. I want to compose and conduct music. I want to contribute to this subatomic particle of an atom we call humanity in any intelligent way that I can. I know that I must have been living out of harmony and eating poorly. I want to change."

And so I changed my life. If you had the physical pain which I had, but conjoined with the desire to be healthy, then it's relatively easy and simple to change. I was fortunate. I rejuvenated myself because I wanted to be productive and healthy for as long as possible. But anyone can do it. If Phillip Lambro did it, any person can do it. You just have to have the correct attitude and desire. I have helped many people whom I hardly knew overcome illness through Japanese Zen Macrobiotics; then many close friends I could never reach and, even today, they suffer, live miserably and eventually die under the continued failures of Occidental medicine. So in answer to my question regarding Sylvia Plath, I really don't know. It would have been up to her. She would have had to have wanted to alter her life. I would like to think that I could have saved Sylvia, as I did one young French shop girl during August 1993 in Toulouse after I gave her a printed invitation to attend a Raelian conference being given at the local hotel afterwhich she told everyone that she had planned to go home and commit suicide because she saw no hope to her existence, but after the conference she saw how she could change and that life was definitely worth living.

Having cursed Sylvia for dying before furnishing me with the monumental texts I had envisioned, and not having the power to get one of her DNA bone cells and have her recreated in a new body with stage three memory transfer cloning, I did the next best thing: I eventually selected four of her poems as the basis for my projected *Four Songs for Soprano & Orchestra*. As I have stated in the preface of the *Four Songs* published piano vocal (optional percussion) reduction score, for the time being I put the idea for this work aside as I had been commissioned to compose and conduct the music for three films; in 1964 I began my *Music For Wind, Brass & Percussion*; in 1965 I finished my *Toccata for Piano*, followed by *Two Pictures for Solo Percussionist & Orchestra*. However, the idea of doing a work in memory of Sylvia with contemporary music haunted me while I was preoccupied with these other compositions.

During April of 1966 I genuinely wanted to embark upon *Four Songs*. I had just completed the music for Universal's *And Now Miguel*, after which I had been fortunate enough to have been able to pay off debts and a bank loan, which had not left me with much financial residue. In spite of this, I did not want to do another film score until after I had composed Four Songs in memory of Sylvia.

One evening I was having dinner at Cyrano's on Sunset Boulevard with Edward "Buzz" Barton (Huntington Hartford's son), and I told him about Sylvia (he had never heard of her, or her work) and the composition I wished to do. Buzz had been a loyal friend and had been interested and supportive of my music. In fact, during 1964 he gave me a beautiful Baldwin Grand Piano expecting nothing in return. So as we spoke, I recited some fragments of Sylvia's poetry from memory (which he liked) and he asked how much money I would need to be able not to do another film score and compose Four Songs. Well, in those days, I was hard pressed to spend $40 dollars a week with all the dinner and social invitations I was receiving, and the comparatively low cost of living. I had a pleasant apartment for only $100 dollars a month at 1419 North Fairfax #3 in a building owned by Sidney Schuman, who was like a brother to me. And many, many months during those years from 1965 through 1979 while I was composing concert music (my rent had only increased to $135 dollars per month) Sidney Schuman would defer my payments. It is safe to say that Sidney Schuman was to composer Phillip Lambro what Michael Puchberg was to composer Wolfgang Amadeus Mozart.

I informed Buzz that if he gave me $3,500 dollars over the next year, I was sure that I could complete *Four Songs* within twelve months, and although I had to dedicate the work in memory of my childhood and teenage friend Sylvia Plath, I would give him credit as Commissioned By Edward Barton. Buzz agreed, and I immediately wrote a letter on 21 April 1966 to Alfred Knopf in New York seeking permission to use Sylvia's poems. Early in May of 1966, Knopf informed me that I would have to contact the publisher William Heinemann Limited in London who, in turn, communicated with Ted Hughes, and Ted Hughes wrote to me from Court Green, North Tawton, Devon, England 9 June 1966 granting me permission to use Sylvia Plath's poems. Directly after this, I began the composition. I selected 1. *The Night Dances*; 2. *The Applicant*; 3. *Mirror*; and 4. *Daddy*. I chose these four texts because of their dissimilarity in style and character.

I also used those four poems because they best represented the disparate qualities of Sylvia's personality. I composed *Four Songs* in my mind as if Sylvia (who couldn't carry a tune to save her life) were the soprano actress. *Four Songs* requires not just a good young soprano, but a good actress as well.

For example, the *Night Dances* (the first song) is impressionistic expressionistic sedately romantic. After three bars of three sets of Japanese Brass Wind Chimes (high, medium and low) breaks the silence in the orchestra followed by a low f-natural octave from the timpani, harp, and piano, the soprano sings "A smile fell in the grass irretrievable." Then reinforced with the cellos and basses the soprano speaks (sprechtstimme) sophisticatedly in meter, "And how will your night dances lose themselves, in mathematics?" In this song, the soprano must half-speak, half-sing, sing, speak and act. "Such pure leaps and spirals, surely they travel the earth forever."

The second song (*The Applicant*) is entirely different and actually shows Sylvia's sense of humor. Regardless of what anyone says, Sylvia Plath, at times when I knew her, did have an excellent sense of humor, and this poem demonstrates it. I perceived this to be the result of how she felt about the ridiculous obstacles society imposes upon one in the pursuit of a commonplace job. And that is why within the symphony orchestra I used in this movement an E-flat alto saxophone, electric guitar, and dance band high hat cymbals. The soprano snaps her fingers seductively as she says, "First, are you our sort of person? Do you wear a glass eye, false teeth, or a crutch, a brace or a hook, rubber breasts or a rubber crotch, stitches to show something's missing?" Then she sings, "No, no? Then how can we give you a thing? Stop crying. Open your hand. Empty? Empty. Here is a hand to fill it and willing to bring tea cups and roll away headaches and do whatever you tell it. Will you marry it? It is guaranteed to thumb shut your eyes at the end and dissolve of sorrow." This movement is sort of jazzy and I think Sylvia would have liked it.

The third song (*Mirror*) tells of a young woman, looking into a mirror ("I am silver and exact. I have no preconceptions.") and seeing herself aging ("Now I am a lake. A woman bends over me, searching my reaches for what she really is."); as Sylvia says, "In me she has drowned a young girl, and in me an old woman rises toward her day after day, like a terrible fish."

I expect growing old was in Sylvia's consciousness; the fear of maturating; because, when I knew her, she was always interested in her youthful appearance; she was continuously immaculate in every aspect from her clear skin and sparkling eyes to her healthy head of natural blonde hair. Sylvia Plath could have easily been a fashion model. I'm sure those last weeks in her life, from what I have heard, she probably looked like a Fellini mannequin, and remembering her in Wellesley, I know that she could not tolerate that.

In the last song, I used *Daddy* which was logical since it was, to my way of thinking rather than chronologically, Sylvia's last poetic statement. In each instance I used the entire poem with the exception of *Daddy* where, due to musical structure, (and the fact that at this point, as Dylan Thomas would have said, Sylvia was at times just ranting and raving), I found it necessary to use only the most powerful half of the stanzas.

This movement is one of extremes from both the solo soprano and the Orchestra. The soprano opens singing with two notes from the Crotales (bells) followed by the Strings and three Vibraphones, "You do not do, you do not do any more black shoe. In which I have lived like a foot for thirty years, poor and white, barely daring to breathe or Achoo." Thereafter there is a great deal of split conflict expressed between the soprano and the orchestra. Orchestral and dynamic activity are quite active throughout the entire movement. Here the soprano is definitely Sylvia: speaking, singing, half singing, and expressing all the obvious years of puritanical repressed trauma in the abreactive schizophrenia of her lines. I selected and used only the choice lines. "Daddy, I have had to kill you. You died before I had time. I have always been scared of you, with your Luftwaffe (and) your gobbledygoo. And your neat moustache and your Aryan eye, bright blue. Panzer-man, panzer-man, O You---."

"You stand at the blackboard daddy, in the picture I have of you, a cleft in your chin instead of your foot. But no less a devil for that, no not any less the black man who bit my pretty red heart in two." And then it goes on in a dramatically schizoid way where the soprano and orchestra sometimes are going in two disparate standpoints. I think Sylvia would have been excited by the results.

I completed *Four Songs for Soprano & Orchestra* 3 December 1967, and a few sopranos have sung the work from the published piano vocal reduction, but why after almost thirty-eight years (as of 2006) the world premiere of this obviously important composition has not taken place is a good question. It's the only completed work in my repertory which has not had a world premiere. I can't understand it. But then again, I also could not understand why Franz Schubert could never get any of his own symphonies performed during his lifetime; or why the Guggenheim Foundation twice refused elderly Arnold Schoenberg a grant causing Schoenberg's *Moses & Aron* to remain unfinished to this day; or why no one could sell a Van Gogh drawing or painting until the day after he died. Or why Franz Kafka never had one of his major works published during his lifetime; or why Bela Bartok always had to struggle for money right up to his death in 1945. I'm hoping to conduct the world premiere of *Four Songs*, with an excellent soprano, before I die. I've offered *Four Songs* on a number of occasions to the Boston Symphony, Chicago Symphony, London Symphony, Los Angeles Philharmonic; I mean, I've lost count of all the orchestras I have contacted over the years. All I can say is that it must be truly an illustrious masterpiece to have received all of the apathy it has engendered.

In the spring of 1982, I gave a copy of the score to the rising American soprano Aprile Millo. She eventually wrote a hand written letter to me, "These songs are an original piece of vocal literature in the true sense of lieder, the perfect fusion of words and music. Bravo." She also sent me two tickets to her recital at Ambassador. I then heard from her the following year, "You honor me greatly by your invitation to perform your *Four Songs*. I am hopeful to perform them very soon as some major recitals seem to be in the offing." Well, that was the last time I ever heard from Aprile Millo. Perhaps she's still in her linguini and clams period with Puccini and Verdi; I don't know.

Other ranking sopranos have expressed interest in Four Songs, but I have to acquire the proper orchestral guest conducting engagements to hire these girls. I was impressed with Dawn Upshaw. I think she could do an exceptional job with *Four Songs*. I gave her a copy of the published score January 1988 after her stunning recital at Ambassador and as I walked away, she called out to me and asked that I return to personally autograph the cover for her.

Perhaps all these divas are waiting for me to die so that they can discover *Four Songs*.

In December of 1981, I wrote Sylvia's English teacher mentor, Wilbury Crockett, in Wellesley (who I'm sure nearly fainted as he had not heard from me since 1953) and I sent him a copy of the published *Four Songs* together with a couple of recordings of mine and my biographical concert brochure. I said in the letter that I wanted him to know that Sylvia wasn't the only artist who came out of Bradford at that time, but she quit and I didn't. He replied to me 16 January 1982. "Dear Phillip, I applaud you and rejoice in your great gifts. The poems you chose interested me. Had you thought of *Edge*? I played the *Two Pictures* tape with a former student of mine who is planning to be a percussionist. Both of us thought the piece brilliant. You were so kind to send me the music. I play the piano and have invited Mrs. Plath to my home to hear the music. Best regards, W.A.C."

I was pleased to have heard from Wilbury Crockett and I responded to him that I was glad to learn that he played the piano, and wrote that perhaps someday I would eventually learn English. Wilbury Crockett was a remarkably intelligent man and I was fortunate to have known him at Bradford.

Over the years, people have asked me what I have thought about the screen adaptation of *The Bell Jar* and if I imagined Sylvia would have been pleased with the results.

As I sarcastically joshed once to my friend and associate Darrell Armstrong after I was invited by the director Larry Peerce (who happens to be the late Metropolitan Opera tenor Jan Peerce's son) to view the final cut of *The Bell Jar* movie as my then agent Walter Kohner had strongly suggested me to compose the score, "It's a good thing Sylvia Plath is dead, because if she were alive and saw what they have done with *The Bell Jar* she'd turn over in her grave."

Fortunately, I was not contracted to do the score and satisfyingly for the novel, the film instantly expired at the box office. The people who had the screen rights did not know what they were doing with *The Bell Jar*. Larry Peerce, who's a clever enough fellow in the finite sense, was absolutely the incorrect director for that story. And Ladies and Gentlemen of the Jury, let me state here for the record, that not only would Sylvia Plath have been altogether disenchanted with the pedestrian script, predictable casting and locations and the unimaginative lighting of the scenes and stock sound effects tracks, but she would have been unequivocally and genuinely pissed-off with the fabricated addition of the lesbian sequence into the story; not that there's anything wrong with lesbians or a lesbian story, but if you are cinematically translating a sensitive novel about the life of a Kodiak Bear during a difficult winter in Alaska, you don't stick in a scene of thirsty Elephants crossing the African plains desperately looking for a water hole.

I knew that *The Bell Jar* had been optioned and renewed a number of times from the middle 1960's on, because I tried to secure the film rights and raise the money myself during 1967 in an attempt to purchase the property outright; but I was constantly informed that the rights had already been optioned and were not available.

No major film studio wanted *The Bell Jar* and that's why it took so long to reach the screen. It was what the Celluloid Moguls here in Never Never Land continually referred to as "a hard sell."

I would have wanted to secure the screen rights to *The Bell Jar* because at that time while doing several feature film scores here in Hollywood I had witnessed a number of exceptional stories get abused and mutilated as they made their tortuous ascents toward the expectant screen. For Sylvia's sake, I wanted to protect her story. Sylvia Plath appreciated artistry and well made films. I vividly recall how much she liked such films as *The Red Shoes*, and *Kind Hearts And Coronets*. I used to see her at the colonial red brick Community Playhouse on Washington Street in Wellesley where all the good cinema was shown when we were young teenagers. I remember Mr. Leslie Bendslev (the owner) who used to take the tickets and do the programming. And Bendslev's, the hand made ice cream parlor, soda fountain and sandwich shop adjacent to it where Sylvia Plath loved to go.

A subsequent chapter in this book, *The Chinatown Syndrome*, deals with my involvement and experiences with the 1974 film *Chinatown* for which Roman Polanski hired me to compose and conduct the original film score. I do not wish to get into it here, save to say that as Polanski was driving me in his car one day, I happened to mention *The Bell Jar* and Sylvia Plath to him. Polanski had never heard of either, but as I was embarking on *Chinatown* I had entertained the notion that *The Bell Jar* might resurrect his career and the novel. But after we completed *Chinatown*, I could see that 1974 Roman Polanski was "finished" as a director. However, the 1967 Roman Polanski might have been an excellent choice to do *The Bell Jar*.

If I could have obtained the rights and adequate financing, I probably would have produced *The Bell Jar* under a nom de plume; hired an unquestionably talented director; done a stream of consciousness film score and effects track using my real name; and cast justified unknown actors and actresses so that the story and film would be the stars.

I still feel that *The Bell Jar* could and should be completely remade someday; however, with the correct artistic and emotional cinematic ingredients. If I weren't involved with music and so many other humanitarian obligations, and had the funds, I'd direct it myself. In fact, one day during the early 1970's at the Japanese Zen Macrobiotic Restaurant in Hollywood

I was startled when I saw a young girl in her twenties who could have passed for Sylvia's twin and who even spoke with a similar voice. The girl was seated near me conversing with another girl, and perhaps since I was almost staring at her, she said to me, "Is anything wrong?"

"No," I replied. "I thought you were someone I knew a long time ago. But you're not." I grinned and she smiled. I never saw the girl again, but if she had been an actress and I were the director, I certainly would have tested her for the part of Esther.

A tragic aside related to my *Four Songs for Soprano & Orchestra* is that my friend Edward "Buzz" Barton who had commissioned *Four Songs* took his own life by blowing out his brains in New York City at the Hotel Fourteen shortly after an argument with his father, Huntington Hartford, in November of 1967. These events are related in a subsequent chapter of this book entitled *Paradox Island*.

A further, but more entertaining episode concerning *Four Songs* occurred during a November 1967 private screening of a couple of dreadful new feature films at the home of renowned actress Jean Simmons and her then husband screen writer director, (*Elmer Gantry* and *Blackboard Jungle*), Richard Brooks. I had met the lovely and gracious Jean Simmons during the summer of 1967 through Kathy Green, John Green's (composer of *Body And Soul* and *I Cover The Waterfront*) tall lovely daughter with whom I occasionally played tennis. Kathy, Jean and I, and usually another man (sometimes dancer director Gene Kelly, cinematographer Conrad Hall, or Richard Brooks) would play mixed up doubles at Jean Simmon's attractive Holmby Hills home on Charing Cross Road. Jean Simmons, although not a tournament player, nevertheless had amazing natural talent for tennis in that she had an innate sense of where to place the ball during a heated exchange in order to force an error. Another thing was that Jean (and Kathy, too), unlike the aforementioned men, never "choked" during a point, or moaned after losing one. I really enjoyed playing tennis with her not only because she was one of the most beautiful women in the world, and one of the elite actresses, but because I found her to be an engaging and delightfully unaffected person; even though I sensed at times that masked behind the soft unparalleled British voice, warm smile, and natural charm, lay some deep rooted unhappiness.

Almost every other weekend Richard Brooks would show a feature film or two in their projection room for a selected list of guests in an informal early evening gathering. The projection room was rather like an oversized living room built adjacent to the main house and beautifully furnished with scatter rugs, large floor pillows, easy chairs and sofas. The screen was fairly large and the 35 mm projection and dubbing equipment was the same as you would find at any major film studio in Hollywood.

That particular evening Jean was away shooting a feature film in Switzerland, but Brooks (after tennis earlier in the day) invited me and my young twenty year old girl friend of the time, Karla (a slender fair Norwegian American beauty with long straight thick flaxen hair) to attend a double feature that evening.

I especially liked bringing Karla along with me when Richard Brooks was around because she rarely knew who any of the celebrities were, or what they did, and since her father had been a Rear Admiral in the Navy she could have cared less. Karla, like me, did not particularly care for Richard Brooks' arrogant abrasive manner, and like me, when he would get a little obnoxious, she told him so. Once Brooks, who continually wore the same old tattered sweat sodden gray baggy warm-up pants and polo shirt to play tennis in, took his sockless tennis shoes off inside the house after serving both Karla and myself some apple juice and crackers. Karla, noticing Richard Brooks' long dirty toe nails, and tobacco stained teeth as he lit his ever present pipe, exclaimed, "Richard, you're toe nails are disgusting. Don't you ever cut them and wash your feet? And look at your teeth. They're gross."

One must understand that, at this time, Richard Brooks (as the result of being super-agent Irving "Swifty" Lazar's close personal friend) was an influential figure in the motion picture industry and everyone from cinematographer Conrad Hall; a nameless broken down Yugoslavian tennis player trying to be a film producer; Jacques Bergerac (Ginger Rogers ex-husband); record producer Quincy Jones; lyricist Alan Bergman; and others, wouldn't have dared make the remarks Karla and I made since they were, metaphorically speaking, continually kissing Brooks' hand and other parts of his anatomy in hopes of landing film assignments, and who knows what else. I particularly informed Brooks on more than one occasion that I did not appreciate (especially on the tennis court) the way he chastised and imprecated his tennis partner, Conrad Hall, for Brooks own lousy play.

"Conrad," I'd say, "why do you put up with his shit?"

"As long as I'm shooting Richard Brooks' films and he's paying me the kind of money he is," Conrad Hall told me, "I'll take anything he dishes out."

On occasion when Brooks would become especially nasty to his partner on the tennis court while I would be teamed up with Jean Simmons, or someone else, I would intentionally hit a medium paced volley or overhead directly at Brooks, and feign astonishment by saying, "Oh, excuse me, Richard. I'm sorry. I hope you're not hurt too seriously."

Well, that November 1967 evening after Karla and I said to each other "Wow, what a terrible picture that was." And the projectionist was setting up the reels for the next feature, Richard Brooks asked me, "Hey Lambro, what are you composing these days?"

"My *Four Songs for Soprano & Orchestra*," I replied.

"Jesus Christ," Brooks exclaimed from the rear of the projection room lighting his pipe with his feet up on the dubbing console, "you were working on that god damned thing the last time I asked you two months ago. Shit, what's taking you so long?"

"That's right," I said, "I've been working on this major composition off and on for over a year now. It's an important symphonic work which I'm doing in memory of my childhood friend the late poetess, Sylvia Plath."

There were about a dozen well known celebrities smiling and attentively listening to Brooks endeavoring to make fun of me. And none of them, including Richard Brooks, had ever heard of Sylvia Plath.

"Son of a bitch, when I was directing at MGM I wrote the whole fucking script to *Cat On A Hot Tin Roof* in twelve days."

"You wrote *Cat On A Hot Tin Roof*?" I exclaimed. "I thought Tennessee Williams wrote *Cat On A Hot Tin Roof*."

Richard Brooks turned red as a beet and said, "I meant the screenplay."

"I read a review once," I continued, "which quoted you as maintaining that you only changed eleven words from Tennesee Williams original play, why hell that's less than a word a day. What took you so long?"

Richard Brooks became so rattled by my retort that he nearly choked on his pipe. That was the only time I ever saw Richard Brooks speechless, and I must say that it was quite becoming.

There was Gene Kelly broadly grinning and trying to break the awkward silence. Of course, he didn't need Richard Brooks, but I always had had the conviction that Gene Kelly had "a thing" for Jean Simmons, and who could blame him. But my main feeling about Gene Kelly (I liked him only in an *American In Paris*) was, as remarkable a dancer as he sometimes was, as an actor and later as a person, I found him to be rather superficial.

Gene Kelly was the type of individual who was habitually beaming and telling everyone how great they looked (or were), and what a wonderful day it was. It seemed to me that Gene Kelly was oblivious to the underlying reality of the people he came into contact with, and the sociological world in general. I mean, he was always courteous with me; save one instance with Karla where he got me into trouble by telling her, half jokingly, the gigantic fib that I was always pursuing many women. However, the main feature about Gene Kelly's personality was that if a person were lying on the floor bleeding and in pain he'd tell them how wonderful they looked, and what a beautiful day it was.

Shortly after that, I just stopped going up to the Jean Simmons home. As Jean Simmons first husband, Stewart Granger, was quoted as saying, "Can you imagine anyone wanting to marry Richard Brooks?"

I'm sure Sylvia Plath would have agreed; giggled; and said, "But Phillip, are you crazy?"

PARADOX ISLAND

Ladies and Gentlemen of the Jury, as I explained within *Dali In Lambrovision*, I first met A & P multimillionaire Huntington Hartford while I was living in New York City around 1962 as a result of an interest Hartford expressed in a painting by Ilja Jefimovitch Repin (a Russian impressionist Rembrandt) entrusted to me by a Swiss associate entitled *Reception At The Court Of The Czar*; an oil on canvas signed and dated 1894 (and authenticated) which we kept in New York City within a bank vault. Ilja Jefimovitch Repin, in my opinion, is probably one of the most underrated impressionist painters of all time. With the exception of his painting *The Cossaks Write The Sultan A Letter Of Rejection* which is hanging at the Louvre in Paris, the majority of Repin's paintings are in Russia at the Museum in Moscow. Had Repin's work been allowed to leave Russia, he would definitely have had a name as significant as Renoir in the West. As a painter Repin's work is every bit as worthwhile as the celebrated French impressionists. However, with very few of his paintings circulating outside of Russia (in the International Art Market) there isn't the active sales trading for Repin which would cause escalating prices, demand, interest and publicity in his work.

Hartford had offered me about $20,000 for the Repin, after I informed him that the firm asking price was $40,000; so there were never any further negotiations.

On occasion, Hartford would invite me to his exclusive trilevel penthouse at One Beekman Place.

We played tennis a few times indoors at the posh paneled ultra-exclusive (1,000 members only) The River Club (East 52nd Street and the East River) with its indirect lighting, excellent indoor Har-Tru naturally green clay tennis court, and carpeted swimming pool.

Although Hartford revealed that he had been on the Harvard University Tennis Team, I was rather surprised how hard pressed I was just to let him win a few games in a set, since during that period he had recently purchased the 625 acre Hog Island adjacent to Nassau in the Bahamas and (pouring 25 million dollars into it) renamed it Paradise Island contracting as his personal tennis pro none other than Richard Pancho Gonzales; in my estimation one of the five greatest tennis players of all time. Even though Hartford's strokes were somewhat fluid, he had the amiss habit of not meeting the ball far enough in front of himself as the result of ambivalent foot work which caused a lot of unforced errors. Having been acquainted with Pancho Gonzales during the height of his overpowering tennis mechanics and in the early 1970's observing him coach Jimmy Connors on occasion with Pancho Segura (Connor's regular coach) at the Beverly Hills Tennis Club, I'm quite sure that Gonzales called these technical deficiencies to Hartford's attention; but as I was to observe rather quickly, Huntington Hartford almost always never adopted good advice.

Hartford subsequently invited me to a few of his companionable gatherings and it was there that I met Salvador Dali, Richard Nixon, and jet-set physician Dr. Louis Scarrone, and as a result of my work at the United Nations and G. Schirmer I reciprocated by arranging invitations for Hartford to a couple of social events including the September 1963 UN Staff Day function where I introduced Hartford to several dignitaries and well known entertainers including Frank Sinatra.

Contrary to what has been said and written about Huntington Hartford's social acceptability and demand for his presence at important gala events up until his purported environmental, personal, metabolic and monetary descent in the mid 1970's, I had a difficult time arranging an invitation for him at the September 1963 United Nations Staff Day as Jeff Sparks actually did not want Hartford there; but since Jeff and I had been such good friends and he felt so indebted to me as the result of my musical and entertainment efforts on behalf of the UN, Jeff finally relented and gave me permission to invite Hartford. I had also asked Hartford's young wife Diane, and questioned Hartford as to her whereabouts when (as described in the previous UN chapter) I noticed he arrived alone claiming Diane did not wish to come. Diane had me paged at the UN after the main proceedings as I was with my last teacher, concert pianist Gyorgy Sandor (who had performed that evening), Jeff Sparks, Hartford, and a variety of other guests sitting on the plushly dark green carpeted balcony overlooking the UN's General Assembly main entrance by the statue of Zeus where the Staff Day Dance was in full swing with Meyer Davis and his Society Orchestra.

"Where are you?" I asked Diane.

"Home... Is Hunt there?"

"Yes," I replied. "Why didn't you come?"

"Hunt made me feel as if I wasn't invited. I'm sure he wanted to go alone in case he might meet another girl."

"Listen, the only people he's met this evening are male dignitaries, Gyorgy Sandor, Frank Sinatra, Jeff Sparks, snacks and refreshments. I was going to introduce him to my favorite female, Madame Nehru, but she didn't show up."

Diane laughed. "What are you doing now?" She asked.

"What do you think I'm doing? I'm speaking with you. Look, why not come down right now," I suggested. "You're only a stone's throw away."

"Hunt might get angry," she said. "We've already had two arguments today."

"To hell with Hunt," I said. "I invited you, so be here."

Within thirty minutes Diane arrived (to the absolute consternation of Hartford) in the most exquisite Venus all white evening gown which framed her attractive twenty-two year old fair skinned brunette features to perfection.

I introduced Diane to everyone available. Diane may have been twenty-two, but she always acted quite mature for her age; especially with her Anglo-Mayfair accent which I'm sure she gathered at eighteen along the Pennsylvania turnpike as she was making her way from Quakerland to the big city of New York in search of the golden egg and ubiquitous priapism. In fact, I was a little disappointed that Jill St. John and Frank Sinatra had already departed because I wanted to introduce Jill St. John and Diane Brown Hartford to one another if only to see who could out Anglicize the other.

Jeff Sparks was totally enchanted with Diane and could not fathom how such a charming young lady could have ever married Huntington Hartford, even with all his millions.

Diane purposely ignored Hartford all evening. Diane asked me to dance and we closely embraced one slow number alone on the balcony above the Meyer Davis Society Orchestra. Afterward, Hartford finally came up to me as I was by myself perusing the snacks and secretly murmured his great dissatisfaction at my having invited Diane to the dance, but I made it quite plain to Hartford that there wasn't much he could do about it since this was the United Nations and not One Beekman Place.

Beatrice Glass, an art collector and dealer with extraordinary taste, with whom I was friendly (and used her apartment and grand piano at 9 East 84th Street while composing and conducting my first film score with the New York Philharmonic, November-December 1963) and who on occasion, against my protestations, would try and seat me next to some wealthy young heiress at one of her assemblages hoping I would marry the girl so that I could be supported the rest of my life (and lose my artistic and personal freedom I'd explain) suggested to me during 1963 that I not associate with Huntington Hartford because of the fact that even with his extensive fortune, he was considered by the reigning

U. S. social eternals of the time to be unacceptable on most guest lists.

Beatrice Glass was a tall engaging middle aged lady of conspicuously good breeding, who possessed an excellent vocabulary coupled with an eloquent manner of speech. When she allowed me to use her apartment and grand piano to compose in, I remember saying to her, "You don't have to worry, Beatrice, I promise not to play too loudly and upset your neighbors; we wouldn't want you to get an eviction notice."

"My dear Phillip," she said assuring me, "you don't have to worry one bit about the neighbors. I'm sure they won't complain to me about your music since I own the entire building."

I actually used Beatrice's apartment for less than two weeks because I got progressively impatient every time I had to leave the flat and return (since she had a priceless art collection from the impressionists to Klein and Kandinsky) and, as a result of insurance stipulations, I had to correctly mount these heavy steel poles into the hallway floor which had to fall into the front steel door a particular way when closing it and then use an additional three different keys to open and close the front door. It got to be like an alpine expedition without the mountains.

Beatrice had a son about my age (an intelligent fellow I thought) who lived out on Long Island and whom she would have liked to have taken after me in some ways; although I informed her that she should consider herself fortunate to have had a son as knowledgeable and well read as he. "Yes," Beatrice would say, "he's intelligent; but he has absolutely no function and direction in his life."

Beatrice's late husband had made a fortune during his lifetime as one of the largest importers of jewelry in the United States. Since Beatrice was fluent in French her husband used to dispatch her back and forth to Europe to select, transact, and secure jewels.

In fact, Beatrice was caught up in a rather harrowing winter escape from the Nazi Gestapo during the outbreak of World War II. Beatrice had bought some priceless gems for her husband's firm in one of the Southern Slavic countries when she received word from her associates that the Gestapo had begun an all out pursuit for her and the jewels. As she explained to me, she walked with her partisan guide about ten miles through the snow bound forest to a makeshift air field where a small plane had been contracted to take her to Switzerland. Beatrice was quite fortunate to have escaped because as the plane took off, the Gestapo had arrived and began firing their small arms and pistols at the lifting aircraft. Fortunately the plane was not hit and Beatrice made her way to Switzerland and then back to the United States.

Toward the end of 1963, Beatrice invited me to a small dinner party at her home where the guests included a European woman whose physical and motor characteristics reminded me of the entertainment personality Zsa Zsa Gabor.

"Phillip is a brilliant composer-conductor," said Beatrice to the European lady.

"Oh really," said the European woman. "You know, my late husband was a composer-conductor and conducted all over Europe before and after the War and was a wonderful composer, too."

As the evening wore on, one of the older male guests had been discussing architecture to which the European madame instantly responded, "My husband was a wonderful architect and designed several prominent buildings in Paris."

"Really," I said quite impressed.

Several minutes later, Beatrice (who had known that I used to play tournament tennis in college) asked me, "Phillip, are you still playing any tennis these days?"

Before I had the opportunity to respond, the continental lady interrupted, "Oh Beatrice, did you know that my husband was a member of the Spanish Davis Cup team in the late forties? Yes, he was such a fantastic tennis player and won many exciting matches. I so loved watching him play."

I was completely startled by the European madame's husband's obvious versatility.

Before another ten minutes went by a medical Doctor at the table began to describe his particular field of practice to us when the European lady completely awed us again by saying, "You know my husband was one of Europe's most famous surgeons and many of his operating techniques completely revolutionized modern surgery."

Well, Ladies and Gentlemen of the Jury, I just could not contain myself, and gently dropping my fork quite politely onto Beatrice Glass's precious China plate, I asked incredulously, "Madame, who is your husband? I have to meet him; he must be the eighth wonder of the world to be a composer-conductor, physician, Spanish Davis Cup player, and architect."

"Oh no, no, young man," laughingly vocalized the European gentlewoman. "You see, it was my second husband who was the doctor; my fifth husband was the tennis player; my third husband was the architect; and my fourth husband was the conductor-composer."

Huntington Hartford had two (what might be quite dissolutely termed) assistants: Sy Alter, a smooth talking pipe smoking former department store detective whose features at that time bore a striking resemblance to author Irving Wallace; and Larry Horn, a rather tall, slender, dim-wit associate of Alter's with a greasy dark brown Elvis Presley hairdo who wore expensive clothes and jewelry, but somehow, in spite of that, always looked cheaply dressed. Larry Horn physically and vocally reminded me of the off-beat character actor Timothy Carey. In fact, after I got to know Hartford, I once remarked, "You know, Hunt, did anyone ever tell you how much you resemble actor Jason Robards? Without the talent, of course," I quickly added.

Diane (usually after a major rumpus with Hartford) would occasionally berate Sy Alter for pretending to be an astute businessman while in reality it was Diane's opinion that Sy Alter was no more than a self-seeking financial parasite who had attached himself to Hartford's fortune. Sy Alter, although not an intellectual, was far from naive; he eventually and quietly milked the Huntington Hartford financial situation for all he could get. Diane thought Larry Horn was "a complete ass" and was hard pressed in tolerating him as much as he was in Hartfrod's attendance. I found Larry Horn to be Huntington Hartford's court jester and his fawning servile flatterer; which was rather futile since Huntington Hartford really had no basic sense of humor; most of the time Larry Horn was the only one laughing at his own jokes. Sy Alter did have a beautiful and charming blonde wife, Dottie, approximately in her mid-thirties, whom I found to be a rational, sensitive and caring person, and Diane seemed to like her as well.

I was led to believe that Hartford kept Sy Alter around for business and introductions to unfamiliar models, and Larry Horn to maintain and accelerate the latter activity.

Speaking of models, there was this rangy blonde paradigm by the name of China Gerard who was a frequent visitor at Hartford's One Beekman Place gatherings. Although I did not know her well, after observing her tenacious networking over a period of several months I can categorically state that this girl socially performed the Lewis and Clark expedition without ever having left Manhattan.

August, September, October, November, December 1963 were unusually active months for me. In addition to being hired by my former University of Miami Tennis Teammate, Nelson Case Jr. to compose and conduct the music for his high budget documentary *Energy On The Move* (devoted to the wonders of natural gas), I had met an elderly, diminutive, impoverished and good hearted Polish-American scientist and inventor by the name of Dr. John Falenks who (along with his associates) asked me to help him resurrect his ingenious stomach camera which he had invented thirty years previously and manufactured fifteen years afterward. I understood that Dr. Falenks was the first person to have ever taken still photographs inside the human stomach. He humbly explained to me how the United States Department Of Health had wanted to buy his patent completely at an insultingly indigent fee with absolutely no royalty arrangement, and how Eastman Kodak also forced him to discontinue manufacturing and selling the stomach cameras (approximately 200 doctors around the United States had purchased the machines) because Dr. Falenks refused their exploitative offer to also purchase his invention without any royalty arrangements whatsoever. Eastman-Kodak then refused to continue processing and supplying the Doctors with the special film and technical procedures required to reproduce such a small negative which was about the size of one's little fingernail.

Dr. Falenks had photographed various stomach cancer outpatients at a few Manhattan hospitals after surgery only to find that in many instances prominent surgeons had missed occasional malignancies. I was informed that the doctors would then rush their patients back in for additional operations, but threatened Dr. Falenks that if he ever advised the public as to what had actually transpired, that they would categorically refute it, and moreover, would file legal actions against him. The patients were required to swallow this very thin small camera which was operated with illuminating light from outside of the body.

I introduced Dr. Falenks to Dr. Louis Scarrone (whom I had met through Huntington Hartford) who asked me to take Dr. Falenks to another one of Lou's Jet-Set Doctor colleagues on Fifth Avenue who was a stomach specialist and had been working on a color motion picture camera principle using Dr. Falenks axioms, but (of course) the patient was only required to swallow a fiber optic mirrored tube and, fortunately, not the entire 16mm motion picture camera itself. That week Dr. Falenks and I were one of the first to ever witness the motion pictures of a human stomach in glorious living color. "It would be great special effects for a horror movie," I remember telling them. I did as much as I could for Dr. Falenks, but I believe this penurious and humiliated elderly scientific genius went on being manipulated to the end of his days.

Earlier that year, I had met an expensively dressed and agitated smooth talking slim youthful middle aged cashmere character by the name of Robert (Bobby) Edwards at the Salad Bowl; a health food restaurant and store on Seventh Avenue almost directly across the street from the Stage Delicatessen. Bobby Edwards apparently lived as if he had a great deal of money with a large apartment on the West Side overlooking Central Park, and one of the most pulchritudinous blonde sensual mistresses you ever saw by the name of Lisa.

"You like that, kid?" Edwards would sometimes tease me about Lisa.

"Well, she's certainly very interesting," I would say.

"You think you could handle that, Kid? That beautiful thing costs me between four and five grand a month."

I ate lunch at the Salad Bowl fairly often where among other things I witnessed comedian Buddy Hackett get evicted for sticking his fingers into and tossing Amazon actress Julie Newmar's salad right in front of her.

The late actor-comedian Dick Shawn (who had had very little musical training) would sometimes frantically seek me out at the Salad Bowl and ask me to help him quickly learn a song for a Broadway musical audition he was about to have within twenty minutes.

Bobby Edwards had advised me that he was interested in importing large quantities of shrimp into New York City from Brazil, and if I could introduce him to the right people, I could make enough money to sponsor my own concert music fellowships. "Kid, do you have any idea how many millions of shrimp cocktails are consumed daily here in Manhattan?"

Bobby Edwards had learned that through my then Peruvian girlfriend, Nellie Castaneda, I had been acquainted with some influential South American businessmen, and in addition he had discovered that I was familiar with Oleg Cassini when he saw me speaking with Oleg on Seventh Avenue one day.

Bobby informed me that Oleg's brother Igor Cassini had staunch and influential ties to South American businessmen and high ranking government officials and quite tactfully suggested that I work on the shrimp deal and forget about having to go through the concert music homosexual political infiltration course I was being subjected to on behalf of acquiring a letter of recommendation for a Guggenheim Fellowship or Prix de Rome from the likes of critic-decomposer Virgil Thomson (whom I unlovingly nicknamed Virgin Thomson) who thought I was a musical genius and promised to help me until I discouraged Virgin's pablum sexual advances toward me; especially during one dinner engagement at his Chelsea Hotel suite complete with wrought iron love seats, piccolo timpani and a bronze bust of Van Cliburn. Virgin had personally prepared dinner for me and two affected male he-she cigarette smoking Columbia University graduate students (who were about my age) who intermittently

107

kissed each other passionately at the dining room table (which I didn't mind at all; at least they weren't fighting) and kept uttering, "Loosen up, Phillip Lambro; what's the matter with you? Why can't a charming and talented boy such as yourself become like us?"

I introduced Bobby Edwards to a tenacious, short, burly and well oiled Ecuadorian merchandiser who drew up a business plan for the South American shrimp venture which I took over to Oleg Cassini's Park Avenue penthouse one afternoon. It had been raining and Oleg, in his bathrobe, was rather frustrated over the fact that the ceiling of his poshly European antiqued penthouse had the unmitigated indignity to be leaking. It was somewhat entertaining there in the living room to see and hear the asymmetrical sounds of a variety of dripping waters descend from the high ceiling into about a half dozen aluminum pots, ceramic bowls and tin cans.

"Phillip, just make yourself at home," Oleg said. "I must take a shower. I'll be with you in about twenty minutes."

As I waited, I perused the spacious living room and its artifacts. I observed a few large oil and pastel portraits hanging on the walls of an uncommonly beautiful young woman who I found out later was the mystical actress Gene Tierney who had haunted millions of motion picture fans with her elusive portrayal of Laura in the 1944 film by the same name. There was also a glass paperweight on Oleg's desk which encased a newspaper photo cutout of a much younger Oleg together with the lovely Gene Tierney and their two horses, but with no caption.

There were two personally inscribed framed oversized photographs of the current President of the United States, John F. Kennedy, and the First Lady, Jacqueline Kennedy. I had often read in the media that Oleg Cassini had been Mrs. Kennedy's personal and favorite couturier. In the coming months, one of Oleg's female employees was to inform me, "Oleg couldn't design a simple shirt pattern if his life depended on it. But don't tell him I said that because I need my job." I was amused as to the tolerably short perfunctory messy inscription which President Kennedy had given Oleg; which, was perhaps why the framed photograph of the President had been relegated partially out of view behind a corner end table lamp. Conversely, Jacqueline Kennedy's responsively warm and favorable dedication caused the First Lady's photograph to occupy the place of visual preeminence upon a special central coffee table.

When Oleg returned he said, "I'm really interested in this fishing venture. It looks very good and perhaps we can do something with it; but first, I'll have to speak with my people and see if I have the time to get involved. The proposal looks fine and I'm sure we could make a great deal of money from it; but, you know, management is the key here. I've made money in my life, but only if I had had the right type of organizational management, I could have made much much more money and kept it."

I nodded as I assimilated what Oleg was saying, and after about another fifteen minutes we concluded the meeting. Oleg sighed slightly as he told me, "I'll be busy the next couple of weeks with my daughter who's coming from out of town to stay with me. She goes to a special school for the handicapped so I won't be able to devote much time to this until after she leaves."

"I understand," I said.

As I was about to depart I asked Oleg, "Who are those beautiful portraits of?"

"That was my wife," he said. "We're no longer married."

By the brevity and tone of Oleg's answer, and the obvious manner in which one felt the gazing mysterious presence from the walled portraits of this unusually stunning young woman, I felt that perhaps Oleg was still captivated by the reminiscences of quality moments from their relationship which since had long passed.

I found out shortly thereafter that Oleg had been a motion picture fashion designer in Hollywood during the late 1930's and early 1940's and had eloped with Gene Tierney to Las Vegas in 1941 which caused a bitter estrangement between Tierney's wealthy insurance parents who refused to accept Oleg Cassini as their son-in-law; considering him simply to be a social fortune hunter. I was also informed that in 1943 a daughter had been born to them with brain damage which eventually initiated the beauteous actress's leisurely descent into a tangled web of emotional disorders. Oleg and Tierney divorced in 1947; reconciled; had a second daughter; and divorced again in 1952.

It was also interesting to note that before the reconciliation with Oleg, Gene Tierney was being romanced by John F. Kennedy who, when his cards played out, eventually told Tierney that he could never marry a divorced woman. Perhaps, Oleg's retributive setting partially out of view behind a corner end table lamp of President Kennedy's personally inscribed framed photograph, and President Kennedy's obviously terse perfunctory messy dedication which President Kennedy had given Oleg, might have been the result of two possessive rival lovers who had captured and ultimately lost the emotions of possibly one of the most unaccountably beautiful women this planet has ever seen.

Several days after my meeting with Oleg Cassini, I received a message to telephone a particular special agent of the FBI. What did the FBI want with inconsequential me? At first, I speculated that, in all probability, it had something to do with the fact that I had been sending my symphonic and concert music to the Minister Of Culture in Russia; but as soon as I contacted the special FBI agent, he began asking me a series of interrogatories about my relationship with Mr. Robert (Bobby) Edwards. It did not take long for me to determine that with the information the FBI agent apparently had on my conversations with Bobby Edwards that my telephone and quite possibly my salad and vegeburgers at the Salad Bowl had been under government high-tech electronic surveillance.

"What do you want with me?" I asked. "I'm just a composer, conductor, pianist trying to get back to my career."

"We know you're not guilty of anything," the FBI agent went on to say. "We just want to ask you a few questions about Bobby Edwards and this South American shrimp venture you people are contemplating."

"What's wrong with that?" I asked.

"How much do you know about Bobby Edwards?" The FBI agent asked. "Do you know what he does for a living?"

"All I know is what he told me; that he trades stock on Wall Street and that he invests in certain business ventures. He gave me a good stock tip on Fairchild Camera."

"Do you think with this shrimp venture of yours that he'll go to South America, especially Brazil?"

"I think that's a little premature," I said. "We haven't even made a deal, yet. But why?"

"Mr. Lambro, Mr. Edwards was indicted last year by the Federal Grand Jury over some allegedly fraudulent and illegally sold stock, and if Mr. Edwards decides to go to Brazil before his trial, there is no legal recourse for the United States Government to extradite Mr. Edwards from Brazil to the United States because this is not considered a serious crime in Brazil. And we don't want Mr. Edwards leaving the United States."

I told the FBI agent what I knew, which wasn't much, and he informed me that I could continue to associate with Bobby Edwards if I wished, and if I wanted to tell Edwards about the FBI inquisition, I was also free to do that, too.

"Oh, by the way," the FBI agent smiled. "You know those sexually explicit telephone calls you've been getting occasionally from an anonymous girl caller the past year from time to time around 3:00 to 4:00 a.m?"

"Yeah," I said a little speechless.

"Do you want to know who the girl is?" The FBI agent asked.

"Yes, I would," I said.

"Bobby Edwards' girlfriend, Lisa."

"You're kidding," I ended in disbelief.

It was Friday 22 November 1963. I had been composing and working in virtual isolation on my first motion picture music score (*Energy On The Move*) for two straight days in a ground level rent controlled garden apartment at 405 East 55th Street (complete with a Steinway grand piano) the use of which had been given to me for as long as I wished by a benevolent Manhattan antique dealer. I appreciated the quietude of the place as I was into many pages of large orchestration paper which I would conduct and record within a few weeks with the New York Philharmonic. Arnold Arnstein and his men were my music copyists and were extracting the orchestral parts from which the New York Philharmonic musicians would play. I had been associated with Arnold Arnstein when I had previously worked for G. Schirmer and Leonard Bernstein that preceding August in assisting Bernstein on the orchestration paper design, extraction of parts, and reproduction of Bernstein's long awaited and overdue *Third Symphony: Kaddish*.

My musically overworked brain needed a reprieve and since I was hungry, I decided to walk to 57th Street and First Avenue and take the bus up to the Salad Bowl.

It was refreshing to get out of doors as I had done some good creative work the past two days and was confidently ahead of schedule.

As I walked along First Avenue, I noticed how unpopulated and quiet it was for this time of the afternoon. Continuing toward 57th Street, I observed coming toward me a fairly tall and heavyset black middle aged lady in an ebony colored overcoat carrying a shopping bag, walking slowly and sobbing and wailing into her white handkerchief.

She had a kindly face with tears streaming down her pudgy cheeks. "What's wrong, Dear?" I asked. "Is there anything wrong? Is there something I can help you with?"

"No, no," she continued to cry walking slowly and not stopping. "There's nothin' anyone can do; there's nothin' anyone can do."

She left me standing there, as she tearfully ambled down the street.

As I walked about another twenty yards a thin little old Caucasian lady was timidly crying into her Kleenex. It was as if I were in a Franz Kafka dream. 'Phillip, get hold of yourself; you've been working too hard,' I thought as I took a few breaths of the crisp air.

When I arrived at the bus stop I noticed how everyone of the dozen or so people waiting, without exception, had a rather impassive or melancholy expression on their faces, but I just attributed this to the fact that perhaps the two days of composing music in solitude had made my senses excessively impressible. We all waited there rather stoically for several minutes until the crowded bus came. There were a few people on the bus weeping, and as I secured a space standing next to a middle aged bespectacled businessman I asked, "What's the matter with everyone? Why is everybody so glum?"

"The President's been murdered," he said.

"What?" I asked not believing my ears.

"President Kennedy's been assassinated, he said to me again.

"You've got to be kidding," I said.

"Someone else said, "He's only been shot, he's not dead."

"Is he dead?" A woman seated nearby asked.

The middle aged businessman angrily yelled, "He's dead. The President's dead."

I had never experienced a Manhattan bus so crammed, yet so passive.

I ate very little as hungry as I was at the Salad Bowl and returned to the garden apartment and turned on the television set. I was so depressed that I completely lost any desire to compose. It was not because John F. Kennedy was our President (I get upset when anyone in our society is murdered), but this act represented the overpowering microcosmic realization to me that regardless of what anyone could say, the fact remained that we here on Planet Earth were still in the most primitive of conditions when we have killing in our society.

I telephoned Nelson Case and told him that I was so dejected over President Kennedy's assassination that I could not compose anymore that day or the next. It was only on the following Monday that I was able to reluctantly return to my normal compositional speed.

That weekend I reminisced how on one warm 1959 August afternoon returning from Europe in the totally vacant waiting room of Boston's Logan International Airport (as I waited for my ride to Wellesley) John F. Kennedy in his dark brown pin striped suit and tie with about a dozen newspapers under his arm (which were folded lengthwise in half before they were again doubled in half) came in and sat directly across from me smiling and nodding a hello as I was studying an orchestral score. A couple of minutes later a diminutive slim elderly lady came up to him saying, "Senator Kennedy, I must have a word with you." Senator Kennedy politely got up and shook the small aged woman's hand as he straightened his tie with the other, and politely listened to her criticism of how perhaps he wasn't doing his best in Washington on behalf of Massachusetts. As Kennedy listened to the old gentlewoman, who reminded me of the elderly landlady in the British film classic *The Lavender Hill Mob*, he caught me quietly laughing out of the corner of his eye which caused him to grin even more broadly as the elderly lady continued to lecture him. Finally, several minutes after the wintery woman had left, the largest brood of relatives I had ever seen descended into the Logan International Airport waiting room: there must have been twenty-five or more rank and files; most of them in beach clothes (including Ted Kennedy clad in Bermuda shorts and clog hoppers) ranging from adults and an inordinately pregnant female to teenagers and a couple of cute toddlers who were yelling and pulling at John F. Kennedy's arms attempting to gain his attention as he was speaking with his older kin. They all left shortly thereafter and I never saw John F. Kennedy again.

Having been weapons trained in the military and having fired many thousands of rounds of projectiles and having tested certain small arms (which, incidentally, I disapprove of and which is probably why today I refuse to own or even touch a firearm), a few things disturbed me about the immediate and supervening conclusions in John F. Kennedy's assassination. If the fatal after shot fired at President Kennedy had come from behind, why then did President Kennedy's head initially go violently backward as is plainly evident on the original Zapruder film? Also, (even in the still pictures which appeared in Life Magazine) why was there a gaseous cloud directly in front of the President's face? Furthermore, if that cataclysmic shot had come from behind, then why would Mrs. Kennedy immediately react in horror and unnaturally go over the back seat of the limousine onto the trunk (as she did) directly into the line of fire? The answers are quite simple. All the shots came from the front and not from the rear. Mrs. Kennedy reacted in horror, instinctively and naturally, to the fatal shot by endeavoring to escape over the rear trunk of the car (before Secret Service Agent Clint Hill her personal bodyguard pushed her back in) because the projectile had come directly from the front; if it had come from the posterior, Mrs. Kennedy would have immediately jumped forward over the transmission to be next to Secret Service Agent William Greer (who was driving the limousine) and Agent Charles Kellerman (Secret Service Chief) who was in the front right passenger seat. The gaseous cloud indicated that the weapon used had to have been one of a special breed of high-tech assassination pistols designed and developed by the Central Intelligence Agency (to dispose of unwanted Foreign individuals) which are electrically operated and gas-powered with the ability to fire any number of explosive toxic pellet bullets, poison darts, or tiny needles (deadly purified and designed at Fort Dietrich, Maryland) which can kill a person almost instantly.

This intelligence was confirmed to me many years ago through William Cooper (a former United States Naval Intelligence Briefing Team member) who despite two attempts on his life during the early 1970's in which he lost part of his lower left leg, valorously struggled for years (until his death November 2001 in a gun battle with law enforcement officers at his home in Eagar, Arizona) to make widely public the fact that the Bilderberg Policy Committee supervised by The Council On Foreign Relations within the National Security Agency ordered the assassination of President John F. Kennedy in Dallas as the direct result of Kennedy's plan to disclose to the American people the truth about the government secrecy surrounding UFO's and extraterrestrial contacts, and additionally inform the United States people about the Central Intelligence Agency's control, development, sponsorship, sale and resale of illegal drugs to finance extraterrestrial and other secret projects. President Kennedy was first shot from the front in the throat by a sharpshooter from the grassy knoll; then immediately thereafter, a second shot from the grassy knoll wounded Governor Connally; the third shot from the grassy knoll hit the curb. At that cue, Secret Service Agent driver William Greer swiftly with his left hand (while Charles Kellerman held the steering wheel) turned in his driver's seat over his right shoulder and fired the special ultra high velocity assassination pistol containing a shell fish toxic explosive pellet which blew away President Kennedy's entire brain instantly. President Kennedy's body arrived at Bethesda Naval Hospital in Maryland (where another brain was substituted) a full thirty minutes before the empty casket which a frightened and threatened Mrs. Kennedy accompanied to the viewing of the duped American public. If you don't believe this then ask yourself why Mrs. Jacqueline Kennedy Onassis who was for many years Senior Editor of Doubleday, and had finished her personal memoirs long before she died, had the manuscript legally sealed by court order which is not to be opened or published until 2040?

In death John F. Kennedy achieved the media veneer of greatness; however, I do not think that when sifting through the authentic (rather than historical) facts that one can honestly consider John F. Kennedy to have been a distinguished leader. To be sure, John F. Kennedy was an illustrious political candidate; but he certainly was not an adequate President. Even though he was not a Thomas Jefferson, this definitely was no reason to murder an individual like President Kennedy or anyone else. In reality,

114

John F. Kennedy did not even approach the executive capabilities and accomplishments of his predecessor Dwight D. Eisenhower. Eisenhower (even though he was forced to make some negative decisions against his will by the hidden government of the military industrial complex which he warned us about in his last address to the Nation) at least enjoys the distinction of being the only President in recent history to immediately stop a war (Korean) and keep the United States out of armed conflicts for the full duration of his eight year term in office. But contrary to popular belief, President Kennedy never paid heed to Generals Eisenhower's and MacArthur's strong counsel against getting involved in Southeast Asia. Kennedy initiated aggressions and exacerbations all over the world from sending 16,000 troops to Vietnam and beginning a massive military and ecological destruction there, to supporting a military coup in Guatemala and backing one in Iraq.

Since the end of World War II many other loyalists have been liquidated by the National Security Apparatus of our secret government under the insane claim that these individuals were of great threat to national security and would seriously jeopardize the stability of our nation in wanting to reveal to the American public the verity about Unidentified Flying Objects and extraterrestrials coming to our planet. When I discovered proof of this, I immediately thought, 'What kind of nonsense is this?' Anyone who uses more than two percent of their brain should know that for a species to be able to travel many times faster than our speed of light in a spacecraft and come and go harmoniously to our planet from incomprehensible distances has to be by all reasoning a benign race; because in order to accomplish such a scientific achievement requires a totally cooperative and peaceful society. The kind of society which would be of great risk to our national security would be that type in which we are currently living; where we exploit and murder each other daily, and where (deducting what comparatively inconsequential advanced technology the visiting extraterrestrials may have already given to our military and intelligence complex) we have not been able to even keep five ants alive in orbit, let alone go anywhere appreciable in the universe without the token scientific aid of these extraterrestrials.

One of those first patriots was Secretary Of Defense James Forrestal who was forced to resign by President Harry Truman. Truman, as ventilated throughout his life among his personal letters, was far from an enlightened individual and stated strong racist feelings referring to black White House waiters as "an army of coons" and in a letter to his wife, "nigger picnic day." James Forrestal, I understand, was a consumedly honorable and genuine person who disagreed with Truman's policy of implementing a greater security system around the alien presence than that of the Manhattan Project (Atomic Bomb) during World War II. Forrestal tried to convince many political and governmental officials (who were ignorant of the facts) as to what was really going on from White Sands to Roswell, but poor James Forrestal was being viewed as distraught and reasonless, until finally he was illegally abducted and isolated by the government from family and friends and dispatched to the mental ward at Bethesda Naval Hospital. It was reported that James Forrestal in the early morning of 22 May 1949 committed suicide by jumping out the window of his hospital room. But in reality, Above Top Secret intelligence sources, including one ex-CIA officer whom I had dinner with, told me that agents from the CIA early that morning slipped into James Forrestal's room, secured a long sheet around his neck with the end tied to a permanent fixture and launched James Forrestal out the window where the sheet tore and he fell to his death before his brother and an attorney could have James Forrestal legally released. Forrestal's diaries were confiscated and due to public demand were altered and expurgated, and eventually published in a highly purified version. However, the authentic story was later vended under the guise of fiction by several CIA writers who in turn gave the finished material to another CIA operative by the name of Whitley Streiber who is erroneously credited as the author of "his" book *Majestic*.

After the Kennedy assassination, I began seeing Huntington and Diane Hartford fairly regularly. I knew that Diane Hartford liked me personally and I genuinely enjoyed her company. We became friends and got to be pals; she was twenty-two and I was twenty-eight. On occasion (with Hartford leaving her alone and not saying where he was going) she would telephone me and I would either meet her publicly or we would have lengthy phone conversations to keep her occupied. One evening (December 1963 after my recording session with the New York Philharmonic) Diane took me to the Plaza Theater where we saw some early Charlie Chaplin motion pictures. Diane informed me half way through the films that two of Hartford's private detectives had followed her and were several rows behind us, and that she was under surveillance most of the time everywhere she went without Hartford. I could not believe this, but it was true.

Many writings have depicted Huntington Hartford as a notorious "womanizer." However, having known him personally in New York City (1962-1964) and having observed him visually from both close and distant purviews, I can unequivocally state that Huntington Hartford with his innate lethargic apathetic personality which at times (although he had a strong masculine speaking voice of good quality) was tinged with an ever so slightly backward slanted effeminate walk, was never a natural pursuer of women even though with his original immense wealth he went through the great effort of others to make the general public (at one time) and those associated with him (at other times) to believe that he was. Huntington Hartford, even though there were physically beautiful women around him much of the time, some of whom found him attractive, was no great womanizer even in the middle class suburbia sense; let alone the Casanova, Errol Flynn, Ali Kahn, or Richard Burton tradition. To be in that select category, one must have in addition to fortune and good looks, a well educated and dashingly energetic individuality; and, at best, Huntington Hartford (although he attended Harvard University and was tall, slim and not ugly) was absolutely void of any intellectually dynamic quality, or dash at all. In fact, the outstanding characteristic of Huntington Hartford's true personality was (as strange as it may seem) that he did not actually possess one.

I was absolutely convinced (and I told him so privately after a couple of exasperating situations where he acted like a complete ass to either Diane or his lovely and bright 13 year old daughter, Cathy) that had Huntington Hartford not inherited all the A & P fortunes which he accidentally had by reason of the insanity in alienated nepotism, I would bet my life that he would not be able to acquire a beginning stock clerk's position in any grocery or department store anywhere. I subsequently found out that my implication had been in fact a reality many years previously when during Hartford's post school years he tried to work for the A & P and was promptly terminated by executives in the very company he owned!

It has been said that Huntington Hartford always avoided confrontations. This is not quite true as Huntington Hartford never could actually recognize an adversative encounter; therefore, his whole life was devoted in trying to extricate himself through associates and attorneys from those habitual personal and financial encumbrances he was most of the time unknowingly hurtled into.

The most amazing reality from my vantage point in 1963 was how Huntington Hartford had ever managed to produce two absolutely glowing children by his marriage to actress Marjorie Steele whom he had met while she was an intelligent, endeavoring eighteen year old acting student (winning a scholarship to Charlie Chaplin's Actor's Lab) and working as a cigarette girl at Ciro's nightclub in Hollywood California 1948: they were Catherine "Cathy" Hartford born 1950, 13 years old; and John "Jackie" Hartford born 1953, 10 years old. I never met Marjorie Steele for she had divorced Hartford in 1960, married an unknown struggling actor who was the stepson of her attorney and ultimately divorcing him, married the distinguished writer Constantine Fitzgibbon and resided most of the time in the United Kingdom. However, I had been acquainted with people who had known Marjorie Steele and I understood that she was a caring person and talented actress until she became an alcoholic during her last years with Hartford.

Daughter Cathy was tall, unusually healthy looking and beautiful, and gave the appearance of being a mature radiant sixteen year old rather than the thirteen year old she actually was. Cathy had the clearest skin, brightest smiling eyes, and healthiest light brown hair imaginable. Jackie I hardly encountered because when I would usually arrive at One Beekman Place early evening he was either upstairs in his room preparing to go to sleep, or pleading his case with Diane to be allowed to stay up a little while longer and watch television with Diane who at twenty-two gave an excellent account of herself as the surrogate mother. Huntington Hartford, to my initial amazement, seemingly did not know how to relate to his children, and that task was usually taken up by young Diane and the governess.

It was Christmas 1963 and at Diane's insistence, I attended a few of the seasonal gatherings at One Beekman Place. After conducting my recording session with the New York Philharmonic, I invested some of my earnings in various Windsor Newton watercolors, sable brushes and large watercolor paper, and produced about half a dozen original landscape paintings which I had matted and gave away among the other Christmas gifts I disseminated that month. In fact, I gave one to Cathy Hartford and (to my surprise) she gave me in return an astoundingly original watercolor and ink which she had painted herself. I immediately showed her work to Salvador Dali who was veritably impressed. Young Cathy had invented a startling assortment of animals and creatures from smiling benign looking serpents with human and animal feet to bird-like elephants over a dreamlike landscape of mountains and clouds with flying Greek sirens and sleeping beauties. Cathy was radiantly pleased at how surprised I was by her artistic originality and talent.

Diane was equally astonished and we summoned Hartford to take a look at what his daughter had accomplished. When he came to look at the painting where everyone (including Salvador Dali) was oohing and ahhing, I could not understand how Hartford actually stood there like a

Soutine dead fish on a plate and did not respond at all. It was obvious that Cathy (who was elated at being the center of attention) was now quietly awaiting for a positive acknowledgement from her father. I could tell that it would have meant more to her than the acclaim she was receiving from Salvador Dali.

Quietly under my breath I said to Hartford, "Compliment her..."

Diane just stared daggers at Hartford waiting for him to embrace his daughter's artistic accomplishments.

Dali pointed and said as I proudly held Cathy's painting, "This show veddy great fantastique imagination; and handling of color and design."

As Hartford ambivalently said nothing and did even less, Diane restrainedly blew her fuse and walked away past Hartford murmuring several recognizable expletives under her breath which Hartford definitely heard as he returned to the living room.

Cathy wasn't stupid, but even though she did not give the appearance, I could tell she was somewhat disappointed and hurt. Young people usually know the truth from four years of age; often times (from what I've seen), they have a greater sensitivity and far more prolific brain power than their parents.

I went to get Hartford. "What's wrong with you?" I asked. "Why didn't you compliment her obvious good work? When your daughter accomplishes something of value you should commend her; when she does something wrong then you must explain why it was incorrect."

But as I was to realize from that moment on, Huntington Hartford was incapable of either praising his children when they had accomplished something of merit, or reprimanding them when they did not behave.

Diane was totally unsettled. When Diane was emotionally agitated at One Beekman Place she would invariably go to the slightly out of tune spinet piano in the living room and pound out about the first twenty bars of Rachmaninoff's famous warhorse *Prelude in C-sharp minor* over and over again, never advancing beyond that point. I think it was the only composition she knew, but it always somehow fit the mood. The more perturbed Diane became, the louder and more proportionately faster she endeavored to perform the Rachmaninoff *Prelude*.

Finally, after Larry Horn advised Hartford how upset Diane had become, Hartford returned and in his own incapacious way commended Cathy's work with even Salvador Dali more wide eyed than usual as a result of Hartford's ambiguous comportment. But the emotional damage had been done. I just could not grasp it; if I had had a daughter like Cathy

Hartford, I would have loved her unconditionally forever.

On one occasion things were quite socially drab in the Hartford living room. Hartford was reading a letter not paying attention to Larry Horn's cacophonic jokes who was adjacent to some vacant Plaza Five Model, and Diane was becoming terribly weary of the company. I could always tell when Diane was sociably disturbed because of the resigned glances she would cast my way. I remember remarking to everyone (Cathy and Jackie had had a few of their young school friends visiting and spending the night with them), "Listen, I think all you adults should go upstairs and go to bed as it seems to be way past your intelligence time, and all the kids should come downstairs and entertain me." Diane burst out laughing, and I could tell that John (the Scottish butler) quite appreciated my comment by the brief wry half smile he gave me.

As lovely and caring a person as Diane Brown Hartford truly was in 1963, there were a few isolated times, usually after she had been ignored by Hartford (who had probably left her to audition a new model) and had had two imbibes, (and Diane was not a drinker) when Diane's petulant behavior arched its back like a hissing cat. I plainly recall one occasion around the 1963-64 Christmas New Year Holidays, where there had been a formal party with all the purported comely people in attendance and where Diane had hired a kind of European Bossa Nova Soft Rock Band (consisting of about six musicians) which performed in the large hallway for the couples who wanted to dance. The group was actually quite good. The lead guitarist was a young tall blond slender German fellow about my age who had just gotten married and his youthful quietly shy bride was sitting in the hallway admiring him and you could tell that the musician and the girl (who was close to Diane's age) were truly in love. Diane, early in the evening, had done everything possible to make the girl and the band feel wanted and at home; however, toward the end of the evening (during the Band's fifteen minute break) Diane had teetered into the hallway from the living room and asked the German fellow who was the Group's leader (and who had his adoring young wife cuddled on his lap) to play a song which Diane had particularly enjoyed all evening.

"Of course," said the young German. "As soon as we finish our break, in ten minutes, we shall be most happy to."

"Oh, would you please play it now?" Smiled Diane. I could tell that Diane had had either a few too many sips, or perhaps an extra tranquilizer.

"My musicians are on a break, Mrs. Hartford. As soon as the break

120

is over in a few minutes, we'll play it twice for you," smiled the young German.

The next instant Diane, as lovely as she was in her white flowing evening gown, quickly lost her grin and yelled grabbing the young German's bride by the arm and jerking her to the floor, "I'm the god damned lady of this house and I hired you and you'll god damned well play that fucking number right now."

Fortunately, I raced over and quickly intervened seizing Diane, pulling her away from the poor bride (who was trying to get up) and her shocked and astonished young German lead guitarist.

"What's the matter with you, Diane?" I asked firmly holding her and shaking her a little from the shoulders. "He's a fellow Local 802 Musician, and the rules are we must give musicians breaks during every session."

"Who the hell do you think you are?" Said the young German in a state of bewilderment as he helped his staggering wife to her feet.

"Just because you are a millionaire," said the shy girl as forceful as she could, "doesn't mean you own us."

"You'll play that song now," Diane yelled with a hiccup over my shoulder, "or I'll fire you."

"You can't fire us because we quit," the young German said firmly and surprisingly rather politely.

As Diane struggled unsuccessfully with me, she demanded, "Phillip, let me go."

"I'll let you go only if you promise to behave."

"Let me go right now, Phillip."

"Alright," I said, "but you behave like the young lady you are. Okay?"

Just as I let her go, Diane went after the German's youthful bride again, but fortunately I interceded once more just in time.

Larry Horn, Hartford, and several other guests came into the hallway. They quickly got Diane upstairs into her bedroom. I summoned Dr. Louis Scarrone from the living room and informed the handsome jet set physician what had happened. He shook his head in bewilderment and asked John the butler to fetch his medical valise from the hallway closet and proceeded to go upstairs to Diane's bedroom where I understand he gave her a tranquilizing hypodermic.

I apologized to the young German and his fair bride, "I'm really sorry that this had to happen," I said. "I've never seen Diane this way. She's really a good person," I went on, "but confidentially she's been having some marital problems, and perhaps in her slightly inebriated state seeing you two newly weds obviously so much in love; well, let's just forgive her this one time. She has so much, that's true; but she also has very little of what you two both have in abundance."

Hartford had the musicians compensated and they left as quickly as they could disassemble their equipment. Dr. Scarrone came down and numerated to me what he had done.

Not too long thereafter, I was in the hallway preparing to leave and return to my dull closet cubicle apartment happily contemplating the fact that in about one month I would be going to Los Angeles to live in adequately spacious quarters and that I really would not miss the abrasive puerile scenes of the super rich when I saw a calmly sedated Diane descending the long winding staircase like a floating white feather. The setting was thinly reminiscent of the closing scene from the film classic *Sunset Boulevard* where a tranquilly crazed fading screen star Norma Desmond (Gloria Swanson) ever so deliberately declines the winding staircase of her mansion after she has murdered her struggling "kept" young screen writer Joe Gillis (William Holden) while he attempts to leave her and the grounds falling face first into the mansion's swimming pool after receiving several bullets in the back.

"I feel so wonderful," Diane said sluggishly drifting down the stairs. I must ask Lou what was in that shot he gave me. Is Lou still here?"

"I believe he went home," I said.

"Why are you leaving?" Diane asked me.

"I have to go," I said. "It's late and I have to get some rest. I'll be leaving for California next month."

We gave each other a friendly kiss, and Diane reminded me that she wanted to personally cook a dinner for me the following week on the servant's night off. John's (the butler's) contract precluded any of the Hartfords from entering the kitchen and servant's districts while he, the maid and their help were in service.

Not only was it evident that Huntington Hartford did not know how to relate to his own children, but it was quite apparent that he did not know how to relate to his wife.

A few evenings later I telephoned and had a late night chat with Hartford. He was speaking in an extremely soft low tone.

"How's Diane?" I finally asked.

"I don't know," he said. "She's not speaking with me."

"Are you in your bedroom?" I asked.

"No," Hartford said. "I'm in another room."

"Why not go into the bedroom and kiss and make up?"

"She's locked the door. What do you think I should do?"

"Do you have a key?"

"Yes, but she's latched it from the inside."

"I think Diane's trying to tell you something," I said. "Why not break the door down like Rhett Butler in *Gone With The Wind*, take her in your arms and subdue her," I went on knowing that Huntington Hartford had a far greater chance of scaling Mount Chimborazo in the Andes than accomplishing that.

"Huhh. Yeah. Huhh," he tried to utter a fraction of a laugh. Poor Huntington Hartford. Here he was, purportedly worth over 500 million dollars in 1963 assets, and bankrupt in sense of humor.

"Well, how about writing her a love letter and sticking it under the door?" I asked. "But with your handwriting the way it is, you had better print because she'll never understand what you've written."

"Yeah. Huhh," Hartford uttered.

Apropos handwriting, several months after I became acquainted with Huntington Hartford he demanded samples of my handwriting which he had analyzed. He told me that as a safeguard and for character examination he always obtained graphological samples from those people whom he came in contact with, and had funded a handwriting institute for this express purpose. I must admit this was responsible for my subsequent interest in handwriting analysis. His graphologists directed me to the definitive texts which I still use in my personal library to this day.

I found out later that Hartford had spent a couple of nights sleeping alone in the downstairs living room hoping for Diane's sympathy which eventually he acquired.

The following Thursday was the servant's day off and I arrived at One Beekman Place promptly at seven for Diane's own personally cooked meal.

Diane had prepared and served me a surprisingly delicious dinner aboard priceless historical royal China and a rare vintage wine in delicate French crystal glasses which (as I recall) dated back to Marie Antoinette. Of course, you must understand that this was about two years before I was to begin practicing Japanese Zen Macrobiotics.

You could have filmed the whole dinner sequence in one take for a motion picture. Dressed for dinner, there we were in that huge secluded dining room and section of the house all alone. Diane (in an off white gown) was at the head of what must have been a twenty foot long darkly rich mahogany dining room table, with your up and coming humble Court Composer at the other end. There was a slight echo as we spoke with one another across the distance and flickering candlelight. Diane, perfectly sober, raised her glass and proposed a toast.

Just then, Hartford opened the door and looked in on us with his usual unemotional expression, and said, "Diane, I have to go out for a little while on a business meeting; Phillip, you take care of Diane, okay?"

Diane, her wine glass still raised toward me, said in a quite teasingly intimate manner which I had never heard her say to me even while we were isolated, "Phillip, you heard what, Hunt said, now, didn't you? Remember, you take care of me; okay? You know what that means." Then putting the priceless French crystal glass to her lips drank her toast giving me one of those wine soaked humming laughs which transformed Diane's demeanor into an Anglicized Southern belle slightly reminiscent of a debauched Tennessee Williams character.

Hartford looked at Diane inexpressively and then at me. I shrugged at Hartford slightly as if to say, I don't know what the hell she's talking about, and then back and forth still expressionless Hartford said, "I'll see you both later" as he quietly closed the dining room door behind him.

Returning to her normal idiom, Diane looked at me and said, "Business meeting, my ass; I'll bet he's going out to meet some model."

I tried to mollify the situation and lifted my wine glass toward Diane. As strange as it may seem, there is actually something quite intimate about two people dining alone by candlelight who are twenty feet removed from each other at opposite ends of a long dining room table.

As I raised the priceless French crystal glass to my lips before eating I felt a thin trickle of wine running down my chin which I immediately caught with the index finger of my free hand and I wondered how this could be as the rim of the glass was in the normal place above my lower lip. I endeavored to take another sip and once more a slight dribble went to my chin which I captured again.

I raised the glass to my eyes examining it as best as I could within the flickering candlelight.

"What's wrong?" Diane asked. "Is there something wrong with the wine?"

"The wine's fine," I said, "but I do believe your priceless French crystal has holes in it."

"That's impossible," Diane said. "Are you joking?"

"I'm not joking," I said inspecting it closely. "This glass is so fine that there are a few tiny holes around the engraved beveled areas just below the rim."

"Oh my god," exclaimed Diane as she raced toward me and I proceeded to show her the minute openings. "The crystal polishers had these glasses last week and must have injured them. Wait 'til Hunt hears about this."

"Diane," I said. "Would it be too much trouble to ask for just a regular common ordinary everyday glass without all the historical provenance which I could drink out of?"

We both laughed. Diane went into the kitchen and fetched far less expensive wine and water glasses.

As generally ambivalent as I found Huntington Hartford to be, it never failed to amaze me how at times he became preoccupied with truly unimportant and frivolous matters.

At one particular party he hosted, there must have been twenty pounds of premium caviar on the buffet table which had dwindled down to about three pounds toward the end of the evening.

"What did you think of the caviar?" Hartford asked me.

"Since I really didn't have any, I don't think I can comment on it," I said.

"I think it was too salty," Hartford told me. "I'm going to return it. I'm not going to pay for it."

"How can you get away with that?" I asked. "Your guests ate practically all of it."

Hartford told John the butler that if the caterer did not give him credit for the caviar, he would never use that caterer again.

When I would attempt to discuss truly humanitarian problems in our society with Huntington Hartford it appeared to be a wasted effort as he seemingly could not relate to the human condition.

I recall arriving at One Beekman Place during a cold winter evening in 1963 after saying goodbye to William "Bill" Cerofeci (one of my closest friends) on his return to his new home in Los Angeles, California from a quick trip to Manhattan where he had visited friends and relatives. I had met Bill in the military (Winter January 1958) at Vicenza, Italy where we were both with the small but powerfully strategic atomic U. S. Army 1st Missile Command attached to the Southern European Task Force. He was in charge of administrating personnel records. Most of the time, I was away playing tournament tennis as a representative of the SETAF NATO Tennis Team as we played all over Europe from Italy to the French Riviera and Germany until my discharge June of 1959.

Bill was full faced, light skinned with brown hair, slightly burly, of medium height, and quite strong and masculine looking; which (if you did not know him) masked his innate sensitivity, generosity and sincerity. Even though our backgrounds came from the opposite environments of affluent Wellesley, Massachusetts versus street tough 106th Street in Manhattan, New York, we shared many things in common from having both been born during the first week in September, to our equal dislike for our biological fathers.

After my discharge, I went to New York City and stayed with Bill and his unhappy about-to-be future-ex-first-wife for approximately a month until I acquired the job as Assistant Director Of Publications for the music publishing firm of G. Schirmer. Bill told me that he had married his first wife in New York the day after he had completed his Military Basic Training late August 1957; falling asleep in front of the priest during the entire Catholic ceremony and having to be awakened by a stiff nudge to the ribs in order to voice, "I do."

While staying at Bill Cerofeci's and endeavoring to keep him from murdering his incompatibly harassing and aseptic young blonde wife, Bill confided in me that he realized his dedicated hard work as a Junior Executive for the American Bakeries Tasty Bread Company wasn't developing, nor was it remunerative enough for him to more than barely survive.

Bill had been brought up in a series of apartment homes in the Italian neighborhoods of Manhattan's 103rd Street to 108th Street where on the one hand flashy racketeers would embrace him as a young teenager introducing him to Mayor Wagner and famous U. S. Senators, and on the other hand his teachers at St. Cecilia's School would instill within him the values of honesty, intelligence and comradery. One thing I quickly found out about Bill Cerofeci in the military was that I could always depend on him and count on his loyalty.

Around February of 1961, I received a telephone call in my office at G. Schirmer from Bill who indicated that he had quit his job with Tasty Bread and had made up his mind that he was going into the clandestine wine cellar to take the financially tempting Sicilian oaths of Il Cosa Nostra.

I implored Bill not to do anything except meet me at Rinaldo's Italian Restaurant on 32nd Street that evening. Between the linguini and white clam sauce, garlic bread, and salad, I tried to convince Bill not to go into the wine cellar where they cross a dagger with a revolver on a wine keg, cut your right hand index finger to exchange blood oaths, and where the elusive underground society demands that you do and obey anything without question (including inhuman torture and murder) as they burn the fraternal commandments in the palms of your hands.

"What the hell am I going to do?" Bill asked. "I'm living in a hotel with Frank Cascio. I have no money; no job. Where's my future?"

"Listen," I said completely without any ideas, "we'll think of something. Anything's better than going into that fucking wine cellar."

"I'm not so sure about that," Bill said.

"What do you mean," I said quietly so that people dining at adjacent tables would not hear our conversation. "What kind of life is that? You know what they tell you, you go in alive and you leave dead. So for a few years you make big money and wear those expensive shiny suits, and have exotic cars and flashy mistresses; but at what price? You're a fair, honest guy. Perhaps you'll make money for them in legitimate areas then one of your fraternity brothers gets jealous of you, lies about you, then one morning you go to your car, turn on the ignition and ten kilos of plastic explodes. Or like tonight; I'm your friend; I invite you to Rinaldo's for dinner; we talk and reminisce about Italy and the old times; then I go to the mens room and somebody comes in and blows you away. Do you want to have to think about that everyday for the rest of your life?" I asked.

As Bill sighed dejectedly, I immediately got an idea.

In Vicenza Italy, Bill had introduced me to Winki and Berkeley Harris. Berkeley, an aspiring tall blond good looking all American actor who was later to become a featured performer on Television soap operas before he prematurely died of cancer, was in the military with us; and Bill (as the result of his position in charge of administrating personnel records) influenced Berkeley's transfer into Special Services. Berkeley's affluent young wife Winki was the maternal niece of Radio Corporation Of America's (RCA-NBC) CEO General David Sarnoff and her paternal relations included the owners of the Lane Bryant Corporation. Berkeley divorced Winki shortly after his discharge in 1959 and eventually married a girl named Susan. Susan Harris went on to create the popular TV shows *Soap* and *Golden Girls*. I knew Winki casually in Vicenza from a few social gatherings we both attended. Although Winki was young, slender, frizzy brunette, and rather plain, she had an interesting, amusing, energetic and bizarre personality and was obviously well educated. Winki had excellent taste, and appreciated the finer things in life including a madly passionate love affair with the beautiful sleepy Italian port village of Positano.

Winki and Bill had remained friends for awhile before Winki had moved to Los Angeles to live. In fact, I never forgot that warm 1960 spring Saturday when Bill (not having seen Winki since Italy) was invited to Winki's apartment and took me along. When we saw the address, we both looked at each other with subtle amazement and sort of laughed. The gigantic apartment house was an about to be condemned building on the Lower East Side of Manhattan where we traipsed up five flights of stairs over trash and underprivileged smudged children of all kinds and colors. After we knocked on the drab door in the dark hallway, Winki opened it and invited us in. Ladies and Gentlemen of the Jury, we were both so startled because it was as if we had walked into an oasis. Winki had gotten the apartment through a friend for $40 dollars a month and had had it completely renovated with pure white walls, bright deeply rich wooden parqueted floors, expensive tiles and fixtures; and with a combination of integrated contemporary and antique furnishings amid a foliage of large and small exotic potted plants, this apartment definitely could have graced the pages of Architectural Digest, or Better Homes And Gardens.

On a subsequent weekend, Winki invited both Bill and myself to her parents summer home for dinner in Tarrytown, New York and before dinner we spent the afternoon at an exclusive all Jewish Country Club where both Bill and I had to adopt false Jewish last names as we signed the register in order to be admitted. Winki knew my acerbic witticisms well enough to remark before entering the hallowed grounds of the Jewish Only Country Club, "And please Phillip, none of your jokes until after we leave; okay?"

"I've got it," I said to Bill at Rinaldo's as I was eating my linguini.

"What..?" He asked

"What we have to do is get you out of New York City and a good job in Los Angeles, and I know just the person with enough influence to do it."

"Who..?" Bill asked

"Winki," I said.

That bitter cold early February 1961 evening I went back to my office at G. Schirmer (the night watchman let me in) and I made several telephone calls until I located Winki in California. After explaining the situation to her, she immediately called Bill and offered to assist him with finding an adequate occupation in Los Angeles.

I also placed a phone call to our mutual buddy Anthony (Tony The Greek) Vulopas who owned a restaurant bar in Lancaster Pennsylvania and who had been with us in Vicenza Italy. Tony was genuinely a fun character and he, Bill and I were together a great deal of the time when I wasn't away playing tennis with the SETAF NATO Team. Tony had made his acting debut in Philadelphia around 1956 under the name of Tony Val opposite James Darren in a teen age exploitation film entitled *Rumble On The Docks* where in one of the scenes Tony rips off the blouse of the young female lead only to get beat up by James Darren later in the final confrontation of the movie. As Tony described it to me one day as we were having a leisurely dinner in Venice Italy, at the premiere of *Rumble On The Docks* in Philadelphia when that scene came on the screen, Tony's mother (who had been born in Greece and was quite religious - Tony's brother was a Greek Orthodox Priest) became so upset that she left the theater with Tony in his tuxedo valiantly pursuing her up the aisle of the darkened theater pleading, "But Ma, it's only a motion picture. It's not real. We were acting. I never actually did any of that stuff." At the supplicating insistence of Tony's mother, who thought Tony's actions on screen were totally disgraceful, he gave up his acting career.

When I revealed to Tony what was happening in Bill's life, I asked him to drive up with his cousin Harry (who was also a friend of ours) and help me get these Mafia temptations out of Bill's system. Tony arrived the following weekend for two days and it really meliorated the situation in the right direction with the two of us firmly convincing Bill that the knife and the gun were no way of life to pursue.

Bill had been seeing his lifelong friend Sheila who had had an excellent paying position with AT&T and who also wanted to transfer her job and move to Los Angeles where she and Bill could live together; but Bill felt it wouldn't look honorable so he offered to marry Sheila before leaving for the West Coast. Even though Bill knew that I did not subscribe to the concept of official marriage, I did not discourage his wish because if the marriage failed (as it eventually did along with their previously close friendship) there was always divorce; however, if Bill took the strict brotherhood vows of Il Cosa Nostra (This Thing Of Ours), I knew that there would never be any possibility for dissolution other than death; or if they liked you, to live out the rest of your life in northern Canada.

Well, there we were; February 1961. It was one of the worst paralytic snow storms in New York history. Mayor Lindsay forbade anyone from travelling the turnpikes it was so hazardous. Most offices and businesses were closed. At that time, you could not marry in New York City immediately; there was a waiting period. The closest place was Yonkers. Clearly, Bill and Sheila had a plane to catch and they had wanted to get married right away.

Another Vicenza Italy SETAF Alumnus and friend of ours, Mike Baggio, had a big brand new Cadillac and offered to attach snow chains to the front and back tires which he guaranteed would make the trip. However, for precautionary measures Mike put two shovels in the rear trunk. Bill and I several years earlier in Italy were, perhaps, instrumental in saving Mike Baggio's burly, coal black curly headed frame as he lay on Lido beach in Venice Italy like a young King Farouk turning yellow instead of tan. We convinced Mike to go directly to a doctor where he discovered that he had had jaundice and was successfully treated. In two more years, Mike Baggio (who told me that he never wanted to have anything to do with criminals) received the ultimate sociological and career stigma as the result of Joseph Valachi's widely televised and revelatory testimony during which Valachi happened to mention Mike's uncle and father. Poor Mike was prevented from applying for a career in Law Enforcement, and then after passing a Civil Service Exam he dejectedly revealed to me (just before I moved to Los Angeles in January of 1964) how he had recently been denied an appointment in Civil Engineering as a result of Joseph Valachi's televised confirmations; swearing to me that he had no idea (other than the Taxi Cab business) what enterprises his father and Uncle were involved in.

With Bill and Sheila bundled under a blanket in the rear of the Cadillac, the heater going, Mike Baggio driving and yours truly in the right front seat, we were off to the Justice Of The Peace's house in Yonkers. With the stiff fines Mayor Lindsay had promised violators, there was not a car to be seen on the entire snow bound Yonkers turnpike; you had to have been out of your mind to attempt driving under such conditions. It was a blizzard. The Cadillac performed admirably until we got stuck about halfway to Yonkers. Mike and I manned the two shovels and began digging. As we shoveled snow furiously, Mike and I looked at one another for a moment and with the bitingly cold wind howling around us I yelled, "If anybody ever told me two years ago in sunny Italy that we'd be shoveling out the Yonkers Turnpike in a freezing snow storm I would have told them that they were fucking crazy."

We both laughed and got the car on its way. Bill and Sheila were married, flew to Los Angeles where Winki was instrumental in annexing a position for Bill with a leading advertising agency before Bill turned to life insurance and eventually opened his own successful agency.

So after I arrived that cold 1963 winter evening at One Beekman Place, subsequently saying goodbye to Bill Cerofeci before his flight departed for Los Angeles, I was rather quiet and reflectively absorbed in my thoughts by the totally disparate situations I had been part of that preceding afternoon.

When Hartford found out that Leopold Stokowski had programmed my music, he periodically asked me to introduce him to the illustrious orchestral conductor. I thought the request rather odd since Huntington Hartford had no natural interest in symphonic, or concert music. Of course, the only way I could ever have gotten Maestro Stokowski to agree to meet Huntington Hartford would have had to revolve around something to do with music rather than Huntington Hartford himself because it was Maestro Stokowski's contention (also shared by yours truly) that the majority of affluent people in actuality have been detrimental to the development and appreciation of art. So since Hartford wanted me to audition the little auditorium in his almost completed Columbus Circle Gallery Of Modern Art, I told him that I would also invite Maestro Stokowski if Hartford would promise that he would not ask or make any nonsensical statements. Hartford agreed and I arranged for the Maestro to arrive early that previous afternoon.

Since that day was Bill Cerofeci's last in New York, I wanted to spend it with him and asked him to come along before we went on our separate ways. Bill loved all good music and in Italy I helped him select a basic library of definitive recordings from the representative symphonic and instrumental masterpieces which he played over and over again. I also invited Harvey Rubenstein my close associate from G. Schirmer; we had resigned together from Schirmer only a few months earlier. And composer-conductor Ernest Gold (who wrote the score for the popular film *Exodus*) was in New York (I had liked his *Songs Of Love And Parting for Soprano & Orchestra* which we published at Schirmer) and I asked him to attend, too.

We were all inside the Gallery; slightly below the street level and just outside the auditorium foyer of this cleverly designed structure by Edward Durrell Stone. This was one of the few correct decisions Huntington Hartford ever made in his life (I'm not speaking about the Art Museum concept) but if any building had to be constructed on that ludicrously tiny island there in the center of Manhattan on the insanely busy intersection of Columbus Circle, no one was better equipped than architect Edward Durrell Stone to design it. Stone did not have an easy task because each dimension of the site was diverse and to comply with the curve of Columbus Circle, Edward Durrell Stone made the north wall facade concaved in the poured concrete building and sheathed the entire structure with Vermont white marble.

I introduced Bill Cerofeci, Harvey Rubenstein, Leopold Stokowski, Ernest Gold, and Huntington Hartford to each other. As usual with Huntington Hartford, something went wrong. He did not have a key to

131

the auditorium. There was Maestro Stokowski with his wind swept *Die Walkure* white hair, impeccable black white pin striped double breasted suit from the 1930's with black shirt, white tie, and warm black gloves to protect his hands. If you did not know that here was perhaps the greatest orchestral conductor who had ever lived, you might have thought Stokowski was an erudite elderly gangster.

"What seems to be the matter?" Maestro Stokowski asked me as he stood quite erect, but a little impatient and ignoring Hartford as Hartford stared at Stokowski from a distance.

"We're waiting for the key to the auditorium," I said.

Knowing the Maestro, I was sure that he would succinctly and politely leave if the key did not arrive within two minutes, so I said out loud to Hartford who looked like a tall little lost boy standing there about twenty feet away in his usual gray flannel suit, "Hunt, is there anyway we can get the auditorium opened a little faster?"

Bill Cerofeci and Harvey Rubenstein nearly fell backwards when Huntington Hartford came up to me and asked to borrow a dime so that he could make a telephone call to one of the custodians. Within several minutes, the guardian arrived and the doors were opened.

Maestro Stokowski and I both clapped our bare hands at isolated intervals so that we could hear and test the reverberation of the acoustics. Since Maestro Stokowski and I had had so many conversations at his 1067 Fifth Avenue Penthouse regarding concert halls and acoustics, and because the Maestro had supported my auditorium design concepts of the future where (among other things) I had conceived a concert hall with three thousand contour chairs asymmetrically executed around movable circular hydraulic stages where there were no visual obstructions and each seat in the hall was excellent and where there were no numbered tickets, seats or rows (first come, take any seat) and where the roof could open up like a flower on summer days, I already knew what the Maestro was going to say when Hartford asked him what he thought.

"Well, it's alright," said the Maestro. "But with only seating for one hundred and fifty four persons there's not much problem with acoustics. It's when you get up over fifteen hundred seats, that's where the problem begins to arise."

"It's fine," the Maestro went on, "for small chamber ensembles and concerts like that, but I'm afraid it's too small even for a chamber orchestra."

Maestro Stokowski thanked us all, courteously excused himself and left.

132

Meanwhile, I said to Hartford that I would see him and Diane later that evening and I left with Bill Cerofeci spending the rest of the day with him until he departed for California.

That evening at One Beekman Place, Diane (noticing how pensively absorbed I was by the totally disparate events I had witnessed that preceding afternoon) asked me what I had been thinking about as Hartford was perusing a January 1964 pre-publication copy of his struggling Show Magazine. Hartford could not believe it when I told him that I had been mentioned in the Calendar of the very edition he was holding in his hands since my *Miraflores for String Orchestra* was to be performed by The Philadelphia Orchestra 8 January 1964. But then again, as I reminded Hartford (who said rather incredulously, "Oh yeah, there it is.") "You don't believe many things which are true."

I explained to Diane that I had been pondering the inequities and sicknesses in our sociological system; with Hartford half listening in the background surrounded by a few of the usual faceless professional models, sycophants and would be socialites. I asked Diane, amid the opulent trilevel mansion setting if she was prepared and wanted to hear what I saw earlier that afternoon not that far from One Beekman Place and what was really going on in the factual world, and she said that she would.

I proceeded to describe to Diane how my close friend William "Bill" Cerofeci who was now living in Los Angeles had visited with me that afternoon and had taken me to the small three room apartment home of an Italian-American mother of one of his male friends whom he had grown up with.

The tiny apartment was located on 1st Avenue between 108th and 109th Streets. As the door cautiously opened, a young, dark haired, attractively plain sad-faced pregnant girl in her mid-twenties who was carrying another crying nose-running baby in her arms seemed astonishingly startled to see Bill as I walked closely behind him into the two foot hallway, directly into a small dingy, but well lit kitchen.

"Ma, will you look who's here?" Said the sad-faced girl. It's Billy. Billy Cerofeci."

"Billy," exclaimed the overweight Italian-American mother who looked much older than her years even though she was a grandmother. "Billy, I can't believe it's you. Will you look at him? How nice he looks? You made something of yourself. Living now in California, I hear. Oh, Billy, you have no idea what I've been through, dear. As god is my judge, I haven't deserved this. I haven't deserved it at all."

As soon as I saw the sad-faced pregnant girl smile as she recognized Bill, I knew that we were in for a tragic narrative. It was one of the few times in my life that I had ever seen such a hopeless transparent smile. Even with her obvious elation at seeing Bill it could not overlay the despondently mournful look on this young woman's aging features.

The Italian-American mother (who was missing some of her teeth and part of her bridge-work) was sitting in the overly warm kitchen in a well worn antiquated easy chair (with some of its sickly dirty white upholstery protruding through the timeworn fabric) next to the stove which was also dangerously serving to give supplemental heat to the three tiny rooms where additional portable electric and oil heaters were functioning to their limit. Both women seemed to be cold even in spite of the fact that they were wearing heavy sweaters and the kitchen was overheated.

The kitchen dining table was covered with a deteriorated sticky oil cloth upon which was a stalk of melting butter, an oversized loaf of cheap bleached air blown white bread, a package of white sugar, an open half-used jar of low grade processed red jelly with a buttered jellied silver knife resting on it, two cans of major brand coffee, and some unwashed egg yolked dishes.

Incongruously, since we were in New York City in the dead of winter, I could not believe it when I noticed that there were about a half-dozen flies soaring around the kitchen. It was only the second time in my life I had ever seen flies inside during the cold winter time; the other isolated experience was a few years previously when one freezing evening in Washington D. C. while on a business trip for G. Schirmer I stepped into a cheap diner in a depressed area for a few moments just to get out of the biting cold.

Bill Cerofeci's childhood neighborhood friend, Pauly, was the son of the Italian-American mother and the brother of the plain sad-faced pregnant girl with the weeping sniffling baby.

It seems that Pauly was basically a good, hard working, financially struggling, Italian-American fellow about our age and he was a good friend of another man who turned out to be the husband of his sad-faced sister. Unknowingly, it was stated that Pauly was set-up by his brother-in-law and the brother-in-law's young mobster friend to drive a get-away car in a robbery that was being committed by the brother-in-law and his youthful mobster friend as poor Pauly (relaxing behind the wheel of the car) knew absolutely nothing about what was actually taking place until a hail of bullets broke loose and the trio were caught in a high speed auto chase by the New York City Police.

As Bill and I were listening to this unhappy episode, it seems that Pauly (even in spite of his innocence), the brother-in-law, and the mobster all were convicted of armed robbery and condemned to Sing-Sing Penitentiary for five years and had just begun to serve their sentences.

The Italian-American mother and her melancholy pregnant daughter with the clamant nasal congested baby were virtually destitute not only because they had lost their obvious means of support, but as the result of their relatives' crime they had forfeited their eligibility for welfare and every other relief program which they had applied for.

Bill and I tried to give solace to the two women, and even though they absolutely did not wish to accept it, we left some money weighted by one of the coffee cans on the deteriorated sticky oil cloth near the stalk of melting butter.

Diane was intrigued by the whole narrative, but Hartford I do not believe was paying any attention at all. He seemed to be more interested in examining the lacquered five color photographs and layout of his Show Magazine, The Magazine Of The Arts; which I condescendingly had referred to on a couple of occasions as Shoe Magazine, The Magazine Of The Tarts.

It was difficult for Diane and I to speak openly about Hartford when he was sitting right there adjacent to us, or even when Diane and I would speak on the telephone because she was certain that the wires were all tapped. In order to circumvent this issue, I gave Huntington Hartford the nom de plume of Hurlingham Bradford, so that Diane and I could accessibly talk about Hartford even if he were in close proximity.

My close friend and producer Nelson Case Jr. was scheduled to get married 27 December 1963 to the former actress Marya Manning, and among my busy social and career schedule (and out of friendship) I accepted the primitive finite honor of being Best Man at their brief wedding ceremony. At the University of Miami, Nelson was quite versatile, and with his remarkable speaking voice and tall good looks, he was hosting and producing commercial Radio and TV shows in the Greater Miami and Coral Gables area while attending the University of Miami as a drama and communications major. His Dad, Nelson Case Sr. (who drove us to the wedding with his new wife and Nelson Jr.'s sister Elizabeth) had been an internationally renowned Radio and TV announcer for Lowell Thomas and other major NBC network programs. Nelson Jr. had been the host of WTVJ's popular Sunday television program University Of Miami In Review which gave the public in depth coverage on all kinds of Southern

United States activities. Also attending the University of Miami (Drama Department) during that time whom Nelson and I were acquainted with was the diminutive dwarf Michael Dunn who was to become a rather popular character actor (before he passed away) starring on Broadway in *Ballad Of The Sad Cafe* and later migrating to Hollywood where he played key roles in the 1965 film *Ship Of Fools*, and the Elizabeth Taylor and Richard Burton 1968 screen version of *Boom*; the adaptation of Tennessee Williams' play *The Milk Train Doesn't Stop Here Anymore*. We were also acquainted with another fellow student whom I felt rather unhappy for: Harvey Firestone III who was the paraplegic billionaire heir who had everything money could buy except the use of his neck and legs. Harvey Firestone, just before Castro's ascension to power, booked the top suite in one of Havana's tallest hotels and (sending his man servant and aide out on an errands) dragged himself to the balcony and committed suicide by letting himself drop over the side to his death.

Meanwhile back at One Beekman Place, Hartford's third marriage to the young Lady Diane was flowing along like one of those intrepid soap operas. This is perhaps the reason why I have had a particular aversion to soap operas and Woody Allen type motion pictures, preferring rather to stimulate my viewing with documentaries devoted to wild animals and insects who seem to have a much more balanced society than we do, when you exclude our overpopulating encroachment on their habitats, which is sometimes more entertaining than wasting one's time watching remanufactured soap operas and films which are distillations of so-called life which, in actuality, exacerbates our society into believing that jealousy (which is really a sickness) is healthy, and revenge (another rampant disease) along with the exploitation of doing just about anything (including murder) on the path to corporate or matrimonial wealth (the ubiquitous mirage of the masses) is the chic way to live and influences men and women into believing that real life should be this way; but which I am sad to inform you kind Ladies and Gentlemen of the Jury is about as humanitarian as putting a carrot stick in front of a donkey.

January 1964 in New York City was cold and it was snowing. The Hollywood film-composer and conductor Franz Waxman had wanted me to wait until the third week of January before moving to California so that we could fly back together. He had an elegant apartment in New York which he frequented on the average of twice each year from his permanent home in Los Angeles. Franz told me that he dreaded the flight from coast-to-coast, and wondered if I would accompany him, so that we could talk about music and things and it would make the several hours in

136

the air pass quicker. Franz had been born in Germany, December 1906 and was educated in both Dresden and Berlin before moving to Hollywood in 1934 where he studied with Arnold Schoenberg and eventually became an accomplished film composer-conductor during the Golden Age of motion pictures winning an Academy Award in 1950 (when they meant something) for his splendid score to the film classic *Sunset Boulevard* which starred Gloria Swanson and William Holden.

About a year earlier, Franz Waxman (knowing my interest in art) asked me to represent the possible sale of an impressionist landscape by the versatile painter Maurice Vlaminck (1876-1958) which belonged to a close friend of Franz's the retired dancer Trudi Schoop who also lived in Los Angeles and whom I never met except over the telephone. I had the painting on display and stored at the famous British antique store Frank Partridge Ltd. which was located just off Fifth Avenue around 54th Street. The Van der Straetens who owned the business were gentlemen of the highest order. Unable to finalize an acceptable sale, I was about to have the painting shipped back to Miss Schoop in Los Angeles when I received a phone call early January 1964 from a Mrs. Robert F. Six who informed me that she and her husband had just returned from California where they had attended a gala party in Hollywood where she said, "Your very good friend Joe Pasternak gave me your telephone number and said I should call you about a Vlaminck you have for sale?"

"Who gave you my number?" I responded.

"Mr. Pasternak? Joe Pasternak, the producer," she sang.

"Although I have a Vlaminck for sale," I said, "I'm sorry to say that I do not know a Mr. Pasternak; although, I've seen his name on films."

"Oh, you must be joking," said Mrs. Six. "The glowing way Joe spoke about you, he's known you most of your life."

Well, I did not wish to get into a land war with Mrs. Robert F. Six, but Ladies and Gentlemen of the Jury, the truth of the matter simply was that I had never met or even spoken with Mr. Joseph Pasternak in my entire life. But now I could see how this entertainment mogul had become the successful producer of such films as *The Great Caruso* and *Love Me Or Leave Me*.

I laughed. "Okay," I said. "How may I help you?"

"My husband and I would like to see the Vlaminck."

I explained to Mrs. Six that she and her husband were free to examine it at Frank Partridge's anytime during their normal hours, but she said that they were so interested in purchasing the painting that they were wondering if I could bring the work by their Park Avenue apartment since her husband was deeply involved with the corporation he owned, Continental Airlines.

Against my better judgment, I went to Frank Partridge's and took the priceless medium sized painting (which today would fetch several millions of dollars at auction, but for which we were only asking $35,000 at that time) wrapped it in brown paper and hailed a taxi cab on Fifth Avenue.

On my way over to the Six's Park Avenue apartment, I thought I would have some fun by testing the intrinsic value of this precious impressionist painting with the cab driver. The taxi operator was an amiable middle aged native New Yorker and I said, "Hey, you know anybody who would like to buy this painting? I need some cash in a hurry."

Since there was heavy cross-town traffic, I had time to unwrap the brown paper and show him the Vlaminck.

"It's pretty messy," the cab driver said.

"Well, it's supposed to be an oncoming storm over a French farmhouse," I told the cab driver, "that's why it looks a little messy in the sky. Storms are messy; what can I tell you? Are you interested?"

"How much you want for it?" The cab driver asked.

"How much are you willing to pay?" I said.

"Nah, I'm not interested," said the cab driver. "Is it hot?"

"Now, do I look like the type of person who would steal?"

"I'll give you twenty-five bucks for it," said the cab driver.

"Twenty-five dollars!" I exclaimed. "I'm looking for at least a hundred dollars," I said.

"Nah," said the cab driver, "that picture ain't worth no hundred dollars."

At the Six's Park Avenue apartment house I thanked the cab driver for his generous offer which, obviously, I was forced to decline; but I gave him a liberal tip anyway.

Robert F. and Audrey Six were waiting for me. She seemed rather graciously charming and showed me into the living room as he (an exceptionally tall large man with a lumbering gait and slightly arrogant manner) was complaining about how extremely busy he had become that he really couldn't enjoy life.

"That's a shame," I said.

As Robert F. Six continued to speak, and I studied the liver lines on his face, my silent inner voice tended to agree with him. All I could think of were W. H. Auden's passages from his Baroque Eclogue, *The Age Of Anxiety*, where Auden says, "The jawing genius of a jack-ass age." And,

"Factories bred him, Corporate towns mothered his mind."

During that time, Robert F. Six's Continental Airlines radio and television commercials saturated the airwaves urging their potential customers to "Fly the proud bird with the golden tail." As the conference progressed, I was wondering which was the proud bird and who had the golden tail.

"What kind of business are you in, young man?" Asked Robert F. Six as I unwrapped the Vlaminck and placed it on a chair.

"Music, Sir." I said. "Music..."

"Music, huh? That's a tough racket," said Robert F. Six as he fell into what I assumed to be his favorite slouching chair. "I ought to know. I used to be married to a singer for many years; Ethel Merman."

"Oh, yes," I said, as I really could not fathom how Ethel Merman and Robert F. Six (two obviously very loud and rocket assaulting personalities) had ever managed to make it to the altar let alone get married to one another. All I could imagine at that moment was that their marriage, perhaps, had been tantamount to a constant war. As the eminent songwriter Irving Berlin used to say about Ethel Merman, "You had better not write a bad song for Ethel Merman because if you do, you'll definitely hear it."

Audrey and Robert F. Six seemed to like the Vlaminck. Mr. Six asked me if he could keep the painting for a couple of days as he told me that he wanted to "live with it" to see if he became "attached" to it. I politely informed Mr. Six that in several weeks I would be leaving permanently for California and that I, too, was extremely busy. He assured me that he would give me an answer one way or the other within forty eight hours, so I agreed to let him keep the painting (assuming full responsibility) provided that he gave me a written receipt for possession of the Vlaminck. At first Robert F. Six did not wish to give me a handwritten deed, but I firmly told him, "Sir, if you want this painting to remain here for a couple of days, I'll have to have a written receipt." Begrudgingly, he struggled out of his easy chair and inscribed the written acknowledgement.

As I was about to leave his apartment, Mr. Six asked me what I thought of his piano. It was a cheap blond spinet he said that he had bought for his brother-in-law Steve Allen when he came to visit. I smiled and said, "Sir, there is nothing wrong with this piano for what it is; but with all due respect, this would be as if I were to present you with an old beat-up piper cub single engine aircraft and asked you what you thought of my airplane."

We both laughed and I started to leave when Mrs. Six inquired if she could share my cab as she had an appointment with her hairdresser.

What could I say? Mrs. Six told me in the taxi that she was surprised that I had not recognized who she actually was (Audrey Meadows) from her many years acting on the popular Jackie Gleason Show. To make her feel better, I pretended to have recalled, but I did not tell her the truth which was when that show was running I was attending High School and I rarely watched it for more than five minutes because that type of crass humor did not appeal to me; I preferred Groucho Marx and the Marx Brothers, and Dean Martin and Jerry Lewis to that of the Jackie Gleason Show.

Two days later, Robert F. Six telephoned and asked me if he might keep the Vlaminck just a little while longer, and against my further better judgment, once more I agreed.

It was snowing again in New York City, and I had shipped my large ocean cargo trunk of books, music scores, clothes and artifacts to myself c/o Bill Cerofeci's home in Hollywood where I would be staying until I found suitable lodgings of my own.

Hartford and Diane asked me to meet them that evening at P. J. Clarke's (a sort of old time saloon) on Third Avenue at 55th Street where they served, in addition to drinks, hamburgers and chili, a bevy of fashion and photographer's models indulging in dilly dalliances because it was considered stylishly chic at that time for the beautiful people to have meetings and be seen there.

With all I had to do, I arrived a little late. Jeff Sparks from the UN (who was ill with the flu) asked me to take an envelope on his behalf containing some money over to his needy loyal friend of many years Veronica Lake (the former golden haired Hollywood screen siren) who was now forced to work occasionally as a hostess in the Restaurant Bar of the Martha Washington Hotel on East 30th Street between Park and Madison Avenues. Even though Veronica Lake was petit and had put on a little weight (she was not fat) I found her to be quite humble and unpretentious; however, I could sense that along with her past Celluloid successes, Veronica Lake had had her share of post Hollywood asperities.

As soon as I walked into P. J. Clarke's I was directed to the semi-private dining room in the rear of the bistro where Diane, Sy and Dottie Alter, Larry Horn and his girlfriend were all seated around a large circular table. Diane seemed in good humor and happy to see me. Hartford had not arrived as yet, but had telephoned in his request which included a Hamburger, French Fries and a glass of milk. We all ordered and shortly after the food arrived, Hartford ambled in taking off his overcoat which he gave to an attentive waiter. He was dressed as usual in his Rumpelstiltskin gray flannel suit and sat down opposite me with Dottie Alter to his right and Diane to his left.

"I'll be right back," Hartford said getting up. "I have to make a phone call."

Sy Alter gave an alert glance to Larry Horn as Diane initiated a seemingly joyful conversation with Dottie Alter, with both girls laughing heartily.

Approximately ten minutes later Hartford returned, sat down and grinned at Diane who with lightning motions and an extinguishing look emptied the contents of a free flowing ketchup bottle onto Hartford's lap. Everyone was startled, but it took Hartford a few seconds to realize what had happened. He slowly looked down at his tomato groin then threw a little of his glass of milk on Diane's breast, after which Diane propelled about half her glass of ice water at Hartford quickly getting up, and grabbing her thick white Cossack coat and hat, exited fleet footed like some tempestuous Czarina.

It was dark and snowing heavily outside as I managed to catch up with Diane who was bundled in her fur hat, overcoat and designer boots trudging along up Third Avenue.

"Diane, what the hell did you do that for?" I asked.

"Do you see how he treats me?" Diane said stopping as she lamented almost sobbing. "Here I am, Mrs. Huntington Hartford and he's off looking for new models to have affairs with. What kind of a fool does he think I am?"

"Listen, Diane, we're friends and I hate to see you this way, but let's be honest; you knew what Hartford was before you married him, so if you're this unhappy about your situation, then why don't you just leave him and begin a new life on your own?"

"Phillip, where would I go? What would I do?"

"That's for you to decide," I said.

"Mrs. Huntington Hartford. What a joke. Do you think I'm the lady of the house? Do you think One Beekman Place is my home? Do you think the estate in New Jersey is mine? Do you know if I leave Hunt what I get?"

I shrugged.

"$250,000 dollars; that's all. $250,000 dollars and I signed my life away before we got married."

"Well, Diane, $250,000 is a lot better than having to get up every morning and go to work like some flesh robot for a hundred dollars a week," I said.

I offered to stay with Diane, but she said it would look better if I returned to Hartford then meet her in about an hour at Sy and Dottie Alter's apartment.

Returning to P. J. Clarke's, I encountered Hartford slowly ambulating along Third Avenue hatless, scarfless and turning up the collar of his overcoat. He looked just as he was: alone and distrait.

"Look, Hunt," I said, "I know it's none of my business, but you know how Diane is; so why do you do things you know will upset her?"

"Yeah," Hartford said as he just stood there in the snow and gaped down like some school boy receiving a reprimand. If you did not know who he was, you probably would have asked him if he needed any assistance and perhaps given him a pair of warm gloves, a scarf, or a dollar to protect himself from the frigid air.

About thirty minutes later I arrived at Sy and Dottie Alter's fashionable ground level sunken apartment. In addition to reviling her own fate, Diane was now berating Sy Alter in front of Dottie and me. Fortunately, there was no one else there.

"Diane, I want you to know I knew Hunt many years before I ever went to work for him," Sy Alter said defensively as he attempted to light his pipe. "All those years I never so much as took a dime from him until he asked me to come to work for him."

"Oh, come on Sy; you call what you do work? It's a joke and you know it. What kind of future do you have with all of Hunt's aimless endeavors? A man with your intelligence could certainly do something far more rewarding than playing at business and losing Huntington Hartford's money."

"What did you want me to do?" Sy asked.

"You could have done something substantial with your life," Diane said. "You could have gotten a job on Madison Avenue with an Ad agency, or gone into real estate."

I felt sorry for Dottie Alter who was almost near tears so I decided to silence everyone's frustration by sitting down at the Alter's newly purchased Knabe grand piano and playing a little Chopin, a little Brahms, and a little Lambro. Sy and Dottie Alter were genuinely surprised that I could play the piano as I heard Diane quietly say, "Oh yes, Phillip is very gifted."

Hartford entered the living room just after the opening bars of the Brahms and Diane told him to be quiet.

The music transformed everyone. Diane was now relaxed and smiling and so were Sy and Dottie Alter; and even Hartford seemed more affable than I had ever seen him.

As the evening drew to a close, I couldn't resist quipping, "Well, I can tell you one thing: I'm glad I'm leaving for California, and even though I'll miss all of you little children, I certainly won't miss your ongoing soap opera." Fortunately, everyone laughed.

I put my affairs in order; including having to go up to Robert F. Six's apartment and repossess the Vlaminck, which after living with for weeks, he elected not to purchase. I did not wish any ill upon Robert F. Six (although he enjoyed the distinction of being one of the most unfavorable individuals I had ever met) because I felt that he had already been punished enough having been married to Ethel Merman.

I relished the flight to Los Angeles with Franz Waxman listening to the recollections of his youth in Germany, his musical studies in Dresden and Berlin, then escaping from the Nazi's after being beaten, and finally settling in Hollywood (1934) where he studied with Arnold Schoenberg and eventually became a successful composer for films. He seemed tired and older than his fifty-eight years and smoked incessantly; bemoaning the loss of the great film directors, writers, musicians and the old Hollywood studio tycoons of the 1930's and 40's. "Hollywood is run by a bunch of hacks now," Waxman told me. "And the films and scorers are the lowest level I've ever seen." From the tone of Waxman's cough, I knew that it was only a matter of time for him; he died a few years later from cancer. If Franz Waxman thought the motion pictures and sound tracks of the 1960's were bad, I'm thankful that his passing spared him from experiencing the subsequent further decline of Hollywood mediocrity.

Apropos Franz Waxman's cough, it made me think of a letter Frederic Chopin wrote to his friend Juljan Fontana from Palma, 3 December 1838 (Chopin was 28) which exhibited the additional greatness of Chopin's character and sense of humor in the face of his imminent tubercular death: "I have been sick as a dog these last two weeks. I caught cold in spite of 18 degrees of heat, roses, orange trees, palms, fig trees. Three doctors---the most famous ones on the island---examined me. One sniffed at my spittle, the second tapped to discover where I spat it from, the third poked about and listened to how I spat it. The first one said I'd die, the second that I was dying, the third that I was already dead."

I was inordinately happy to return to California as I had not been there since 1955 when I received my scholarship to The Music Academy Of The West in Santa Barbara. Bill Cerofeci met me at Los Angeles International Airport and I briefly introduced him and Franz Waxman to each other as Franz was departing. I was glad to see Bill and happier still that he had settled in Los Angeles and had not united himself with Il Cosa Nostra.

As Bill drove us to his home (the top quarters of a spacious thick walled pink Spanish stucco duplex house) at 6909 1/2 Bonita Terrace in Hollywood, I could not believe how much I had missed the intoxicating perfumed foliage of Southern California's jacaranda, magnolia and jasmine umbrage.

With Bill working actively for Provident Mutual Insurance, and Sheila continuing her ranking position with AT&T, I was fortunate enough (in addition to living there) in being able to use their place everyday as a studio-office from which I was trying to launch a career composing and conducting music for films so that I could support my concert music endeavors.

Other than Bill Cerofeci, Franz Waxman and Ernest Gold, I did not know anyone else in Los Angeles. However, before I left New York City, Leonard Bernstein had given me the telephone number of John (Johnny) Green whom I had met on several occasions while at G. Schirmer after John Green had conducted the musical sequences for the film version of *West Side Story*. As soon as I called him, he affably invited me to his attractive home at 903 North Bedford Drive in Beverly Hills on different occurrences where he introduced me to a number of people including his two lovely daughters Kim and Kathy (by his tall wife Bonnie Walters), and subsequently to another beautiful daughter by his former wife Betty Furness. John Green was a brilliant songwriter who wrote the music for such celebrated songs as *Body & Soul*, *I'm Yours*, *I Cover The Waterfront*, and *Out Of Nowhere*, before he became captivated with the executive position in charge of music at MGM from the late 1940's to the mid 1950's which earned him fourteen Oscar nominations and five Oscars for such films as *Easter Parade*, *An American In Paris*, and *West Side Story*.

John Green was an intelligent fellow (having graduated from Harvard University 1928) who could talk ceaselessly about virtually any subject. In fact, many considered him to be the surrogate Mayor of Beverly Hills with as many after dinner speeches as he was giving at that time.

I remember one particular evening John Green had invited me to his home for dinner shortly after I had arrived in Los Angeles where the only guests were the debuting singer actress leading lady to John's current television project (Rodgers & Hammerstein's Cinderella) Leslie Ann Warren and her mother. The young Ms. Warren was absolutely enchanting throughout that one evening, but as I was to view her actions occasionally at the various elite private clubs and discos during the

144

supervening months and years, I told John Green that, perhaps, Richard Rodgers had made a mistake and should have appropriately cast Leslie Ann Warren as one of Cinderella's inconsiderate step sisters rather than Cinderella herself.

Meanwhile, during a long distance telephone conversation with Huntington Hartford, he suggested that I see if I could sell his theater on Vine Street and his sizable 133 acre estate at the north dead end of Fuller Avenue which had been the largest parcel of privately owned real estate in Hollywood. Hartford had bought the land in 1942. The manor had originally been built by coal baron Carmen Randolph Runyon and had also been purchased in 1929 by Irish tenor John McCormack after McCormack's proceeds from his role in the film *Song Of My Heart*. I also found out later that the English mansion and grounds additionally had been used by screen idol Errol Flynn during 1957 and 1958 when Flynn was an indigent uncontrollable alcoholic and was being financially supported by Huntington Hartford under the guise of employment contracts (which Flynn never fulfilled) for Hartford's ambiguous and inept theatrical stage ventures.

"I thought you didn't want to sell those properties," I said to Hartford.

"I've changed my mind," Hartford said. "I need the money."

Hartford also suggested that I contact an Edward "Buzz" Barton who he said could introduce me to a number of people in the entertainment industry and gave me his number.

I phoned Edward Barton and he proposed that I meet him at Hartford's estate on Fuller the following early afternoon.

After walking up approximately a quarter mile of the two lane driveway deeply set within the Hollywood Hills, flanked by portions of unspoiled mountain wilderness, rundown gardens, tall pines and palm trees, Edward Barton received me at the virtually deserted main mansion where he was playing billiards with two of his friends, Larry and Wayne.

"Edward, very pleased to meet you," I said.

He smiled and politely said, "Just call me Buzz; my friends call me Buzz."

Edward "Buzz" Barton had a mild pleasant manner about him. He was twenty-six years of age (I was 29) approximately five feet eight inches tall, and with sandy brown hair he looked like a cross between a young Alan Ladd and James Dean.

"Do you shoot pool, Phillip?" Buzz asked.

"No," I said. "Tennis is my game. I'm afraid I'm not very good at pool."

"We'll have to teach you," Buzz said.

"Did Hunt send you to spy on us?" Buzz smirked as he sank a ball into the corner pocket with professional accuracy. Seeing Buzz grin caused Wayne (a tall closely cropped muscular socially awkward type) to beam, and Larry (a short long blond haired lean nervously introverted character) to chortle.

I laughed as Buzz chalked the point of his cue stick. "Are you serious?" I asked. "Why the hell would Hartford send me to spy on you?"

"Well, if you don't know," smiled Buzz who then laughed a little. "We're not going to tell you."

Wayne and Larry snickered on cue.

Buzz missed his shot. "Your turn, Wayne." Buzz said as he came over to me.

"I'm here in Los Angeles to try and compose and conduct motion picture music," I said, "in hopes of supporting my concert music career. And Hunt thought that you might be able to introduce me to some influential motion picture people."

"He said that, huh," Buzz said shaking his head. "Well, we have to tell you one thing: we don't particularly like Hunt very much; in fact, at times we out and out despise him."

"Yeah," big Wayne added as he missed his second shot, "we think Huntington Hartford's a big shit head."

Flimsy Larry began chortling and trembled slightly as if he were trying to begin a gigue like some jittery Elizabethan court jester.

"Calm down boys," Buzz said. "Calm down. You'll have to forgive Larry and Wayne."

For the next twenty minutes the dialogue continued to unravel inconsequentially around me as I had the feeling (from the way I was passively being scrutinized) that Buzz Barton and his friends actually thought Huntington Hartford had sent me to report back to him which, of course, was not the case.

Several days later Buzz and I met for lunch. It was a beautiful warm sunny California day. Buzz came around alone and picked me up in his convertible Jaguar. He seemed just as congenial and amiable as before, but more relaxed.

"Where's your chorus?" I asked with a smile as we drove west along Franklin Avenue.

He gave me a slight inquisitive look.

"Your two friends," I said.

146

"Oh, Wayne and Larry," Buzz grinned. "They're out there doing their things. I've known them ever since High School. They're like the two brothers I've never had. I've tried to help them out because they come from poor unfortunate backgrounds."

"And what kind of a background do you come from?" I asked.

"Are you putting me on?" Buzz asked.

"What do you mean?" I countered.

"You really don't know who I am," Buzz said shifting gears as the traffic light turned green. "Didn't Hunt tell you who I was?"

"Look," I said. "All Hartford said to me was that I should look you up and that you knew a lot of people out here who might be able to give me a few motion picture scoring assignments."

Buzz chuckled, "I'll be a son-of-a-bitch." He glanced back and forth from the road to my face, "You mean to say that Huntington Hartford never told you that I was his bastard son?"

"Really..?" I asked as my mind flashed several years in reverse to when I first met Hartford's two children and I had asked Diane how many children Hartford had and she alluded in a whisper, "Hunt has another son, but sshhh, he doesn't want anyone to know." However, I thought, perhaps that he was closer in age to Jackie and Cathy, and lived in the East.

"Just look at my face, Phillip. Do I look like Hunt, or do I not look like Hunt?"

I studied Buzz's face. "Come to think of it, you do; but," I smiled, "you're better looking and at least you have a personality. How come Hunt's taller than you?"

"I took after my mother who was about five eight."

"Where is she now?"

"She died when I was a baby."

I nodded.

"Well, now you know," said Buzz as he grinned masking his melancholy feeling. "I'm the bastard illegitimate son of the famous multimillionaire Huntington Hartford." Buzz paused and laughed.

"What do you mean illegitimate?" I asked. "You seem pretty legitimate to me. In fact you seem more legitimate than Hurlingham Bradford."

"Who's that?" Asked Buzz.

"That's the pseudonym I gave Hartford when Diane and I want to talk about him without his knowing whom we're referring to."

"Hurlingham Bradford," Buzz said giggling. "That's pretty good. I like that. Yes, how is my step-mother, Diane?" He went on. "I've spoken with her at length on the telephone. She sounds absolutely charming."

"She's fine," I said.

"Isn't that something?" Buzz said. "My step-mother is even younger than I am." He laughed. "She said that she'd like to meet me and get to know me better. Wouldn't that be some shit if she fell in love with me and we had an affair?" Buzz laughed, "Wow, that would really blow the roof off; wouldn't it? How would my father, Hurlingham Bradford like that?"

Buzz took me to a narrow little rundown restaurant with a creaking screen door at 8229 Sunset Boulevard (corner of Hilldale & Sunset) which was operated by a struggling theatrical husband and wife team of Marilyn and Harry Lewis who named their little eatery, Hamburger Hamlet. Buzz raved about the food, and particularly the lobster bisque with garlic toast; and I could see that he wasn't wrong. We subsequently ate there often where the both of us kept reproaching Harry and Marilyn Lewis for not expanding Hamburger Hamlet into other larger locations. Several years later, they must have heeded our advice because that original tiny forty-plus seating capacity Hamburger Hamlet eventually augmented into a successful chain of twenty-six Hamburger Hamlets with eighteen in Southern California; six in Washington D. C., Virginia and Maryland; and two in Illinois.

Buzz and I quickly became good friends to the consternation of Huntington Hartford. Buzz liked quality music and literature and, I understand, he was a suitable enough golfer to have played on the amateur tour for a couple of years, and unlike his father, was keenly intelligent and quietly personable.

Meanwhile back at 6909 1/2 Bonita Terrace, Bill Cerofeci's marriage to Sheila was dissolving rapidly along with their previous friendship since Bill had now become romantically embroiled with his Provident Mutual Insurance secretary, Ronette (whom he ultimately married and is still with today) which caused Bill and myself to eventually get evicted. Bill introduced me to Sidney Schuman (who was to become a life long friend) who owned an apartment house at 1419 North Fairfax and I immediately moved into the attractive apartment #3 at the princely lease of $100 dollars a month.

Although Buzz was living off the reported several million dollar trust which Hartford had his attorneys set up and expanded for Buzz, he was not the least bit ostentatious and, in reality, did not want people to know that Huntington Hartford was his father. Buzz was a member of the exclusive Beverly Hills private club The Daisy and he introduced me to all the unique and interesting night-spots from The Luau in Beverly Hills and The Whisky-A-Go-Go and Cyrano's on Sunset Boulevard to Barney's Beanery on Santa Monica Boulevard. One of the reasons Buzz liked going out on the prowl with me was usually the idiosyncratic things I would sometimes say to attractive girls whom we were trying to meet. For example, once Buzz was driving his convertible Jaguar down Sunset Boulevard on an early Friday evening and there were two attractive girls in their convertible Ford Mustang driving along side of us. Buzz said, "Phillip, quick; say something to those two girls." I courteously shouted, "Hi, I'm Phillip and this is my friend Buzz. We're from out of town and we're completely and totally lost. Would you be so kind as to help us find our way? And perhaps a little later try and cure our sexual impotence?"

Another time I asked this girl and her female friend who were motoring parallel to us if they would like to take out a subscription to the International Tuba Journal and meet us later for dinner. And, do you know, they met us subsequently that evening for dinner.

A comedian acquaintance of mine (Herb Eden) introduced me to a former Las Vegas show girl by the name of Pat who possessed an uncommonly beautiful face and figure in the alluring classic Hollywood persuasion with whom I had had a short romantic encounter. Pat lived in a cute bungalow on Larrabee just north of Sunset Boulevard and supplemented her income from posing for Playboy and other exotic magazines by dancing at a local Sunset Boulevard restaurant stripclub called The Body Shop. It was difficult sleeping at Pat's home when several times a week at about 3:00 a.m. a police car would invariably flash its searchlight on Pat's bedroom window and she would have to get up, put on a robe, go over to the corner of the bedroom where she had a three foot stack of magazines, bring them out to the police officers and personally autograph them. Pat was deathly afraid of being raped or killed because several months previously a strange man had unexpectedly approached her from behind the shrubs of her bungalow when she returned home late one evening, so she asked the police and sheriff's department to patrol her area from time to time. I was totally shocked within a few weeks to discover that this flawless beauty was secretly taking drugs, and coupled with the fact that I believe she found my introspective world of Steinway pianos, concert and symphonic music perhaps not too terribly appealing, we parted; although I was appreciative of Pat introducing me to the film director Samuel Fuller with whom I had many telephone conversations.

Pat had befriended a spindly limping craggy faced middle aged Hollywood hustler known as Freddie "The Weasel" who would run errands for Pat and do just about anything she asked. Pat reciprocated by occasionally playing checkers with Freddie and letting him watch television at her home. After I left, she hired a young personable blond Californian black belt martial artist who worked at a local lumber company (whom I was acquainted with) by the name of Ron to live in an extra bedroom in exchange for nightly protection. Ron was engaged to be married within six months, but his fiancee was understanding of the rent free situation and not jealous.

Shortly after this, I had had an afternoon appointment with a motion picture producer at his office in the building across the street from The Body Shop on Sunset Boulevard and was on my way there (dressed in my best French suit and attache case) when I noticed Freddie "The Weasel" hobbling toward me in the distance. I always felt rather sorry for Freddie and that's perhaps why I went out of my way to be congenial with him.

"Hi Freddie," I yelled. "How are you?"

As soon as Freddie noticed me, he immediately limp-ran away from me across Sunset Boulevard nearly getting killed in the process by an oncoming automobile screeching to avoid hitting Freddie.

"Freddie, what's the matter?" I shouted. "I just want to say hello to you. Come here. I want to talk with you."

Freddie "The Weasel" left so fast that I feared he might have a heart attack because of his age, physical and anemic condition.

Several weeks later the incident became rendered after I happened to meet Ron the martial artist. It seems that one evening Ron was asleep in his room, and Pat at around 2:30 a.m. was watching TV and playing checkers with Freddie "The Weasel" when Freddie informed Pat that he could not take their relationship any longer and that he was hopelessly in love with her body and wanted to have sex with her instantly. At first Pat thought it was a joke until Freddie pulled out a revolver and threatened Pat. Pat called for Ron, but before Ron could get out of bed Freddie went to Ron's room, opened the door and with his pointed revolver said in a hushed crazed manner, "Don't get out of bed Ron until after I leave. I don't think it'd be a good idea."

Ron told me that he just quietly said to himself, "Oh shit." And then pulled the sheet up over his face until Freddie "The Weasel" closed the bedroom door.

"Freddie, please put the gun down," Pat said. "I'm not going to have sex with you and that's final. I don't care if you kill me, I'm still not going to have sex with you."

After about thirty minutes more, Freddie "The Weasel" left. Pat did not call the police; however, when Freddie telephoned later to justify the incident, Pat invented a story about how she had just spoken with me and that I wasn't only a composer conductor, but also a high ranking member of the Mafia and that if Freddie so much as ever contacted Pat again that I was going to have a contract put out on Freddie's life.

Buzz took an interest in my music career and when I bemoaned the fact that I did not own a piano, he said that I could have his Baldwin Grand to keep which he had had in storage from his childhood. It was an exceptional 1928 small Grand which sounded much larger in tone than it actually was and which I ultimately had restrung and completely rebuilt and upon which I practiced, composed, and tested some of my best compositions. I eventually sold the Baldwin Grand in 1981 to the UCLA School Of Music and invested the proceeds into the Concert Grand which I own today. UCLA assured me that the piano which Buzz had given me would go into a new school building special artists room under lock and key and would only be used by advanced students and faculty. I think that you might get the impression that I consider fine pianos to be like living things; which, of course, they are.

As the months went by, Buzz introduced me to the tall attractive blonde Cynthia Stone who had come from a wealthy family; became an actress in New York City during the early 1950's; met, promoted and married Jack Lemmon; generated his motion picture stardom (they eventually had one son); divorced Lemmon and afterward took the unknown actor Cliff Robertson into her fold and forged Robertson's career; married him (they had one daughter); then ultimately divorced Robertson. Cynthia was leasing the large beach house directly on the Santa Monica sandy shore of Pacific Coast Highway from silent film star Harold Lloyd and taking care of her son Chris Lemmon who was about ten and her daughter Stephanie by Cliff Robertson who was almost four years old.

Buzz arranged to have me invited to several of Cynthia's social congregations at the beach house. There was one in particular where Buzz, his engaging Swedish blonde date Pieta (pronounced Peetah), his friend Larry, and I went to. It was a Sunday afternoon swim lunch event where a number of Cynthia's cinematic intimates were having a difficult time networking because of their children and their children's abundantly disorderly friends. Cynthia introduced me to Cliff Robertson who (although not intoxicated) perhaps had had one drink too many as he (obviously feeling quite sorry for himself) sat on the large living room floor (as part of his legal visitation rights) and played with his and Cynthia's adorable four year old Stephanie.

One of Cynthia's pretentious Anglicized female confidants was conspicuously looking for her moppet son and vocalizing at the top of her voice as she floated around the area, "Peetah. Peeetah, dear. Peetah. Where are you, darling?" I immediately thought this lady was looking for Buzz's Swedish date Pieta, and so did Pieta herself who went up to the lady and responded, "Yes..?"

"You're not Peetah," said the mannered lady. "I'm looking for Peetah."

"Yes, I am Pieta," said the young Swedish girl.

Before anymore Byzantine dialogue occurred, I immediately intervened explaining to Pieta, "Dear, she is looking for her son, Peter."

"Yes," said the stilted, but attractive lady. "I'm looking for my little boy, Peetah."

Pieta said, "Then madame why do you not say Peter? Pieta is a girls name."

The affected lady turned on her heels and left quite fazed as we all endeavored to refrain from laughing.

Cynthia was always quite congenial, engaging and helpful and often went out of her way to recommend me for motion picture scores. But later in the year she told me that she had decided the efforts required to forge the careers of two Hollywood film stars had been too debilitating, so Cynthia decided to move to Florida and marry her recently divorced former High School sweetheart who had won custody of his three children and with Cynthia's two children they hoped to live their lives happily ever after. I had spoken with Cliff Robertson several times over the telephone about film projects, but the last time he phoned me during that period was to lament about the fact that Cynthia's taking his daughter to Florida represented an unusual encumbrance upon his visitation rights and, incredulously, he wondered if I might persuade Cynthia not to move to Florida. I told Robertson that it neither would be appropriate for me to get involved, nor would it be legally permissible.

During the next year Buzz invited me quite often to the stylish private club The Daisy on Rodeo Drive in Beverly Hills. They had a pool table there where Charles Bronson and Steve McQueen valiantly tried to teach me how, why, when and where to hit the white cue ball; but I must admit that, unlike Wolfgang Amadeus Mozart, who loved the game and allegedly played rather well, I just have never had any affinity for billiards.

One Friday evening during 1965 Buzz asked me to The Daisy where at our personal table he introduced me to several friends of his including Omar Sharif the Egyptian actor who had gained distinction in David Lean's 1962 film *Lawrence Of Arabia*, and the just completed David Lean production *Doctor Zhivago* which was having its prosperous release. During the course of the discussion where everyone was deliriously ecstatic about *Doctor Zhivago*, Omar Sharif (whom I was seated next to) sensing my reluctance to offer any comment one way or the other about the motion picture, turned to me and inquired in his quiet gentlemanly manner, "And what did you think about the film?"

I smiled. "Well, do you want a Hollywood answer; or would you like a truthful response?"

Omar Sharif grinned. "A truthful answer," he said.

"Boris Pasternak was Russian," I said. "His story is Russian."

"Oh, Omar," chimed in one of the starlets at the table, don't listen to him."

"Yeah," said another seductress primping herself in front of her portable mirrored compact. "He doesn't know what he's talking about."

"Let him finish," said Omar Sharif gesturing with his hands. "Let him finish." Buzz gave me a slight nervous look of disapproval as he smoked his cigarette.

"As I said," I continued. "Pasternak was Russian. The story is Russian. And for all of David Lean's innate sensitivity and mechanical and technical brilliance, the whole film comes out very British in spite of the wonderful cast. I think you were the closest to being Russian in character with your Arabic-French accent, but even here I'm not so sure that you were totally convinced about your role."

"How the hell can you say that, Phillip?" Moaned Buzz. "That picture was great."

Omar Sharif quieted the whole group who were about ready to have me lynched and said, "You know, it's amazing but you are absolutely correct. I kept telling David Lean all through the production exactly what you have said. I told him that I didn't feel right in the part and that what we were doing was not Russian and did not reflect Pasternak's wishes, but David kept telling me, 'Trust me. I know what I'm doing. Please trust me.' So," said Omar Sharif putting a glass of his favorite red wine to his lips, "I trusted him."

Everyone at the table seemed stunned that Omar Sharif had agreed with my veracious commentaries about *Doctor Zhivago*.

"Some imaginative Russian director like Andrei Tarkovsky or Sergei

Bondarchuk should have directed Zhivago," I said, "and it should have been shot in Russia with more of a Russian cast who could speak English."

"That would have been very nice, but I'm afraid impossible with the Russian Government," Omar Sharif said.

I maintained that if enough of a financial participation had been diplomatically offered the Soviets, that eventually they would have agreed to a coproduction; but who shall ever know?.

Omar Sharif concluded, "You know, Phillip, I receive thousands of letters each week from *Doctor Zhivago* and I read some of them; and some of the ones I read bring tears to my eyes. So maybe, David Lean was right and we are wrong. I don't know, but it's something to think about."

The next evening at The Daisy I encountered Omar Sharif again standing immaculately tailored in his European vested suit at the bar with a glass of burgundy wine and as we watched all the comely girls gyrating to the blaring music on the disco floor, I said, "Omar, I've been seriously thinking about what you said yesterday evening regarding *Doctor Zhivago* and I've come to the conclusion that we are definitely right and David Lean was wrong."

Omar Sharif smiled and patting the top of my head said, "Yes, you are right, Phillip. You are right."

I only met Omar Sharif a few times after that and we briefly spoke about his passion and tactile affinity for cards and gambling. He seemed convinced that he could never lose; another aspect which I told him I could never subscribe to. Eventually, I understood that Sharif (even though he was a world class bridge player) lost millions gambling which I heard he ultimately recouped by acquiring part interest in a small seaside French casino and by giving up cards and betting altogether.

Another evening at The Daisy, Buzz presented me to the handsome actor-photographer John Derek and his new wife a then unknown very young thin blonde actress by the name of Linda Evans. We were all seated at a table: Linda Evans to my right, Buzz to my left, and John Derek directly across from me. John Derek was in the process of directing Linda Evans in an extremely low budget film for which Buzz was attempting to get me to do the score and the conversation was amiable until John Derek (who had retired from acting years before) deplored himself for ever having become an actor to which I responded, "I didn't think you were that bad, John. In fact, I remember *All The King's Men* with Broderick Crawford which I saw my 'first year in High School and I thought you were actually quite good."

Even though I was only about twenty-nine at the time, young Linda Evans was so startled she exclaimed, "John, you aren't that old, are you?"

John Derek pensively nodded his head slowly and said, "Yeah, he's right. He's absolutely right."

Linda Evans was John Derek's third wife, and once while having a subsequent conversation with John I thought he told me that his second wife's name was the actress Ursula Undress to which he corrected me to Andress; adding, "However, in many respects you're really not that far wrong, you know."

I used to also have lunch occasionally at Bud Thompson's Hollywood Natural Foods store on Hollywood Boulevard where I met a number of characters from Percy Kilbride whom I had remembered from my childhood with Marjorie Main in the *Ma & Pa Kettle* motion pictures. I also encountered an ill and out of work elderly tall distinguished looking former Broadway actor with a shock of white hair and a mellifluous speaking voice named Ken who had also been supported by Huntington Hartford from time to time after a series of surgical operations and who miraculously (shortly before his death) married a young girl in her twenties and became for the first time in his life the proud father of a baby boy. Ken used to pester and coerce me into taking him to the Polo Lounge of The Beverly Hills Hotel for lunch so that he could consort with all the wealthy people in spite of the fact that I would often caution him by reciting the Buddhist proverb, "Those who associate with Mandarins, lose their trousers."

Two mildly distraught girls by the name of Lee (who apparently had been romantically intimate with Frank Sinatra, since I noticed in Lee's bathroom a tenderly inscribed framed picture of Sinatra which had been torn into a hundred pieces then meticulously pasted back together like some puzzled collage) and Tonya (who was a former Playboy centerfold and was being retained by the aging comedian George Burns as a therapeutic supplement to his wife Gracie Allen) used to come and pick me up and insist upon giving me a guided tour of Hollywood despite my protestations at not being the least bit interested in seeing the apartment on Doheny Drive where Marilyn Monroe used to live. Although as an antidote, I reciprocated by forcing the both of them to look at where F. Scott Fitzgerald had struggled in 1940 with his writing, drinking, and Sheilah Graham (probably in that order) at 1403 North Laurel Avenue in West Hollywood.

I used to let Tonya chauffeur me to my interviews with producers at the various studios in the new blue Cadillac convertible which George Burns had given her until it became a detriment to my music career because the executives would often become more interested in dating Tonya than in hiring me to do the music score for their current production. Poor Tonya, I understood that she died from a drug induced heart attack about a year after I had met her and six months after we had lost contact with each other.

Buzz became remotely interested in tennis and when I had the time, I would give him a few lessons after which he sometimes took me to the golf driving range and attempted to teach me the proper golf swings. Usually after that, we'd go have a Swedish Sauna and chat before going to dinner and perhaps tally upon some agreeable girls. I especially remember one afternoon in the Sauna where we were discussing Ernest Hemingway and his work.

"How did Hemingway die?" Buzz asked.

"The same way as his father did, I understand."

"How was that?"

"When Hemingway realized he couldn't write anymore; all his friends were dead; his back was in pain; and he couldn't fuck anymore; I was told by my friends in Key West who had known him that he put his affairs in order, went upstairs and put a favorite shotgun into his mouth and blew his brains out."

"Wow," said Buzz. "What a fucking way to go. Can you imagine that? Putting a shotgun to your mouth and pulling the trigger? Man, that must have taken a lot of guts." Buzz laughed. "Well, maybe someday when the going get's too rough, that's how I'll go."

"Hemingway must have been really suffering," I said. "It doesn't take much guts to kill yourself when you're suffering; but who knows?"

"I want you to do me a favor," Buzz said reflectively. "An important favor."

"What's that?" I asked.

"I want you to introduce me to Rita Hayworth."

"Rita Hayworth," I exclaimed. "I don't know Rita Hayworth."

"But you know Jean Simmons; you play tennis with her," Buzz said.

"Yes, I know Jean Simmons. But what does that have to do with Rita Hayworth?" I questioned. "Why the hell do you want to meet Rita Hayworth anyway?"

"I understand that she knew my mother. They were both dancer actresses and I was told that they were friends."

"Buzz, your mother's dead. She's been dead ever since you were three years old. What good is it going to do now to try to dig up the past? We have to live for the present and future not the past."

"Phillip, don't you understand? I was too young to remember my mother except through what her stepmother, my grandmother who raised me, kept telling me all my life. I want to find out what my mother was really like from another perspective, that's all."

I sighed and looked at Buzz.

"That's all; just do me this one favor," Buzz said.

"Alright," I said. "I'll see what I can do."

"Besides," Buzz said, "I don't feel that my mother committed suicide as they say and as the papers reported. I believe that Hunt had something to do with my mother's death."

"I'm sure that he did, but you're not intimating that murder was involved are you?"

"That's why I want to talk with Rita Hayworth," Buzz said.

Buzz told me that he had eventually found out that he was, in all probability, conceived when Hartford took his mother Mary Barton (then about twenty-one) on a supposed 1937 fling to Paris, France where he maintained that there had been a marriage certificate which eventually Hartford never acknowledged because it would have made him a bigamist inasmuch as Hartford had been married to Mary Lee Epling since 1931. Buzz also on rare occasions implied that there had been enough conflicting evidence from witness and newspaper accounts to the coroner's report about his mother's suicide to where he thought the case should be reopened and, at the very least, studied.

Over the next few years, it became obvious to me that Buzz wanted to know as much as possible about his mother and what actually happened to her (while not wanting even his friends to know about this interest) if for no other reason than to ascertain the truth about Mary Barton and where he came from. Buzz was intelligent enough during his early teens to realize that from all the deception he had endured during his childhood from both Hartford (who engineered the young Buzz into believing, at first, that he was his "uncle" while Hartford had the child moved to Los Angeles where he openly used baby Buzz as a progeny showpiece to privately fortify himself as a stud with the starlets and movie stars he was dating) and from Buzz's now late step-grandmother who obviously was a party to this deception until Buzz grew older (as she played off the gratuity of Huntington Hartford on the one hand and Buzz's growing financial trust on the other) that with so many conflicting accounts about his mother and father which he had been subjected to, Buzz recognized that he had never and would never be able to annex the truth out of his only 100% blood relative, Huntington Hartford. However, when the opportunity afforded itself to where there was a remote and incongruous chance (as in my case) where an introduction to Rita Hayworth might lead to new and startling revelations about what really happened to his mother, Buzz became passively aggressive about it. Buzz had never been sure about the accuracy of what his step-grandmother had said over the years about his mother, because his mother's (Mary Barton's) parents had both died when she was approximately thirteen and young Mary was adopted by Buzz's step-grandmother Florence Grundhoefer and her husband William. When Buzz was born, Hartford not only saw to it that his name was kept off the birth certificate, but Mary Barton's as well. Edward "Buzz" Barton's birth certificate inscribed Florence Grundhoefer Colt and her now new husband John Colt (an ex-felon) as Buzz's parents and within thirty days baby Edward "Buzz" Barton was carted off to Florida to be raised by Mary Barton's stepmother Florence Grundhoefer Colt who eventually would take another husband and become Florence Brangenberg.

I was hoping that Buzz would forget about his mother and Rita Hayworth and get on with his own life as he went off to Europe for several months. He wanted me to go along with him, but as I was knee deep in orchestration paper and working hard on a film score, trying to secure others, and composing concert music, I politely declined. However, upon Buzz's return to Los Angeles, he revealed to me that the real reason he wanted to meet with Rita Hayworth was because he had discovered over the years that supposedly Rita Hayworth, upon learning how contemptibly Mary Barton had been treated by Hartford (who was now seeing another woman in addition to dallying Mary Barton along), had introduced Mary Barton to another wealthy man who had become quite enamored with Mary and that they were planning to return to Los Angeles and get married in Las Vegas which (according to Buzz's deductions) sent Hartford into internal indignation whereby Hartford (in Buzz's mind) could have quite possibly choreographed his mother's suicide.

When I heard this, I remembered one of Hartford's friends informing me about how Hartford (while he attended Harvard University around 1931) had been investigated concerning the murder of a young girl in which one of Franklin D. Roosevelt's sons had been implicated and Hartford, supposedly had put up the major portion of the legal fees to legitimately extricate Roosevelt's son.

When Buzz reached maturity, he eventually obtained information and press clippings which he referred to several times during our dialogues summarizing his mother's reported suicide in September 1941 at her apartment in New York City. I had heard that Mary Barton wanted to regain custody of Buzz from her obviously Trust hungry exploitative stepmother who was using most of the income designed to support infant Buzz for her own personal use rather than baby Buzz. Mary Barton (by all accounts) was an active career minded and self sustaining individual when you consider that she had been working and supporting herself in her own apartment in Manhattan and Los Angeles since her teens until her untimely death. Furthermore, consider her personal life from the end of 1937: Mary Barton married divorced actor George De Normand who was involved in a bitter court dispute over custody of De Normand's seven year old daughter by his previous wife. Subsequently leaving him, Mary Barton worked in the chorus line at The Roxy Theater in New York City where Huntington Hartford bombarded her with flowers, offers, and late night telephone calls which eventually led to the breakup of Hartford's marriage with Mary Lee Epling. After Buzz was born 18 August 1938, Hartford tried to make financial resolutions with Mary Barton; however, she decided to wait until Hartford was divorced from Mary Lee Epling who was suing Hartford and who in turn had the dashing and handsome screen star Douglas Fairbanks Jr. waiting for her in the wings. After Hartford's divorce, Mary Barton realized that Hartford was not going to publicly recognize her or her son, so she settled with Hartford financially for herself and an initial trust for Buzz (with Mary Barton's stepmother as trustee), and according to Buzz, was preparing to go to California and marry this affluent man Rita Hayworth had introduced her to.

During this time, Hartford (through political connections) induced his way into the Coast Guard to fulfill his military duty, but still had enough leave time to keep in touch with Mary Barton and other girls.

The Sunday before Mary Barton's death in her Manhattan apartment, the club where Mary Barton was appearing maintained that she had told them that she would be leaving for California. The police said that she had been dead since Monday, but her body was not discovered until several days after that as the result of a series of unaccountable telephone calls from a man claiming to be Mary Barton's friend to the landlady relating to the fact that Mary Barton's apartment windows had been open. That Monday the landlady sent the superintendent of the apartment building to check on Mary Barton whom he found presumedly sound asleep in her bedroom and left. Three days later the unexplainable caller phoned again and beseechingly caused the landlady to go once more to Mary Barton's apartment where she found her dead amid strewn roses which according to the superintendent were not there the previous Monday. How the roses got into the room no one could explain.

One evening during 1966 Buzz and I were having dinner at The Aware Inn on Sunset Boulevard when the beautiful screen star Loretta Young walked in and seemed rather astonished when she noticed Buzz and stopped by our booth for a few minutes. I was equally surprised as Loretta Young floridly said to Buzz, "Why, hello. How are you?" Buzz responded politely and introduced me to Loretta Young who when she flashed her sparkling eyes and ravishing smile was (to my great amazement) still wearing her orthodontic retainers at approximately age fifty-three. After Loretta Young left our table, I told Buzz the amusing story of how several years before at age twenty-two in Paris France I broke my own lower orthodontic retainer which I had put in my left shirt pocket as I impatiently wagered my friends that I could beat them up to the restaurant near the top of the Eifel Tower by racing up the confined spiral steel staircase while they wasted their time waiting for the interminably slow elevator. As I bolted up the Eiffel Tower stairs, somewhere near the apex a young lady who was descending slipped and as I caught her to prevent her fall, she tumbled into my arms and cracked my lower retainer which I had to air mail back to my orthodontist in Dallas, Texas for repair. I was upset at my stupidity even though I won the useless bet.

Not wanting to bring up Rita Hayworth's name as it had been many months since Buzz had asked me if I had been working on an introduction, I thought to myself, 'If Buzz knows Loretta Young, then why doesn't he ask her to present him to someone who could arrange an overture to Rita Hayworth?'

As we ate our meal, Buzz divulged that he had met Loretta Young when he was fourteen years old at a particularly depressing period in his life. Hartford was covertly selling the beautiful house where Buzz had been brought up out from under him and his step-grandmother to Loretta Young in August 1952; eventually moving Buzz and his step-grandmother (Mrs. Brangenberg) and her family to a Los Angeles suburban tract home somewhere in Westchester. Hartford had purchased the house at 1308 Flores (the corner of Flores and Fountain Avenue) in February of 1949 (listing his secretary Agnes Hardecker as owner) in order to be within proximity of Buzz, and had it sold to Loretta Young August 1952 when he needed some quick liquid capital. Loretta Young had her husband at that time (Tom Lewis) listed as the purchaser.

Several days after meeting Loretta Young, Buzz and I were driving along Fountain Avenue when he suddenly turned up Flores, parked the car directly in front of 1308 and said, "This is where I used to live when I was growing up. Boy, do I have a lot of memories about this place. I wonder who lives here now?" Buzz asked as he got out of his Jaguar.

"What the hell are you doing?" I asked. "Let's get going," I said.

"Phillip, you think I'm crazy, don't you," he grinned.

I just shook my head from side to side.

"Come on," Buzz said. "I just want you to see where I used to live, that's all."

"What's the point of all this?" I asked. "Who cares where you used to live? Even Loretta Young doesn't live here anymore. Now, if Loretta Young still lived here and was home and she invited us in for tea, that would be different. That would be a lot different," I said. "I'd really like that."

I couldn't believe what Buzz was doing because it was so uncharacteristic of him as he walked up to the front door, rang the bell and explained to the present owners how he had grown up in this house and if they wouldn't mind, he would like to come inside and see it again. The owners said that they would mind, but informed Buzz that he could walk around the outside grounds, if he wished. To conciliate, I walked about the back yard with Buzz where he showed me where he used to play basketball with his friends and then I finally persuaded Buzz to leave.

During this period I usually accompanied Buzz throughout the local Hollywood and Beverly Hills night spots mainly on weekends as I was too immersed with my music career during the week.

One evening at The Daisy I became reacquainted with Anthony Newley whom I had met a few years previously in New York City through my good friend Broadway show musical conductor Milton Rosenstock. Milton had suggested that I come and see Newley's novel musical immediately (whose title had so intrigued me) because they had received terrible reviews, and attendance had been less than fifty percent and most assuredly the show would close within a few weeks. The name of the musical which had fascinated me (because it sometimes expressed my sociological sentiments) was *Stop The World I Want To Get Off*. I saw it and Milton Rosenstock asked me afterward to have dinner at Sardi's with him, Anthony Newley and his beauteous young wife British actress Joan Collins. I thought the revue was excellent and Milton invited me a few more times until word of mouth overcame the apathetic press and made it an almost impossible ticket to get. *Stop The World I Want To*

Get Off ran for several years on Broadway.

Buzz and I also used to frequent P.J.'s on the north west corner of Santa Monica Boulevard and Crescent Heights in West Hollywood. P.J.'s had a disco in the rear with usually a multitudinous number of alluring girls rotating on the dance floor to the Rolling Stones blaring "I can't get no satisfaction" and in the front room a stellar latino jazz pianist by the name of Eddie Cano played everything from Cole Porter to Antonio Carlos Jobim.

One hot summer day while Buzz and I were at the beach in Malibu, Buzz told me an amusing story about how he had been personally visited at the Black Fox Military Academy in Los Angeles (where he went to school for a while) by none other than dashing screen star Errol Flynn. Buzz grasped that Hartford had set up the whole scenario not only to impress Buzz, but more importantly, to influence Buzz's peers and teachers at Black Fox. Buzz remembered how Errol Flynn said to him while they were alone, "Now, you wouldn't really want to sue your father and bring all this nasty business to the attention of the public, now, would you, Buzz?"

With the prodding and legal assistance of Buzz's maternal step-grandmother (now Florence Barton Brangenberg who was 60 at that time), when Buzz became 17 years of age, he brought suit against Hartford in November of 1955, and again in December of 1955. Hartford was out of California for good and with his money and the fact that he had already financially provided handsomely for Buzz, Hartford was to successfully avoid subpoenas, extradition and even negative press. From 1949 Hartford had not been paying too much attention to Buzz largely due to Hartford's rivalry pursuit in the affections for and marriage to the beautiful young actress Marjorie Steele who was to bear Hartford daughter Cathy in 1950 and son John "Jackie" in 1953. Hartford's main rivalry was not really with, as commonly thought, Sydney Chaplin (Charlie Chaplin's son), but with Marjorie Steele's own adoring father who had been so totally emasculated all of his life by Marjorie's mother that he devoted the majority of his energy to lovingly raising his daughters. Friends of Marjorie Steele informed me of how much Marjorie idolized her father (Marjorie's father loved all of his daughters deeply, but Marjorie was his favorite) and that the marriage to Huntington Hartford was of great disappointment to Marjorie's father despite the fact that Hartford bought and gave Mr. Steele a ranch in California which eventually became the ultimate psychological castration prompting Marjorie's father to finally commit suicide. After her father's self-destruction, Marjorie's relationship with Hartford began to deteriorate and their marriage crumbled into divorce.

The first suit which Buzz filed and which was never settled was designed to compel Hartford (then 44) to acknowledge the paternity of Edward "Buzz" Barton. The suit was dismissed without explanation in order that a new suit could be filed in which the like issue of Buzz's futile life long attempts to have his rightful paternal name given to him be settled even though he expressed to me on many occasions that he really did not want anyone to know that Huntington Hartford was his biological father.

This may seem strange, but I was a witness to an event which supports that contention. Buzz and I were sitting at Jack Hansen's (the owner of The Daisy private club and Jax clothing stores) personal table one evening at The Daisy when one of his security guards came to the area and said to Jack Hansen, "A young gentlemen is at the door claiming to be Huntington Hartford's son and wants to be admitted."

Buzz and I quickly glanced at and away from each other as Jack said, "Phillip, you and Buzz know Huntington Hartford, don't you?"

"Yeah, we know him and we know his son," we both said as a matter of fact. "I believe his son is living in Europe now," I added.

Jack Hansen said, "Would you both please go to the door and look through the peep-hole and let me know if it's him?"

"Sure, Jack. Yes, of course," we both said as we started to the door.

"Do you believe this shit?" Buzz asked as soon as we got out of hearing range. "I want to see the fucking ass hole who would ever want to be Huntington Hartford's son."

We both took a look through the peek-out to keep up appearances. "No, that's not him." I said to the security guard who was dressed in black tie and evening wear. "This guy is too good looking. Hartford's son looks like a mole."

"Yeah," laughed Buzz. "This guy is absolutely not Hartford's son. He doesn't even resemble him."

During this time I met an attractive former model and Vassar graduate turned novelist by the name of Jeanne Rejaunier who lived not far from me. Jeanne had known Hartford, and to some extent Buzz (largely through our conversations), and she knew me casually from accompanying me to a few dinners and a piano recital which my last teacher, Gyorgy Sandor, gave in Los Angeles. Jeanne had an abundance of intelligence and beauty, but rather poor judgment when you consider that she admitted to me that several years before she had attended a Canadian hospital with movie star Cary Grant where they both were voluntarily strapped into beds and given LSD by practicing psychiatrists. Jeanne would sometime come over to my apartment with portions of her novel in progress imploring me to read them; after which I would usually utter, "Wait a minute is this character supposed to be me?" She would laugh and say, "Are you going to sue me?" "No," I remember responding, "because I would never do or say such things." In addition to me, Jeanne also had portions of Buzz and Hartford prototypes in her soap story. A couple of her books were published: *The Beauty Trap* and *The Motion & The Act* both of which I never read.

Toward the summer of 1966 (immediately after finishing the music score to Universal's *And Now Miguel*) Buzz asked me again to go along with him to Europe; however, I was still compelled to decline because I was intensively working on my symphonic compositions and trying to acquire another film scoring assignment.

Buzz wanted me to give him music lessons just before he departed to ascertain whether or not I felt he had enough musical talent to become a professional musician. I laughed. "Why the hell would you ever want to become a professional musician?" I asked. "I certainly would never suggest that life to anyone in our society the way it is; but with your trust fund, you can do just about anything you please without any pressure. So while you're in Europe why not go to a music school or private teacher and see if you would like it for your own appreciation and enjoyment?"

On other occasions when Buzz (now 27 years old) would ask me what I thought he should do with his life, I would invariably say, "Look, Buzz, you'll have to decide that for yourself. I'm a composer conductor pianist. I was offered a position to go into the oil business a few years ago, but even though I realized I was turning down millions of dollars, I knew that I would not be happy unless I were composing and making important musical statements; in spite of the fact that I was totally cognizant of the financial and personal deprivations I'd be encountering. A person should go where their roots go; like a tree."

I assume the certain amount of publicity which I had been gaining coupled with major symphonic performances I was now receiving may have made Buzz feel professionally inadequate and purposeless in his life even though I would relay to him what my ex-tennis doubles partner Frederick von Sousten III (who had inherited millions by virtue of his great grandfather inventing that over-the-counter toxicant called aspirin) used to tell me when I was twenty after I would exclaim to Freddie,

"What are you going to do with your life? You can't just continue to play tennis and go to parties all the time. Jesus, Freddie, you're almost thirty years old now."

"Why not?" I remembered Frederick von Sousten III telling me with great disdain as we were practicing for another tennis match. "Working interferes with living."

Buzz returned later that year from Switzerland and eventually arranged for a heady Swiss girl to follow him to Los Angeles by the name of Herta. It was now obvious to me (especially after Buzz had asked me what I thought about the idea) that my friend (the most pleasant, kindest, generous of persons; a prince among gentlemen) was desperately searching for a true emotional attachment with the opposite sex which could genuinely assuage the life-long albeit intermittent ping-ponged rejection he had experienced as the result of having been Huntington Hartford's first born and never having known his biological mother.

"What difference does it make, Buzz, what I think about this girl, Herta, whom I've never met? It's what you think about her and what she thinks about you that counts. I'm not going to be having a relationship with her, you are."

Although Buzz was not one to dwell fretfully upon his childhood or the barrier to his rightful name, periodically during our friendship, mostly on isolated occasions, I would say, "Look Barton, things could have been a lot better for you, I know. You could have been born a bastard in the ghetto with no mother, no father, no education, and no trust fund; not to mention, no memberships to these exclusive Beverly Hills private clubs, no attractive girl friends and having to get up five o'clock every morning and go to work in a sweat shop for two dollars an hour."

Usually, after I would say something like that, we'd have a good laugh and I would reiterate that he actually did not recognize how lucky he had been to never have to worry about earning a living, being responsible for his mother, and not to have known his father (one of the richest men in the world at that time) well enough to realize how fortunate he was to have never been reared by him.

After Herta had arrived, Buzz informed me that he had made a mistake in thinking he was actually romantically inclined toward her, but he said, "I love her like a sister and I'll continue to support her until she can become independent."

Subsequently, Buzz moved into another spacious apartment in Brentwood just West of Barrington on Sunset Boulevard with a nice sauna. He was excited about a young nineteen year old pretty model whom he had met in the neighborhood and was about to have a date with that evening by the name of Erin Gray. The next afternoon while we were taking a sauna, Buzz said, "Erin Gray is one of the most beautiful girls I have ever met, but somehow we really didn't hit it off; but I told her about you and she said that she'd like to meet you."

That evening I called Erin Gray. She sounded absolutely dreamy over the telephone and I informed her that I had been invited this coming Friday for an early evening dinner at La Scala Restaurant in Beverly Hills and a symphony concert afterward at Royce Hall UCLA by my good acquaintance Jack Borman and his wife Fritzie. Erin said that she would love to go and I drove to her apartment that following Friday and picked her up in my new Ford Mustang. Buzz did not exaggerate; Erin Gray was extremely good-looking in addition to being immaculately groomed and dressed. I noticed at once that Erin Gray would eventually become a model because she seemed to have those wide eyed inwardly dazed, and somewhat petrified qualities of a department store mannequin. I attempted to put her at ease as we drove to La Scala Restaurant by telling her that my friends Jack and Fritzie Borman were quite youthful for being in their late sixties and were absolutely one of the rarest breed of unassuming super rich individuals I had ever known. "So Erin, please just relax and have a good time," I said.

"Oh, Erin; just one more thing," I added. "Fritzie usually wears a very large diamond ring, so please, whatever you do, please don't stare at her jewelry. It's real and it's paid for."

"What do they do?" Asked Erin.

"They don't have to do very much," I said, "because they own the Pennsylvania Life Insurance Company."

"They must have a lot of money," Erin Gray said in her stupefied manner.

"Well, yes, you might say that," I said. "But it never has affected them. I was in Jack's office last week just before he invited me to lunch where he took a call from a bank and loaned the bank twenty million dollars for the construction of a building."

"Wow," said Erin. "Twenty million dollars. I can't even imagine such an amount of money."

The dinner and conversation went along congenially and Erin (although broad eyed and mutely smiling) seemed less tense but still somewhat socially insecure. We were all sitting in a circular booth at La Scala Restaurant with Erin to my left, Fritzie to my right and Jack Borman (with his natural smile and handsomely tailored dark blue suit) to Fritzie's right.

During the pasta Erin (to my dismay) could not contain her gaze away from Fritzie's large diamond ring which was literally bigger than an oversized almond which caused Fritzie to kindly remark to Erin, "Dear, you seem to like my ring the way you keep looking at it. Would you like to hold it for a little while?"

I nearly choked on my pasta after Erin fondling Fritzie's diamond ring said, "Is it a real diamond?"

"Well, dear it better be," said Fritzie laughing, "or Jack will be very unhappy."

"But it's so large," Erin said. "I've never seen a diamond this large."

"Oh, I had one bigger than this," said Fritzie, "but a cat burglar stole it a couple of years ago from our top floor condominium at The Churchill. We never got it back. That burglar was smart because he only took that one ring and left everything else as it was. It was a week before I noticed that it was even gone."

During the concert Erin had trouble translating the open program on her lap even though it was in English. There was a soloist performing Beethoven's *Piano Concerto No. 1* as Erin whispered into my left ear, "What are they playing now?"

I pointed to her open program and whispered back, "Beethoven; *Piano Concerto Number One.*"

"Who's he?" Said Erin Gray.

At first, Ladies and Gentlemen of the Jury, I thought that this good-looking flesh robot was joking as I smiled at her; but Erin Gray was not smiling in return.

"Are you serious?" I quietly breathed.

"Yes," she confided having trouble pronouncing Beethoven's name. "Who's this Beethoven?"

"Sshhh," I said. "We'll discuss it later."

As I was driving Erin Gray home that evening, I asked her as courteously as I could, "Did you graduate from High School?"

"Yes," said Erin. "Last year."

"And you never learned who Beethoven was?" I asked.

"Look," said Erin as her latent Tom-Boy qualities began to surface. "I'm sorry. I'm not into your kind of music; I'm into rock and roll."

"Well, if you're into rock and roll, you should have at least known Chuck Berry's hit record *Roll Over Beethoven.*"

Erin Gray divulged that she had just signed a contact with The Ford

Agency in New York City and that she was confident that she was going to become a top model, and that she was very much in love with a boy who was going to marry her and that they planned to live happily ever after. I wished her the best, but suggested as tactfully as I could that perhaps she take a few minutes each day to expand her informative horizons as I'm sure that even Revlon would want their models to look as if they knew who Beethoven was.

The next morning I went over to Buzz's apartment. "Jesus Christ, Barton," I exclaimed as Buzz smoking a cigarette on his couch was laughing so hard he began to cough. "What the hell kind of ding-bat did you fix me up with last night? This girl is so uneducated, she not only couldn't follow the program, she didn't even know who the hell Ludwig van Beethoven was."

One evening as I was having dinner with Buzz at Cyrano's on Sunset Boulevard, I told him about my teenage and childhood friend Sylvia Plath (he had never heard of her, or her work) and the composition I wanted to do. I had just completed the music for Universal's *And Now Miguel*, and I was fortunately able to pay off debts and a bank loan, which had not left me with much ready cash; but as I intensely wished to compose *Four Songs for Soprano & Orchestra* for Sylvia Plath, I definitely did not want to do another motion picture score. As we ate and spoke, I recited some fragments of Sylvia's poetry from memory (which Buzz enjoyed) and he asked me how much money I would need to be able not to do another film score and stay home and create *Four Songs*. With the low cost of living then, I apprised Buzz that if he gave me $3,500 dollars over the next six months, I was sure that I could complete *Four Songs* within the next year, and although I had to dedicate this work in memory of Sylvia Plath, I would give him credit as Commissioned By Edward Barton. Buzz agreed, and if it had not been for his commission, one of my best and most important compositions would never have been written.

Buzz was not really an alcohol drinker, but I noticed that he had been imbibing more and that he had been smoking additionally which seemed to make him a trifle melancholy.

At times when we were together he would ask, "Phillip, if you had all the money you ever needed. What would you do?"

I told him that I would begin a music publishing and book publishing company which would disseminate all types and forms of quality literary and musical works. I would produce films which might influence society into a more peaceful and harmonious direction while still being filled with entertainment and action. I declared to Buzz that violence was altogether acceptable and permissible on screen as long as we kept it completely out of our society. I would build auditoriums of the future where everyone would have the best seat, and create my own symphony orchestra with players from all over the world and call it the United States International Orchestra. Not to mention instituting a Japanese Zen Macrobiotic Center and Restaurant in every major city of the world.

Buzz enjoyed my ideas and said that he wanted to form a production company which could financially implement these concepts and that the only way he could see doing it was to confront Huntington Hartford and demand that he, Buzz, (by virtue of being the first born) be legally entitled to the A & P fortune.

I did not laugh. However, I said, "Buzz, look, it's great to fantasize, but why don't you just forget about Hurlingham Bradford and forge your own way in life. By the time Hartford dies, the way he's pissing his fortune away from Paradox Island to Shoe Magazine, if you're next in line, all you'll probably receive will be a pile of debts, subpoenas and law suits."

I began to sense an ever growing dissatisfaction Buzz was now realizing within himself. He seemed to feel as if he had not prepared himself adequately for any valued course in life. Buzz also confided to me that he probably had been responsible for letting the personal friendship he had had with Wayne (whom he now disparagingly referred to as "the plumber's son") let Wayne exploit Buzz's income from his Trust against Buzz's better judgment. I also heard the same remarks from their mutual friend Larry.

I was now beginning to receive telephone calls from Wayne (whom Buzz had never brought around socially at all) and Herta informing me of what Buzz was doing, or what Buzz was not doing. Herta phoned and asked to see me privately at my apartment. "Why can't we just discuss what it is you wish to talk with me about over the telephone," I asked, "as I'm extremely busy with my work."

"No, I must see you in person," she said. "Please, if you are Buzz's friend, you'll see me. It won't take very long. But you must promise me that you will never tell Buzz."

I relented and Herta came to my apartment. She was quite high-strung and shaken, and almost near tears. I offered her some Mu tea to calm her as she began to unfold her story as to how she thought in Switzerland that Buzz truly loved her and wanted to marry her. Now that Buzz had moved Herta to Los Angeles, he had slowly distanced himself from her even though he was financially supporting her.

"Well, look," I said, "people change. We're in a world of change. You should accept whatever happens and try to agree with it and remain friends."

It seems that Herta did not wish to harmonize with the situation, but rather wanted me to convince Buzz to marry her.

I laughed.

"Why are you laughing?" She asked. "This is a serious matter."

"What can I do? I don't interfere with Buzz's life. He does what he wants; I do what I want."

"You have a lot of influence over him," Herta said. "He quotes you all of the time."

After awhile, I managed to persuade Herta that she should take up her romantic exacerbations and private matters directly with Buzz and not through me or anyone else.

Around the beginning of January 1967, Wayne called me saying that he was altogether troubled by Buzz's behavior because Buzz had spent close to $40,000 dollars the past month on just renting office space in Westwood, sending young girls whom he had accidentally met on Hawaiian vacations, and a number of other impetuous flighty expenditures, and would I go over to Buzz's apartment and "try and talk some sense into him."

I drove over to Buzz's apartment early that afternoon. It was a warm radiant day. The rooms were in a state of turmoil. "I'm in here, Phillip," said Buzz. Buzz was in his bedroom lying stretched out upon his disheveled bed neatly dressed in a white dress shirt and a pair of tan gabardine slacks with brown shoes. The windows and shades were wide open and the room was bright as day. Buzz was staring vacantly up at the ceiling and had two cigarettes burning simultaneously in his hands. It was obvious that his thoughts were millions of miles into infinity.

"Hi," I said casually as if nothing were wrong. "How are you doing?"

"Hmm," Buzz said laughing with his lips and mouth closed. "I'm just fine; ...just fine. I couldn't be better."

Even though Buzz appeared relaxed, his heart was beating so forcefully I could see it pulsating through his white shirt.

I suggested that he seriously consider giving up smoking, and Buzz said that he definitely wanted to; and I also proposed that he contemplate taking up Japanese Zen Macrobiotics. "Yeah, you're right, Phillip," Buzz said. "I should quit drinking and smoking and get on a better diet. I'm losing weight."

Wayne telephoned me a few more times and said that he had spoken with Hartford about Buzz's condition in hopes that Hartford would perhaps do something. "What the hell did you do that for?" I asked Wayne. "Hartford doesn't even pay any attention to his wife and the two children he's recognized and living with." It had been quite obvious to me that Wayne, although he was acquainted with Huntington Hartford, never actually knew him.

Wayne phoned me again wanting me to induce Buzz to check himself into the rest home called The Westwood. "Wayne, what are you talking about?" I said. "The Westwood is no rest home, it's an expensive psychiatric hospital where the likes of really disjointed people go like Judy Garland and Oscar Levant. I know Buzz is disturbed," I said, "but what he needs is to go to a Japanese Zen monastery in Kyoto, Japan and not the booby hatch in The Westwood."

Finally, the evening of 14 January 1967, Wayne called me from The Westwood and put Buzz on the receiver. It was the first time I had ever encountered Buzz intoxicated. Wayne legally could not have Buzz committed to The Westwood, Buzz would have to sign himself in and Wayne was having trouble convincing him to do that. So when Buzz came to the phone to see what I thought about the idea (even as muddled as he was Buzz still did not trust Wayne), I said, "Buzz, just do what Wayne says. A few days there at The Westwood will do you good. Just sign the forms and everything will be okay. Then after you're rested and get out, we'll get you on a good macrobiotic diet, and start you playing tennis and golf again, and go to the beach."

You must understand that Buzz was not the type of person to ever get extremely acrimonious no matter what the situation was unless he were physically assaulted as was the case a year earlier in Paris, France where actor Peter O'Toole at a private club (who was rather drunk and did not know Buzz) pushed Buzz off his bar stool attempting to get an introduction to Harold Lloyd who had accompanied Buzz to the club after which Buzz indignantly asked Peter O'Toole, "What did you do that for?" I understand that Peter O'Toole made some pejorative remarks and bulldozed Buzz again upon which Buzz hit Peter O'Toole and broke his nose with a stunned Orson Welles watching from the balcony and Harold Lloyd bewilderingly looking on. O'Toole was immediately ejected and permanently restricted from the club; and as the result of his injured nose, the multimillion dollar film production Peter O'Toole had been acting in with Audrey Hepburn, *How To Steal A Million*, had to be suspended until Peter O'Toole's nose sufficiently mended.

A couple of days later, Buzz telephoned me from The Westwood and was he angry. You might have thought that he had been illegally abducted into the military and was being shipped to war-torn Vietnam. After what Buzz disclosed was going on, perhaps he might have had a better chance of escaping the armed forces than getting released from The Westwood. Buzz informed me that he would phone again as soon as he could get permission and wanted me to come down there immediately and get him released.

The Westwood psychiatric hospital was located at 2112 South Barrington in West Los Angeles. The structure was originally the home of William Randolph Hearst's actress-mistress Marion Davies who bequeathed the property to UCLA. A group of wealthy doctors purchased the ownership from UCLA in 1960 and converted it into a psychiatric hospital and named it The Westwood.

The day after, Buzz called again and asked me to contact his assigned psychiatrist Dr. Ralph Obler who eventually was to become one of my lifelong friends. Dr. Obler did not want Buzz to have any visitors for the next two weeks in spite of the fact that Buzz was contacting me at every opportunity when rare communication privileges were being granted to him.

"Jesus Christ, Phillip," Buzz lamented over the telephone. "Will you please speak to Dr. Obler and come and get me out? These people down here are fucking crazy. They cry and moan all night long, and hallucinate in their sleep. I haven't had a decent night's sleep since I've been in here."

"Look," I said, "I've spoken with Dr. Obler and he said that the sooner you cooperate with the program and everyone down there, the sooner you'll get out.

"Well, fuck him and his chicken-shit programs. I'm not going out and mowing the lawn and raking-up leaves and working in the laundry room with all the money I'm paying to be in this fucking crazy house. I'm no janitor, or maid. It's bad enough that I have to make my own bed every morning."

Ladies and Gentlemen of the Jury, even though it was not a laughable matter, I was silently amused because I could see that The Westwood was, perhaps, giving my friend some benefit after all; in that it was quite obvious Buzz had realized he was surrounded by people most assuredly in far worse emotional and mental distress than himself.

"It's all god damned Wayne's fault," Buzz went on. "And the Doctor knows it, and I know it. I was tricked, doped and drugged by Wayne, into committing myself in here because I finally after seven years was breaking away from Wayne's influencing me on how I should spend my money and the plumber's son couldn't stand it."

I endeavored to settle Buzz and suggested that the only way to get out of The Westwood was to cooperate wholly with everyone and I informed him that I would visit him at the first opportunity Dr. Obler would allow me to. Buzz told me that as part of his psychiatric program he was assigned thirty minutes every day at the typewriter to express himself and that in addition to a short story he was writing, that he was typing an important letter to James (Jim) Taylor, Buzz's trust attorney which he wanted me to personally deliver.

Within about ten days Dr. Obler allowed Buzz to have me visit him. The Westwood from the periphery of the outer reception room and beyond looked perfectly appealing and peaceful, but as I was admitted into the security of the locked passageways within the inner sanctum it began to remind me of a top secret military installation.

Buzz was waiting for me in the interior reception room where he seemed elated to see me. He introduced me to a young teenage girl with long dark brown hair, in her mod jeans and brightly colored psychedelic T-shirt, chewing bubble gum and continually brushing her hair.

"This is Joanie Phony," said Buzz. "And this is my friend, Phillip."

"Hi," Joanie Phony said as she eyed me over, continuing to brush her hair and crunch her bubble gum.

"Hi, how are you?" I said.

"Joanie," Buzz asked, "when the hell are you going to change your clothes? You've been wearing that same damned outfit for two weeks now."

"Not until my fucking father let's me leave this place. I came in with these clothes and I'm keeping them on until I leave this place, regardless what he or the shrink says."

It seems that Joanie Phony had rebelled against her wealthy father socially and politically; having been arrested during a heated anti-Vietnam War confrontation with the Los Angeles Police Department in the riot at Pandora's Box (a popular teenage disco on the tiny island where Sunset Boulevard and Crescent Heights meet) which caused the club to be completely decimated and many protestors arrested and thrown in jail (including Joanie Phony), upon which her father had had her legally committed to the confines of The Westwood.

As Buzz took me on a guided tour of the ward (past amiable male orderlies both white and black dressed in their all white uniforms) he introduced me, in the cafeteria, to another one of his fellow patients, the actress Patty Duke. From the dialogue and the way Buzz and Patty Duke hugged each other, it was apparent they had become fast pals. I was to find out later that the reason Patty Duke had been in The Westwood at that time allegedly stemmed from the fact that she had been continuously working professionally as an actress ever since childhood and now as a young adult having taken her first extended vacation, she could not emotively cope with the inactivity.

Buzz then ushered me into his large room where he slept and which he shared with another male patient who was sitting on the side of his bed adjacent to Buzz's, perhaps in his late sixties and entirely catatonic from the way he was just staring intently at a distant portion of the floor with complete muscular immobility.

"Hi, Eddie," Buzz leaned over and yelled at his catatonic roommate. Then turning to me Buzz said rather softly, "He has a little trouble hearing, but he understands everything we're saying." Buzz paused and smiled laughingly at Eddie.

"How are you today, Eddie?" Buzz yelled. "It's a beautiful day today, isn't it?" Buzz paused again. "You know, you're looking much better, Eddie."

Eddie may have heard Buzz, but you would never have known it from Eddie's absolute catatonic gape: just continuing to stare at that distant portion of the floor, Eddie didn't move an eyelash.

Buzz began to lecture me (and catatonic Eddie) as I sat in a chair and reiterated what he wanted to do with his life; every once in a while, getting a hallucinatory confirmation from vacant immobile Eddie by saying, "Isn't that so, Eddie. You see, Phillip? Even Eddie, as fucked up as he is, knows I'm right." And, quite frankly, some of what Buzz ranted and raved about did make a great deal of sense (such as simplified and accelerated education; speed reading and comprehension; making quality films) even though his wanting to nominate film star Burt Lancaster for the Presidency of the United States, and propose marriage to *Lolita* film actress nymphet, Sue Lyon whom he had never met were in my candid estimation a little bizarre; although we must admit that Buzz's thoughts did predate another actor's ascension to the Presidency, and Sue Lyon did (I understand) a few years later exchange marriage vows with a convict in a penitentiary who kept writing her love letters while permanently incarcerated.

Buzz wanted to smoke so he took me to the smoking area of the internal reception room with a large round table and folding chairs.

"Buzz, you have to give up smoking," I said. "It's not good for you."

"I know," Buzz said. "You're absolutely right; and I will, just as soon as I get out of this place."

"And I can't believe that they serve you people white sugar, white bread and synthetic salt. The diet here is atrocious. Nobody will ever get mentally well in here unless there's a biological improvement."

As we continued to speak, Buzz seemed to think that I had some sort of influence with Dr. Obler and could get Buzz released from The Westwood before his tour of duty had been completed.

"Look, Buzz," I said, "I want you out of here as much as you do, but I can't do anything. I hardly know Dr. Obler."

"I'll give you fifteen hundred dollars," Buzz said, "if you can get me out of here."

"Come on, Buzz. Just do what they tell you to do and you'll be out of here within a few weeks."

"Two thousand five hundred dollars, Phillip. I know you can use the money."

Buzz paused. "Five thousand dollars. I'll write out the check just as soon as you get me out of here."

"Buzz," I said, "I'm your friend. You know you can't buy me."

We were both smiling at each other; and then in an instant Buzz darted out of his chair with such speed throwing all of his weight behind a forceful right hand coming toward my face that it was only my unusually fast athletic reflexes which caused Buzz to miss my head saving me from serious injury. "What the hell are you doing? I'm Phillip, your friend," I said ultimately trying to contain Buzz (who was exhibiting phenomenal strength for his slight size) as we both ended up grappling on the floor. Fortunately two tall muscular orderlies (one black and one white) saw by way of the observation windows what had happened and barged through the swinging doors and had a difficult time themselves restraining Buzz as he yelled at me, "Phillip Lambro, I'll fucking kill you if you don't get me out of this place."

Several days later, Buzz telephoned me as if nothing had previously happened and said in his normal behavior, "I've been thinking over what you said, Phillip, and I've told Dr. Obler that I'm going to be cooperative and do everything he wants me to do. I even went out in the back yard today and helped with raking the twigs and leaves, and picking up the trash."

Buzz made notable progress and I visited him again at The Westwood when I was allowed.

Around the middle of February, Dr. Obler apprised Buzz that if I would assume responsibility for him that he would let Buzz leave The Westwood for a Saturday morning Sunday evening liberty pass. I told Dr. Obler that I would presuppose accountability for him and Dr. Obler made me promise that Buzz would be in my attendance for the whole duration.

As soon as we were in the car Buzz said, "Phillip, I haven't had any sex in over two months. I know you promised Dr. Obler that I had to be in your company the entire time, but listen, I know this girl who really likes me and I want to spend the night with her."

I looked at Buzz. "Only if you promise and give me your word of honor that you won't touch a drop of alcohol, cut down on your cigarettes and be back at my apartment by noon tomorrow."

"I give you my word of honor," Buzz said. "I won't drink, I'll have as few cigarettes as I possibly can, and I'll be back at your apartment before noon."

"Okay," I said. "I'll take you to a small party a film director friend of mine is giving at his home tomorrow afternoon."

Buzz kept his word and was at my door thirty minutes before noon on Sunday.

I had been invited by a struggling up and coming motion picture writer-director named Francis Ford Coppola to a small afternoon gathering he was giving at his rented home in Mandeville Canyon, Brentwood. Francis Coppola had read a letter I had written to producer Phil Feldman which caused a delirium at the Seven Arts film studio offices in New York City where the personnel had made a number of photo copies and circulated them widely. Coppola contacted me while I had an office at Columbia Studios in Hollywood and told me how much he "admired my guts," and "wanted to meet me" when he returned to Hollywood.

I had been recommended by my then agent, Sy Marsh at the William Morris Agency, to score producer Phil Feldman's new off-beat comedy *You're A Big Boy Now* which had been written by Coppola and was to be his debut as a feature film director. Obviously, Feldman asked what my last assignment had been and Sy Marsh informed him that I had just finished the music for Universal's contemporary western *And Now Miguel* to splendid music reviews. At the Morris Agency one afternoon Sy Marsh notified me that Phil Feldman had run *And Now Miguel* and exclaimed to Sy Marsh, "This isn't the type of music I want. This is western music. This is sheep music. I want New York music."

Well, Ladies and Gentlemen of the Jury, when I heard that unenlightened remark, I dictated a letter which read, "Dear Mr. Feldman, I should like to apprise you of the fact that as I was scoring the music for Universal's *And Now Miguel*, I was not thinking about writing music for anything else except that motion picture; and most assuredly not your Manhattan comedy *You're A Big Boy Now*. As your career progresses, I certainly hope the criteria which you've applied to me as a composer is never applied to you as a producer because all you would be capable of producing would be Manhattan comedies on 42nd Street between Seventh and Eighth Avenues. Very truly yours, Phillip Lambro"

I particularly asked Buzz as a favor not to go into his eccentric political, romantic or motion picture rhetoric with the guests at Francis Coppola's assemblage as it might offend someone and cast a negative aspersion against me which, with all the invectives already in my account, I could hardly afford.

It was a small gathering. Francis seemed glad to see me and introduced me to everyone including his wife and two children who were wholly occupying and down to earth. The new film director William Friedkin was there bitching about the political tactics a director was forced to go through within the Hollywood Studio System in order to direct a feature film. I particularly remember fidgety William Friedkin who sat next to me if for no other reason than he accidentally spilled a little ketchup on my quality gabardine slacks and frantically endeavored to get someone to clean the spot.

The stage, film actor and comedian Robert Morse was there thoroughly congenial and beaming. I had always liked Robert Morse in *How To Succeed In Business Without Really Trying* and *A Funny Thing Happened On The Way To The Forum*.

Elizabeth Hartman the gifted actress who had shot to stardom in MGM's *A Patch Of Blue* was there sitting all alone in the center of a divan where behind her breathed a large bay window which looked out into the Mandeville Canyon foliage. After meeting her that afternoon, I was surprised that Francis had cast Elizabeth Hartman as the schizoid psychotic go-go dancer in his comedy *You're A Big Boy Now*. Comedy..? Francis Coppola, as tenacious as he was in the motion picture jungle, was never an indigenously humorous person. When I finally saw *You're A Big Boy Now* (I don't think I laughed once) only then did I fully appreciated the enormous ability which Elizabeth Hartman possessed as an actress: to play so convincingly an out of tune extroverted go-go dancer when in actuality, the genuine Elizabeth Hartman was so introvertedly shy completely startled me.

While the others remained downstairs, Francis Coppola took me upstairs to his writer's work room where he wanted to show me that he, too, had suffered from artistic discrimination and exploitation. "Seven Arts told me that if I ever wanted to direct *You're A Big Boy Now*, I had to help Gore Vidal with the screenplay for *Is Paris Burning*. Phillip, look at all these wonderful scenes I wrote for *Is Paris Burning* while I was defending myself from Gore Vidal's sexual advances in a hotel room in Paris."

"No kidding," I said.

"Yeah, but finally Gore got smart and left me alone in Paris to work while he went off to Greece to find some willing boys. I did all the work, and Gore Vidal got all the money and credit. Look at these great scenes never used," Francis said shaking his head dejectedly. "I argued with the producer Paul Graetz who told me, 'Young man, I was producing motion pictures before you were born; I know what the public wants.' So I told him, With all due respect, Sir, I'll be producing motion pictures after you die. I felt really bad," Francis went on. "He died the next week of a heart attack."

We went downstairs and joined the gathering. Buzz came up to me and said, "I thought there might be some girls here."

"What difference does it make," I said. "You're going back to The Westwood in several hours anyway; and besides you've already had your fling."

Buzz and I joined in a stand-up conversation William Friedkin, Robert Morse and Elizabeth Hartman were already engaged in. Finally, Robert Morse turned to Buzz and asked, "What kind of work do you do?"

"I'm in the process of formulating a motion picture production company," Buzz said. "And I'm making a third national party to draft Burt Lancaster for the Presidency of the United States."

I sighed and gave Buzz a quick negative glare.

Robert Morse's jaw dropped slightly as he partially smiled at Buzz with that incredulous and appealing countenance which he so hilariously used in all those Broadway comedies.

"You can't be serious," Friedkin said.

Elizabeth Hartman looked at Buzz and then quickly glanced at both Robert Morse and Friedkin, and fractionally smiled.

Buzz, realizing that I was a little more than unsettled by what he was saying, shifted the theme toward explaining his other intended company, Theory Dynamics (which he knew I approved of) based upon accelerated comprehension in education which Francis Coppola (who now joined us) and Elizabeth Hartman thought was a good idea, but which Robert Morse and William Friedkin seemed politely ambivalent about.

Dr. Obler released Buzz from The Westwood 24 February 1967; however, Buzz was required to have psychiatric visits with Dr. Obler at his private office from 27 February 1967 until Buzz quit 24 March 1967.

Buzz rented expensive offices in Westwood and asked me to peruse them. As soon as I examined the blank offices with its nude furniture, desks and walls, I endeavored to restrain myself from laughing in front of Buzz and Larry which agitated Buzz.

"Now, what's wrong with this?" Buzz asked in frustration.

"Nothing's wrong with the office," I said. "But before you have offices, you have to have something of value coming out of them. You, Wayne and Larry have always been more interested in the frame rather than the picture. These offices are the frame, but where is the portrait?"

As disturbed as Buzz was, he admittedly saw my point and soon thereafter terminated the lease.

I was hard at work composing *Four Songs for Soprano & Orchestra* and was pleased with what I was accomplishing; thanks to Buzz's commission.

On the weekends and occasionally during the week, I continued to accompany Buzz to the preferred nightspots of the time: the Luau and The Daisy in Beverly Hills with all their supposedly beautiful people; The Whisky-A-Go-Go where famous athletes to British film star Laurence Harvey slightly inebriated (who tried to kiss Buzz) being followed by wealthy Joan Cohn and her girlfriend came to dance, watch the Go-Go dancers, and listen to Johnny Rivers and his rock band sing *Memphis, Tennessee* to "Let the Midnight Special shine its light on you; Let the Midnight Special shine its ever-lovin' light on you."

One Friday night at The Whisky-A-Go-Go, a young alluring dark haired girl dressed up as an American Indian pursued me and indicated right in front of Buzz that she wanted to go home with me that evening. Edward "Buzz" Barton was inherently never a pretentious, narcissistic or jealous individual; if a girl did not particularly care for him, Buzz always, in a gentlemanly fashion, accepted it; which also held true for me. However, since Buzz did not have the music career which I had, and circulated and socialized more often than I did, he naturally had many more lady friends following him than I ever did. Where Buzz might have had two girls chasing him a month, I was fortunate to have had two a year. Buzz seemed to be enjoying himself that evening, but I observed that he began smoking more and having a few too many alcoholic beverages again. About an hour afterward, the attractive dark haired girl came up to me virtually near tears saying, "Is that guy really your friend?"

"You mean Buzz?" I asked.

"Yes," she said.

"Yes, he's one of my best friends."

"He's not a friend."

"What do you mean?"

"Do you know what he said about you?"

I shrugged as I noticed Buzz watching us from the other side of The Whisky-A-Go-Go dance floor (like a little boy who had just been caught raiding the cookie jar) with all the strobe lights pulsating to the music and undulating dancers.

"He told me, Don't go home with Phillip, he's gay; you come home with me."

I laughed.

"It's not funny," she said. "That's a terrible thing for a friend to say."

"You have to understand Buzz has been having some deep rooted emotional problems recently which stem from a whole life of rejection. He's had a breakdown and just got out of a rest home. He didn't mean what he said. He couldn't help it," I said.

"You're not gay are you?" She asked.

"If I were, I wouldn't be having the trouble I've always had in my concert music career, I can tell you that."

Buzz again tried to prevail upon the girl to go home with him until she became quite indignant and stayed away from the both of us. Buzz came over to me and said, "Phillip, I really like that girl in the Indian dress. I know she likes you, but convince her to go home with me, will you?"

I just glanced at Buzz then pretended to divert my attention to the dancers on the disco floor.

"Come on," said Buzz. "You always get the girls."

"I always get the girls?" I asked. "Look, Barton, you're the one with the Trust Fund, the Jaguar, and all the fucking time in the world to pursue your aimless interests, with girls after you all the time. I'm just a 1967 version of a struggling Mozart trying to contribute music and earn a living from my apartment on Fairfax Avenue."

Buzz went over to the maiden in the American Indian dress and made one last futile attempt; then failing, left The Whisky-A-Go-Go without even saying goodbye to me.

The girl in the Indian dress asked me to drive her home. She was extremely sensitive and had been distraught by what had happened; not only for me, but for Buzz as well, especially after I (sitting with her in my car for over two hours) had explained to her what Buzz had been through in his life and how, actually, he was essentially a worthwhile person in an emotionally rundown state. She kissed me good night and I went home.

The next afternoon Buzz called me as if nothing had happened. I told him that I thought it would be best if we did not see each other for a while, and made one last desperate attempt to persuade Buzz to forget about trying to reconstruct a mother whom he never knew, forget his comatose father Huntington Hartford, and since Buzz wanted to make a great deal of money on his own, to change his lifestyle, go out and get a berth with an investment firm, make millions of dollars and completely ignore his father. I wished Buzz the best.

About five months had passed (it was either the last week in October 1967 or the first week of November 1967) and my telephone rang early one evening as I was lying down in silence next to my grand piano after having had another productive day with my *Four Songs for Soprano & Orchestra*.

"Hello..?" I said.

"Phillip, do you know who this is?"

"Yes, of course," I said. "Buzz..."

"That's right," Buzz chuckled. "How are you?"

"I'm fine," I said. "More importantly, how are you? You sound so far away; where are you?"

"I'm fine," Buzz said. "I'm in New York City."

"I hope you're working on Wall Street, making millions of dollars and have found a nice sexy girl," I said.

Buzz laughed then paused for a long moment. From his demeanor and the tone of his voice, he seemed like the normal Buzz I had remembered before The Westwood.

"Hello..?" I said.

"I'm still here," Buzz said. "Listen, I want you to do a very important favor for me, Phillip."

"What's that?" I asked. "Loan you fifty dollars?"

"No," Buzz ever so slightly laughed, "it's more important than that."

"What is it?" I asked.

"I want you to forgive me."

"For what?" I asked again.

He sighed. "I did a terrible thing that night against you at The Whisky-A-Go-Go with that girl," Buzz said, "and I want you to forgive me."

I laughed.

"No, it's very important to me that you forgive me," Buzz said.

"Of course, I forgive you, Buzz," I said.

"You do forgive me," Buzz said again.

"Yes," I chuckled slightly, "I forgive you."

Buzz let out a big sigh of relief.

"Where are you staying?" I asked.

"The Beekman," Buzz replied.

"Why the hell are you staying there?" I asked as if I didn't know.

"Look," Buzz said, "I'm the first born from Huntington Hartford and I'm going to get my name and all the money that goes with it so that we can do all those great humanitarian things you've always wanted to do."

For more than the next hour that we spoke, I endeavored to prompt Buzz to forget about my altruistic visionary plans because as I explained to him even though our society needed and was ready for a new utopian orderly way of life (provided we controlled our population and did away with the concept of money), the unenlightened primitive governmental and political leaders our planet had would make this type of society impossible to achieve.

Twice more during our lengthy conversation, Buzz interjected, "Now, you do forgive me, don't you, Phillip?" To which I quickly responded, "Yes, of course; will you forget about that?"

"Maybe you're right, Phillip." Buzz finally said. "Barton is a good name, and I should forget about Hunt and just forge my own way in life."

We eventually said goodbye to each other and Buzz said that he would call me again and that we would see each other soon; adding, "You do forgive me, Phillip."

"Will you please stop with this forgiveness Odyssey?" I asked. "How many times do I have to tell you? Yes!"

We both laughed and ultimately hung up the telephones.

A moment later, as I reclined on my Japanese futon a telepathic thought hit me with overpowering force. "Oh, my god," I said to myself. My brain echoing, immediately replayed the scene where Buzz and I were in the Swedish Sauna a few years earlier. It was as if we were there again.

"How did Hemingway die?" Buzz asked.

"The same way as his father did, I understand," I said.

"How was that?"

"He put his affairs in order, went upstairs and put a favorite shotgun into his mouth and blew his brains out."

"Wow," said Buzz. "What a fucking way to go. Can you imagine that? Putting a shotgun to your mouth and pulling the trigger? Man, that must have taken a lot of guts." Buzz laughed. "Well, maybe someday when the going get's too tough, that's how I'll go."

"Oh, no, Buzz," I said to myself. "That was why you kept asking for my forgiveness."

I immediately tried to call Buzz back. There was no Edward Barton registered at The Beekman. "Do you have a Buzz Barton? An Edward Colt?" I asked. The desk clerk at The Beekman informed me that no one by those names was registered.

I phoned Wayne who gave me a list of all of Buzz's other known legal names and aliases. I called every hotel I knew in New York City where I thought Buzz might be staying with positively no results.

I found myself doing absolutely the last thing I wished: telephoning Huntington Hartford. I had not spoken with Hartford in over a year largely due to (unbeknown to Buzz) several benign long distance arguments I had had with Hartford over his not, at the very least, recognizing Buzz legitimately as his son and giving him his rightful name. I reached Hartford at home.

"Hunt, Buzz telephoned me yesterday evening and I'm worried about him."

"Yeah," said Hartford in that lethargic low tone of his. "I know; he's been calling me, too."

"Do you know where he is?" I asked.

"No, I don't," Hartford said.

"Can you find out for me?"

"When I hear from him, I'll tell him to call you."

"Hunt, I'm afraid Buzz is going to do something drastic."

"No, don't worry. He'll be calling me within a few days. Everything will be okay. Don't worry."

"Look, Hunt, please," I said. "You can get Buzz a job on Wall Street. He's an intelligent young gentleman. You'll be proud of him. All he wants is his name; is that too much to ask? His name is Edward Hartford. Just give him the god damned name and recognize him. What's so difficult about that?"

"When I hear from Buzz, I'll tell him to call you," Hartford said.

"Hunt, I have this awful premonition because he asked me several times to forgive him about some inconsequential thing."

"It'll be alright," Hartford said. "How's everything else?"

I could not imagine how Hartford could ask me that. "Hunt, unless we get to Buzz right away something terrible is going to happen to him; I know it, and if it does it'll be on your conscience."

"Don't worry," Hartford said and we hung up.

Within a few days I received telephone calls from a TV news anchor, a newspaper reporter and Wayne practically simultaneously recounting how Buzz had blown his brains out in a rented room at the Hotel Fourteen. I had been to the Hotel Fourteen once in 1960 while I was working for G. Schirmer and Leonard Bernstein to endeavor to persuade Johnny Mathis who was staying there while performing at The Copa to record some of Bernstein's songs from West Side Story. It seems that Buzz had met with Hartford for lunch and the maitre d' overheard Buzz demand getting up, "Are you, or are you not going to give me my name?" To which Hartford was described as saying, "No, never." And Buzz throwing his napkin down on the table, turned and stormed out of the restaurant. I asked the media not to use my name as I had nothing to say except that I had lost a good friend and comrade with whom I had had some fun times. I understand that Buzz left a short letter to the effect that life was just too difficult for him to endure. In it he stated that he wanted Herta to have the $500 dollars cash in his wallet, and to be sure that the piano he gave me was legally mine.

I wrote a castigating reprimand to Hartford who responded with a letter to me in his own illegible handwriting where, perhaps, the only thing of value was contained in his first sentence: "Dear Phillip-- If death can do any good whatever in the midst of all the sorrow it leaves behind, is it not to make us a little kinder to one another?" Too bad Hartford didn't follow his own advice.

I contacted Dr. Ralph Obler who was saddened by the news.

Wayne called me several weeks later to inform me that he and Herta were getting married.

Several months afterward while going down the elevator of the new Hollywood private club The Factory, there was Patty Duke in the company of several formal elite, looking as if she were ready to be photographed for the cover of Vogue in her dark evening gown, expensive jewels, up-swirled dark blonde hair and painted face.

"Oh, hello," she sang. "How are you?"

"Fine," I said. Then after a slight pause I added, "You remember,

Buzz."

"Buzz..?" Patty Duke said quizzically.

"Edward Barton..? Buzz..?"

"I'm afraid I don't remember him," she said.

Had Patty Duke not been in the companionship of such a cadre of gentility, I probably would have said, 'Don't you remember when you were in the crazy ward of The Westwood? Your good pal, Buzz?' But I could not say that, so I did the next best thing.

"Buzz passed away a few months ago," I said.

"Oh, that's too bad," said Patty Duke. "I wish I had known him."

CLOSE ENCOUNTERS OF THE WORST KIND

It was November 1965 in Hollywood, California. I remember it distinctly as it rained blessedly for twenty days that month, and even though the population bomb was loudly metering, it had not yet mushroomed and one could still avoid the interminable Hollywood and Ventura Freeway traffic congestion if you did not drive on them from 8 to 9 a.m. and between 5:30 to 6:30 p.m.

I was completing my music score to *And Now Miguel* at Universal Studios and was assisting the competent and seasoned sound engineers with the transferring of music onto the synchronized dubbing tracks of voice and sound effects (a long and tedious job under the best of circumstances) but unfortunately with our producer, Robert Radnitz, who was struggling to play motion picture dictator, (incidentally, I have yet to meet the actual director of that picture to this day) the task grew many times longer and more arduous because of Robert Radnitz's inability to generally listen to his sound technicians and your humble Court Composer and make correct dubbing decisions in the monstrous Dubbing Room One: a large screen theater with dubbing and recording consoles at the rear and completely without the rows of seats on the entirely flat carpeted floor which (while waiting for the next determination and take) I would sometimes run around, or play baseball catch with an editor to get a little exercise.

In order to avoid my eyes and ears from becoming overtaxed and stale, I would inevitably take extra long lunch hours (usually an hour and one half) and go over to a nearby Sound Stage where Paul Newman and Julie Andrews (if you can imagine such a screen combination) were filming the even more interminable Alfred Hitchcock motion picture *Torn Curtain* which, after having seen some of the filmed portions of the daily rushes, I affectionately nicknamed *Torn Turkey*. My nickname seemed to have stuck with some of the Universal technicians as they all, in time, also referred to this 1966 production as *Torn Turkey*.

There was an attractive young lady (Julie Andrews' stand-in) whom I met on the Torn Turkey set and eventually asked for a dinner date which she politely refused after she found out that I was only a composer-conductor instead of the rising Irving Thalberg producer-tycoon she had thought I was. Anyway, I found the "stand-in" more interesting than Julie Andrews; especially, after I had witnessed how difficult it was for Ms. Andrews (even with blonde hair) to convincingly fall in love with Paul Newman on screen. Newman seemed a little bit more persuasive, but one was also hard pressed to imagine Paul Newman's performance as a Nobel Prize atomic space scientist. Consequently, it gave me some daily semblance of relief to trade the insanity of *And Now Miguel* with the banality of *Torn Curtain*. Although, there was this extraordinary Californian actress by the name of Carolyn Conwell (who played the East German Peasant Woman) who was so authentic with her German accent that I was totally astounded when she told me in her natural unaccented American speech that she was from the San Fernando Valley. Also, there was a German character actor by the name of Wolfgang Kieling whom Hitchcock imported to play the gum chewing leather jacketed villainous East German Agent who I was astonished to find out spoke almost no English and had memorized most of his dialogue entirely by phonetics. Away from his character, he was a kind gentleman who on the set sat patiently in his chair reading his German newspapers. And, as I was to find out during my Hollywood tenure (confirmed by Jeff Sparks at the UN), it always seemed to me, with very few exceptions, that the movie villains in real life were genuinely the nicest of people, while the heroes and the supposedly "nice" people on screen were in actuality the nastiest of individuals with the least consideration for others.

I used to occasionally see Alfred Hitchcock in his limousine and also waddling around the lot during that time. In fact, since I had composed and conducted the music for the forgettable Joseph E. Levine, Embassy Pictures release *Git!* (December 1964), one of the editors on that picture had been Doug Robertson a masterful Canadian-American technician who had worked for the celebrated English director Sir Carol Reed and who had introduced me (by way of several charming dinners at his home) to his British wife of many years, Peggy Robertson, who was Alfred Hitchcock's Executive Secretary, and (no joke) "Right Hand Man." Doug and Peggy had met in an underground London World War II bomb shelter during a Luftwaffe air raid. Peggy Robertson had been with Hitchcock since his early London years and it was rather obvious (after I got to know Doug and her) that Hitchcock relied eminently upon Peggy's judgment. I was at Doug and Peggy Robertson's home several times when in the middle of dinner Hitchcock would call her for an impromptu telephone discussion. Doug revealed to me that Hitchcock even called during the middle of the night on numerous occasions over the years interrupting the Robertson's marital sex life for conference calls.

At the first dinner gathering Doug and Peggy Robertson invited me to, there was a married couple about my age by the name of Peter and Polly Bogdanovich; the famous Russian prima ballerina and actress Tamara

Toumanova and her mother "Mama" Toumanova; and Mary Tomasini (the former actress Mary Brian) the shyly charming and tearful wife of the famed late Hitchcock editor George Tomasini who had just passed away a few weeks earlier from a massive heart attack at only 55 years of age. George Tomasini had been working on Otto Preminger's In Harm's Way and from what I learned from friends of mine who had worked for Otto Preminger, I'm sure that Preminger's overbearing and explosively harsh personality had hastened any cardiovascular or arteriosclerotic condition which George Tomasini may have possessed.

After I became familiar with Alfred Hitchcock's work on *Torn Curtain* (having as a youngster attended all of his previous films) and discovering some of the inner sanctum mainly from Doug Robertson, as Peggy told me almost nothing about Hitchcock's personal and private life (which was a lot for Peggy Robertson; as Doug used to declare, "Why hell, Phillip, I'm her husband and she tells me damned little.") it was obvious to those who knew, that when Alfred Hitchcock's masterful film editor George Tomasini died 22 November 1964 (he had edited all of Hitchcock's pictures), the successful box-office Alfred Hitchcock had perished with him. Hitchcock's many subsequent films after *The Birds* and *Marnie* never were as prosperous, but since Hitchcock owned such a massive block of MCA stock, and had become fabulously wealthy, he was powerful enough to do whatever he wanted to do within the motion picture medium.

I also noticed from *Torn Curtain* that Alfred Hitchcock was not actually a hands-on-the-set director; as he delegated everything to a number of subordinates and seemed to direct the entire production from his bed, easy chair, desk, and telephone before waddling on to the set where he would even instruct a secondary to yell, "Action!"

I recall one scene in particular where the friendly German character actor Wolfgang Kieling (the gum chewing leather jacketed villainous secret police agent) having followed Paul Newman to Carolyn Conwell's German farmhouse was trying to use the telephone and where a little wet cement and the cement bag was supposed to miss The Agent, and hit the telephone, and after special effects and the entire film crew had worked everything out all morning for this sequence, and I watched Hitchcock (just before lunch) waddle up beside the Panavision camera like an aging beached Sea Lion, give the signal for someone to yell, "Action!" how the wet cement and wet bag missed the telephone entirely and hit the poor German character actor squarely in the face. The mild mannered Wolfgang stayed absolutely still and did not complain at all, as Alfred

Hitchcock said (after a lengthy pause) in that calm basso profundo, "That will never do... Clean him up." Whereby, Hitchcock ambulated off the set and back to his office. Incidentally, having visited Peggy Robertson several times in the Hitchcock bungalow offices, it was interesting to note that Hitchcock's offices were not like offices at all; they were plushly decorated living room quarters used as offices.

One afternoon in Dubbing Room One (as we waited for Radnitz to return from lunch) I was having some fun with the sound technicians who in addition to lamenting over *And Now Miguel* were now also working on *Torn Curtain*. Well, the doors were open and my back was to the doors, all the lights were on, and there I was ascribing amusing incidents pertaining to *Torn Curtain* as *Torn Turkey* and we were chuckling until I noticed that all of the technicians who were facing me had abruptly stopped laughing. As I turned around there was the deadpan rotund Alfred Hitchcock next to Peggy Robertson five feet directly in front of me.

"Hello, Phillip," said Peggy Robertson. "How are you?"

"Peggy," I exclaimed. "Fine. How are you; and how is Doug?"

"We're all fine," she said. "We'll have to get together again soon."

Since I had never been introduced to Alfred Hitchcock, I carried on this brief colloquy with Peggy Robertson as if Alfred Hitchcock were not there. Peggy also did not introduce me to Hitchcock who just stared at me. They were looking for a particular soundman who was not in Dubbing Room One.

As Hitchcock left the room slowly with Peggy Robertson, we could all hear him say in that low monotone of his, "Who is that dark young Italian looking gentleman you were speaking with?"

"Oh, that is Phillip Lambro. He's a very talented composer who is doing the score for *And Now Miguel*."

"Oh, I see," said Hitchcock.

I remember how we were all wondering if the illustrious Alfred Hitchcock had heard us referring to his 50th major motion picture in progress as *Torn Turkey*.

Peggy Robertson told me an amusing story one day about a letter which Alfred Hitchcock had received from a dismayed parent. The father wrote to Alfred Hitchcock saying, "Dear Mr. Hitchcock, When my teenage daughter saw the film *Diabolique* she vowed that she would never again use a bathtub. Now she has seen your motion picture *Psycho* and she refuses to take a shower. What should I do?" Peggy Robertson said that Hitchcock dictated a short reply: "Dear Sir, Perhaps you should consider having your daughter dry cleaned."

During that first dinner party (December 1964) at the Robertsons, this fellow Peter Bogdanovich (whom I had never heard of before) kept up a nonstop cinematic tirade from soup to salad regarding how many gunshots were fired in reel-six of John Ford's last western, to who held the fourth spear in the second remake of *Ben-Hur*. I was so astonished at all the motion picture trivia that Bogdanovich was spewing forth like the Fontana di Trevi that it caused me to exclaim after ten minutes of listening to him, "You ought to be a film critic and write movie reviews with all the motion picture knowledge you seem to have."

"Well, I do," said Bogdanovich somewhat amazed. "I write film articles for Esquire Magazine. Don't you read Esquire?"

"No," I said trying to lighten up the conversation, "I just look at the pictures."

"Peter, please eat," said Peggy Robertson. "We're all ready here for the main course and you haven't even touched your soup."

Bogdanovich further tried to impress me with his writing credentials while chewing his soup, "I'm doing monographs on John Ford, Cary and Hitch, but what I really want to do is direct."

"Very good," I said. "The cinema really needs better motion pictures now."

Mary Tomasini timidly smiled; she was such a charming, quietly shy, lovely slender middle aged lady who occasionally broke into tears when she thought of her recently departed George Tomasini. Mama Toumanova (a short plump Russian elderly woman) looked at Bogdanovich with the eyes of a shrewd Czarina who had seen, perhaps, everything in life that there was to see. Tamara Toumanova flashed her beautiful *Swan Lake* smile, and since I had met famed cinematographer James Wong Howe through my good friend Bourdon von Brecht (owner of Vita Health Foods on Sunset Boulevard), Doug Robertson broke the silence at the table by asking me, "How's Jimmy Wong Howe these days, Phillip?"

"Fine, I replied. "He looks great for his age. He and Bourdon von Brecht took me to the fights last week."

Well, Ladies and Gentlemen of the Jury, as soon as Doug Robertson mentioned that I was acquainted with the legendary master Academy Award cinematographer James Wong Howe, Peter Bogdanovich immediately said, "After dinner, I want to speak with you."

Mama Toumanova, I could tell, saw through Peter Bogdanvoich as if he were a piece of crystal.

As soon as dinner was finished, Peter Bogdanovich escorted me out onto the patio area with his ever obedient wife of the time (Polly Platt

190

Bogdanovich) not far behind.

Bogdanovich implored me to introduce him to James Wong Howe, and when he found out that I had also met the celebrated cinematographer Haskell Wexler, he wanted an introduction to Wexler as well.

"Do you have anything which I could see?" I asked. "Even if it's been shot in sixteen, or super-eight. I have to have something before I can go to them on your behalf."

"I have nothing," Bogdanovich pleaded, "but I have a couple of ideas for properties and a script which I've written which I'd like to talk with them about. I know I can direct."

"Listen," I said. "I know how you feel. I've just finished my second film score myself. A person has to have an opportunity to start somewhere."

The more I spoke with Peter Bogdanovich that evening, the more I could sense that, in actuality, he had no real idea at that time what being a true motion picture director entailed. So I said, "Look, Peter, your script may be quite fine, and of course, a motion picture must have an absolutely first rate story and shooting script; but to be a good film director (in addition to story) you must know the camera and what it can do; you must know editing, you have to know lighting and how to light a scene properly, and you must know how to communicate with actors, actresses, and a myriad of other technicians, just for starters. Why not enroll in the cinema department at UCLA or USC?" I asked. "Or go to the Cinematography Institute in Santa Barbara."

It seemed that Peter Bogdanovich was beyond going to school, or even learning. He told me he did not need to go to film school as his school had been managing the New Yorker Theater in New York City. I complimented Bogdanovich on his programming skills and told him that the New Yorker Theater had been one of my favorite movie houses which I had frequented many times during those years, but I added that even though I had conducted the New York Philharmonic, and had major performances and splendid reviews from being one of the youngest composers ever to have been performed by The Philadelphia Orchestra, and also stellar performances by Leopold Stokowski, that I considered myself a beginner and studied every day as if I were still in music school.

Since Polly Platt Bogdanovich was also now pleading on Peter's behalf, and after she had confidentially informed me as to how difficult life had been for them and how she and Peter had been evicted from their apartment on Riverside Drive in New York where poor Polly had to carry ("Peter didn't lift a finger to help me.") the thousands of books in their collection, I gave them my telephone number and said that I would do my best to present them to James Wong Howe, and Haskell Wexler; or help them in any way that I could.

I eventually got to know Mama and Tamara Toumanova fairly well. Although they lived in the elite part of Beverly Hills, they were unaffected people and equally at home with aristocracy, or peasant farmers; individuals after my own heart. Toumanova had been one of the most exciting and famous prima ballerinas of all time, but I could tell that she had a particular amount of sensitivity and consideration for any unfortunate person. Tamara Toumanova was about to return to the cinema after an absence of twelve years in Alfred Hitchcock's *Torn Curtain* where she more or less would play herself in the role of a Ballet Dancer and would do an abridged version of Tchaikovsky's *Francesca di Rimini*. Mama was indeed Russian and tough; elderly cute with a low raspy voice of fractured English, and smoked a rare occasional cigarette not because she enjoyed it, but more as a defiant public prop. Tamara, although she was born in Russia and spoke Russian fluently, was more aristocratically European French-English in demeanor and upbringing since that is where Mama had brought Tamara Toumanova as a child to live and dazzle the principal cities of Europe with her genius for Russian ballet.

If Mama Toumanova had been two decades younger, she would have been the best international concert manager I could have ever hoped for because she had an infallible nose for undiscovered talent. I found out that she was the one who had given Antal Dorati his first symphonic opportunity as a conductor (1934-1940) in the pit of the Ballet Russe De Monte Carlo after Mama Toumanova went to the management and forced them to use Dorati.

I understand that she used to tell people about me by yelling, "God gave that boy Lambro talent. That boy is genius. I tell you as god is my judge that boy has greatest of talent."

Mama Toumanova thought famous impresario Sol Hurok was a joke and a crook, and used to tell him so in Russian to his face. Even though Tamara had been represented by Hurok for a time, they both did not like him because of Hurok's devious ways and his pathetic criteria for only seeking gifted artists to represent after they had achieved a great measure of success on their own.

Mama Toumanova also thought Peter Bogdanovich was of weak substance as a person, and it was her contention that he would have little to offer the world of cinema and absolutely nothing to humanity. She warned me not to waste my abilities trying to help him. After I got to know Peter a little better, I subscribed to Mama Toumanova's initial prognostication. In fact, I told Mama Toumanova that I felt his wife Polly Platt was the only one with aptness in that family of two.

James Wong Howe, the diminutive Chinese-American declared, "Look Phillip, what can I do for this potential Bogdanovich director? They hire me. A director or producer tells the studio I want James Wong Howe; they call my agent, and I go shoot the picture. What can I do? I can't do anything for him; so there's no sense in my even meeting him. Tell him to go to UCLA; I teach there sometimes. They've got a good cinema department."

During that period, Peter Bogdanovich was telephoning me on the average of four to five times a week. I called Haskell Wexler. I had been to Wexler's office, his house in the Hollywood Hills, and his beach home on Latigo Shore Drive in Malibu. He was thinking about producing a documentary which I might have scored, but he said that he had to go off and make enough money shooting major motion pictures so that he could do his envisioned documentaries. Wexler said that he could not see Bogdanovich because he was about to film the Elizabeth Taylor, Richard Burton production *Who's Afraid Of Virginia Wolf?* and that (to my amazement) he was taking the Hollywood Cameraman's Union to court over the fact that they would not let Wexler join. I understand that the Hollywood Cameraman's Union finally settled with Wexler (who was in the Chicago Union) after several years of appeals and just before the case was to be reviewed by The United States Supreme Court. I was disappointed with Haskell Wexler for not letting his case go before the U. S. Supreme Court and thereby possibly establishing a precedent in allowing other discriminated cinematographers open access to enter the Hollywood Cameraman's Union. It was rather common knowledge that it was almost impossible and exceedingly difficult for any cinematographer to get into that Hollywood Local.

I had been on occasion chumming around with a resourceful Italian cinematographer by the name of Mario DiLeo. Mario had worked in Italy with a number of the Italian master film makers and had just returned from Brazil where he had shot the film *The Gentle Rain* for Paramount on extremely dangerous Amazon locations. Mario and I would usually meet mid-evenings at Cyrano's on Sunset Boulevard where we would try and pick-up some interesting young ladies; you could do that in those days. In fact, Mario and I met two attractive Swedish girls who invited us to their pleasant apartment on Doheny Drive the very next evening for dinner. Mario's date had prepared most of the food and was quite nervous as she nearly burned Mario's neck with hot food and almost dropped a plate on me. My Swedish date was apprehensive, but less jittery than her friend as they both conversed in Swedish when they obviously did not want us to know what they were saying.

Finally, I asked (as Mario and I glanced at one another), "Is there anything wrong? I have the feeling that something is bothering you girls."

Eventually, my Swedish date said in English, "Why don't you tell them why you're so nervous?"

Mario's date closed her eyes for a moment and sat down at the dining table holding her blonde head with her right hand before revealing to us how dreadful she felt because the posh apartment she led us to believe was hers was in fact her boyfriend's (film star Tony Curtis') hideaway who was keeping her and was supposedly out of town, but who had just telephoned shortly after we arrived informing Mario's Swedish date of Curtis' unexpected return and if he could get away from his wife, that he would be over as soon as possible.

Then too, there were these drab primitive oil paintings hung all over the apartment which the Swedish girls had previously asked my opinion about, but which I told them (as tactfully as I could) were really the height of amateurism.

Since Mario and I had suddenly lost our appetite, we politely left both girls who apprised me that all the paintings which I had dismissed earlier had been painted by Tony Curtis; to which I responded that perhaps they might suggest to him that he either go back to art school and try a little harder, or do himself a favor and give up the visual arts completely.

Fifteen minutes later Mario and I were back at Cyrano's having a salad and some garlic toast when I said, "Mario, I have a favor to ask of you."

"What is that my friend?"

"There's an aspiring film director by the name of Peter Bogdanovich I recently met who has a film script he's trying to get off the ground which he tells me needs a special kind of cinematographer. I haven't read his script; I can tell you that he really doesn't know the camera and directing, but I think he's willing to learn. Caro mio, please do this favor for me and see him; perhaps something might come of it, and maybe you could help him in the process.

"Okay," Mario DiLeo said. "For you Filippo Lambro, my friend, I'll see what I can do to help him.

Mario at that time along with his friend and partner Faoud Said were building a prototype high-tech streamlined film location bus called the Cinemobile and working on it everyday. It would shortly revolutionize the motion picture industry by saving studios many hundreds of thousands of dollars in location filming since everything a major motion picture would require on location Mario DiLeo and Faoud Said designed compactly into that one Cinemobile. Faoud Said later sold the company and went back to Saudi Arabia where he ventured into the petroleum business and I was told made an extensive fortune.

Since Mario and Faoud were operating behind South Sunset Plaza, I telephoned both Mario, and Peter and Polly Platt Bogdanovich and arranged to introduce them to one another at the nearby Old World Restaurant the following afternoon for late lunch.

I brought Mario to the Old World Restaurant where an anxious Peter and Polly were waiting for us in one of the booths. After approximately ten minutes I felt secure enough to where I excused myself and went back to my studio to compose.

About two hours later I received a telephone call from Mario DiLeo. "Hey, Filippo. I just finished with this Bogdanovich and his script. I know you tell me that this guy doesn't know anything about directing and the camera; but you tell me that he is willing to learn. This guy doesn't want to learn, because if I do with the color camera what he wants me to do, the screen, for sure, she comes out black."

Ladies and Gentlemen of the Jury, it was somewhat of a minor miracle that I was even assigned the score to Universal's *And Now Miguel* because producer Robert Radnitz had never heard of me (not that that should have ever meant anything because I had never heard of him either) and he had wanted to use his previous composer Paul Sawtelle (who worked with pianist-orchestrator Bert Shefter) and used to irk Radnitz by continually falling asleep during the initial screening of the Radnitz picture Sawtelle was scheduled to score. The only reason I was eventually awarded the assignment was because Universal Studio's Music Department Head, Joseph Gershenson had the ultimate decision, and felt that I was the best composer for the film.

I found out that Robert Radnitz was in a fog concerning the quality of my music for *And Now Miguel* until Arthur Knight from the Saturday Review (whom I have never met) told Radnitz that my score was the best Radnitz had ever had in any of his motion pictures. Arthur Knight also praised my soundtrack publicly in the Saturday Review as did other critics from the Christian Science Monitor to Film Daily. I even had tourists from the Universal Tours to Disneyland telephoning me at home a year after the picture had been released, wondering if they could buy a tape directly from me of the music for *And Now Miguel* since Universal had never released a soundtrack album, but gave the inquiring tourists my home telephone number! I had to tell both the dozens of people who called and finally the studio that all the master recordings were in the Universal vaults and definitely not in my closet.

Secondly, I was a little apprehensive every time I would see MCA-Universal Board Chairman, Jules Stein, or President, Lew Wasserman, walking in my direction on the studio lot because a year earlier my Jewish Godfather, Shaya Bronstein (Sidney Brown was his Bel Air name), had entrusted me with the sale of a few of his priceless French impressionist paintings (a small Renoir, an Untrillo, a Modigliani, a Vlaminck, and a Valtat) which Jules Stein had telephoned me about through a mutual acquaintance. I met Stein in his office with Wasserman and gave Stein the provenance and beautiful color photos of the paintings.

"Where are the original paintings?" Demanded Jules Stein. "I thought you were going to bring by the paintings."

"If you're seriously interested in purchasing them," I said, "then you'll have to view them at Mr. Brown's home in Bel Air. Sir, it would have been physically impossible for me to carry the actual paintings here, plus the insurance agreement would not permit me to take the paintings out of Mr. Brown's home."

Jules Stein looked at me sternly (with Lew Wasserman apathetically perusing the color photos) and said pointing, "Do you see that bulging brief case over there, young man?"

"Yes, Sir," I said. "I do."

"Do you see how full of legal briefs and contracts it is? Do you see this desk and the thousands of people in this Studio who work under me? Do you think a man in my position has time to go and see everything I'm interested in? People bring things to me. I don't go to them."

"I'm sorry, Mr. Stein," I said as courteously as I could, "but Mr. Brown has instructed me to tell you that if you are interested in buying any of the paintings, that you would have to come to his home in Bel Air and purchase them."

"Young man, get out of here," Jules Stein said in exasperation.

Lew Wasserman, at least, smiled at me. I took the photos, documentation, authentications and left before the mighty Jules Stein erupted.

For nearly four weeks while scoring *And Now Miguel* I had been successful in avoiding both Jules Stein, and Lew Wasserman. I had visions of Stein and Wasserman remembering me and having me fired on the spot. I felt increasingly secure until one day, after Radnitz had been receiving raves about my score, he demanded to take Joe Gershenson and your humble Court Composer to lunch in the Universal Executive Dining Room.

As I was about to order, Radnitz screamed "Jules, Lew, come here. This is our composer, Phillip Lambro, I was telling you about who's doing the music for the picture."

My heart stopped beating for a few seconds. I looked up and there in front of me, Ladies and Gentlemen of the Jury, was Jules Stein and Lew Wasserman. But they were smiling. I started to get up to shake their hands, however Jules Stein said grasping my hand, "Please, no need to get up; enjoy your lunch."

Stein, Wasserman, Radnitz, and Gershenson were all talking with each other in rapid-fire succession for about twenty seconds with the rest of the Dining Room focused on our table. As Stein and Wasserman were about to leave, Wasserman said to me, "Haven't we met someplace before?"

"He's been on the lot for over a month," Radnitz said for me as I smiled.

Stein and Wasserman left, and fortunately for yours truly, Jules Stein had completely forgotten me and Lew Wasserman was vaguely trying to remember. From that day on, until the completion of the picture, I continued to avoid the last of the Hollywood Tycoons unless it was an occasional unexpected encounter at which time I greeted them politely and succinctly.

Another diverting incident as I was working on *And Now Miguel* occurred one day upon my tardy return from lunch, when the doors to Dubbing Room One flew open and a livid Radnitz, having nearly bitten through his ubiquitous pipe almost physically threw out a young gentleman who was doubtlessly hurt and embarrassed.

"If I catch you around here again, kid, I'll call the police. Now, get out of here." Then turning to me Radnitz said, "Where the hell have you been? We've been waiting for you."

As Radnitz went inside, I tried to console the young man, who informed me that he was just a serious film student from UCLA within a special program at Universal (I subsequently found out that there was no "special program"), harmlessly wanting to observe the intricate technical goings on in Dubbing Room One. After a few minutes, I asked him what his name was and he said, "Stephen Spielberg" (he has since changed the spelling of his first name to Steven) and when he found out who I was, he unleashed a barrage of superlatives about how effective my music was (partronizing has never affected me), but because his raw infectious enthusiasm for the cinema was so ebullient it made me want to take an even further curiosity in Spielberg and what he had to say.

"Oh, Mr. Lambro," said young Steven Spielberg, "your music for this picture makes the whole film as far as I'm concerned."

"Gee," he went on, "I'd love for you to see the films I'm working on; but, no, I shouldn't even ask a man of your importance to look at any of my little films."

"Why not?" I asked. "They're probably more interesting than this wide screen Technicolor Turkey I'm working on now."

"Really..? Wow; you'd be interested in seeing my little sixteen millimeters and super eights?"

"Sure," I smiled. "Why not? What are they about?

"There's one I'm thinking about doing soon," Spielberg went on. "You promise you won't laugh when I tell you my concept?"

"No, I won't laugh," I said.

"It's a documentary short about puddles."

"Puddles," I echoed. "What about puddles?"

"The film opens, and that's where your music would play such an important part in this picture, with an extra-close-up of a bead of water. In fact, it will be such an extreme diffused close-up that the audience, at that moment, won't even know it's a solitary bead of water. Then we focus back further until we see that it's one of hundreds of beads of water on a car windshield with the wipers going; then we cut to the rain and puddles; all kinds of puddles; and where these puddles go: into cracks and crevasses and little streams, then bigger streams, then into rivers and oceans. Well, Mr. Lambro what do you think..?"

"It's a fascinating concept," I said, "and of course I would be interested in quite possibly doing some music for your puddles."

"Oh, Boy, Mr. Lambro," said Spielberg. "Wow, you've made my whole day."

"You don't have to call me Mr. Lambro" I said. "Phillip is good enough."

Just then, Leonard Peterson, the new music sound engineer poked his head out of Dubbing Room One and said, "Phillip, Radnitz is waiting for you, we're about to make a take."

"Okay," I said, "I'll be right there."

198

I looked at this Steven Spielberg who was about twenty at that time and thought to myself with all this overflowing enthusiasm and high spirited excitement for motion pictures that there must be some spark of originality and talent under this apparent passion for the cinema; and I, of course, did not like Radnitz's way of throwing the young man out of Dubbing Room One, so I said to Spielberg, "Look, since you're obviously such a serious film student, and you care so much about the motion picture medium and want to learn, I'm going to take you back into Dubbing Room One. How's that?"

"Oh no, Mr. Lambro, I mean Phillip," Spielberg sputtered, "I'm not going back in there; Radnitz will kill me."

"No he won't; because you'll be with me. Come on, it's okay; I guarantee it."

Well, Ladies and Gentlemen of the Jury, when I walked into Dubbing Room One with young Steven Spielberg in trepidation a little behind me, I thought Robert Radnitz was going to swallow his pipe by all the reflected stunned expressions on his and the Universal technicians faces.

I did not give Radnitz a chance to speak, "Look, Bob," I said, "we're not making a military classified pentomic picture here. Steven's a serious film student, and he's a friend of mine, and he only just wants to observe what we're doing technically, that's all. And who knows, in ten years you might want to hire him to direct one of your future pictures."

Since many people had been enthusing over my film score, Radnitz acquiesced; then not wanting to be upstaged by your humble Court Composer, Radnitz said to Spielberg, "Okay Kid, but you sit back there in the corner and not a peep out of you, understand? Or it's out you go."

I winked at Steven who beamed and shook my hand, loudly whispering, "Thanks, I'll never forget this."

I nodded and slightly raised my hand affirmatively and got one of the technicians to give Steven a chair where he sat quietly for hours in the corner as we patiently dubbed *And Now Miguel*.

Leonard Peterson was the engineer on the dubbing console assigned to consolidate the music tracks. During the entire dubbing (being the composer) I had to sit next to Leonard with my score and guide him to the correct balances of the relatively small orchestra I was forced to use. I noticed that Leonard had been a bit nervous, and I continually gave him confidence as I could tell that he was a remarkable engineer; however, within a couple of days, I asked Leonard (so that the other soundmen would not hear) to tell me if there was anything wrong. That day we went to lunch, and he relayed to me in confidence that this was the first motion picture which he had ever dubbed, and that he was on probation for the position; and with a wife and two small daughters, he had left his less paying engineering job at a local Los Angeles radio station to gamble for this much more lucrative engineering job at Universal Studios.

I said to him, "Leonard, I can tell that you're a good engineer; but you're going to have a heart attack if you fret over whether or not you're going to get past your probationary period. You just relax and leave everything to me. I'll go to Bill Hornbeck" (he was head of the entire Universal Sound Department) "and I'm sure you'll get the job. In fact, I'm willing to stake my life on it, because I've complained so much about the studio recording the past two months that when Bill Hornbeck hears me praise you, it will shock him into giving you the position as it'll have been one of the few times I've said anything complimentary."

Ladies and Gentlemen of the Jury, this was true. The equipment in the recording studio (not to be confused with Dubbing Room One) was terribly antiquated and after I heard the first playbacks I civilly expressed my disappointment, but was told to shut up, or I might lose my contract. Julie Andrews, a few months later, as she was about to record her songs there for her new Universal musical *Thoroughly Modern Millie* (which I also affectionately nicknamed *The Unsinkable Modern Millie*) did not even hear one playback; Ms. Andrews just took a look at the squalid barn-like walls and said that she was going to record at RCA Studios, so mighty Lew Wasserman placated Ms. Andrews and gave the order to have the outdated studio gutted and rebuilt immediately into a brand new multimillion dollar high tech state of the art motion picture recording facility. So much for the benign influence of Phillip Lambro.

Later that day, during a Union Break, I went into Bill Hornbeck's office after speaking with his Assistant, Phil Scott. Bill Hornbeck was a late middle aged distinguished looking gentleman with rimless glasses and a 1940's moustache.

"Hi, Bill," I said.

"How are you," he replied cautiously. "What can I do for you?" He asked. "Is there anything wrong?"

"Who's that guy?" I pretended. "What's his name; the new music engineer, in Dubbing Room One?"

"You mean, Leonard Peterson?"

"Yes," I said. That's him. Leonard Peterson."

"What's wrong?" Bill Hornbeck asked.

"Nothing's wrong," I said. "I just want you to know that this Peterson fellow is absolutely one of the best soundmen I've ever worked with in my life."

Bill Hornbeck, I could tell, was definitely astonished. "Well," Hornbeck went on, "that's very gratifying to learn because he's on probation for that position."

"Probation," I exclaimed. "Listen, with all the mediocre engineers floating around Hollywood these days, you had better not lose this Peterson fellow; he's definitely first rate."

"Well, coming from you," said Hornbeck. "That's quite a compliment."

Leonard Peterson relayed to me a few days later that Bill Hornbeck had informed him that he had lifted the probationary period and that Leonard was firmly engaged into the Universal Sound Department with all the financial benefits that implied.

Steven Spielberg and I immediately became friendly; not due (as one might think) to Steven's enthusiastic patronizing of my musical abilities, but largely as a result of the fact that I thought with his passionate energy for films, even though I began to sense that he might not have the necessary mechanical, technical and visionary amenities to become a truly great director in the Akira Kurosawa, Sergei Eisenstein, Orson Welles sense, but with such ardor I felt certain that he would definitely be eager to learn and distill these discoveries into something unique.

I took Spielberg to lunch and dinner many times where he told me his ideas for future films. There was a black and white film short devoted to Nazi demonstrators Steven informed me about which he had filmed in Phoenix Arizona while he was attending High School. Steven described how he had hid the camera inside a truck with one way glass windows where from the outside you could not see that there was a camera filming the entire action, and how he had rented Nazi uniforms and flags and enlisted some of his friends and High School classmates to play the parts of proclaiming Neo-Nazis in the Jewish part of that city which eventually caused pandemonium to break loose with elderly women actually beating up his surrogate Nazi actors with umbrellas, canes, grocery bags, and flying purses.

I remember Steven asking me once if I had thought there had ever been any good Nazis during the Holocaust; to which I replied that I had heard of several who had saved Jews from either going into concentration camps or did their best to keep some Jews from dying in them. So it was not surprising for me to learn twenty-nine years later that Steven was making a film about Oskar Schindler.

At this time, Steven did not have an apartment, but was more or less staying with a variety of friends. He telephoned or contacted me at least five or six times a week. The telephone number he had given me was that of his father with whom I would leave messages and who would sometimes leave messages with me for Steven. One time Steven's father (who was an articulate engineering businessman) called asking me if I knew where Steven was that particular day, to which I responded, "Perhaps, he's out at UCLA."

"What would he be doing at UCLA?" Asked Spielberg's father.

"Doesn't he attend school there?" I asked.

"Hell, no; he's supposed to be in school at Cal State Long Beach."

It may be interesting to note, in view of all the press devoted to Steven Spielberg's mother and Steven's relationship with his mother, that from the end of 1965 through 1968 (the years in which I was associated with Steven Spielberg) although he mentioned his father from time to time, when I once asked him about his mother and where she lived and what she was like, Steven quickly changed the subject. In fact, during all those years, I do not ever recall Steven Spielberg once mentioning his mother.

Perhaps the most pivotal and prophetic moment in Steven Spielberg's entertainment career may be traced to the day (about three weeks after I had met him) where I saved Steven from being physically thrown off the Universal Lot by the Security Guards.

Scotty, the Security Guard, and his muscular associate, had a loudly protesting Steven Spielberg by each arm with Steven's shirt tails under his sport jacket compressed upwards like an accordion all above his bare navel. The Security Guards had Steven's legs dangling about two inches off the floor and were clamorously transporting him down the hallway outside the studio where we were recording the balance of my *And Now Miguel* score. The studio doors had been open because I had been complaining to the engineers about a faint hum on the playbacks which nobody heard at first, except me, (including the engineers and Robert Radnitz) which we eventually traced to a system noise emanating from an air conditioner in the studio. I convinced the engineers to have the air conditioner turned off while we were recording, but we had to keep the heavy hallway doors of the recording studio open so that the orchestra musicians would not faint from lack of air.

"Hey, Scotty," I yelled running into the hallway. "What's going on out here? You've just ruined a take."

They dropped Steven Spielberg to the floor.

"What are you doing with Steven?" I asked.

"Mr. Lambro," Scotty said in his calm Scottish brogue, "we've been getting a lot of complaints about this young gentleman and he's not supposed to be on the lot at all."

"He's okay," I said. "He's part of a special film student program here," I lied. "Let him go."

"Are you sure, Mr. Lambro?" Scotty asked.

"Yes, I'm sure," I assured Scotty and his muscular associate. "Mr. Wasserman knows about the program," I lied again.

"Okay, Mr. Lambro, we'll let him stay on the lot; but you're responsible."

"You don't have to worry," I said. "I'll assume responsibility."

Scotty gave Stephen a suspicious stare and putting his index finger quite close to Steven's flushed face said, "And you had better behave and keep your nose clean; understand? Because if we hear anymore complaints, it's out you go, young man."

"I didn't do anything," Steven said quite embarrassed."

As the guards walked away, Steven sighed, "Thanks, Phillip, that was a close call," and proceeded to tuck in his badly rumpled shirt and straighten his creased sport jacket.

I told Steven to come into the recording studio, sit down and be quiet so that I could finish this film and go on to composing more important things like my *Four Songs for Soprano & Orchestra*.

The last time Steven Spielberg called me was in 1975 to tell me how much he liked the soundtrack album from my score to *Murph The Surf* and to inform me how well *Jaws* was doing at the box office.

"You know, Stephen," I said. "I wonder what would have ever happened to you if I had let the Security Guards at Universal throw you off the lot that day?"

"Phillip, please don't ever tell anybody that story. I don't want anyone to know about that."

"Why not?" I replied. "It's true; it's part of your life. I think it's very amusing."

Had I let the studio guards throw Steven Spielberg off the lot that day, most assuredly he would not have met Sid Sheinberg, John Cassavetes, and others who were to become instrumental in launching Steven's career at Universal Studios.

Although I brought Steven to many agents and managers, and predicted his inaugural financial success, "Look, he's no Kurosawa; he's not even a Kubrick, or Lelouch" I told Irv Schechter, Sy Marsh and others at the William Morris Agency after I took Steven virtually by the hand to see them. "But he's very clever and he's going to have big initial successes followed by big financial failures; so why not sign him now?" I asked.

"I can't do anything for you, kid," said Irv Schechter, "you don't have a big enough name."

Steven Spielberg, to his credit, remarked politely, "How big do you want my name, Sir? I can come back today with my name painted in two foot high letters, if you want."

After I left the William Morris Agency, I took Steven to my new representatives, Sam Adams of Adams, Ray & Rosenberg, then when I went to Ashley Famous Agency which became International Famous Agency (and ultimately cloned itself into ICM) I tried to get them to represent him, too. I must have taken and spoken about Steven Spielberg to, at least, thirty agents, personal managers and publicists from David Mirisch and Rick Rosenberg to Richard Carter (Jack Lemmon's publicist) and super-agent Ben Benjamin. All the agents would do was either tell me to forget Spielberg, or look at me, as if I were reasonless.

Then I suggested Steven to producers like Harold Hecht, George Englund, Alan Pakula, Ronald Lubin, and many more whom I had met for possible scoring assignments to try and give Steven an opportunity to direct his first feature film so that he could have a little income because (although he hated to admit it) I knew that Steven Spielberg was living only on the small allowance his father had been giving him. In fact, I clearly remember Steven's father telephoning me once just before Steven's twenty-first birthday wanting to know where Steven was.

"I really don't know where Steven is," I said.

"Well, when you see him," the elder Spielberg said, "you can tell him that his check is here, but in a few weeks he'll be twenty-one, and that's it. I'm not supporting him anymore. He'd better go out and get a job, and get this whole crazy movie business out of his head."

Shortly after this, I brought Steven with me to dinner at Nick and Ciel Cravat's home in Woodland Hills. Nick Cravat was as close with his boyhood friend Hollywood tycoon Burt Lancaster as anyone, and I wanted Nick to go to Lancaster on behalf of Steven, but Nick told Steven quite bluntly at the dinner table, "Unless you become a big name director like Frankenheimer, I can tell you that the way Burt is, he won't have the time of day for you." It was a depressing soiree for Steven, because during his conversation with Nick Cravat, Cravat said toward the end of the evening, "Steven, you've got a lot to learn, my friend; a lot to learn." As I drove Steven home on the Ventura Freeway, I told him not to let these Hollywood situations get his spirits down, and to persevere toward making the types of quality films which had attracted him to motion pictures in the first place.

As much as I did not wish to, as a desperate measure, I even took Steven to the aging producer-director Charles Martin whom I had met at Producers Studio in 1964 (now Raleigh Studios). Charles Martin always reminded me of a cross between George Sanders and Zero Mostel: he seemed to be emulating the dialect and mannerisms of George Sanders (whom he had directed in Death Of A Scoundrel for RKO starring, in addition to George Sanders, Yvonne DeCarlo, Zsa Zsa Gabor and Victor Jory), but with his lightly made-up face and banded girth he was leaning more toward Zero Mostel. Charles Martin began his Hollywood career at MGM where he wrote and directed *No Leave, No Love* starring Van Johnson, and the Esther Williams picture *On An Island With You*. Charles Martin also wrote the screenplay for David O. Selznik's *I'll Be Seeing You* which starred Ginger Rogers, Joseph Cotton and Shirley Temple.

However, all Charles Martin had to say to Steven Spielberg, after Steven had enthusiastically told Charles Martin about a project involving bicycle racing he wanted to film, "My boy, you have a lot to learn about the motion picture business, and what the public wants." Well, as little as Steven Spielberg knew about films at that time, he was miles ahead of producer Charles Martin in 1967.

All of 1966 and 1967, Steven Spielberg was really hustling on his own, too. I had left the Universal Lot, but Steven I understand had broken into Cary Grant's dormant private bungalow (Grant was never there) and was exploiting Grant's telephone and ordering what other items Steven could get away with in order to give himself the motion picture corporate profile and image he was desperately seeking.

In August of 1967, I signed a letter of agreement with Steven (which I still have in my files to this day) to furnish the music for a 35mm Technicolor featurette about California bicycle racers entitled *Slip Stream* which was to star Tony Bill and John Ireland, Jr. Stephen had introduced himself to Tony Bill and that is how I eventually met Tony. Steven had raised very little money for the production, so Tony (who was shooting *Ice Station Zebra* with Rock Hudson during weekdays) worked weekends on a deferred basis for Steven.

Serge Haignere (the excellent French-American cinematographer) who was filming *Bob & Carol, Ted & Alice* at Columbia Pictures furnished the cameras, lights, sound and raw color stock to get the project going for nothing in advance, and totally on a deferred basis. Serge was an absolute cinematic craftsman and a gem of a person, and helped Steven

Spielberg immeasurably. Mike Medavoy who was just beginning his career as an agent within a small Beverly Hills Theatrical Agency also helped Steven.

I specifically recall Tony Bill calling me 7:00 a.m. one Saturday morning from the *Slip Stream* shooting location in Malibu genuinely upset.

"Do you know where Steven is?" He asked.

"No," I replied. "Isn't he there?"

"No, he's not here, yet; and we've all been waiting for him since 6:00 a.m. I mean," I remember Tony going on, "I work hard all week on *Ice Station Zebra* and then I bust my ass nights and weekends to learn this script for nothing, and show up here on time; the least Spielberg can do as director is to also be here on time."

I found out from Serge Haignere that Steven would appear about 8:00 a.m. wondering why everyone was so upset.

Slip Stream was about half completed and I saw all the rushes and rough assembly. The film had commercial possibilities, but needed an additional $40,000 dollars to finish it. I took Steven to everyone I knew within the industry (about a dozen meetings) and everybody turned us down from the major agencies to Mickey Rooney's business manager. We ran the partial rough color assembly of *Slip Stream* so many times at rented projection rooms, I lost count. *Slip Stream* was never concluded, but I've always had the suspicion that it eventually transmuted into the highly successful film *Breaking Away*.

It was during the *Slip Stream* production that I realized that Steven Spielberg (as much as I wanted him to become an illustrious film director) just did not have the inherent qualities of ever becoming even a fundamental motion picture director; which, on occasion, Spielberg has readily admitted himself. Steven actually has never been anything but an extremely good exploitative Executive Producer who (like Peter Bogdanovich to a lesser extent) has always had the capacity to take the abilities and ideas of other more creative and technically adept people and get these individuals to produce and develop these concepts into a product which he can call his own. Underneath that immature naive "Gee, Golly, Wow" personality lay the manipulative personality of a young male who began reminding me of the famous Anne Baxter screen character Eve Harrington from the film classic *All About Eve*. I always knew that Steven was going to be financially successful in films because as he explained to me while we were doing *Slip Stream*, "Phillip, even if the picture fails, we can merchandise bicycles from the film and sell racing gear."

"What do we have here?" I argued with Steven. "A motion picture; or a Celluloid promotional vehicle to sell your bicycles and T-shirts?"

Steven had bicycles, T-shirts and merchandising on the brain; and in practically every feature film he's ever done, he has inserted an idea or product from one of his thirteen year old teen age home made fantasy films which he told me about when I first met him November of 1965. He finally got his wish to merchandise his *Slip Stream* bicycles in *E.T.* I am sure authentic extraterrestrials had a good laugh over that premise because real extraterrestrials would never use anything as primitive as a bicycle let alone a primordial internal combustion automobile for local travel. Advanced extraterrestrials use transportation belts which harness carrying waves in the atmosphere for quick short distance travel, and electromagnetic disc shape crafts travelling over twenty-seven times faster than our Earth speed of light for intergalactic travel.

Tony, Steven and your humble Court Composer remained friendly during that period.

Tony had a development deal over at Warner Bros. and Steven would get Tony to book the Warner Bros. studio theater and a projectionist, and we would watch many of the old great movies from Hollywood's Golden Age of the 1930's and 1940's. One day Tony and Steven exhausted me completely: they ran four or five feature films from about 10:00 a.m. until we staggered out of our private theater late that same evening.

"You guys are fucking crazy," I said. "You're movie junkies. You need to go to Film Goers Anonymous."

Originally, they invited me to see two films; which is more than enough for any normal person to see at one sitting. Then they said, "Just stay for one more." And then, "Oh, Phillip, you've got to see this one."

As we left, I remember Steven saying to me that he'd like to make a film someday utilizing some of the best parts of all the eminent adventure films of the past. I suggested that he'd never be able to do as well as the originators (so why try?), and what he should do is just make a film containing all the original best parts edited together with narration. The public who thought Indiana Jones was exciting are now able to realize through the medium of cable, video cassette and DVD how much more exciting the originals were than Steven Spielberg's and George Lucas' pathetic cinematic regressive caricatured plagiarism. Ladies and Gentlemen of the Jury, please realize what the public doesn't know, they never miss.

Since I had the feeling that even though with all the activity surrounding

Slip Stream and our lively efforts to raise the necessary processing fees that *Slip Stream* would never be completed no matter how assiduously we tried to raise money, and no matter how tenacious Steven Spielberg was. So during the same time, I was ensconced within a production company named Gotham-Rhodes at Columbia Pictures where the corporation was fighting for survival trying to make a monumental epic about the last famous battle of World War II tentatively titled *The Final Guns* for which I was guaranteed to compose and conduct the music. The whole story revolved around The Battle Of The Ardennes 1944-45 which was considered by Allied forces to be an impenetrable wooded forest plateau vortexed in North East France, South East Belgium, and Luxembourg. However, the Germans toward the end of the War developed a unique suspension tank (unknown to Allied Intelligence) which could easily travel over fallen logs and boulders and under the guidance of General Hasso von Manteuffel, one of the few German Generals to stand up against Hitler and live, and who never allowed an SS detachment within any of his Divisions, spearheaded the final assault against the Allied Forces.

The Final Guns could have been an epic motion picture had it been made, and made properly. We were trying to get David Lean or William Wyler to direct and Robert Bolt to do an historical screenplay based upon Department Of Defense chronicled documents. We had access to President and General Dwight D. Eisenhower via his son John Eisenhower; I can prove that, because many of the sixty-five minute telephone calls to President Eisenhower's home in Gettysburg, Pennsylvania (after Columbia Pictures took away our long distance telephone privileges) were charged to my personal account.

Laurence Olivier was to have played Hitler, and James Mason would have played Manteuffel, but our producer who was not a screen writer (not even an acceptable letter writer) set out to save money by attempting to design the screenplay himself; which predictably and ultimately turned out to be a disaster. John Levingston, a British chap with an excellent voice who had had a few small parts in *King Rat* and other Hollywood films was dispatched to the United Kingdom to try and secure actor James Mason on the basis of our producer's script which I strongly opposed showing anyone; let alone someone as literate as James Mason. Well, James Mason was rather courteously amusing in his lettered response which was followed up by the terms of his agent Al Parker. Unfortunately, James Mason got John Levingston's name incorrectly and referred to him as James Levingstone:

JAMES MASON. 24, RUTLAND COURT,
LONDON, S.W.7.

October 7th. 1966.

James Levingstone, Esq.,
C/o Miss Trudy Westley,
Columbia Pictures,
142, Wardour Street, LONDON.W.1.

Dear Mr. Levingstone.,

I read the script "THE FINAL GUNS" and it
is certainly a very interesting piece of work and I have no doubt
that it is madly authentic. When you were telling me about it,
describing it as 'an intimate drama of conflicts between the leaders
concerned' I imagined something perhaps a little bit more enthralling,
but that's a quibble. Undoubtedly Hitler comes out as the most
interesting character and Manteuffel comes out strong. I can't quite
see why your friend Eisenhower should say 'This film must be made'
because, if anything, I would say that the strongest effect of the
film would be to revive the image of Adolph Hitler genius.

In practical terms my own reaction is this:

If I am free at the time when they need the
services of an actor to play Manteuffel. If they are prepared to pay
me adequately, and if the film is directed by Wyler or David Lean and
Lawrence Olivier plays the part of Hitler I shall be happy to string
along - but I can make no definite commitment at this moment.

It is all very splendid and I wish nothing
but the best of luck to the enterprise. I am sending the script back
as requested to Trudy Westley at Columbia and I am sending copies
of this letter to both my Agents, Al Parker in London and Hugh French
in California. If there comes a time when we need to negotiate and
if the film is to be made in the U.S. then Hugh French would be the
one that you must contact.

Yours sincerely.,

JAMES MASON.

C/c. Al Parker.
Hugh French.

AL PARKER LTD.

LICENSED ANNUALLY BY THE G.L.C.

DIRECTORS:
AL PARKER (U.S.A.)
  MANAGING DIRECTOR
M A. M. JOHNSTON
  SECRETARY & TREASURER
JAMES SHARKEY

ᴸᵖ A R ᴋᴇʳ
HOUSE
50, Mount Street
Park Lane
London, W. I

TELEPHONES
GRO. 4232-3-4-5
GRO. 1131-2

CABLES
ALPARKER, LONDON-W I

INLAND TELEGRAMS
APARKERLIM, LONDON

CONTINENTAL TELEGRAMS
APARKERLIM, LONDON

REPRESENTATION IN NEW YORK, HOLLYWOOD AND CONTINENT
MEMBER OF THE PERSONAL MANAGERS ASSOCIATION

11th October 1966

John Levingston Esq.,
Columbia (British) Prods. Ltd.,
142 Wardour Street,
London, W.1.

Dear Mr. Levingston,

Re: James Mason - THE FINAL GUNS

Yesterday by the first post I received a copy
of a letter Mr. Mason wrote you on the 7th October
and by the second post, yours of the same date
arrived.

I have sent the copy of yours to our client
with a letter I am writing him.

I am of the opinion it is adivsable to
acquaint you with Mr. Mason's established terms
which are

$200,000 (Two hundred thousand dollars) for ten
consecutive weeks and pro rata for any additional
ones after the guaranteed period and the daily
rate for any last and incomplete week up to and
including the last day whether he stands by or
works: first class return transportation for two
from Switzerland to wherever the film is being
made: $1,000 (One thousand dollars) weekly living
expenses and a chauffeur-driven car whenever he
requires it.

Cordially yours,

Al Parker

AP/pdw
cc James Mason

210

The only person I realized who had any ability to reason correctly within the Gotham-Rhodes organization was that of the associate producer, Darrell Armstrong, who was an immensely intelligent fellow with a superlative command of the English language and an uncanny and witty way of expressing himself lucidly and concisely. Darrell had graduated from the prestigious Boalt Hall, The School Of Jurisprudence, within UC Berkeley, and spoke German fluently as he had been a member of the U. S. Counter-Intelligence Corps, in addition to being so exceptionally adept with the camera that he became Marcel Marceau's favorite photographer.

Through Darrell, I had met the seasoned actor Perry Lopez, whom I had remembered from such film classics as *Battle Cry* and *Mr. Roberts*, and the film noir *Violent Road* starring Jack Palance and Shelley Winters which I had seen during my teen age years at the Community Playhouse in Wellesley, Massachusetts. Perry Lopez had also been a close personal friend of screen idol James Dean since they both double-dated with the actress sisters Pier Angeli and Marisa Pavan; Perry Lopez with Marisa Pavan, and James Dean with Pier Angeli.

Perry and I became friends and one afternoon during July of 1967 he showed me some historical documentation about the famous Mexican Robin Hood bandit who had terrorized Southern California during the late 1800's by the name of Joaquin Murietta. After I read the material, I knew that it had the potential to be an exciting motion picture and that it would be a perfect role for Perry Lopez as Joaquin Murietta. Historical data revealed that Captain Harry Love of the United States Cavalry had been assigned by the U. S. Government to track down and kill the elusive Murietta (a formidable task under any situation) but the predicament was made immeasurably difficult by the historical phenomenon that Joaquin Murietta always surrounded himself with a group of follower bandits who physically resembled him (medium height, with swarthy dark skin, and long black hair) whom he ordered to dress like him. Captain Harry Love frustrated by years of defeat, finally killed one of Murietta's men, cut off his head, and proclaimed amid much fanfare that he had been finally successful in killing Joaquin Murietta. However, the public believing that Murietta had been dead (when in actuality he was not) now began to believe that the ghost of Joaquin Murietta was still roaming the Southern California desert when Murietta would strike with greater infrequency.

Perry Lopez and I began formulating a pre-production package which we hoped we could get into the development stage. Since Perry had acted in four TV-*Tarzan*s with Ron Ely (the tall good looking blond Tarzan of the time) it was decided that Ron Ely would be perfect for the role of John Bow, the fictionalized overlay based upon Captain Harry Love. I suggested that Darrell Armstrong be the producer and I introduced Perry and Darrell to Steven Spielberg and convinced them both that we give Steven an opportunity to direct John Bow (the working title of the picture) as Steven's debut into the world of theatrical releases. It was agreed that I would compose and conduct all the original music, and in exchange for my production expertise, I would retain all the publishing rights to my score, and (if need be) would act as an associate producer using a nom de plume.

Later in July of 1967, we all (Darrell Armstrong, Perry Lopez, Ron Ely, Steven Spielberg, and your humble Court Composer) met at the Polo Lounge of The Beverly Hills Hotel. Steven was terribly excited about going to the Polo Lounge because he had discovered how many big Hollywood deals had been formulated there. I was more calmly optimistic about making a development deal for John Bow to where we could get a major studio to bank the entire project. During this time (in private) I would suggest to Steven that he perhaps become more interested in learning the medium and development of creating worthwhile motion pictures rather than the peripheral aspects in the lifestyle and business of Hollywood; such as, as Steven described to me one day at Universal, whether I knew the executive power difference and implied comparison of having an end office as opposed to a corner office, or an inner office within the Black Tower at Universal. It was Steven's dream to have a corner office in the Black Tower, "The Tower Of London" as I nicknamed it, (with all the unnecessary career beheadings which took place there, I wasn't wrong) with five telephone lines and two attentive secretaries, because if MCA Universal gave you a corner office, you knew that you had arrived. The next in power would get end offices, and the least powerful would be relegated to inner offices, Steven enumerated.

"What the hell does this have to do with making an exciting motion picture?" I would ask Steven. "I don't need a corner office to compose quality music," I said.

Meanwhile, back at the Polo Lounge of The Beverly Hills Hotel, Steven Spielberg was sandwiched in the middle of a large posh booth between Tarzan Ron Ely, swarthy Perry Lopez, myself, and tall bespectacled Darrell Armstrong. Steven looked a little like Jiminy Cricket from *Pinocchio* as I could definitely tell that Ron Ely (who was extremely interested in the project) was not satisfied that Steven Spielberg could direct anything, let alone a motion picture. As Steven spoke about the undertaking and how he visualized it, being quite careful to agree with everything Ron Ely and Perry Lopez had to express about their characters, it was decided that Steven would bring in a treatment writer whom he knew by the name of Jerry Wish. I subsequently convinced both Perry Lopez and Ron Ely (after a series of telephone calls) that Steven Spielberg was more than adequate to direct this picture.

Steven, Jerry Wish, Perry Lopez, Darrell Armstrong, and I all had several story meetings and Darrell drew up a preliminary agreement which we all signed.

Jerry Wish did a workman-like treatment which we could never persuade any studio to do. Steven tried with Universal; Darrell attempted with Columbia; I endeavored with United Artists; and Perry Lopez continued for four years before Steven asked to be released because Universal was now going to give Steven something to direct.

During January 1999 I happened to rent the wide screen video of the 1998 Amblin Entertainment Universal Pictures feature release of *The Mask Of Zorro* with Antonio Banderas and Anthony Hopkins which I noticed Spielberg had executive produced and fortunately did not direct as it turned out to be a rather favorable action picture. Ladies and Gentlemen of the Jury, as I watched this film from the comfort of my bedroom I was jolted to discover that the majority of the *The Mask Of Zorro* sizable production was a complete rip-off of the Joaquin Murietta story which I had initially introduced Steven to during July of 1967, and which incidentally had very little to do with the original Zorro allegory. At that time, Steven did not even know where Murietta Springs was let alone who Joaquin Murietta was until I told him.

Any civilized person who reads this faithful account must immediately envision how utterly insignificant it would have been for multimillionaire Steven Spielberg during the preproduction stages of *The Mask Of Zorro* to have picked up the telephone and say, 'Phillip, I'm extremely grateful to you for having introduced me to the Joaquin Murietta project in 1967 and for having fought for me to have directed this feature (which would have been my first directorial assignment) when initially Ron Ely, and Perry Lopez had grave reservations about my directing abilities. So now I am going to take this material and have my writers incorporate it into my new production of *The Mask Of Zorro*. I think it only fair to give you, Perry Lopez, Darrell Armstrong and Jerry Wish, who worked so hard initially on this project, token payments of $50,000 dollars each as a gesture of my gratitude.'

But Ladies and Gentlemen of the Jury, did Steven Spielberg do this? No he did not. None of us ever got as much as a thank you note. When Perry Lopez viewed *The Mask Of Zorro* at a screening in the Academy Of Motion Picture Arts And Sciences Theater, he told me much later that his first emotional instinct was to confront Steven and "punch the little weasel out." Darrell wanted to file a law suit. Jerry Wish informed me after all these years that (unknown to all of us) he had ultimately expanded the treatment material we had given him in 1967 into a full length screenplay, and through an introduction Spielberg had given Jerry Wish, it eventually got to sometime producer Ron Dunas (whom I originally introduced Spielberg to as I used to play tennis with Ron Dunas in Beverly Hills) who could not ever get the Joaquin Murietta story into production for Jerry Wish. Jerry did not want to file a law suit against Spielberg. And I, of course, having so many more invaluable artistic and humanitarian projects yet to do, told everyone that I did not really wish to spend my precious time in court, but that in my soon to be completed memoirs I would tell the truth for future historical accuracy.

Apropos Steven Spielberg's directorial debut, I recall his telling me, "Gee, Phillip, can you imagine? I'm going to be directing Joan Crawford; can you imagine that? Me, directing Joan Crawford in a Rod Serling episode of *Night Gallery*."

Well, Ladies and Gentlemen of the Jury, I couldn't really imagine that, but I said, "Why, that's wonderful, Steven. I wish you every success."

"I mean," he went on, "I'm so nervous about it, I don't know what I'll do. Perhaps, I'll get a large blow-up of her and ask her to personally inscribe it to me before we begin shooting."

"Steven," I sighed. "You're talking about one of the great Hollywood screen legends of all time; you can't go in there like a star struck movie fan and ask Joan Crawford for her autograph. Why, if you did that, she'd probably go to Lew Wasserman and ask to have you replaced. Steven, you're talking about directing a real professional actress; a lady who locked horns with Jack Warner and Harry Cohn. If, as a director, you go up to her and ask her for her autograph before you begin shooting, she'll chew you up and spit you out while she's brushing her hair."

"God, what'll I do?" Spielberg asked. Quite frankly, I could not believe this conversation.

"You tell Miss Crawford what you want, scene by scene, and within the framework of what you want just yell 'action' and let her do the rest. Then at the completion of filming, if she's still speaking with you, you can bring out the roses, and a blow-up and ask her to autograph it for you."

Relevant to Steven Spielberg's innate naiveness, I'll never forget when, through the kind graciousness of cinematographer Serge Haignere (who was quite obviously gay in his Gallic and likable disposition), he let Steven live with him for over six months free of charge at Serge's nicely furnished modest apartment in the San Fernando Valley (just East of Laurel Canyon Boulevard), how (when Steven would invite me to come over and meet him at Serge's place) Steven, after having lived there for at least five months, one particular Sunday afternoon asked me, "Do you think Serge is gay?"

"How would I know?" I asked. "You're the one who's been living here five months."

"He sure has some strange friends," Steven said shaking his head.

Serge had the most uniquely huge male brown cat I had ever seen which, because of its size, Serge walked on the street like a dog with a leash, which caused a great deal of attention everywhere they went because of the cat's abnormal size and striking looks.

About a year after Steven Spielberg introduced me to Tony Bill, I went to have dinner at The Aware Inn on Sunset Boulevard opposite Tower Records (its no longer there) and, of course, The Aware Inn was packed; and although the maitre d' Elmer was a good acquaintance of mine, he said, "Phillip, you should have called; I won't have a table for you for at least an hour and a half."

Even though I was well dressed, I was hungry, and I guess the disappointment showed on my face. As I was about to walk out of the front door, Elmer called me to return.

"Mr. Lambro, there's a gentleman who's about to eat alone who'd like you to join him."

Elmer introduced me to this slightly bald, tanned very well dressed middle aged man in his sixties who had just been seated and who I could immediately sense was an Italiano Americano. He spoke English rather softly with almost no trace of an accent, but having lived in Italy, I could tell that this gentleman's mannerisms were either from Naples or further south to Sicily.

I remember that although Elmer presented my name to the well oiled Italiano Americano that he told Elmer, "Just call me George."

After I sat down, and menus were given, George smiled at me. I could tell that he liked me because of my Italian looking features. As I quietly spoke with him, I had the feeling that, perhaps, George was not his real name. In fact, as I looked into his eyes, I could see that this kindly, very polite, and respectful Italiano Americano had perhaps seen and experienced all the unspeakable things in life.

"I'm in from Vegas on a little business," George said. "That's why I'm eating alone."

He asked me if I ever went to Las Vegas; and when I told him that although I had lived in Europe and had travelled over most of the United States, but (at that time) had never once been to Las Vegas, he found that rather uncommon.

"I guess you don't like to gamble." he said.

"No, I don't gamble; I don't smoke; I don't drink. But I've seen pictures of a few of your show girls I wouldn't mind meeting."

We both laughed. I could tell that he had a good sense of humor.

In his quiet way, he asked me what I did for a living; and I told him that I was a concert composer and conductor, and that I was also doing a film score from time to time. As dinner progressed we talked about Italy, sports, women and the entertainment industry.

"Do you know Dean Martin?" He asked toward the end of dinner as he lit up an expensive cigar.

"I've met him at The Daisy, the private club, a few times," I said. "I really don't know him, but he's nice enough to let me use his tennis court a couple of times a month."

"Dean's a good friend of mine," he said.

He then asked me if I knew Frank Sinatra; and I explained how I had met Sinatra through my work at the United Nations and how he had had some of his associates try and assist me when I first came to Hollywood.

"Frank gave me this watch several years ago," he said, as he took off his gold wrist watch and showed me the intimate inscription on the back from Frank Sinatra.

"Do you know Frank, Jr?" He asked.

"No," I said. "I've never met him."

"What about Tony Bill?"

"I was just with Tony today," I said. "We're pretty good friends. Do you know Tony?" I asked.

"No," he said faintly smiling, "but I know all about him."

I returned the smile, but said nothing.

"Ever notice the resemblance between Frank, Jr. and Tony Bill?" He asked grinning a little broader.

I paused and nodded silently; the way I had been trained by the Albanians and Italians from the old country who had sometimes taken care of me as a small child. "Yeah, you're right," I said. "There's a tremendous resemblance. I never thought about it before."

"When Frank first became a big star he met this young society lady. They fell in love and she had a kid. She had plenty of money and didn't want Frank to get a divorce and marry her."

We spoke about twenty minutes more. George paid for the entire meal, saying that he enjoyed my company, and wished me luck with my music career. I offered my telephone number and suggested that he call me when he was next in Los Angeles, but he said that he probably would not be in Los Angeles again for a very long time although he took my name and phone numbers. I never heard from, or saw the man again.

A few days later, I was in Tony Bill's office at Warner Bros. Steven Spielberg was there having a discussion with Francis Coppola who was beginning his career and had just stopped by from his Seven Arts Productions offices down the hallway, and I was slouched in one of the easy chairs looking at Tony's face.

"Why are you staring at me that way?" Tony asked.

"Tony," I said wanting to see his reaction, "did anyone ever tell you how much you resemble Frank Sinatra, Jr.?"

"Yeah, Tony, he's right," agreed Coppola and Spielberg.

"Nobody's ever said that before," said Tony who quickly changed the subject.

Perhaps the most interesting film idea I had ever heard from Steven Spielberg came around 1967 when I had driven Steven to that fateful meeting at the William Morris Agency in Beverly Hills. Since neither of us had any coins for the parking meter, we went inside the William Morris lobby where I endeavored to change a dollar into coins. As soon as Steven and I returned, there was a Beverly Hills Meter Maid writing up a parking violation for yours truly. As Steven and I were pleading our case to the Meter Maid (who could have cared less) Steven told her that he would like to have her telephone number because he was a motion picture director and wanted to do a film short about *A Day In The Life Of A Meter Maid.*

Ladies and Gentlemen of the Jury, I gather by now you must realize that in all honesty, I emphatically wanted Steven Spielberg to succeed as a motion picture director; not just financially, but as a cinematic artist as well.

There will be those who shall cite Steven Spielberg's various films which by contemporary standards have done remarkably well at the box office. However, I am not here to remind you of Steven's bloated critical and financial disasters such as *1941*; *Always*; *Hook*; and *A.I.*; or to argue with the cash register; save to point out more importantly, that when and if you consider population factors, actual cost and dollar to purchasing power ratios, instead of numerical grosses, Steven Spielberg films are definitely not the top money making motion pictures of all time which his publicity factory would have you believe. Steven's films will never financially capture *Gone With The Wind* and *Snow White And The Seven Dwarfs* (just to name two out of many); and what Spielberg film has played in theaters (First Run) consecutively to an admiring public for over one year as have Orson Welles' *Citizen Kane*; Stanley Kubrick's *2001* (which kept MGM financially solvent for over two years); James Dean's three films *East Of Eden*, *Rebel Without A Cause*, and *Giant*; and *West Side Story* which I personally remember playing First Run continuously for over one year at the Rivoli Theater on Broadway in New York City; not to mention the James Bond films which took home money in bushels full and still remain actively popular today.

Ladies and Gentlemen of the Jury, I am here on behalf of the power and artistry which not too many years ago people took for granted when they went into motion picture theaters which seems to have all but vanished from the American scene. Then too, the public likes what it sees and hears, but the public can never like what it does not see and what it does not hear. However, we have to be truthful and say that whatever financial successes Steven Spielberg may have achieved in motion pictures (at horrendously inflated ticket prices), as a cinematic artist he has not really contributed any substantial directorial landmarks at all.

In a sense, Steven Spielberg may be loosely compared in tennis with Bjorn Borg and John McEnroe. Borg and McEnroe won for several years because the players they faced during that time on the way to their many championships never really had the big punishing serves and volleys of a Pancho Gonzales, Jack Kramer, Frank Sedgman, or Lew Hoad; or the big canonball forehand of a Pancho Segura. Likewise, Spielberg came along when all the authentic directors were either dead, retired, or could not get financing or completion bonds. Metaphorically speaking, Spielberg (for all his tenacity and male *All About Eve* characteristics; he could badger you to death to do things for him even when it was against your own principles) never faced the big vintage competition of an Edward Dmytryk, Frank Capra, George Sidney, David Lean, Orson Welles, Alexander Korda, Fred Zinnemann, Michael Curtiz, Raoul Walsh, John Huston, John Ford, etc. In other words, Ladies and Gentlemen of the Jury, it was not that Stephen Spielberg motion pictures were so good, it was that the rest of the film product released was so bad as to venture little or no competition at all.

If I had known the cinematic mediocrity Steven Spielberg would eventually become responsible for, I guarantee you all that I would have let the Universal Security Guards throw Steven Spielberg off the MCA lot that fateful pivotal day.

By the end of 1968, after three years, I had had it with Steven Spielberg. I never really wanted to do the music for any of his films; (perhaps for several million dollars I would change my mind because I could use the money for my artistic, educational and humanitarian projects) even today his films lack depth, and he never heeded my suggestions to expand his horizons and study literature, music, drama, cinematography, and art.

It's quite evident to see that Steven Spielberg, for all his natural superficial cleverness, has difficulty handling actors and actresses in a scene; and he does not actually know how to successfully transfer a story into effective cinematic terms. Even with *Schindler's List* (which I have to happily admit is a marked improvement for Steven) each time he gets insecure with the Celluloid rendering of this notably poignant story (as beautifully scripted by Steven Zaillian) you are conscious of this insecurity especially in master shots to camera-shaking medium close-ups of chaotic mob scenes where it was quite apparent that realizing Spielberg's inability to adequately recreate and direct the mass confusion, he was forced to shake the camera in a vain attempt to synthetically achieve the desired effect.

The undeniable qualities of *Schindler's List* as a film is first and foremost in the great story and admirable screenplay which exemplifies how a Nazi party member's unique humanitarian morality can grow, amid inhuman adversity, to where it eventually consumes him, overpowering his own material and personal interests; then in the superlative acting by Liam Neeson, Ben Kingsley, Ralph Fiennes, and others; the authentic production design by Allan Starski; the editing by Michael Kahn; and the cinematography by Janusz Kaminski.

The directing of *Schindler's List* owes a great deal of influence from the style achieved previously in perhaps the best holocaust film ever made: *Europa Europa*.

Several years ago I had the Japanese assistant director from Spielberg's abortive film *1941* as a house guest for a couple of weeks. In citing Spielberg's obvious directorial obstacles, the Japanese assistant director revealed to me that his particular job was to keep the celebrated Japanese actor, Toshiro Mifune, happy and to translate Spielberg's wishes and directions to Mifune; who I understand was playing a Japanese World

War II submarine commander. The assistant director recounted to me one evening at dinner that "Mr. Mifune was really becoming exasperated with Spielberg's direction and told me in Japanese, 'Nobu-san, we've been in this stinking submarine for two weeks now; I don't think this Spielberg fellow knows what the hell he is doing.' And Mr. Mifune walked off the set." The celebrated French director Jean-Luc Godard when asked his opinion about the work of Steven Spielberg said, "It's all fakery. It's false. I know the difference between Beethoven and Spielberg."

Steven Spielberg is purported to have said that each time he sees a David Lean film, he feels as if he should go down on one knee and bow in reverence. I should like to suggest that, perhaps, in his particular case he should reconsider and go down on both knees.

During January 1964, having just concluded my first motion picture music score, which saved my life financially, I jubilantly vacated my New York City closet-cubicle apartment and decided to move west to Los Angeles in an attempt to secure more film scores which I felt would support my concert composing and conducting careers, and might even afford me the luxury of practicing the piano once again. Maestro Leopold Stokowski, who had programmed my music, liked the plan and encouraged me to implement it.

Through the consequence of my musical administrative work for Jeff Sparks at the United Nations, I had met Nat Kalcheim a major executive-owner of the powerful William Morris Agency in New York City who wrote a stalwart letter of recommendation on my behalf to his nephew Sid Kalcheim who was about my age and worked as an agent for the Morris Agency in Beverly Hills. Toward the end of 1964, as a result of Sid Kalcheim's benevolence, I signed a contract to do my first Hollywood motion picture. Although I was appreciative in receiving the assignment, I was grossly disappointed by this innocuous contemporary Technicolor western drama entitled *Git!* which became an eminently forgettable film although it had a viable premise and was released by Avco Embassy. I did the best I could with forty barking dogs who were actually the most convincing actors in the whole production. Moreover, I was forced to accept some pedestrian lyrics from the director producer who concocted them to my main theme which I had guitarist Laurendo Almeida prerecord. Since the main role had called for a youthful actor to portray a wandering Elvis Presley character who had to be able to at least sing a few simple ballads and who in the opening scenes gets arrested for the major crime of trespassing [?] (my how times have changed), I had to audition several male country and western vocalists (for the purpose of dubbing) because the young thespian who had been cast could not really sing and had been contracted simply because he bore a distant resemblance to the late screen idol James Dean; unfortunately, what this picture needed was James Dean.

There was one guitarist singer who impressed me (whom I had met through lyricist songwriter Carol Conners) who came to my apartment on Fairfax Avenue and genuinely wanted the job. He was a rather facile country music guitarist who not only had a unique singing virtue, but his natural speaking voice, demeanor and western Americana good looks caused me to suggest to him and the director producer that we, perhaps, pay off the remote James Dean look-alike and charter this young gentleman; because in my estimation all he would have had to do would have been to just read his lines as he was definitely the convincing personification of the character which this movie was hopelessly seeking. The singer and I rehearsed my song and I asked the director producer to come down to my flat and hear him, but he said that he was too busy reshooting certain sequences and asked that we perform the tune over the telephone. Amply, Ladies and Gentlemen of the Jury, I put the receiver on my grand piano and with the vocalist gently plucking his guitar and yours truly softly filling in the contrapuntal harmonies at the keyboard the both of us brought more quality to the song than the monotonous words deserved.

"Well, what do you think?" I asked. "Isn't he good?"

"Look kid," the director producer said to me. "He's okay, but I never heard of him. What's his name again?"

"Glen Campbell," I said. "He's very talented. You should put him in the film. He is that character. And we wouldn't have to dub in somebody else's voice."

"Kid, I don't think so. I really don't hear anything here. I'm going to stick with what I've already got."

Ladies and Gentleman of the Jury, I did everything I could to get Glen Campbell that assignment, but I was overruled at every juncture. Glen Campbell intensely wanted the assignment so that he would not have to take to the road again playing one night stands and be away from his wife. Several years later, after he had had various hit recordings and a major television show, I casually crossed paths again with Glen Campbell who said to me, "Boy, I really had wanted that job."

"I know," I said, "and I wanted you to get it. But it's a good thing, in a way, that you didn't do the picture," I went on, "because it probably would have ruined your career."

We both had a good laugh; although if the director producer had listened to my initial instincts and added the then unknown Glen Campbell (even with the feeble script) that picture would be at least playing extensive local television today instead of the two dollars and twenty-eight cents ASCAP royalties I'm receiving from the film's current play dates in South Africa.

I did the spotting and timing of the music cues for *Git!* with the production's two masterful editors Don Tate and Doug Robertson at Producers Studio which was opposite Paramount Pictures; it has now been transformed into Raleigh Studios. Don Tate was a favored film editor for Bob Hope, and Doug Robertson had worked closely with the illustrious British master, Sir Carol Reed. Both of these gentlemen did not relish laboring either on *Git!* or with our director producer whom they considered unsuitable for the Celluloid medium; but as they said, it was employment. Don Tate was quite adept in getting rid of our director producer whom we nicknamed Eeek so that he could edit the picture in peace. But he advised me that it was much easier in clearing Bob Hope out of the editing room because Don would usually say to Hope, "You know Bob? I was just studying some footage of your golf swing here and I do believe you've acquired a little slice to the left on your follow through." Since Bob Hope was a golf addict, he would inwardly become alarmed and then apprise Don Tate of some important meetings he had to attend to and abruptly leave the studio for the golf course and his PGA touring professionals for two or three days at a time.

One warm morning as we were synchronizing the music tracks (our editing cubicle door was open) I heard this repeated hoarse ill sounding cough not too far away. Feeling concerned, I went outside to see if I could be of any assistance and when I turned to the right of the doorway, approximately twenty feet directly in front of me, I saw that the sick man was none other than Buster Keaton. He was smoking outside the sound stage door. "Are you alright?" I asked. He was coughing so much and expectorating that he couldn't really answer as he looked at me with such pain in his eyes gesturing that he was okay even though I knew otherwise. "You'd better stay away from those cigarettes," I said as he nodded and I returned to the editing room.

"Gee," I said to Don Tate and Doug Robertson, "that's Buster Keaton out there. What's he doing here? He should be in a Health Spa." I found out that Buster Keaton was appearing in one of those *Beach Blanket Bingo Bikini* surfboard pictures because he needed the money. You could tell that he was undoubtedly quite ill. I thought, at the very least, that he should be resting at the Motion Picture Health And Welfare Home in Woodland Hills; even though at that time there wasn't the facility they have there today. Both Don and Doug told me that 'Buster Keaton probably doesn't have enough credits.'

I said, "What do you mean, credits?"

Don Tate said, "You know, now when you do one film you receive a certain number of credits. When Buster Keaton made most of his silent films they did not have the Union or the Motion Picture Health And Welfare Home. So he probably doesn't have enough points to qualify going there."

"Enough points to qualify," I echoed, "He and his colleagues made Hollywood."

Doug Robertson agreed, "Yes, well he probably lost all of his money like most of those silent movie stars."

Several months later there had been a taped national broadcast of my second Philadelphia Orchestra performance which had taken place earlier in 1964 with William Smith conducting that great ensemble in my *Miraflores for String Orchestra*. I had been one of the youngest composers ever to have been performed by The Philadelphia Orchestra season 1960-61 when Smith had conducted my *Dance Barbaro for Percussion*.

An acquaintance whom I had met through Edward "Buzz" Barton telephoned me one day saying, "Harold Lloyd heard your music over the radio and would like to meet you."

I said, "Harold Lloyd, Harold Lloyd; isn't he the fellow who used to hang from clocks in silent movies?"

"Yes," he said.

I had never seen any of Lloyd's films, but I had glanced at reference photos and articles about his daring cinematic feats in motion picture reference books and magazines. "Well, fine," I said. "Bring him by. I'm busy scoring this film, but bring him by anyway."

I had the feeling that Harold Lloyd was basically like all the other silent movie stars who I'd been told had lost all of their money, and were as impoverished as church mice and had to do all sorts of other things in order to survive. In fact, I vividly remembered during my teens watching a humorously sensitive Groucho Marx trying to coax the noted silent screen star Francis X. Bushman on the television quiz show *You Bet Your Life* into winning a badly needed few hundred dollars.

Several days later Harold Lloyd came to my composing apartment, which was then at 1419 North Fairfax Avenue #3, not far from Sunset Boulevard, and this acquaintance nervously introduced us as soon as I opened the door and immediately left.

As it was around lunch time, I asked Harold Lloyd if he would like to have some natural vegetable soup which I had just prepared. He said yes, and I gave him a couple of large bowls with organic unyeasted whole wheat bread and the way he ate it all led me to believe that he hadn't eaten in a week.

After the soup, he sat on the couch near my grand piano and asked me quite politely if I would play something for him; because he said that it would mean so much to him. I played, a little Chopin, a little Brahms, a little Lambro, as I could sense how genuinely Harold Lloyd adored good music.

"Do you know anything about me?" He asked after I finished playing.

"No," I said. "I've never seen any of your motion pictures."

"Yes, they're very difficult to come by now," he said.

I added that I had occasionally seen testimonials in foreign film magazines about him, but he explained to me that he actually wasn't that interested in motion pictures anymore and now he just loved to spend his time listening to good music and taking stereo photographs.

"You have to come up to my place and listen to some music," Harold Lloyd said. "I have a record player and some records."

"Oh, of course," I said. "I'd like to."

I had an excess copy of Arturo Benedetti Michelangeli performing the Rachmaninoff *Fourth Piano Concerto* with the Ravel *Piano Concerto in G* on the other side so I said, "Here is a wonderful recording by an exceptionally great pianist. I have an extra copy, and I'd very much like for you to have it."

"Oh, I might already have this," Harold Lloyd said.

"I don't think you have this recording," I said, "because it's difficult to get."

Harold Lloyd said, "Well, I'll take it only on the condition that if I do have it, that you'll take it back. I'm kind of sure that I have this recording."

I thought to myself, 'this poor fellow's mind must be failing.' So I just humored Harold Lloyd along and said, "Of course I'll take it back if you already have it."

"Here's my number" he said, "and I'll answer the phone here."

I could not quite fathom the remark because I had visions of Harold Lloyd living in a one room apartment.

I neglected to call Harold Lloyd as I was finishing the score to *Git!* which took longer than expected because our unskilled director producer had to continually re-shoot certain sequences; the money for which I found out was being extracted from our music budget.

About a week later Harold Lloyd telephoned me. "Phillip, when are you going to come up and listen to some music?" He asked.

I said, "Well, I have about another week or two on this film and then I'll call you."

"Oh, please do," he said, "I enjoyed meeting you and getting together and talking."

I phoned Harold Lloyd a couple of times to reassure him that I had not forgotten and to inform him that I also appreciated our meeting and that I definitely would visit within the next ten days. Now, I was new to Los Angeles; I didn't have his address; and even if I had, I wouldn't have known exactly where it was. The inquisitive thing was that each time I called Harold Lloyd he not only answered the telephone before the second ring (or not at all), but he did not answer it with the customary "Hello," but rather with an exclamatory, "Bucket!"

This time I blurted out, "Bucket? Crumpet, Bucket!"

Harold Lloyd said, "Bucket, bucket, bucket! Who is this?"

"This is Phillip Lambro," I said.

"Oh, Phillip, when are you going to come up?"

"Well, I'll be up; when would you like me to come up?"

"How about tomorrow?"

I said, "Okay, tomorrow's fine. Could you give me your address?" He told me 1225 Benedict Canyon, and we agreed upon a time early the next afternoon.

I did not know where Benedict Canyon was because I had only been in Los Angeles a brief time. I just knew where Fairfax Avenue was and Sunset Boulevard and maybe part of Hollywood and a trifle of Beverly Hills.

Harold Lloyd said, "Do you know where The Beverly Hills Hotel is?"

"Yes," I said, "because I've had several interviews there for potential motion picture scoring assignments."

"Well, I'm not far from there," he explained. "You just take another right, and you'll see Benedict Canyon.

I said, "Fine." The following afternoon I drove up Benedict Canyon. There were many opulent homes, but I calculated that Harold Lloyd must live further away where, perhaps, there were one or two room apartments. But then the numbers abruptly jumped and did not correspond to the figures he had given me. I arrived at the closest equivalent by going back and forth a couple of times; and since it was a rather pleasant day, I proceeded to one of the nearest homes and rang the chimes. The screen door was closed, but the main entrance was wide open and I could see inside. Nobody answered. I pressed the doorbell again and a middle aged lady reticently staying her distance approached and said, "Yes, what do you want?"

"I'm looking for 1225 Benedict Canyon," I said. "Can you help me? I've gone up and down the road several times, and yours is the closest number to it."

"Whose house is it?" She asked, coming a little closer.

"Harold Lloyd's," I said. When I mentioned Harold Lloyd the woman's whole demeanor transformed and she opened the screen door and came out and asked, "Oh, are you a friend of Mr. Lloyd's?"

"Yes," I said.

"Well, come here, dear," she said leading me by the arm down her green lawn and driveway. It's over there," she said pointing to a large clump of trees. "That's the Lloyd estate." Lloyd estate? I thought to myself.

I got back into my car and drove to the gated opening where I could see that the dense shrubbery had covered the stone with the numerals.

They were expecting me. There was an armed guard in his little Buckingham Palace stone cubicle just inside to the left of the wrought iron gate. And when I motored up this quarter mile driveway I could scarcely believe the horticultural beauty; it was like being among the Hanging Gardens of Babylon.

There were geese running around a pond amid roughly sixteen acres of Italian Mediterranean gardens with twelve fountains. And having lived in Italy, I found it comparable to a large Palladio villa. The residence had over forty major rooms; with a twelve car garage; Olympic sized tile inlaid swimming pool with a huge cabana you could actually live in complete with a kitchen and theater size motion picture screen; a nine hole golf course; Davis Cup sized tennis court and small club house; and a canoe water course. And there he was, Harold Lloyd, at the top of the courtyard waiting for me. In fact, I was to find out afterward that he called this manor, Green Acres. Part of it was in Los Angeles and the other portion was in Beverly Hills.

"Phillip, come on up," he said.

Ascending the stairs, we went in. There was an eminently large foyer and hallway with highly polished dark maroon tiles and a deeply burnished wood spiral staircase to the right with a black wrought iron banister. It was immaculately clean and well preserved; however, with the lavish dated antique museum furnishings which I had been certain were purchased at notable expense, I could not help feeling as if I had stepped into a time machine and suddenly perambulated into 1927.

We went down an Oriental carpeted particularly long hallway with a high ceiling and eventually into a huge sunken living room. I never knew the exact dimensions of the living room, but it was colossal. Later that afternoon Harold Lloyd was to explain to me how the Beverly Hills and City Of Los Angeles dividing line went right through this enormous living chamber. "Phillip, do you know that I'm sitting here in Los Angeles and you're over there in Beverly Hills?" He asked.

To give you an idea of how big the mansion was, that day while we were listening to some new recordings and Harold was looking for a disc which he had misplaced, the house telephone in the outer foyer was ringing and Harold asked me if I would please go and answer it because nobody was home. I started running (and I was a pretty good sprinter) from the living room, up the few stairs and along the carpeted lengthy hallway, and finally into the vestibule where I ultimately picked up the receiver to a dial tone because the telephone had rung about seven times and whoever it was had finally hung up.

Yes indeed, Harold Lloyd did have "a record player." At the time it was hand made by his friend, Sol Marantz, whom he had met at a Hi-Fi Show. It was about 150 watts per channel. Now, we are speaking about 1964 and the sound was insatiably spectacular by even today's standards.

It was just the most incredible surprise to me. He also had two sets of huge theater speakers; and yes, Harold Lloyd did have some records: he had more recordings than the average major retail record shop. In fact, he had a secretary just for the express purpose of cataloging his recordings.

I could sense that here was a faithful audiophile. Harold Lloyd knew the names of most of the major composers: he knew who Chopin was; he knew who Brahms was; he knew who Beethoven and Bach were; even though he did not know much about their actual lives in depth. Some compositions and composers he would sometimes forget; but I recognized immediately that here was a genuine music devotee, in that the music itself was the most important entity for him and because he appreciated and would love to play all kinds of different types and styles of music. For example, he would say, "Now, here, this is an aria from an opera -- oh, I forget the opera's name -- let's see. Oh, yes, *Lucia*. And it's Maria Callas. What do you think of this? I like it."

Harold Lloyd had little books about composers and artists lives which he would read. He actually could not understand why most composers had lived in poverty when they had written such eloquent and stunning music. And, indeed, he did have the Arturo Benedetti Michelangeli recording. I nearly fell off my chair. He explained to me that listening to recorded music and taking stereo photographs had been his passion since retiring from motion pictures. Harold Lloyd disclosed that he did not like going out to social gatherings anymore; and he emphatically did not wish to meet anyone connected with the entertainment industry. I found out a few years later that it took Peter O'Toole many years just to accidentally force his drunken introduction upon Harold while in Paris. (That incident is contained within my Paradox Island Chapter). During that time, all Harold Lloyd seemed to want was to encounter on isolated occasions intriguing people connected with music, or photography.

Apropos Harold Lloyd's answering his private telephone "Bucket," is an interesting chronicle. I never questioned him about it until several years later. In a sense, I was correct: Harold Lloyd did live and spend a great deal of time in one isolated small room; even though this chamber (approximately ten feet by ten feet) was right next to his unusually large upstairs master bedroom within an enormous villa. In this bedroom he would sleep, lounge around and watch Television. The unlisted telephone number which he had originally given to me was his own personal one within that sequestered room which no one ever answered but he. This upstairs cubicle adjacent to his bedroom was totally off-limits to everyone except Harold. It was where he used to have confidential phone conversations and look at his immense collection of stereo photographic slides. These negatives were all contained in many brown leather attache cases which fitted into specially constructed wall shelving housing thousands of all kinds of stereo color and black and white photos. You had to look through a large viewfinder in order to see these spectacular nature panoramic color renditions of Lake Louise and the Rose Parade which Harold Lloyd attended incognito every year.

Harold invited me into that inner sanctum several times after we got to know one another. And since he knew that I appreciated feminine beauty, he also showed me hundreds upon hundreds of stereo slides which he had taken of comely female nude models, including a young Marilyn Monroe.

They were rather well produced and I thought rendered in extremely good taste. Perhaps during 1965 they might have been deemed pornographic, but they were all of exceptionally pretty and in some instances unquestionably pulchritudinous maidens in artistically seductive poses.

I remember Harold saying (one day after he had shown me about a hundred and fifty photographs of naked models), "Oh Phillip, you must look at this one. What do you think about her? Isn't she beautiful?"

As I was becoming a trifle bored from eyeing all the three dimensional gentlewomen as attractive as some of them were, I said, "Harold, couldn't we perhaps meet some of these girls in person, sometime?"

He told me that he used to employ figure models by the day and sometimes through the weekend. They would venture out on location with him, now and again into the desert where he would take hundreds of stereo photographs and the best ones would ultimately end up cataloged in the brown attache cases within this smaller room where his private telephone was. Of course, I also had the main telephone number of his mansion (which was also unlisted), but Harold Lloyd almost never answered that phone himself; leaving it either to the servants, his daughter Gloria, or his cute Lolita-type grand daughter, Sue; or Sue-Sue, as he used to refer to her.

The several times I recollect his inviting me into his privy room over the years, the telephone would ring and he would always answer it "Bucket!" Now and again, "Bucket! Bucket, Bucket, Bucket." Just as he would invariably respond whenever I would call on that line. After the session where I had become a trifle indifferent about viewing the photos of all the undressed paradigms, we went downstairs and out onto the spacious back lawn in the middle of his sumptuous Italian gardens where we sat down on wicker chairs with Harold's two small French poodles in nervous attendance. The sun was shining. It was a beautiful Southern California day.

"You know, Harold," I said. "It's really none of my business, but why do you always answer your private telephone Bucket?"

"Well," he said, "I know you can keep a secret; but while I'm alive, you must never, never repeat what I'm going to tell you to anyone. Agreed..?"

I said, "Fine. I won't repeat it to anyone while you're alive."

"I've always been a very close friend of Howard Hughes." "Really?" I said. "I've heard that he's dead."

"No, he's not dead; he's just not feeling too well."

At the time Harold revealed to me that Hughes was living and commuting in penthouse isolation from Las Vegas, Nevada to Managua, Nicaragua.

"I hear from him about two or three times a year," Harold said. "I never know when the hell he's going to call. He's called two in the afternoon and two in the morning. He could telephone anytime. And we talk and reminisce for about an hour or two; and we've had this bet for many years. If I answer the phone, Hello, I have to pay him $2,000 dollars. But if he calls and I answer Bucket, he has to send me a check for $2,000 dollars."

So Harold said, "I'll be damned if I'm going to pay Howard Hughes $2,000 dollars! So I answer the telephone, Bucket every time."

And of course, while Harold Lloyd was alive I honored his confidence and did not mentioned this story to anyone.

I never brought up Howard Hughes name while speaking with Harold Lloyd because I had not known Hughes. However, there were several occasions when I was having an extended conversation alone with Harold where he would refer to a story involving Hughes; but it was only when we were totally alone. Harold Lloyd never brought up Howard Hughes' name, or spoke about him while his family or other people were around us.

I recall one day as we were conversing about hospitals and doctors when Harold told me how Howard Hughes during a test flight in one of his experimental fighter jets during the 1940's crash landed the craft on a residential tree lined street in Beverly Hills. "Damndest thing you ever saw, Phillip. Right there in the middle of Beverly Hills. Nearly killed, Howard. Luckily he didn't kill anyone. Some serviceman pulled him out of the plane. I went to visit him in the hospital several times. He hated hospital beds and continually complained about how uncomfortable they were; and he apologized that he had to greet me lying flat on his back, but he said that he was thinking about inventing a more comfortable hospital bed. Well, a few days later when I returned to visit him, he was raised up, but lying down. I was amazed. He had designed and had his engineers develop and deliver to him the prototype hospital bed we all know today: whereby you can raise a portion of the bed just by cranking it up to the desired position."

Another interesting account Harold related to me about Howard Hughes was how they used to like to go bowling together during the 1940's.

"Howard and one of his friends, Gene Mako (the tennis champion) and myself used to go bowling quite often," Harold said to me. "And, of course, we used to bet a little on the side. Gene Mako and I would usually beat Howard and whoever he brought along with him. But one day Howard felt really confident that he and his partner would beat us so he raised the ante. It was a very close game, but Gene and I barely won. I tell you, Phillip, I never saw Howard so angry. I went over as he was changing his bowling shoes and swearing to himself."

"Come on, Howard," I said, "it's only a friendly little game among us. Why are you so upset?"

"Why am I so upset?" Hughes exclaimed. "Do you know who the hell my partner was?"

"Why, one of your usual friends," Harold said.

"That was the current United States Bowling Champion!"

Howard Hughes genuinely relished Harold Lloyd's films. I understand that Hughes personally considered Harold Lloyd the superior comedic genius over Chaplin and Keaton. Harold told me that it was Hughes who continually baited him into coming out of retirement against Harold's own initial better judgment during 1946. "I never wanted to return to motion pictures," I remember Harold telling me. "It was Howard Hughes who kept after me for so long, that I finally relented to do *Mad Wednesday*. I never should have done that picture; it was awful." *Mad Wednesday* was finally released 1950.

At this time, I could not comment one way or another because I had never seen even one Harold Lloyd motion picture. I eventually did see *Mad Wednesday* after Harold's death and noticed why he was so disenchanted with it; although, he did tell me the plot line when I asked him and I do recall his speaking glowingly about his female co-star Frances Ramsden.

"I could never understand why Frances never became a big star," Harold remarked once. "She was beautiful; she had a wonderful voice; she was intelligent. I just don't understand it."

Apropos Howard Hughes, I had met and become friends with an attractive and rational blonde young lady by the name of Pat Crosby. Pat had initially been a Las Vegas show girl who eventually married and divorced Dennis Crosby (one of Bing's sons); and to give you an idea of her unparalleled character, Pat accepted only one dollar in alimony at a time when in California if you married a man for twenty-two minutes and then divorced him, the Court usually awarded the woman the entire man's financial holdings in addition to most of his red blood cells. Since Pat had borne Dennis Crosby two sons, she did accept minimum child maintenance. Several years later, Dennis Crosby endeavored to have the nominal child support payments reduced in Court. Pat never asked to have them augmented and tried avoiding any legal confrontation. However, after the Judge reviewed the low monthly disbursements the court ordered Dennis Crosby to pay an increase.

One afternoon while Pat and I were chatting about money and the terrible things we had seen people do to get it, she told me a narrative about how Howard Hughes had noticed her working in a Los Angeles nightclub during the 1950's and assiduously pursued her for a date.

"At the time," Pat said, "I was living in an apartment near Gardner and Sunset and I had to support my first son by my teen-age marriage, and I informed Howard that I would be happy to go out for dinner with him on my day off provided that he pay for the baby sitter."

"How much will that cost?" Hughes asked.

"About ten dollars," Pat replied.

"That's no problem," Hughes said. And Pat and Howard Hughes made arrangements to meet that week.

"Well, Phillip," Pat said, "on the afternoon of our dinner engagement, Howard telephoned saying that his chauffeur would be by with the baby sitter money because he did not want me to be late. The chauffeur came by and handed me an envelope with ten brand new one hundred dollar bills in it. I immediately called for the chauffeur to come back and told him to go around the corner to Mimi's Kitchen and break one of the hundreds into twenties. While he was gone, I wrote Howard a note saying that twenty dollars would be more than adequate to take care of the baby sitter and that I hoped he would not be offended, but I was returning the rest of his money."

Pat said that when she and Hughes finally encountered each other for dinner that twilight, he was absolutely disarmed over what she had done.

"You're the first girl who's ever refused my money," said Hughes. "I don't know if I can accept that. In every relationship I've ever had with a woman, I always pay for everything."

Pat revealed to me that when she informed Howard Hughes over the table that all she had agreed to do was meet and have dinner with him, neither of which entailed a relationship, that Hughes ego was so deflated he spent the entire evening explaining to Pat why they could never conclude a romantic association.

I discovered another Howard Hughes chronicle from Herbert Flam, the late former U. S. Open Tennis finalist and 1950's Davis Cup player who disclosed to me around 1965 that one of his wealthy building contractor friends used to play poker for relatively high stakes at a regular weekly game in one of The Beverly Hills Hotel bungalows where most of the participants often times did not know each other. Herbie informed me that the contractor told him that this man (who they later found out was Howard Hughes) would occasionally come and play. However, this particular day he said to everyone, "Come six o'clock, whether I'm winning or losing, I have to leave because I have an important engagement." It seems that the unknown Howard Hughes was winning quite a bit when six o'clock arrived; but as he was leaving, one of the players who had lost heavily began to mumble things about people who depart when they're way ahead. The contractor who had been in the game further stated to Herb Flam, "We didn't know who he was, until he nonchalantly pulled out his check book and wrote a check."

"Here," said Hughes, throwing his personal check for one million dollars down on the table in front of the disgruntled poker player, "I'm tired of your complaining. I told you I had to leave at six o'clock whether I was winning or losing. So I'll give you a chance to win more than you've ever won before; I'll let you cut the deck for a million dollars. Put up, or shut up."

When everyone saw the name on the check and the amount, the whole room fell silent.

"Well..?" Asked Hughes.

The fussing poker trouper embarrassingly apologized as Hughes picked up his check and left the room.

The only other person whom I ever met who knew Howard Hughes was Bill Reynolds, one of William Hornbeck's editorial and sound technicians at Universal Pictures during late 1965 and early 1966 as I was concluding the dubbing to my music score of *And Now Miguel*. I used to order late lunch when it was impossible for me to leave, and I happened to ask Bill Reynolds if he wanted to be my guest for a sandwich and some apple juice. He seemed flattered that I was considerate enough to think of him.

"Mr. Lambro," said Bill Reynolds, "let me tell you a story about when I was working for Howard Hughes at RKO. He was making *The Outlaw* and was personally supervising me with the dubbing and editing. One day we were especially having a long and difficult time, because Howard really didn't understand the mechanics of film making. We must have been in the editing room eight hours without a break when Howard suddenly said he was hungry and instructed me to order some food. When the food arrived, he further directed me not to touch it. He proceeded to open it himself and began eating as we worked. I waited a while to see if he would offer me some, but he didn't. After about ten minutes I said, "You know, Howard, I'm hungry too.""

"Oh yeah," Hughes remarked. "Don't touch any of mine, but why don't you order some food for yourself."

Bill Reynolds also told me that for long periods of time Howard Hughes would not visit RKO Studios which he owned. It seems that one day Hughes tried to get onto the lot driving one of his old cars, dressed rather shabbily and sporting about two days growth of beard. The young guard at the gate refused to believe that Hughes was who he said he was and further demanded some identification. When Hughes advised the young man that he did not have any, the guard declined to let him onto the RKO lot. Bill Reynolds declared that Howard Hughes also did not even have any money to make the phone call to him, and had to go all the way back to his Romaine Street office and telephone Bill to meet him at the gate so Hughes could finally be admitted. Bill Reynolds said that when Hughes returned, he ordered that the young watchman be given a sizable increase in wages for strictly observing security procedures.

In addition to my being a concert and symphonic composer, I believe that Harold Lloyd liked me at this time because I represented the younger generation. I think he enjoyed my personality, and I found out that he appreciated the fact that I could not be seduced by money.

The acquaintance who had introduced Harold Lloyd to me was involved in a subtle extortion plot with another friend of his to try and blackmail Lloyd for about $1 million dollars shortly after I had become friendly with Harold.

They telephoned me several times and tried to enlist my aid in this attempt to extort the $1 million dollars offering me an equal share of the money. They had confronted Harold informing him that if he did not give them $1 million dollars, they were going to go directly to Harold's wife (Mildred Davis, the socialite and former silent screen star) and inform her of all of Harold's extramarital activities with figure models and other denuded women whom he was supposedly advocating on the side. I, of course, got disgruntled at their seeking to take advantage of Harold and told them so when they would phone me. "Look, this is not right," I remember telling them. "Whatever he does is his own business as long as he's not harming anyone. I don't believe in blackmail and extortion; it's an atrocious crime." I said, "I just don't believe in it, and if I were you, I'd forget the whole thing and leave the man alone."

Years later, I found out that Harold had called in agent friends of his from the FBI who quashed the extortion attempt. Evidently there was a phone tap on all of the conversations (including mine) so when the FBI played the tapes for Harold, I understand that Phillip Lambro stock went up immediately.

A lot of people were after Harold Lloyd's money. In fact, I recall once while I was with Harold one afternoon in his personal bunker, the then Governor of California, Edmund Pat Brown, calling him about donating, or investing some money. And Harold said, "I told you not to call me asking for money. I'm not going to give you one red cent. I give money to the Shriners and that's enough." After that, he politely cut off Governor Brown; hung up the telephone; and turning to me said, "I'd like to see you talk to the Governor of the State of California that way."

I also remember Gloria Swanson phoning Harold a few times struggling to get Harold to invest in opening a health food restaurant she had in mind. He used to make fun of her natural food intake and especially my Japanese Zen Macrobiotic Diet, too.

"Now, Gloria," Harold said. "Tell the truth. Wouldn't you really love to have a nice, big, thick, juicy T-bone steak with plenty of mashed potatoes and gravy on it, rather than all that grass and carrot sticks you people eat?"

I was laughing mutely in the background as Harold was beaming at me while satirizing Gloria Swanson over the telephone.

"You should meet my friend Phillip Lambro; he eats all the same kind of grass and rice as you do."

I never encountered Gloria Swanson through Harold, but I was eventually introduced to her and her medical doctor friend about a year after that conversation by the maitre d' at The Aware Inn restaurant on Sunset Boulevard. Evidently she was having a dinner date with her plastic surgeon. I was quite surprised to discover how diminutive Gloria Swanson actually was.

Harold Lloyd disclosed to me that he was a Grand Potentate of the Shriners, and I understood that over the years he had bestowed a great deal of financial assistance upon that organization. I do not think that he donated very much of his fortune to anything other than the Shriners.

Although he was mythologically affluent from all kinds of tenacious investments, and the rare phenomena of being perhaps the only opulent person in Hollywood to have escaped the 1929 Stock Market Crash, when it came to money, Harold Lloyd was unquestionably closefisted; even with himself. I think that this was another reason he liked me. I never asked him for money. In fact, there were a few times when we went out to eat, where I picked up the check. Obviously, Harold Lloyd had had the best of everything which legal tender could buy; and he had a generously pleasing and rather folksy personality, but when it came to monetary matters, he was exceptionally frugal, to say the least. There was the occasion Gloria Lloyd (Harold's daughter) wanted me to take her to the Old World Restaurant while we were at the mansion, and as we were about ready to leave, I noticed that I had left all of my ready cash back at my apartment. Gloria confronted Harold in the foyer asking for enough money for dinner. Harold pulled out a few hundred dollars from his pocket desperately looking for a ten dollar bill after which Gloria snatched one of the twenties from his hand, running out the door yelling,

"Phillip, hurry up; let's go before he catches us." Harold was actually quite peeved by what Gloria had done.

After I had known Harold for about five years, he said to me on one occasion, "Phillip, you never knew the old Lloyd, did you?"

"What do you mean?" I remarked sarcastically. "I'm looking at the old Lloyd."

"No, no," he laughed. "I mean the movie star Lloyd."

"No," I said, "I've never seen any of your films. Are they any good?"

He said that he wished he could show me a few of his silent movies because he wanted to see what I thought of them. Harold knew me well enough to know that, if asked, I would always inform anyone of my honest opinion. He had a large motion picture screen and a projection room right there at his villa; but, unfortunately, the 35mm theater projector wasn't working as it had been broken for several years. When I suggested that he hire someone from Birns & Sawyer to fix it, he told me that the part did not exist anymore. When I further proposed that he employ somebody to duplicate the piece, he informed me that if he could not have the exact replacement as originally manufactured and intended, he preferred that it stay collapsed. He was adamant in that respect. If Harold could not find the correct substitute item for anything in his life, he wouldn't manufacture one, he would just let the object stay unworkable in its original format.

Because I only knew him as "Harold Lloyd Real Person" as opposed to "Harold Lloyd Famous Silent Movie Star" I think he found that refreshing and valued it.

Harold eventually invited me to see one of his films. He telephoned me one particular week shortly after the broken down projector discussion (late 1969) and I met him at his estate about 11:30 a.m. Thursday 8 January 1970. Harold had his part time driver take us in his station wagon to the home of Richard Simonton, the Chairman of Muzak, out in Toluca Lake who had a 35mm theater projector and small screening room and that's where I saw my first Harold Lloyd film: *Grandma's Boy*.

I was amazed. There was no question about it; Harold Lloyd was absolutely a remarkable athletic comedic genius. The astonishing element from my perspective was that the Harold Lloyd I personally knew (like my experience with Jack Benny) was basically not a naturally funny individual at all. Even after that entire time, the movie which had been shot in 1922 (with few exceptions) held together rather well even though it was only about five reels; which, as Harold told me, "was a long moving picture for comedy in those days."

"Well, what did you think?" I remember his asking me.

"Hey Lloyd," I said, "you were amazingly talented. You were a real artist."

Harold was so happy that I esteemed his work, not only because he knew how candid I was, but inasmuch as this respect and praise was coming from a concert musician of the younger generation.

Apropos Harold Lloyd's appreciation of concert artists and how he isolated himself from the Hollywood community during his later life, Garson Kanin had invited him to parties probably in excess of two dozen times and Harold would always decline. During the time I was with Harold, I recall his rejecting Garson Kanin at least two times over the telephone.

"Oh Garson," Harold would say. "Thank you for thinking of me, but I really wouldn't fit into one of your parties...Why..? Well, because you always have all those Hollywood types there who ask me a thousand questions, and quite frankly I really get bored."

However, about a year before Harold died, he told me, "Garson Kanin called me again. You know I never go to his parties because they always have those Hollywood types there. But I just happened to ask him out of curiosity, 'Well, who's going to be there, Garson?' And he mentioned Artur Rubinstein." Harold disclosed that this was the only time he had ever ventured to a Garson Kanin function because he coveted the opportunity to meet famed concert pianist Artur Rubinstein. Harold recounted the story to me like an enthusiastic little boy. "Oh, I met Artur Rubinstein. You know how many recordings I have of his," he said. "I told Rubinstein how much of a fan I am of his playing and how I own practically all of his RCA recordings; and you know what? Rubinstein embraced me and said, 'You don't know what a fan I am of yours; and how many times, during the 1920's and 30's when I was depressed over my concert career, I had such great joy watching your motion pictures, especially in Europe,' he said. Can you imagine, Phillip? Artur Rubinstein was a fan of mine. I couldn't believe it." Harold was so excited.

Having been correspondingly pleased by my reaction to *Grandma's Boy*, Harold invited me to view another one of his silent films. The following Wednesday (14 January 1970) at noon I picked Harold up at Green Acres and drove him to the Simonton's where he ran *The Freshman* which was a seven reel feature made in 1925. I was altogether surprised once again by the quality of this motion picture. You must realize that these films were produced before I was born, and I viewed them not as contemporary Panavision Dimension 150, but as pictures related to what I knew to be, historically, a reflection of that era. Harold had come from a poor mid-west family that continually, from what I gathered, suffered a lot of social and financial humiliation as had a large segment of our population at the time; so his ability to mirror in his screen characters this drive to overcome and succeed within the social mores of the day (amid all the personal comedic humiliations) was, I think to a large extent, the reason he attracted millions of adoring admirers world wide.

Over the years, I discovered from Harold how he had become a movie star. Harold Lloyd did not mind telling me about his early life because he sensed that I was actually more interested in "Harold Lloyd Person" than "Harold Lloyd Famous Silent Movie Star."

In fact, one day I asked him how he happened to get into acting? I was not surprised when he declared that he had come from rather unprosperous beginnings in Nebraska. I felt that this accounted for two significant entities in his life: one, the legendary Italian Renaissance mansion which he had constructed for himself during the early to middle 1920's where no amount of money had been spared to purchase the very best available during that time; and two, the preoccupation of being quite overly frugal with his financial assets. I believe psychologically Harold Lloyd had this trepidation that one day he would awaken from this luxuriant dream world he had built and find himself again in abject poverty. The Harold Lloyd I knew was a somewhat commonplace "down home" individual who tended to mask the intelligence which he naturally possessed. In fact, if you happened to be on his estate and encountered him unknown among all of his workers, you'd have a difficult time singling him out as you would have probably thought that he was just one of the help.

He revealed to me that during his teens he and his father had planned to depart for either New York City, or California, where there was substantial activity. And since they could not decide which way to go, they flipped a coin and California won. They bought a ticket to go to San Diego where Harold's father had a slight business opportunity and Harold could finish High School. But Harold told me that the fare absorbed all of their extra funds, so in order to survive, they made popcorn on the train and sold it in bags to the weary travellers.

After Harold completed High School and his Dad forfeited the enterprise he had had in San Diego, Harold described how they arrived here in Los Angeles, renting one room downtown, after which Harold then acquired a menial job working for Southern California Edison while pursuing his theatrical ambitions after hours.

Harold explained the frustrations he had experienced at being habitually rejected by all of the Hollywood casting directors and studios who were producing the silent one-reelers of the time.

One day, however, somewhere near MacArthur Park, Harold saw a group shooting a film which he tried to infiltrate in front of the camera during one of the mob scenes. A production crew member noticed him and immediately proceeded to throw him off the set.

In those days Harold advised me (to my initial surprise) that they did not film from written scripts. The director would appear with his cast; an actor; an actress; and some extras; and they would just improvise and make up stories and situations as they went along. It seems this was the operational process from which these one and two reelers were spawned, which eventually were shown in nickelodeons. My education of the silent movie epoch, what limited knowledge I have of it, I owe to Harold Lloyd.

Harold mentioned that even though he had been dismissed several times from Hal Roach Studios, one morning he observed that they were filming a picture with large masses of extras. Harold made himself up and crawled under the fenced tarpaulin, and managed to get in front of the grinding camera where everyone thought he was one of the supernumeraries.

When they developed and ran the rushes in the projection room the following days, Hal Roach happened to remark, "Who's that wiry bastard over there?"

The director said, "Oh, my god, Mr. Roach, I'm terribly sorry, that guy's been sneaking in..."

Roach said, "No, go get him. I like him. Find out who he is."

Hal Roach's subordinates finally located Harold and offered him a contract. Harold's first film shorts became unquestionably popular. He and Roach did additional ones, which also were tremendously appealing with the public.

Shortly after this, as Harold Lloyd became a well-known star, he began to receive major offers from the other studios which forced Hal Roach to accept Harold's condition precedents of ownership participation; with the possession of each film reverting to Harold after a stipulated amount of time. According to what Harold told me, he took less money in exchange for proprietorship of his motion pictures; and that way, he was able to amass a fortune at the box office from first dollar; especially since, as he revealed, "at that time, U. S. Federal Income Taxes were minutely voluntary."

Everyone thought Harold Lloyd was crazy to take such a gamble, but Harold fathomed otherwise.

One afternoon while we were sitting outside in the rear Italian foliage of his manor, Harold described to me what a stunning estate and gardens Adolph Zukor (the owner of Paramount Pictures) also had in New York.

"Zukor had been trying to sign me to do some pictures for him at Paramount," Harold said, "so I accepted a summer invitation to go meet him in New York. In those days, it was a long trip by train. I remember after I got there having to wait about 45 minutes for Zukor in this large gazebo over a natural stream that went right through his property. It was really quite beautiful."

Out of curiosity, I asked Harold what kind of man was Adolph Zukor.

"He was tough as nails," Harold said. "He kept telling me that I was crazy to want to produce and retain my own films, and split the profits with him. At first, he said that he wouldn't even consider it; then after I got up, politely shook his hand, thanked him for a wonderful afternoon, and proceeded to leave, he called me back and we eventually came to an agreement. Zukor wanted to sign me to an exclusive contract. Since I was fairly popular in those days, I got him to agree to a non-exclusive contract. He also wanted me to commit to a number of films. I agreed to do one film at a time, and see how each film was received. I did not want to have to do more films than I thought I could."

That is what Harold Lloyd disclosed to me, and how he arrived at accumulating a formidable amount of currency from moving pictures which he further invested shrewdly into a variety of other real estate and business challenges.

Harold demonstrated individual pride in the reality that he was one of the very first to have a feature length motion picture comedy (seven reeler) with *The Freshman*, because at that time the industry never had had a comedy picture of that length with an extensively scripted story. In fact, Sid Grauman (owner of Grauman's Chinese Theater) would not even consider putting Harold's film into his movie house because Grauman believed that the public would not sit through humor of that length. So Harold explained how he went downtown Los Angeles and rented one of the other motion picture palaces himself where the film ran for nearly a year.

On occasion, I would spend a great deal of time at Lloyd's Green

Acres mansion; but it was intermittent from 1964 through 1971. These were my formative creative years as an artist, and I was composing symphonic and concert music; studying unique orchestral repertory for my conducting career; and making a living by composing and conducting a scarce motion picture score now and again; going on interviews and business appointments; and occasionally dating an interesting girl; so there were extended periods of as much as two months where I would not frequent the Green Acres estate at all, but I would invariably telephone Harold and we would chat irregularly and stay in communication.

Within his public and social exterior, Harold Lloyd continuously gave the impression of being a happy and lighthearted man. Privately, as I grew to know him, I discerned otherwise: even behind that unequaled grin he was actually a deeply troubled and disenchanted human being. Firstly, during August of 1919 when he was twenty-six years old and had just begun his popular ascent to stardom, Pathe Pictures requested an assortment of still photographs from Harold to be used by their publicity department in fostering his movies. One of the shots required Harold to light an extended cigarette from a holder with the lit fuse of a false prop bomb. While Harold was making himself up for the shoot at Witzel's Photography Studio on 8th and Hill Streets in downtown Los Angeles, Frank Terry the property manager had selected all the necessary items for the photo session from a nearby film studio property department. Harold held the lit fuse near his face as the photographer began taking the pictures; however, the fuse had suddenly extinguished itself so Harold abruptly lowered his right arm stating that a new fuse should be inserted when the supposed counterfeit bomb massively exploded. Fortunately, the force of the blast went vertically destroying the ceiling, fracturing the photographer's false upper teeth in half, and blowing away Harold's right thumb and index finger. It was thought that Harold would also lose the complete sight of his right eye, but in time both of his eyes miraculously healed. He felt totally depressed and acrimonious over the loss of his right thumb and index finger as the result of this egregiously careless accident, and as he lay in his hospital bed he considered his career as a movie star to be over. Even though he came to realize that from another aspect it was rather providential, as he explained to me one day, "Why hell, if I hadn't dropped my right arm when I did, it would have probably blown off my god damned head." The general public was to never know about the privation of Harold's right thumb and index finger; they were just informed about the recovery of his eyesight. To Harold's surprise, the comedic popularity of his initial films during his convalescence led

242

to an unprecedented demand for additional motion pictures. On camera and in public during that time he wore an assortment of flesh toned prosthetic devices and gloves which disguised this painful loss but which he secretly cursed until the end of his life.

Secondly, Harold Lloyd privately blamed himself for what he considered to be a disappointing family life. Although he had achieved fifty times the ordinary success of any film star and businessman throughout his illustrious motion picture career and trade enterprises, he could never understand why his son, Harold Lloyd Jr. (who was a polite, intelligent and shyly personable gentleman) chose to live with a man in a homosexual relationship. Harold Jr. almost never came to the house while I knew Harold Lloyd, but I eventually did speak with him in depth one New Year's Day dinner to which I accompanied Gloria Lloyd to her adopted sister's (Peggy Lloyd's) home in the San Fernando Valley. On several occasions during the years I was acquainted with Harold Lloyd he would say to me in trust and only while we were alone, "Phillip, why is Harold Jr. that way? What on god's earth did I ever do to make him live the life that he's leading?"

"You didn't do anything wrong, Harold," I would say. "It's not your fault. Harold, Jr. is a good person. That's the way he is. Accept it. Let him be what he is and let him lead his own life the way he wishes to live it."

But Harold Lloyd never sanctioned it, and internally he not only damned himself for not having thoroughly checked the supposed fake bomb which destroyed part of his body, but he also condemned himself for Harold Jr.'s homosexuality as well. Gloria informed me that the consensus of family opinion was that when Harold Jr. was born (which astounded everyone because it had been medically diagnosed that Mildred Davis Lloyd could never conceive again after Gloria's birth and that is why Peggy Lloyd had been adopted) that Harold was rarely around Harold Jr. while he was growing up due to his screen popularity, business investments and overly active social calendar. "There were only nannies, aunts, female servants, housekeepers, and us girls around Harold Jr. all the time," Gloria said. "And that's probably why he turned out the way he did." Of course, I told Gloria that I did not subscribe to that theory and still don't because I have known similar environmental cases where the child turned out to be heterosexual.

Concerning that New Year's Day dinner party at Peggy Lloyd's home during the late sixties (Harold Lloyd was not there), I had the opportunity to have an extended discussion with Harold Jr. (to the envious consternation of his boyfriend who proceeded to get drunk) and I learned a multiplicity of things regarding what Harold Jr. thought about Harold Sr. It was obvious that Harold Jr. (we had met fewer than half a dozen times the preceding years) knew from whatever source that I was acquainted with the inner sanctum of family differences so he expressed to me, rather surprisingly in view of his basically reserved demeanor, many of the sensitive personal issues he felt associated with having been born Harold Lloyd Jr.

"You don't know what it was trying to grow up being Harold Lloyd Jr.," he said. "The shoes were just too big. I tried so hard to please Dad and become a success in my own right, but I guess I didn't quite have what it takes. I tried acting; I tried singing. Have you heard my album that I made years ago?"

"Yes," I said. "Harold played parts of it for me once and I thought you had a rather good voice."

"The album just never went anywhere," he said matter of factly.

As we conversed, Harold Jr. occasionally asked for my counsel. I intimated that, perhaps, the stress he had always endured stemmed basically from his name: Harold Lloyd Jr. I told him that I would have changed it to Peter Lloyd or James Lloyd, if he wished to keep his last name. "I mean, there are so many Lloyds in the world, if you wanted to keep your last name, no one would have associated you with your father if you had just changed your first name. You could still do it," I encouraged him, "because you're still young enough to pursue any career you choose, and you haven't been active in nearly a decade. Why don't you just change your name? I would."

Harold Jr. said he would think about it, but felt it was too late because even though casting directors and the industry had altered, he thought someone would eventually find out who he really was and then the tension would yield again.

I then proposed that he perhaps consider a career behind the scenes such as a writer, director, agent, producer; or if the entertainment industry had been too painful a voyage for him, that he go into an entirely different vocation.

Harold Jr. I knew received an allowance from Harold Lloyd in the vicinity of $450 dollars a month; which, in those days, was just about enough to cover his rent and incidentals, and also support Harold Jr.'s slightly older gay live-in whom Harold Sr. especially did not relish. I also knew that after Harold Jr. had initially brought his homosexual associate several times to Green Acres, the companion began accusing

Harold Lloyd openly in heated discussions of being the genuine cause of Harold Jr.'s alcoholism and professional and sociological failures to the extent where Harold Lloyd demanded that Harold Jr. never bring his consort to the mansion again.

That evening was the first time I had ever met Harold Jr.'s inverted lover; and, as the night wore on, he began making scratching feline remarks to both Gloria and myself which we endeavored to ignore. "Ah, Gloria, my dear. You've always reminded me of a young Garbo. You look so lovely tonight. Who's your new boyfriend?"

About twenty minutes later, as Gloria and I were calmly seated on Peggy's living room sofa, Harold Jr.'s slightly inebriated running mate unexpectedly was standing and gloating directly behind us and said, "Look at their beautiful Roman noses, I bet they both went to the same plastic surgeon. Who did your noses?"

"Nobody did my nose. What about you, Filippo?," Gloria said tranquilly to the rest of the guests. Gloria had been undergoing treatments with a Brentwood M.D. psychiatrist and based upon my previous observations, I gathered she had taken a whole Valium before the dinner party instead of her usually prescribed half.

"This is the nose I was born with," I said while making a remotely satirical facial gesture toward the company in reference to the muddled immaturity of Harold Jr.'s gay companion.

"You're both lying," he snapped. "Nobody could be born with noses like those. And look at his hair. What do you put on your hair? Who does your hair?" he said endeavoring to touch my head from behind as I quickly got up and faced him.

"Only my hairdresser knows for sure," I said lampooning the Miss Clairol Madison Avenue slogan of the day, "and he's a fruit like you," I added as several of the guests chortled at our increasingly obnoxious guest.

Peggy Lloyd came out of the kitchen and Harold Jr. stood up as they both reprimanded Harold Jr.'s consort telling him that he had better behave or be prepared to leave.

The gay companion feebly tried to cast several verbal remarks against me under his breath which we all disregarded.

As dinner was being served, Harold Jr.'s concomitant made one more valiant attempt to gain my attention by hurling an additional barb toward me which we continued to overlook and after which he said, "See..? You're not as bright and clever as you think you are. You can't say anything, can you?" He sneered. "Mess with me and I'll cut your balls off!"

"At least I have some," I said immediately.

Our offensive homosexual friend became so incensed at my counter remark that he now wanted to brawl with me at which time Harold Jr. and another gentleman restrained him and at the insistence of Peggy and Harold Jr. arrangements were made for a taxi to take him home.

Although Gloria did indeed remind one of a young Garbo, at the time, (actually more attractive than Garbo ever was) she was on the sunny side of her forties and had had a disappointing marriage to Billy Guasti (the heir to a winery which produced -remember the Radio ads?- "Virginia Dare... Say It Again... Virginia Dare... It's A Delicious Wine") and I know in her sedated way she wanted to discover an interesting man and have a joyous loving relationship. With Guasti the conjugality did not turn out the way Gloria had envisaged and eventually it thrust her into a state of nervous depression. Harold also unveiled his bafflement, but informed me that he had not been entirely surprised by the matrimonial outcome; especially from the way he described the epic production costs of the wedding and reception at the Green Acres gardens; although "Sue-Sue" (Suzanne Guasti) was born from that union which was kind of a miracle in itself after Gloria told me how desperately she tried to abort the pregnancy. In fact, it used to amuse me when Sue-Sue was approaching her teens and would whine to Gloria about not having a proper bicycle, life or car, how Gloria would jokingly remark to her, "Listen, kiddo, be happy with what you've got. You're lucky to be here at all; especially if I tell you all the things I did to try and not have you."

I knew that Gloria did find me appealing, but since I enjoyed her as much as I did as a friend, and inasmuch as she was having these emotional problems, I did not want to have a casual affair with her because, in view of the activity of my developing music career, I made certain that all I ever experienced in those days were occasional fleeting romances with girls and women who did not place an inordinate sentimentality or contractual value upon their love making. So I specifically avoided any exotic involvement with Gloria Lloyd. Harold was the one who had introduced me to her and several years later suggested that I marry her; I nearly fell over after he mentioned it. I think the main reason Harold wanted me to wed Gloria was that he appreciated the fact that I was a rather stable person who was not impressed by material wealth and that although I was a generous person by nature, I was logical and simple in my spending habits. Whereas Harold never actually said so to my face, Gloria told me on a number of occasions over the years, "Dad, really likes you."

Gloria, at this time, was being pursued by several international gigolos and that's another reason I believe that Mildred and Harold Lloyd paid for her visits to the Brentwood Psychiatrist.

I was the one who finally convinced Gloria to stop sleeping until two in the afternoon, get up early in the morning and go get some kind of job or activity, and move out of the mansion.

Harold telephoned me terribly upset. He informed me that one of the house painters who worked for the outside firm Harold had engaged to repaint the windows and sashes of the villa had struck up a conversation with Gloria from his ladder as she opened the window to her second story bedroom and eventually asked her for a date which Gloria accepted. I calmed Harold down and told him not to worry. Fortunately, for Harold and Mildred the relationship only lasted that one rendezvous.

Harold also called me shortly thereafter mortally disillusioned over the fact that I had persuaded Gloria to move out of the manor and into a small Santa Monica apartment after she was able to acquire a position as a salesperson with one of Los Angeles' leading department stores. Gloria's allowance from Harold was only $350 dollars a month during the mid-sixties so I prompted her to stop feeling sorry for herself; go to bed at a reasonable hour during weekdays and arise early; go out and win her own position; and leave the mansion. I specifically prevailed upon Gloria to depart from Green Acres after she had shown me a couple of delusive love letters written to her by some Mexican gigolo who had visions of marrying her and inheriting Harold Lloyd's entire estate.

"Gloria," I said. "As long as you meet people and you either take them up here, or they come and meet you here, you'll never know if they really like you for yourself or for what they fantasize they think they're eventually going to gain from you after Harold goes. If you get a simple little apartment, and you bring them there --they won't know who you are, because there are thousands of Lloyds in the world-- then you'll know who is really interested in you for yourself and not for sixteen acres and an Italian villa in the middle of Beverly Hills."

I also instructed Gloria never to invite any of her new friends and co-workers from the Department Store to the mansion, or ever tell them who her father actually was.

"Why the hell did you make Glo move out into that tiny Santa Monica apartment when she has all this?" Harold indignantly exclaimed to me over the telephone.

"That's precisely the point," I said. "Harold, you came from poor beginnings. That's why you love your estate. Gloria was born in that mansion. She needs a change. She needs her own place so she can have meaningful relationships with people who'll like her for herself. Do you think that Mexican gigolo would send her flowers and love letters if he called for her at that apartment?"

A few days later, after Gloria stated that Harold and Mildred had consulted the situation with Gloria's psychiatrist, Harold telephoned me and said, "Well, maybe you're right, Phillip. We'll see." It seems that the Doctor told both Harold and Mildred, "That Lambro fellow is giving Gloria the right advice." In fact, when either Harold or Mildred wanted to prompt Gloria about something, they would invariably ask me to do it for them. I recall on several occasions how Mildred would stop me in the upstairs hallway and whisper her solicitations to me.

As for Mildred, I remember once staying over at the mansion after Gloria and I had returned late one evening from dinner and a movie. I fell asleep in the downstairs library and awoke about 2:30 a.m. There was this silver plated swan dish on one of the end tables in the library which I always liked because it had a particularly resonant gong-like quality when I hit it with my fingernail. So I slowly walked through the dimly lit hallways of the manor striking the silver swan like a deep bell in a clock tower until I arrived upstairs near Gloria's room where I saw the apprehensive figure of Mildred uttering, "Who's there..? Who is it..?"

Gong...Gong..."It is only I, Mildred; Hamlet." Gong...Gong...

I practically scared Mildred out of her wits.

Gloria's health improved amid her novel surroundings. She became the leading salesperson in her area of the Department Store and generated new friends. She stayed at the Department Store for several years, until she made the fateful oversight which I had feared. One Monday, Gloria's car broke down near work. Assuming her auto would be impounded and without thinking beyond her predicament (she had left her dirver's license and Auto Club Card in her room at the mansion where she had spent the previous weekend) she asked her salesgirl friend if she would give her a quick ride to her parents home so she could retrieve the license and auto card in order to have the vehicle "jumped" or towed. When the salesgirl (who Gloria thought was an intimate) saw the Lloyd estate, she went that week to all the other salespeople and in concert they demanded that Gloria be terminated deeming that she really did not need the job. Gloria was asked to leave. To Gloria's credit she immediately acquired another situation within a Westwood fashion boutique.

Around 1967, I went to Harold a couple of times on behalf of increasing Gloria's allowance to at least $400 a month, but he complained that with all the psychiatrist invoices and other accounts he had to satisfy for her, he could not manage it at that period.

Gloria did, shortly thereafter, receive an increase to $400 dollars. Gloria's good friend (whom I only met once) was the wife of actor-writer Peter Ustinov who socially humiliated Harold into augmenting Gloria's allotment to $400 dollars.

I encountered Mrs. Ustinov that solitary time when, during a heavy rain storm, Gloria prevailed upon me to drive her to The Beverly Hills Hotel where she was to have lunch with Mrs. Ustinov. I parked on Hartford Way adjacent to the Hotel since the auto attendants were backed up with over activity all the way to Sunset Boulevard, and under my umbrella Gloria and I ran up the inner sidewalk of the exclusive grounds where a gardener was washing the sidewalk with a hose as buckets of rain were falling. I couldn't believe this, so we stopped and I asked the gardener what was the purpose of hosing down the sidewalk while a torrential rain storm was in progress. The Beverly Hills Hotel gardener revealed that his instructions were, regardless of the weather, on specific days to wash the sidewalks; even in the rain. Well, so much for common sense, management and water conservation.

I once asked Harold Lloyd what caused him to retire from motion pictures. Harold told me that he realized, although he was able to make the change from silent films to sound movies without too many complications (he did not have a bad voice; but not a mellifluous one) that he could sense when his popularity as a movie star began to wane in the 1930's. By the time World War II arrived, he was firmly entrenched into many other business demands and, as I remember his saying to me, "I just lost interest in making motion pictures."

Harold Lloyd had invested his earnings shrewdly. In addition to being one of the few who completely avoided the 1929 stock market crash because, as he explained, he sold practically all of his shares well before the collapse, he then bought large parcels of land from the desert in the San Fernando Valley (when it was thought to be worthless without water) to Santa Monica beach fronts, and further real estate in Utah, New York and other areas of the country. He once revealed to me how his business associates thought he was totally insane to build his Italian villa upon the then 1922 sandy desert of Beverly Hills when, in fact, the only other structures there were Will Rogers home and The Beverly Hills Hotel.

Eventually, all of Harold's sagaciously amassed real estate holdings became, with the advent of water, corner lots for gas stations, apartment houses, and major buildings.

Harold unequivocally regretted coming out of self imposed retirement to appear in Mad Wednesday. He only did so against his better judgment because Howard Hughes, who was not only a close confidant but a great admirer of Harold's, "pestered me to death," as Harold said. Harold revealed to me that he immediately saw Mad Wednesday was going in the wrong direction. He felt it was not really comical because the script tried to reprise antiquated formats from his successful old silent films and coupled with the dated dialogue he knew it would never be successful with a more sophisticated and demanding public. Harold also thought that director Preston Sturges actually did not have a natural affinity for comedy. His prognosis being accurate caused Harold to subsequently lose total fascination with making movies and go into permanent seclusion.

When Harold Lloyd initially suggested that I consider marrying Gloria (shortly after his wife Mildred Davis Lloyd's death), I was utterly astonished. He brought it up a couple of times in rather oblique ways. The first time, we were lounging out in the garden and he altogether surprised me by saying, "Now, what about you and Glo?"

"What do you mean?" I asked.

"You know," he went on. "Is there anything there? Wouldn't you like to marry her? I think you'd be really good for her."

I was completely astounded. I knew how much he loved Gloria, so I chose my words heedfully. I told Harold that in my sphere of endeavors as a symphonic and concert composer, conductor it was an exceedingly arduous life, and since I cared so much about Gloria's well being, I definitely would not be the right person for her because I could never devote any semblance of marital attention which she deserved.

And even with many millions in trust dangling in front of my face, I just could not quite lose my emotional freedom and I believe, although he did not say so, that Harold Lloyd admired my opinion. I advised him that I truly did not accept the legal concept of marriage; that I thought a person should be independent and if a physical and mental relationship ceased to exist that people should care enough about one another to part amicably as acquaintances and continue to assist each other and not feel acrimonious and have to go to court (or worse yet, become vindictive and physically abusive toward one another); and, specifically, not marry and divorce for money. And so I remember from his facial expressions and affirmative nods, that Harold Lloyd seemed to value my convictions.

Of course, I personally have never embraced the concept of contractual marriage. And to those moans I hear in the background, I respectfully point out that statistics (eight out of ten marriages end in divorce) support my contention; with, perhaps the other two being thinly held together either by extreme wealth and pre-nuptial agreements, or extreme poverty. I think wedlock is a pagan ritual; because it forces, especially the woman, to love by immured contract. If two people wish to romance each other and stay together all of their lives then they should be free to do so, but without the imprisoned contractual obligation of a license. Whether you put a ring on a finger, or a bone through a nose, it's all the same thing: possession. The concept of marriage in all of our various earth societies has rarely, if ever, been based upon the principle of love; but rather upon the theorem of ownership and amourous exploitation by transaction.

One of the things which Harold Lloyd did not respect was my Japanese Zen Macrobiotic diet. At appropriate opportunities, he never failed to make it the object of his special brand of humor; that is, until about eighteen months before he died. Hardly anyone knew that Harold Lloyd had cancer at that time. Just his brother-in-law, John H. Davis who was a doctor at St. John's hospital whom I believe I only met once in passing, and who, I was subsequently informed, was one of the original members in the Our Gang motion picture comedies.

I had a feeling that Harold might be terminally ill because (even though he attempted not to show it) he suddenly became interested in the macrobiotic regimen. At the time, I had Toyo Nakayama and her mother, Miyoko, cooking my meals six days a week at their knowing little Japanese Zen Macrobiotic Restaurant on Hollywood Boulevard (unfortunately it closed in 1975) several blocks west of Western Avenue and Harold asked me to take him there. I brought him to the restaurant about half a dozen times.

"Oh, Phillip," he would say to me. "I just feel so punk. Do you think your diet can help me?"

Even though I sensed he had some form of cancer, I wanted him to voluntarily admit it to me; but he never did. Instead, he would just say, "it's nothing really serious."

It was quite bizarre when you think that I offered to come up to the mansion and cook for him (free of charge) in his large kitchen with wonderful gas ranges, but here he was, hierarch of his sumptuous manor and terminally ill, saying that he could not risk it because he was afraid of what his cooks might say, and quite possibly get upset and quit. I simply could not understand Harold's reasoning.

Harold Lloyd was quite a sportsman in his day (although when I knew him, he did not participate in any athletics at all), but in addition to bowling with Howard Hughes and Gene Mako, he told me that he used to play handball and tennis quite actively wearing a special prosthetic glove on his right hand.

He had a sunken championship sized tennis court with a small clubhouse, dressing rooms, and a drinking fountain at the rear of the estate. When he found out that I had played tournament tennis in college and the military, he revealed how during the 1930's and 40's he used to have a special professional tennis tournament every year at Green Acres for charity directly after the stellar USLTA amateur Pacific Southwest Championships which would occur at the Los Angeles Tennis Club. "Oh, I had Bill Tilden, Ellsworth Vines, Don Budge, Gene Mako and all the major professional tennis players," Harold said. "And I offered them good prize money, too."

After inspecting the tennis court, which was one of the finest I had ever seen (it had been constructed in the mid 1920's and it was perfectly flat and didn't have a crack in it after all that time), I asked Harold if I could have it resurfaced green, a net put up and white lines painted since the entire top surface had completely faded into the original sandy concrete color. He said that he would take care of it himself as he did not want me spending any of my hard earned money. A few weeks later, he informed me that it was ready for me to play, so I remember bringing up Mexican player Eduardo Martinez-Lanz (whom my good buddy Rafael Osuna asked me to practice with) and we were shocked to find that Harold had only installed a new net and had the lines painted white. The court remained its eroded sandy cement color. The back and side fences had a thick deep growth of natural solid green ivy which was good for seeing the tennis ball (even though we would lose one now and again) but I was disappointed that Harold had not resurfaced the entire court grass green as we both had agreed. What I suspect was that when he made the initial inquiry, he perhaps was expecting a 1926 quotation; and when he got the projected cost from whoever painted the lines for resurfacing the entire tennis court, he opted for just repainting the lines. I offered several times to compensate him for it, since I was, practically, the only one using the court, but Harold said it was good enough to play on the way it was. Sue-Sue used to ride her bicycle all over the court until I told her not to after it had been cleaned, washed and the lines painted.

I also persuaded Harold to repair the scaled down fairy tale miniature Irish estate playhouses and brick castle which he had built on the left side of the rear gardens for Gloria, Peggy and Harold Jr. when they were youngsters. Harold had always feared ransom kidnapping of his children (especially after the Lindbergh incident) so he felt obliged to devise ways to keep them and their selected playmates (such as Shirley Temple) entertained for long periods of time. Harold had had a Command Performance for the King and Queen of England afterwhich they invited him to Buckingham Palace where he became impressed with the Royal Family's charming pixie narrative playground which had been constructed to accommodate the Royal offspring. Harold told me that the King and Queen furnished him with duplicate plans of the model brick castle and dwarfish Hansel and Gretel houses with their quaint thatched roofs, beveled glass windows, hot and cold running water, and small garden yards.

One day I said, "Let me bring up some children to play on certain mornings and afternoons."

Harold said, "Fine." So I would, on occasion, find a couple of deserving moppets and introduce them to this diminutive Disneyland where they would play and have the time of their lives.

I had met actor Nick Cravat (who portrayed the deaf mute in *The Count Of Monte Cristo* films and with Burt Lancaster in *Flame And The Arrow*) and he and his wife Ciel would ask me now and again if I would please take care of their two lovely young daughters Marcelina and Tina; which I did on many occasions. I brought the two girls to the estate several times to swim in the inlaid mosaic tiled wading pool next to the Renaissance Olympic sized swimming pool with its gigantic cabana. I remember once while Marcelina and Tina were enacting their important fantasies in the bantam fairy tale houses how they called me to come and have lunch with them. They were under eight years old at the time.

"Phillip," they yelled. "Come and have something to eat. We made you a salad."

I was not far away sitting in a garden chair on the lawn reading the newspaper. I walked over to the miniature Irish estate and went inside and sat down to what I thought would be a make believe lunch; but to my astonishment, Marcelina and Tina had prepared a real salad for me out of Harold Lloyd's prized tulips and other rare flowers on the original pewter plates with all the utensils still there from the 1930 cupboards. As we sat down on the tiny chairs next to the little table, I thanked the girls very much for their beautiful thought, but I had to tell them that there was a sleeping giant who lived in the big chateau over there who would be exceedingly irate if he saw us eating his flowers and plants so we had to destroy all the evidence immediately before the giant woke up.

I said, "You girls may play, but you leave the flowers and plants alone. Okay?"

I recall a couple of amusing incidents involving Harold Lloyd's children when they were juveniles. Gloria revealed to me that when the Doctors informed Harold and Mildred that they thought Mildred could never have another child, how they adopted Peggy. Gloria said that when Peggy arrived at the Green Acres mansion they immediately showed her to her bedroom and proudly exhibited all the toys and her fresh stylish wardrobe of pretty dresses, but little Peggy unfazed by the new opulence thrust upon her uncompromisingly refused to wear anything but her drab orphanage garment for two whole months.

A couple of years later, Gloria and Peggy found out that the leading French star of the day, Maurice Chevalier, was going to attend one of Harold's lavish evening parties, and they both pleaded with Harold to let them stay up past their scheduled bed time so that they could meet their favorite luminary in person.

"Well, I don't know girls," Harold said. "It'll be too late for you to meet him. But you know, Mr. Chevalier is a big star and people pay good money to see him. What are you girls prepared to pay me to introduce you to him?"

"Ten cents," they said.

"If you girls can pay me fifty cents," Harold said. "I'll bring Mr. Chevalier up to your bedroom before you go to sleep."

Gloria told me that she and Peggy shook fifty cents out of their piggy banks and gave the money to Harold. That evening Harold brought Maurice Chevalier (who had had a few too many drinks) and his equally inebriated and disheveled girl friend into their bedroom.

"We were so disappointed," Gloria said, "that we demanded our money back the next morning at the breakfast table."

Another entertaining incident which Gloria disclosed took place when she was about five years old and first taken to see one of Harold's movies at Grauman's Chinese Theater in Hollywood. There she was watching Harold on the screen about to be hit over the head with a club by a big brute. Young Gloria thought the whole episode in the movie was actually taking place and she started to cry, and yelled out at the screen, "Don't you hurt my Daddy!" They had to escort little Gloria out of the theater because she was causing such a disturbance.

Harold Lloyd, on occasion, did tell me which actors and pictures he enjoyed from the 1950's and 60's. He would mention a film he had seen and either liked, or disliked, and state why. He sometimes would take Sue-Sue to a matinee of a first-run feature now and again. Not long after I met him, he telephoned me regarding a current article in Life Magazine where he had been mentioned.

"Who the hell is this Gene Paul Belmundo?" He asked.

"Oh, you mean Jean-Paul Belmondo," I said. "He's a wonderfully talented French actor. You must see him in *That Man From Rio*. It's a very entertaining and well made film."

"Yes, well they're talking about him and that picture in this latest issue of Life Magazine that I have here."

"Well, what do they say?"

"They say that this Belmundo..."

"Belmondo," I politely corrected.

"Belmondo, yes; is a combination of Humphrey Bogart and Harold Lloyd. If that's true," Harold went on, "he must be one hell of a screen star."

I said, "Oh yes, that he is. That he is."

Harold did go to see *That Man From Rio* and was quite impressed with Jean-Paul Belmondo's athletic, comedic and acting abilities. Harold Lloyd also admired Laurence Olivier. And when he found out that I had been playing tennis occasionally with actress Jean Simmons at her home, he expressed how much he had always enjoyed her motion picture performances. He also particularly liked the acting and screen presence of Jean Simmons former husband Stewart Granger.

After suggesting to Harold that he go see Stanley Kubrick's film *2001* he telephoned me and said, "Yes, Phillip, you're right, it's a very interesting and well made film. The photography's brilliant; it's well edited; the acting's good; but I'll be damned if I know what the hell he's trying to say."

Harold Lloyd felt that the motion picture business during the 1960's was slowly deteriorating. He thought that the industry, although it had improved mechanically and technically by leaps and bounds, was "short-changing the public." He told me that not enough emphasis was being placed upon the construction of an interesting story with characters you actually cared about, and that the studios were "making films to just make films." He also believed that ticket prices were far too costly. "Why, hell," he once told me, "I went to Grauman's Chinese Theater the other day with Sue-Sue and paid $3.50 for my ticket" (a high price at the time) "and the theater was over half empty. Now, if they would make a really good picture and charged only a dollar, the place would have been packed."

I rarely brought anyone other than myself to Green Acres; although I had been offered large sums of cash for social introductions to Harold

Lloyd from business people who had found out that I knew him. Of course, I responded that I could not do that for any amount of money.

During a blistering summer day in the late 1960's I was with one of my closest friends, Sidney Schuman, at his Shell Station which he owned (at the Northwest corner of Highland and Melrose in Hollywood) visiting with Sidney and his old Chicano mechanic-helper Spanish Joe who looked younger than his years although he probably was well into his sixties. Spanish Joe had a wonderfully lethargic personality, a full head of dark black-gray hair, and a swarthy complexion. Although Spanish Joe would get an amazing amount of work done, it looked as if his every move were like the aftermath of a marathon runner. Sidney told me that Spanish Joe's easy disposition had perhaps been molded from the sporadic beatings he had taken from his indignant wife when Spanish Joe would come home too late and a little too intoxicated from time to time.

"Jus' remember, Amigo," Spanish Joe would often say to me and Sidney, "the first hundred years are the hardest."

As I was about to leave, a small car wheeled in smoking from the radiator being driven by a young girl with long dark hair, and a mild case of acne over her light complexion. Since everybody was so preoccupied, I tried to help the baffled female who admitted to me (after I flooded her radiator with cold water and found it almost dry) that she had never even bothered to examine the fluid levels of her vehicle ever since she had purchased it. After assisting her, with support from Spanish Joe, she thanked me. I asked her what her name was and what she did for a living and she declared that she was an actress in Hollywood endeavoring to get some work and that her name was Karen Valentine. Even though I wasn't captivated by her, and I don't think she was allured toward me, I introduced myself as I thought that I might be able to quite possibly initiate her to Macrobiotics which would most assuredly clear up her acne and brighten her eyes. We exchanged telephone numbers and later that week I called her and asked if she would like to go out for lunch. The places I posed were the Japanese Zen Macrobiotic Restaurant, the Old World, and the Polo Lounge at The Beverly Hills Hotel. She opted for the Polo Lounge where I endeavored to politely inform her about Macrobiotics. After I courteously cited that if she modified her diet, and that her acne condition most assuredly would clear up, she became a bit irritated even though I attempted to explain to her that what I was confidentially suggesting was for her own health and benefit. As the conversation wore on and our potential familiarity wilted, along with Ms. Valentine's salad, I noticed that I would not have time to take her back to her car without being late for an appointment I had had with Gloria Lloyd who was expecting me to deliver to her my watercolor paints and sable brushes which I hadn't used in years so that Gloria could implement my proposal and begin painting to occupy her mind during off hours.

I took Karen Valentine with me and presented her to Gloria, but I told Karen (after giving her a quick tour of about five acres of the estate's gardens) that I would never be able to introduce her to Harold Lloyd because of his aversion toward meeting Hollywood actors and actresses. I also informed Karen Valentine that the only way I could ever be able to acquaint her with Harold Lloyd would be if she were to give up acting and go out and acquire a commonplace occupation. I believe we saw each other once after that, and we never communicated again; except on a rare occasion at a trendy private club where she pretended not to observe me to my complete satisfaction.

I understand Karen Valentine became somewhat of a minor television personality on a situation comedy show for a brief period of time, but since I disliked the insipid driveling dialogue of those manufactured shows I never saw her. In fact, I was so immersed with composing and so disenchanted with the mediocrity of television and the newscasts during this period that I ultimately sold my TV. I only bought another television set after accidentally viewing *Saturday Night Live* in the mid 1970's at a friend's home which was to become my favorite program.

I did bring to the Lloyd estate my good friend Darrell Armstrong, a strikingly intelligent and cultured person who had graduated Law School from the prestigious Boalt Hall, The School Of Jurisprudence, within the University Of California Berkeley, and loved concert music and who was also at times a professional photographer. Since Darrell was a cameraman and an aficionado of good music, Harold definitely wanted to meet him. I brought Darrell up to Green Acres a few times where we all listened to music in the enormous living room with Harold, as usual, presiding as Disc Jockey.

During 1969 and 1970 I would occasionally arrange some social doubles matches on the Green Acres tennis court. I recall one with record producer Don Blocker (whom I had known from my office building) and former USC Tennis Team member Horst Ritter (a German born player, trying very hard to become an international business tycoon), and Horst brought along comedian-actor Jerry Van Dyke (Dick Van Dyke's brother) as the fourth. I made it quite clear to everyone that I would not be able to introduce them to Harold Lloyd because he was not feeling particularly well. The truth of the matter was that even if he had been in the best of health, I would not have been able to acquaint them with Harold.

Since I had brought Gloria along with me on several occasions when I would have dinner at Nick and Ciel Cravat's home in Woodland Hills, Gloria and I invited the Cravats to the mansion once while Harold was out of town. The Cravats and Gloria liked each other and had gotten along exceedingly well. Whereas Nick had not been working in films much during those years (only bit parts in some major pictures), he was forced to accept a humiliating, but steady corporate disbursement (enough to make ends meet) from his childhood preeminent Burt Lancaster with whom he had run away from home during their juvenile years in New York City and had formed an acrobatic circus act together. This situation seemed to eat away at Nick's liver and make him, at times, the most embittered man one would ever want to meet. Nick was invariably suggesting I marry Gloria so that I would not have to acquire motion picture scores anymore and could just devote myself to concert music. I kept telling Nick that if I married Gloria, I'd be so immersed with her ambiguous tranquility that I would never have any time to compose.

During January 1971, I brought along an alluring girl named Jessie and endeavored to teach her tennis and see if she, perhaps, might become romantically interested in me. Well, Jessie fell in love with the estate, but not yours truly. Although I did make one concluding attempt by inviting Jessie months later to USC's Town & Gown where I was being honored by The Sierra Club (along with the producer Bruton Peterson, and the director, James Rascoe) for having won the National Board Of Review's Best Music For A Documentary Award for the film *Mineral King* which ultimately became instrumental on the floor of the United States Congress in ecologically saving that wondrous agrarian region of Yosemite Valley's majestic Sierra Nevada Mountains in Eastern California from an intended Disney growth enterprise. There was a dinner followed with a screening of the picture which had been narrated by Burgess Meredith. When I went to pick up Jessie at her parent's home, she looked absolutely stunning, however I became totally disappointed when I noticed that she was wearing her mother's silver fox fur coat.

"How do I look?" She asked doing a 360 degree turn.

"You look fine," I said. "But do you think you could wear a cloth coat instead of that fur coat?"

"What's wrong with my coat? This is a very expensive silver fox fur coat."

"This is California and not the North Pole," I said. "And if you saw what they did to those silver foxes, I don't think you'd want to wear that coat."

Jessie immediately lost her smile. I felt she wasn't intrigued with me exotically, but now I could sense an extraordinary possibility that she might even grow to dislike me before the evening concluded.

"Look," I said. "There will be 3,500 Sierra Club conservationist animal lovers there and since I'm being honored we'll be seated at a long raised dais having dinner. You'll be stoned to death."

Jessie refused to leave unless she was permitted to embody her fur coat. Finally, we came to a truce: she would wear the garment to the Town & Gown, but not have it on inside. As she carried the silver fox within the Town & Gown I instructed her to tell anyone who gave her a detrimental stare that it was a coat made out of synthetic fur. Although she was quite impressed with my music score and the attention I received, we never dated again.

The only time I ever deceived Harold Lloyd was when actor-producer Tony Bill implored me to introduce him and his then associate Vernon Zimmerman to Harold. I had met Tony Bill during 1967 through Steven Spielberg. Since Tony Bill had gone through as many problematic issues trying to aid Steven Spielberg as I had, and considering how he so genuinely wanted to meet Harold Lloyd, I agreed to take him up to the mansion with me (Monday 9 February 1970 at 7:30 p.m.) where Harold and I were going to listen to music anyway, solely on the condition that Tony and Vernon Zimmerman agree to pretend that they were graduate students majoring in film who wanted to listen to good music. Harold liked students and sometimes exhibited his silent movies to schools and colleges for nothing.

If you're wondering why I never took Steven Spielberg or Peter Bogdanovich, it was simply because those two were perhaps the greatest personal exploiters who had ever entered my life. They could have never pretended to be cinema undergraduates at that time; their striving egos would not have permitted it. I believed they most assuredly would have betrayed my confidence once in the company of Harold and immediately would have tried to impose upon him for their own personal benefit.

Tony Bill and Vernon Zimmerman convincingly played their roles as quiet, polite, serious motion picture graduate students, and I could tell that Harold liked them both. There was no entertainment industry talk for the first hour and a half inasmuch as Harold said as we walked down into the sunken living room, "Now what kind of music would you boys like to listen to?"

"Anything you wish to play, Mr. Lloyd," said Tony.

"Yes, anything you wish," echoed Vernon Zimmerman.

I just smiled at Harold.

"Well," Harold winked at me, "I suppose you boys would like to hear The Beatles. I have a Beatles album, but it's by the Boston Pops with Arthur Fiedler. I can't take all the noise of the regular Beatles albums so you'll have to forgive me, I just don't understand rock and roll."

We all laughed.

I don't remember exactly what Harold played for us, but I seem to recall his selecting portions of a Mahler Symphony, a Brahms Piano Concerto, and a Tchaikovsky Symphony, with a bit of the Boston Pops Beatles, Tony Bennett, the Scots Guards, and Peggy Lee thrown in for good measure.

As we approached two hours, I decided to give the cue that it was time to leave because Harold I could see was getting a trifle fatigued, although he would never admit to it in front of new young acquaintances.

"Phillip, tells me that you boys are graduate students in film. Well, I hope you go on to make good pictures because it's pretty lean out there."

Tony had previously informed me that he wanted to produce a prime time television special devoted to Harold Lloyd utilizing all of Harold's famous visual signature clips, and I said to ask him about it as we were leaving; which, to Tony's well educated comportment he did most tactfully.

"Well," said Harold. "If you boys can get the networks to pay me $150,000 dollars for one prime time showing, I think we can talk business. Now, remember, it's $150,000 dollars and one showing; and no negotiations to the contrary. If everything goes well, then we can talk about repeating it."

I was surprised when Harold told them, "If the networks are interested, have them contact, Phillip. He'll know what to do and how to properly put them in touch with me."

As I drove Tony and Vernon back to their cars, they thanked me profusely for what they termed "an historic evening." Both of them had been unequivocally affected by the mansion and at how sincere they found Harold Lloyd to be.

Regarding Harold Lloyd's massive record collection, Harold used to imprint his name with a big blue stamp on the back of every recording. Since he had so many albums (I believe it was in excess of 20,000 at one point) he was afraid some might get stolen, so he had them inscribed with his name on each one that he bought and decided to keep. He was also a shrewd record buyer, too. He rarely paid the standard price, and if he suddenly disliked a recording, he returned it. These demands were usually met because he purchased albums in such large quantities and had them stored within specific closets of the villa. At the time, Music City was the largest record store in Los Angeles (this was just before Tower Records), but Harold actually had more LP's than Music City. And as his agglomeration grew, he was forced to have a professional card catalog system devised because it got to the point where sometimes he couldn't find a particular recording when he wanted it. He had a full time secretary just typing up cards and cataloging his discs.

Tony Bill proposed the Harold Lloyd documentary concept to the television networks several times; however, the network executives felt that the price was too excessive. After that, I lost social contact with Tony Bill; although, he went on to co-executive produce the highly popular film *The Sting*, which I heard made him relatively wealthy. Gunther Schuller's unique personal arrangements of Scott Joplin's Rags were blatantly engaged within Marvin Hamlisch's *The Sting* soundtrack score, and after legal copyright clarifications were proved, the transcription royalties appropriately reverted back to Gunther Schuller which also made him fairly affluent.

As for Gunther Schuller, I attempted to convince Schirmer (while I worked for them during 1961) to publish Gunther, who was comparatively unknown at the time (having had the ignominious distinction of being an American composer first published in Germany), but I was overruled in the Board Room by Hans Heinsheimer who said, "Who the hell is this Gunther Schuller, anyway?" Several months later, after Antal Dorati conducted Gunther's *Seven Studies After Paul Klee* with the Minneapolis Symphony in Carnegie Hall, Heinsheimer came running into my office the following morning (armed with the glowing review from the New York Times) screaming, "Get me Gunther Schuller!" I said, "You had your chance; it's too late. He's with another publisher."

Gunther appreciated my sincere efforts on behalf of his work and invited me a few times during that period to small recitals where his pieces were being performed. I remember once where he took me via the New York City subway to a concert in Greenwich Village given by his friends who formed The Modern Jazz Quartet. Gunther introduced me to John Lewis and all the members of The Quartet. However, it's interesting to note that Gunther (as we were riding the train) asked me if I had ever heard of the black piano ragtime song composer Scott Joplin. I told him that I hadn't and he proceeded to enumerate enthusiastically about Joplin (who had been born 1868 in Texas and died in New York City 1917) and his Rags, and how this music had influenced Igor Stravinsky. Gunther told me that he wanted to eventually make arrangements of Joplin's music and a recording; which he ultimately did causing the widespread popular resurrection of Scott Joplin's ragtime tunes.

I had known Harold now for about five years, and one summer afternoon while we were sitting in the living room, young Sue-Sue (who was blossoming into an ebullient teenager) came into the area in her tantalizing way. Harold adored Sue for many reasons: she was undoubtedly cute, and had a bubbly personality; but mainly, I believe, because she skillfully made him feel more like her father rather than her grandfather. I don't recall how the two brought up the subject of the Christmas Tree, but Sue and Harold were having a discussion about it and I remember saying, "What Christmas Tree?"

Then Sue-Sue said rather surprisedly, "Phillip, you mean to say you've never seen the Christmas Tree? Daddy, don't tell him," she snapped at Harold.

"What Christmas Tree?" I asked again.

"The little, itty, bitty, teeny, tiny, small Christmas Tree that's this high?"

Harold began laughing as I was smiling, but Sue-Sue was now having the time of her revenge in retaliation for all those countless occasions where I teased her at every opportunity and sometimes called her Lolita.

"Where is this Christmas Tree?" I asked.

"Daddy, don't you say anything."

"I won't," Harold laughed.

"Phillip, you stay right here and don't you move."

Sue-Sue ran the hundred out of the living room and down the long hallway and returned in a few minutes with a large handkerchief and proceeded to blindfold me in my chair.

"Now you sit right here for about ten minutes; we'll come back for you when we're ready; and you have to promise not to move or peek. Okay?"

"Okay," I said.

"Promise?"

"I promise."

They were gone for about ten minutes. I did not know what was going on, or what would happen. I couldn't see anything and all I heard were the birds and insects musically sputtering from the outside trees and gardens.

"Alright, Phillip," said Sue taking my hand. "You may get up now and come with me; and no peeking."

"I can't see a thing," I said. "I'm totally in the dark."

Just to make sure everything was more difficult, Sue turned me around in place (like Blind Man's Bluff) before leading me by the hand up the few steps and out of the living room and along the hallway. We stopped part of the way down the corridor and turned right into another room with an unusually soft luxurious carpet which I could sense that I had never been in before. As soon as I was positioned, Sue said, "You can take off the blindfold now."

I could not believe my eyes. I was in this empty room which was about as large as two oversized living rooms and at the end of the chamber before me was a lit colossal Christmas tree about fifteen feet high and six feet deep at its widest base with so many exotic and precious large and small Christmas ornaments and colored light bulbs that you literally could not see one branch. I was absolutely astonished to the glee of Sue-Sue and Harold who were both reveling at my amazement. Harold told me that he and Sue had been discussing how many more years this particular tree could stay up before they had to dismantle and replace it.

"The whole process takes about two weeks," said Harold. "This tree's been up for about three years."

"Three years!" I exclaimed. "Isn't it a fire hazard?"

"Not at the moment," Harold explained. "When the tree is selected, we reinforce it with steel rods and anchor it, and then treat it with a fire retardant material which preserves it anywhere from three to seven years. We had one that lasted seven whole years before we had to take it down."

Harold proceeded to tell me when and where he had acquired many of the rare ornaments on the tree. Some of them had been purchased in the United States, but many of them, he said, were secured during his numerous international travels from China to Europe. Harold (ever the business man) one year sold a photo session with the Christmas tree to Playboy Magazine.

Harold also informed me that he let Paramount Pictures rent for about two weeks one of his ostentatious vintage autos at a prepaid fee of several thousand dollars for a motion picture starring William Holden. When I asked him which film it was, he couldn't seem to recall although I have found out recently from Suzanne that it was the Silver Cloud Rolls Royce used in the 1954 Billy Wilder film *Sabrina* starring Humphrey Bogart, Audrey Hepburn and William Holden. Harold also said that when World

War II broke out, that he never wanted to drive these classic automobiles because he felt that it was too flamboyant and kept these cars covered and stored within his twelve car garage. Harold also acquainted me with the fact that Paramount paid for the entire rewiring of the royal auto, to bring it up to current vehicle codes, before they used it.

According to my log, Harold Lloyd died 8 March 1971. He was about a month and a half shy of 78 years old.

During January of 1971 (through a Ford Foundation recording grant) I was able to conduct and commercially record my United States International Orchestra here in Los Angeles in performances of Ramiro Cortes *Meditation for String Orchestra* together with my *Structures for String Orchestra* and *Music For Wind, Brass & Percussion.*

Harold was delighted by the fact that my recordings were taking place, but when I heard his weak voice over the telephone utter that he could not attend any of the sessions, I knew that he did not have long to live. Knowing what you already now know about Harold Lloyd and his veritable love for music, I think it's safe to realize that had it been a year earlier, he definitely would have been at some of my concert recording sessions.

Since I understood that Harold was dying, I specifically avoided going up to the estate after the 30th of January 1971.

There was a note in my calendar book 14 July 1970 where I had telephoned Harold at St. John's Hospital (Room 382). I was a bit startled to have learned that he had been in the Hospital, but Harold assured me that it was nothing serious, and he was just there at the insistence of his brother-in-law, Dr. Jack Davis, for a routine check-up.

Another previous circumstance which indicated that Harold might be terminally ill occurred shortly after he had returned to Green Acres from St. John's. It was a pleasant sunny day and we were outside sitting in wicker chairs on the back lawn. He amazed me by saying, "What do you think I ought to do with this place,.Phillip?"

"What place?"

"This place. The estate."

"Why, is there something wrong?" I asked.

"No, there's nothing wrong, but it's a helluva expense you know keeping it up; about $250,000 a year. And a lot of time and energy; and I'm not getting any younger."

"Well, Harold," I went on, "it's really none of my business what you do with this place," I said.

Harold burst out laughing, "For years everybody's been trying to tell me what I should, or shouldn't do with this place, and I've told them it's none of their damned business. Now, when I ask you for your opinion, you tell me it's none of your business."

We both laughed.

"Really, I'd like your opinion," he went on.

Since I began to sense an indication that something might be amiss, I did not answer as Harold continued. "Do you think I ought to leave it to the kids? Harold, Jr.; Sue-Sue; Glo and Peggy?"

"No," I said.

"Why do you say that?"

"Because they wouldn't be able to handle it, for one thing. They don't have the income or the expertise to fend off tenacious developers who'd want to make a gigantic killing by cutting up all of this and making an expensive series of tract homes." And I said, "I would hate to see this beautiful estate get decimated."

"Well, how could we avoid that?" Harold asked.

"You could do what your good friend William Randolph Hearst did," I said. And I knew that he had known Hearst fairly well (and here is an example of how everything is relative) because Mildred and Harold, when I first became acquainted with them, once said to me, "Oh, if you think this house is something, you should have seen Hearst's estate. We used to go up there for week long parties. That was an estate."

Harold and Mildred were like two excited youngsters vocalizing about Hearst's San Simeon Castle and especially how long the dining room table was. Harold and Mildred Lloyd's dining room table was approximately 15 feet, but when they described how they ate off of Hearst's 38 foot long dining table, I told them I had difficulty comprehending how it would be to ask William Randolph Hearst at the head of the table to pass along the whole wheat bread.

"Oh, this place is nothing, you know, compared to Hearst's place," Harold and Mildred used to tell me.

I said to Harold, "You should do what Hearst did and make a museum out of it."

"A museum for what?"

"It could be for the arts, or music; you love music." And then I said, "You're known for your famed contribution to silent movies. Why don't you make this estate into a Hollywood Silent Film Museum and have the silent pictures shown here and artifacts of Keaton, Lloyd and Chaplin and all of your great colleagues from that Golden Era?"

"That's an excellent idea." Harold said.

Harold telephoned me several days later and said, "I don't know about your idea. I've investigated it and we don't have a permit for enough parking."

I said, "Well, you could do what the Getty Museum does in Malibu." At this time, before the revised and new Getty Museums had been constructed, it was mandatory to make reservations sometimes two weeks to a month in advance because of the restricted number of parking allotments. After I acquainted Harold with the procedures at the Getty Museum, this led to his renewed interest. I also stressed that it was imperative Harold devise a way, before hand, to project and guarantee the financial and operating arrangements for the Museum, "Or else," I said, "it will end up like the never realized Hollywood Museum near the Hollywood Bowl." I reminded Harold how around 1965 the Los Angeles Police Department, amid gun fire, had forcibly evicted a young veteran defending his cute little cottage, wife and child, to make room for the proposed Hollywood Museum. After they ejected him and his family, the city leveled his home and trashed it away the following week; and to this day, nothing has never been constructed upon that land. "So good ideas, are fine, Harold," I said, "but it's the materialization of the thought which takes rare ability; and quite frankly, I do not have faith in your Board Of Trustees as long as you're not there to guide them."

I also think that, in his slow debilitating cancerous end, Harold really did not have much confidence in his Board Of Trustees either; because I understood that he included a stipulation in his will that in the event the Board Of Trustees abandoned the project, the entire Green Acres Estate was to be turned over to UCLA, USC, the City Of Beverly Hills, the City Of Los Angeles, the State Of California, the United States Of America, or any other charitable organization which could operate the Museum.

True to the cast of all notable business men from John D. Rockefeller to Aristotle Onassis, Harold Lloyd believed in O.P.M. (Other People's Money) for investing and his will, I was informed, did not provide for the necessary funds to manage the Museum.

Unfortunately, Harold's Board Of Trustees were completely thrown out of their element to deal with the perspicacious Iranian real estate investors who were perched patiently in the wings like vultures waiting for the Trustee prey to finally expire: Dr. John H. Davis, 18 year old Sue-Sue, nephew Gaylord Lloyd, Muzak's Richard C. Simonton, and Thomas R. Sheppard just did not have the adequacy to take the estate and formulate it into anything much less a Museum.

The Iranian investors were eventually able to manipulate a purchase to Harold Lloyd's estate at an auction for one million six hundred thousand dollars cash (less than what it originally cost Harold to build the place in 1926) and of course, they made a gargantuan return by exploiting the property.

One weekend evening I accidentally encountered Sue at Pip's, the exclusive private disco and dinner club when it was on Robertson Boulevard. This was not too long after Harold had passed away and a few months after Harold Jr. had destructively succumbed. Sue revealed to me that Harold had left most of the remainder of the funds in trust: Harold Jr., Gloria, and Sue each receiving two-sevenths, and Peggy receiving the remaining one seventh. Now, she informed me that with Harold Jr.'s death she and her mother (Gloria) each were apportioned three sevenths, and Peggy was still dealt only the remaining one-seventh. I told Sue that Harold had divulged to me years before that Peggy had done something which he did not approve of and that he had warned her that if she did it, when it was time for him to "go" that she would not receive as much as the others. I apprised Sue how I had argued with Harold on Peggy's behalf (even though I hardly knew her) and I thought that she and Gloria should give Peggy more of their share. I also advised Sue that it's a good thing I did not have anything to do with the entire estate because I would have taken all of the funds and made the manor into an animal and bird sanctuary and not given them anything. Sue thought I was joking, but I wasn't. I probably would have done what I had heard Jascha Heifetz did before he died: to make sure and not leave a penny to any of his children.

As you have perhaps surmised by now, Ladies and Gentlemen of the Jury, I do not believe in the primitive monetary system which we have in our society, and therefore, I also do not accept the concept of inheritance as valid because it puts an inordinate emphasis upon how much money a person has rather than the humanitarian contributory talents an individual possesses. Historically, people who have been given large sums of money rarely, if ever, have benefited either themselves or mankind.

How could we replace money, you are probably asking. The answer is relatively simple: by vastly reducing and ultimately controlling the birth rate to coincide with the death rate. No two people should be allowed to have more than two children within our current populi (no matter how rich or influential they are) because of the rapid irreparable damage overpopulation is creating from food and farmland erosion; energy consumption; water contamination; loss of species, fisheries and forests;

famine; global conflicts and war; to garbage and pollution; massive traffic and living congestion; crime; graffiti; and disease. With the birth rate matching the death rate, we could eventually eliminate currency, purge the continued use of deadly fossil fuels, and proceed toward the clean free electromagnetic energy which Nikola Tesla discovered and envisioned for the entire earth at the turn of the 1900's. Thus by containing world population we can then progress to the absence of cash, which would eliminate most of humanities governmental and sociological disorders and reduce the abnormal stress acquiring legal tender has placed upon our planet's raw materials. We need to have an altruistic structure where cooperatively everyone can have the best of everything and not live in the primitively inhabited dangerously abrasive society which places radical emphasis upon profit and over consumption rather than value and excellence.

Harold Lloyd knew about overpopulation. Even though he wanted his beloved Green Acres to survive, he told me (after I warned him about the real estate appropriates and proposed the Museum concept to save it), "Well what can we do? With so many babies being born every year, places like this will never exist. The demand for houses will be too great. Why, hell, in 1926 this place and Will Rogers home were the only houses in all of Beverly Hills. Now, look at it."

When Harold Lloyd died, I did not want to go to the funeral, but Sue telephoned me several times. The first call was to inform me of Harold's death. The second call came the next day when she asked, "Phillip, do you know where Daddy kept his Mad Money?"

"What Mad Money?" I asked.

"You know," she said. "The ten to fifteen thousand dollars in cash that's hidden upstairs somewhere."

"I don't know about any ten to fifteen thousand dollars, Sue." I said. "All I knew about was the five or six hundred dollars he used to carry in the pocket of his bathrobe."

"No, we already found that," she said. "Are you sure Harold didn't tell you where he kept his Mad Money?"

"Look," I went on, "I don't ever remember Harold mentioning any ten to fifteen thousand dollars he had hidden in the house. But why don't you look in his private room where all the stereo slides are? Maybe it's in there somewhere; or behind one of the paintings around the house."

Sue telephoned me several hours later informing me that they had finally located Harold's Mad Money.

"Phillip, you will be coming to Daddy's funeral, Thursday, won't you?"

"I don't think so," I said. "Phillip Lambro never attends births, weddings, or funerals; not even his own."

"Oh please, Phillip; please come. It's not going to be like a regular funeral; Daddy didn't want that. It's only going to be thirty minutes with a little organ music (you know how Daddy liked the organ) and he would have wanted you there."

So to gratify Sue, I attended the thirty minute funeral (10:30 a.m. to 11:00 a.m.) 11 March 1971 at the Scottish Rite Temple 4357 Wilshire Boulevard. There were quite a number of people in attendance. I was ushered to a seat about eleven rows from the rear of the large auditorium where about five empty seats to my right was the tanned Palm Springs face of movie mogul Jack Warner who smiled at me. I nodded and returned the smile. Although, I felt like telling Jack Warner (whose Beverly Hills house was adjacent to the end of Harold's estate) 'that if it hadn't been for me after the City had taken a small part of your property, Harold Lloyd would never have finally sold you that piece of land to expand your yard.' Harold was complaining to me that Jack Warner was so upset by what the City of Beverly Hills had done that he had been begging Harold to sell him a small portion of Green Acres so Warner could have a slightly larger yard. I finally persuaded Harold to let poor Jack Warner buy the parcel, saying, "Harold, out of sixteen acres you're not going to miss that piddly plot in the far corner which is overgrown with dead vegetation anyway."

After Harold died, I never went up to the estate again. In fact, I never even went by it until about 1985. I had played tennis with my long time friend and coach, Alex Olmedo (the 1959 Wimbledon, Australian and Davis Cup Tennis Champion) on his courts at The Beverly Hills Hotel. I had had an appointment in the San Fernando Valley and at 4:30 in the afternoon I knew the Freeways would be gridlocked bumper-to-bumper. Since Alex lived in the Valley, he told me of a convenient way through Benedict Canyon over Mulholland Drive where it would be possible to circumvent all the Freeway congestion and not be late for my engagement. As I drove up Benedict Canyon I was shocked (although not surprised) to see what had been done to Harold Lloyd's beloved estate. Developers had cut up and subdivided the front and sides of the Italian gardens and paved a common asphalt road through it called Green Acres Drive erecting opulently oversized tract papier-mache barn-like homes on proportionately very small lots the baseness for which the contractors endeavored to camouflage with an overabundance of exotic palms and vegetation. It looked to me like an overgrown pink asymmetrical Las Vegas housing project. As I went by, I remember saying, "Harold, you smart son-of-a-bitch, I told you so; didn't I?"

This was a microcosm of what is continuing to happen all over the United States (the third most populated country in the world after China and India): carving up nature and our ecosystems as a result of a burgeoning population beyond our scientific and sociological attainments. Instead of controlling our population where two equals two and making circular complexes, where inhabitants could comfortably live within a minimum of at least 2,000 square feet of ample living space and be right within nature, and go toward pollution free electromagnetic energy, we are sundering every available division of soil. And we who cannot, as yet, create the complex DNA physical ecological entities which we are destroying every minute should respect and protect that precious macrocosm which is left. Because once you annihilate the essence of something, there's no going back and retrieving it with our present primitive technology.

As an artist, I forewarned Harold Lloyd in 1969. This is all an artist can do; like the function of a dog, to bark and sound the alarm of oncoming peril. My premonition that Green Acres would eventually be dismantled if Harold did not do something to prevent it before he departed became an actuality.

In addition to Green Acres, Harold Lloyd loved good music and delighted in horticulture; and, I presume, that's what we had in common and how we became friends.

He appreciated quality plays and acting, like Shakespeare; although he was never a Shakespearean actor. As he once said to me, "You know, they call me an artist now, but all we ever did in those days was just to try and make good, wholesome, entertaining movies."

Harold would show his films for nothing to students at Junior and Senior High Schools, Colleges and Universities; but he felt that if someone wanted his pictures for commercial television, that they would have to pay $150,000. And if they were to be shown in motion picture houses, the distributor had better be prepared to remunerate him.

I recall driving Harold north along Fairfax Avenue once where he said, "Phillip, stop the car. Go back."

I said, "What's wrong?" (We were driving by the Old Silent Movie Theater on Fairfax Avenue below Melrose Avenue) and he said, "Quick, let's go to your apartment. I have to make a telephone call."

Harold phoned his confidants at the FBI to investigate the theater to see if they had been exhibiting a bootlegged copy of one of his films which they were advertising. It seems that they were; so Harold had his FBI intimates confiscate the movie from the theater's projection room and had it returned to him.

Whatever frailties Harold Lloyd may have had, I have to admit that he was a unique person from every aspect and I certainly enjoyed knowing him; and I think he actually appreciated knowing me.

THE CHINATOWN SYNDROME

Since the automated biography *ROMAN by Polanski* has done me the honor of citing my association with the original music score to the film Chinatown on pages 355 and 356 (in addition to misspelling my first name), I feel it my obligation to let the film historians, critics, motion picture industry and general movie going public alike learn the veritable truth about my experiences and what I personally witnessed during this 1974 Paramount Pictures production.

In the first edition of Thomas Hardy's *Tess Of The D'Urbervilles* the author, in his explanatory note, quotes St. Jerome's proverb, "If an offense come out of the truth, better is it that the offense come than that the truth be concealed." It is ironic that Mr. Polanski, who has made a picture out of this piece of literature, neglected to discover Thomas Hardy's sincerity of purpose.

I first encountered Roman Polanski on the set of *Rosemary's Baby* during 1967 at the insistence of John Cassavetes (the film's leading man) who had been after me to compose some partial music cues for his low budget black and white experimental feature *Faces*. John was the type with whom you could speak candidly (a rarity in the Hollywood entertainment community I was finding out) and he was a little disappointed over the fact that I did not wish to create any music for his movie after having viewed the rough-cut a few weeks earlier. John had mentioned to me in passing that he had spoken about my composing abilities with Roman Polanski and had suggested that he contract me to do the score for *Rosemary's Baby*. I told John to forget it because, one: I was composing my concert work *Four Songs for Soprano & Orchestra* (which I completed the end of that year on commission and in memory of my childhood and teenage friend Sylvia Plath, whose texts form the basis of this work), and two: I knew Polanski was now using his Polish jazz pianist friend Christopher Komeda, who (although he had no original flair for composition) by the plebeian eclectic film scoring standards which motion pictures were now accepting, Komeda was more than adequate. Then too, I had always detested the Hollywood tradition of having to be forced to socially and politically maneuver in acquiring an assignment. I informed John that I would not come down to the set of Rosemary's Baby and meet Polanski, and that was final.

John waited several days before asking me over the telephone to help him pass out some *Faces* auto bumper-stickers and posters in order to promote his picture.

I said, "Okay, I'll pick them up at your home on the weekend."

To which he responded, "Don't wait until then, I have them down here in my dressing room at Paramount, and I need everyone's help to distribute these bumper-stickers right away because there's an important screening in a few weeks."

I did not want to refuse John again, because in originally declining to do his score-cues, I began by saying "no" at his house around one in the afternoon of that day (with periodic harassment from John and his two echoing pals, Seymour Cassel and Jack Ackerman, and after about two dozen interesting stories interspersed with more pleading to now just assist John with one important music cue) the next thing I noticed was that Seymour and Jack had left, and Gena Rowlands (John's wife) was asking me to stay for dinner as it was past 6:30. John promised that he would not introduce me to Polanski and not mention me for the score to *Rosemary's Baby* if I would only just come down and wait in his dressing room and between takes he would give me the *Faces* bumper-stickers with instructions on how to disseminate them.

An hour later I was on the Paramount lot where I received directions to the *Rosemary's Baby* sound stage. John was shooting a scene, and since it was virtually impossible to see anything of what was going on (because the set was a production design of a New York City apartment with the fabricated outer walls facing me) I decided to wait in John's mobile dressing room where I found one of his co-stars, a bearded Mr. Ralph Bellamy, sitting in a chair passing the time awaiting his next call. We struck up a conversation and within about ten minutes John walked in throwing a towel on the dressing table in disgust.

"What are you doing here?" he asked me with his characteristic half-smirk.

"John," I droned, "you left a pass at the gate for me and told me how important it was to come down right away and pick up your god damned bumper-stickers."

"Oh, yeah, bumper-stickers," he mumbled, then adding that half-laugh of his, which he sometimes used so effectively on screen, he opened his dresser drawer and pulled out about two hundred, eight-by-four-inch, pressure sensitive, black bumper-stickers with the lone word *FACES* all in white upper case.

"Here, how many can you get on people's cars?" he asked. "John, just give me fifty to start," I said. "I don't want to waste them. What about the posters?"

"The posters are too expensive. They're only going in key store windows, restaurants and places like that."

"Okay," I continued, "I'll give these stickers to my girlfriend and have her give them out to her friends; then I'll pass along the rest to my friends, who I know for sure will, at least, put one on their cars."

"What about you?" John asked.

"I never put bumper-stickers on my car," I smiled.

"Fuck you," he said.

Bellamy laughed while trying to light his pipe.

"John," I implored, "tell me some more of those Gregory Ratoff stories you told me up at your house the other day."

Bellamy was amazed that John had known Gregory Ratoff, because Bellamy had also been acquainted with the colorful Russian actor-director-producer, illustrious Hollywood Golden Age impresario-con-man. John enumerated how Ratoff had given him his first break into motion pictures with a bit part in a film shot in New York City; and how after it became somewhat successful for Ratoff, Ratoff had felt "that god damned Greek," whose name had escaped him had brought him new found luck. Ratoff finally tracked down John again and said, "Look here you no good, god damned Greek bastard," in what Cassavetes described as a humorous fractured Russian accent, "even though you don't know anything about acting or motion pictures, I Gregory Ratoff, the great actor-director-producer will teach you everything you need to know."

John proceeded to retell some of those fascinating stories I had originally heard at his home: about how Ratoff had convinced John that the only way he could ever hope to achieve flying colors within the motion picture industry was to work with Ratoff for free as his Man-Friday, which, incidentally, John did for several years.

One of my favorite accounts was how Ratoff, almost totally out of money, went to the south of France and conned 20th Century Fox's Darryl F. Zanuck out of $10,000 dollars (big money in those days) to develop a screen treatment for a story which Ratoff had extemporaneously contrived to Zanuck. After about a year, and Ratoff had depleted the money on other things, one of Zanuck's aides contacted Ratoff, saying that Zanuck was wondering where the synopsis was. "Jesus Christ, Greek," Ratoff had exclaimed to the youthful Cassavetes, "there I was in big trouble. Zanuck wanted to see the treatment for the story I told him about in the south of France, however, the only thing was I couldn't remember what the hell I had told him!" John continued to relay how Ratoff ingeniously began to construct a scripted treatment which eventually (after a series of writers developed a screenplay) became *The Man Who Broke The Bank*

At Monte Carlo, which Zanuck himself produced.

Polanski came into the dressing room as we were laughing over the chronicle and John promptly introduced me as, "This is the composer I was telling you about; he's really great. You owe it to yourself to listen to his music; he could write a fantastic score for this picture." Polanski looked a little intimidated by John Cassavetes' sudden exclamation and he responded rather shyly that he already had a composer.

"Christopher Komeda," he said to me. "Do you know him? Most Americans don't."

"Don't listen to him," I said. "You have a fine composer and I'm sure he'll do a good job." I gave Cassavetes a cutting glance as if to say, 'Shut up Greek and leave this poor guy alone.'

Polanski had wanted John back on the set for just another short take before everyone left for lunch. John asked me to wait and have lunch with him.

As the scene was being redone, I went outside and milled around, observing the cast and crew in this overgrown barn called a sound stage. There was Richard Sylbert, to whom I had been previously introduced some months earlier at the home of United Artists executive, Sandy Whitelaw, arrogantly posturing in his safari apparel and pipe, attempting to appear like some sophisticated great white hunter from Kenya, rather than the ubiquitous production designer he actually was; William Castle, the producer, whom I had remembered during my teens from his many movie coming-attractions, pacing the floor and chomping nervously on a Havana cigar; and Howard Koch Jr., an assistant who asked if I would be a fourth at the ping-pong table between the set and dressing rooms. I said okay, and we played a few fun doubles games, after which Polanski came over and took away the paddle from Koch's partner and proceed to have a go at rallying with us. I was surprised to see what little hand-eye coordination Polanski had and to notice that he was a bit awkward as well. After a few rallies, he threw down the paddle, saying something to the effect that this game was no good and a waste of time.

As I was leaving to meet John for lunch, Polanski stopped me and said, in that rapid centripetal manner of his, "Look, I'd really like to hear your music sometime, but I already have a composer on this film." I told him to forget John's remarks and that I had come here to see John on another matter, but that I did enjoy meeting him, and I had seen all of his films and personally thought he had great cinematic vision. Polanski thanked me and we conversed for another minute during which time he asked me where I lived. I explained that I was now living in my composing apartment on Fairfax Avenue not far from Sunset Boulevard. Polanski said that he had had so many visitors staying and wanting to linger at his house that he could hardly get into the place at night, and would I be interested in putting up one of his friends. He was a bit startled when I replied that I had been letting a young Frenchman, whom I had met at the Old World Restaurant (a natural food hangout on Sunset Boulevard) by the name of Henri Sera stay at my apartment from time to time, because he was one of the people Polanski had been thinking about. He asked if I knew his brother Simon Hessera (who was also in town) and I said no. We exchanged goodbyes and I went to seek out John Cassavetes, who was speaking with an Israeli writer by the name of Eliyahu 'Amiqam who had arrived to visit with Cassavetes. Eliyahu 'Amiqam was one of the most truly humanitarian individuals I had ever met. His philosophy was that we live in one world which does not have to be chaotic if we avoid the forces of destruction and follow the order of life. John and I were completely fascinated by 'Amiqam's ideals and thoughts and we asked him to join us for lunch at the Paramount commissary.

While we walked, Polanski ran up behind John and made some last minute acting suggestions which obviously could not wait. As soon as we all reached the front of the commissary, Robert Evans (looking quite handsome in his dark blue continental vested pin-striped suit) confronted John and Polanski with, "Gentlemen, I saw the rushes this morning and I'm very impressed; very, very impressed, indeed." John grinned and inclined his head as Polanski, biting his lower lip, with his eyes blinking rapidly, nodded nervously. Evans continued, "I'm very, very pleased, and very impressed; yes, I couldn't be happier with the rushes."

I began thinking to myself, 'This is the Head of Production at Paramount Pictures Corporation?' I furtively glanced at Eliyahu 'Amiqam, who faintly smiled at me, but remained stoically polite and immobile. We were like a group of mute, Kafkaesque characters staring at one another until Cassavetes made the first move toward the steps of the commissary and terminated an encounter I would have had trouble believing had I not witnessed it.

Once inside, Polanski left for his table where he looked like an animated Sultan in blue jeans holding court. Cassavetes, 'Amiqam and I went to another dining table off to the side where we began to assimilate 'Amiqam's altruistic philosophy and his ideas for a forthcoming book. Having begun my Japanese Zen Macrobiotic way of life shortly before this, there was little I could eat. However, I became rather startled when Mia Farrow (whom I did not know nor had ever met) came up behind

276

me, grabbing my shoulders, and in reference to John, loudly whispered into my right ear, "Don't believe a word he's saying, he's full of shit." I sort of smiled at her and she left beaming.

After that day at Paramount, I never returned to the Rosemary's Baby set, but continued to see John Cassavetes at his home, and I did correspond with 'Amiqam every now and again. Sometimes I would accidentally encounter Polanski on Sunset Boulevard, where he seemed fascinated by the Vietnam protest marches and Flower Children, and just West Hollywood life in general.

I recall his approaching me and shaking my hand as I was about to enter Cyrano's Restaurant (a favorite Sunset Boulevard rendezvous where you could meet a lot of interesting girls) as he was leaving with an exceedingly attractive blonde who walked about six paces behind him like some obedient French poodle. It was just one of those "Hello, how are you, nice to see you," quick introductions and goodbyes and I smiled at the charming statuesque blonde in her well tailored, beige gabardine mini-skirt and white-laced blouse. She yielded the grin coyly and left on Polanski's cue, hurriedly treading several steps after him along Sunset Boulevard. I was to see Polanski a few times now and then at a variety of places; sometimes at the Old World, here and there on the street, but usually in the company of an entourage, and most of the time with that captivating young lady remotely back of him who I later found out from Henri Sera was a new actress by the name of Sharon Tate.

Artistically, 1967 was a fertile year for me because I was able, through a commission from Edward "Buzz" Barton, to complete my *Four Songs for Soprano and Orchestra* 3 December 1967. I had not done another film score since Universal's *And Now Miguel* (1965-66), however, I really hadn't minded because, although I had always composed distinctive music scores (regardless in the quality of the film) my heart was with concert music. With symphonic music I could compose anything I wished. I could make deep and personal statements and contribute without having to hold an unenlightened director's or producer's hand like a child's through ten reels of music cues.

During 1968 and 1969 I had become friendly with Henri Sera (who years later was to introduce Polanski to the thirteen year old bubble-gum chewing San Fernando Valley nymphet whom Polanski photographed and admittedly seduced in Jack Nicholson's pool) and I tried to help Henri, since his brother, Michel Abesera had cured himself of a serious illness through Macrobiotics and was a well known leader in the Macrobiotic cause, having written one of the first Macrobiotic cookbooks. I endeavored to influence Henri by suggesting that he return to Macrobiotics and eliminate animal and dairy products from his intake, returning to grains, miso soup and vegetables. Henri would want to come and stay at my apartment when either he had had a fight with one of his many vacant girlfriends, or wasn't feeling that well from indulging in an unsatisfactory way of life.

Henri (who was rather slim anyway) once told me how he avoided the military draft in France. He went on twenty days of just eating natural brown rice and when he appeared for his physical examination, the doctors took one look at his cadaverous state and rejected him immediately. Adding soups and vegetables to his system again, and eating more, Henri's weight returned to normal within two weeks. Henri and I would sometimes meet at the Old World Restaurant where in those days you could get natural brown rice, vegetables, and a non-meat vegeburger all for about $3.50, and meet an interesting assortment of people. Some of the waiters were French and were friends of Henri's and we usually had one or two tables going in animated discussions with a lot of the French Contingent holding court. I did meet a level-headed young Frenchman by the name of Jean France Mercier, who was to become one of my closest friends. He later married Lynda Gold, the daughter of an affluent Santa Monica businessman, who changed her name and became a sometime actress, and the three of us always had a lot of laughs and good times when we were together.

Jean France (who had developed into an excellent photographer) had some motion pictures and still photos taken of his wedding, which after his divorce, his ex-mother-in-law asked if she could have. Jean France agreed and personally delivered all the prints to Mrs. Gold's home since he told her that he would have no future use for them anyway. When Mrs. Gold thanked Jean France (whom she had always liked) Jean France humorously, but with an expressionless face, gave her the bride and groom ornament top which had been left from the giant wedding cake. "Here," he said, "you might also want to have this."

A few times Polanski came into the Old World with either Sharon Tate still ambulating latterly, the Sylbert brothers, or with Henri's brother Simon Hessera whom I still did not know, who was shooting a picture for Paramount to a script by Polanski entitled *A Day At The Beach*, which to this day remains somewhere in the bowels of Paramount's unreleased disaster vault.

During 1969, Henri, through association, also began to view himself as a film director, since he revealed that he had appeared in several cameo parts within French movies, and wanted to know if I would be interested in doing the music for his new 16 mm short film which he planned to produce and direct with Jean France in the title role. I said that I would have to see the work-print before I committed, but I would be happy to read his script. Later, I found out from Jean France that there was no script; Henri had just planned to make up the story as they went along.

Henri and Jean France drove to San Francisco to scout for locations and were involved in a grave auto accident; which left Jean France with some head injuries and continual migraine headaches and Henri with a dislocated shoulder and a broken leg in a humorously large white plaster cast. Henri subsequently moved into Jean France's cute little garden cottage up in Laurel Canyon, but it was too small and Jean France's attractive girlfriend (who was coming and going) tried valiantly to nurse the both of them. Henri had no car and Jean France's was "totaled," so on occasion I would pause from composing and deliver the both of them to the doctor's office in Beverly Hills.

A few days later, Henri was back holding court at the Old World. It was amusing to see him still chasing and auditioning young Hollywood starlets with his hobbling oversized cast and cane. One day while Henri was verbalizing about his sexual exploits with an interesting looking girl (who I knew had a crush on Jean France) I incredulously asked Henri, "How on earth did you ever fuck that girl in the condition you're in?"

Jean France quietly replied, "Once with the cast and twice with the cane," obviously still in pain, holding his head between both palms with two burning cigarettes extending from each hand. I could not stop laughing for about two minutes, to the consternation of Henri. Even Jean France, as physically distressful as it was for him to even chortle, had difficulty not laughing at his own humorous remark.

Moreover, during that summer of 1969, I was taking time off from composing and learning new scores to add to my conducting repertory, by playing tennis again. I had played a little on the famous University of Miami Tennis Team (1953-1955) where the 1950 Wimbledon Jr. Champion, Johann Kupferburger of South Africa, was number three and I was anywhere from number ten to twelve; and where I had had a 6-1, 6-1 upset win over Yale number one Richard Raskind during the annual University of Miami and Yale round robin tournament in Coral Gables. Raskind, you may recall was later to achieve fame with a sex change and became Rene Richards, which surprised the hell out of me because this big guy was quite masculine, liked the girls, and had some wieldy shots.

In the Army I had also been a member of the four-man SETAF Tennis Team within the European NATO Team during 1958 and 1959. My friend Alex Olmedo (the Wimbledon, Australian and Davis Cup Champion) was helping me considerably with my tennis technique on his pleasant courts at The Beverly Hills Hotel and my other buddy, Rafael Osuna (1963 U.S. Open Champion) had asked me (before he died during June in that air crash) to practice with his close friend and new University of Southern California student, Eduardo Martinez-Lanz, also from Mexico.

Macrobiotics had helped me cure a terrible case of sacroiliac arthritis and from the medication a form of leukemia so you can imagine how appreciative I was at just being able to move my body and run again. I did not mind when, or if, I lost; just being able to breathe, exercise, and hit a tennis ball without pain was compensation enough. Since I was practicing tennis again after many years (and especially with Eduardo who was trying for a berth on the elite USC Team) I was not at my Fairfax apartment and composing studio too often; so Henri Sera, who presently had nowhere to go, asked if he could move in once again until his gigantic cast (which now had been on for several months) was finally removed and he could collect about $2,500 insurance settlement money. I relented, but told Henri that I did not relish some of his friends making a mess of the apartment and finding cigarette ashes all over my compositions in progress and in my grand piano. He promised that he would live better and try to return to Macrobiotics.

The summer passed quickly. Henri was now dating the younger sister of singer-TV personality Cher whom he was to eventually marry and divorce and who, on more than one occasion, I would sometimes ask to leave when I came home. It seems she was under the erroneous impression that I was staying with Henri and I should abandon my own apartment. Henri was beginning to become a problem because I could see, as engaging as he was, that he had no genuine talent for motion picture directing, and he refused to enter UCLA Medical Center to change his cast as the insurance doctors had requested.

It was Friday 8 August 1969, and I was getting ready to go with Eduardo to Santa Barbara to play in a weekend tennis tournament. As I was packing my gear, I said, "Henri, I'm going to Santa Barbara to play tennis. This place is a mess. I want you to stop procrastinating and check yourself into UCLA Medical and get your cast removed today." "But I can't," he said. "Sharon's throwing a party."

"Sharon who?" I asked.

"You know, Sharon; Roman's wife."

"I thought you said she was having a baby in London."

"She and Roman had some sort of disagreement, I don't know, and she's having the baby here, and Roman is still in London. She's having a party tonight and I'm going."

"Look," I continued, "if you're not checked into UCLA tonight, and you go to that party, when I come back from Santa Barbara, all your stuff is going to be out on the street; and if you know one thing about me, Henri, when I say something, I mean it."

Henri looked at me with displeasure and said no more because Eduardo had just entered the apartment and we were preparing to leave.

Eduardo had misunderstood the entry requirements when he telephoned the tournament; and since he had not mailed the entry fees (thinking we would pay upon arrival) we found ourselves not even in the draw. We stayed the day and I took Eduardo to the Music Academy Of The West, where in 1955 I had received a scholarship to study with concert pianist Gyorgy Sandor and composer Donald Pond.

The director, Maurice Abravanel, was still there and he received me graciously, since he had remembered me and in fact had conducted my *Miraflores for String Orchestra* during 1965 in a televised concert with the Music Academy Orchestra. Abravanel was also conductor of the Utah Symphony Orchestra for many years.

We decided to return to Los Angeles Saturday afternoon. As Eduardo sped his Mustang down Pacific Coast Highway, I became bored with the music on the radio and tried to find a better station. Switching frequency-to-frequency, I heard the clipped phrase, "Sharon Tate murders..." I quickly returned the knob back to that position and could not believe what I was hearing. As the newscaster described the sketchy details of the homicides, which had reportedly taken place during the previous evening's party, I wondered if Henri Sera had disobeyed my strict demand about admitting himself into UCLA and getting his cast removed. The announcer added that there had been an unidentified body of a young male found in the garden cottage, which I hoped had not been Henri.

As soon as we arrived at my apartment on Fairfax Avenue, I raced up the stairs ahead of Eduardo and called the UCLA hospital. I was informed that Henri Sera had, indeed, checked in. I spoke with him later by telephone and he said in that slight French accent of his, "My god, Phillip, I would have gone to that party had you not been so strict with me, but I knew you meant what you said and not having any other place to stay right now, I did not want to find all my belongings out in the street; you saved my life, probably."

It's a good thing you're at least half-Macrobiotic," I said, "otherwise you wouldn't have listened."

Henri and I talked briefly about the tragedy, which in the world of Oriental Diagnosis, we could in part analyze: the person who commits a crime is ill; the person who receives that crime is equally ill for having attracted it.

Many years later I occasionally noticed Henri Sera from my car because for a while we lived on the same street here in Los Angeles where he had become an Orthodox Jew, married again and had three children. Ultimately, he went to live in Israel.

The next time I encountered Roman Polanski was the early part of February 1974. I was giving a ride to my friend, Ellen Gameral (an exceptionally bright, hardworking and literate administrator who worked for 20th Century Fox) when I noticed Polanski waiting along side of us in his white Corvette as the traffic light was about to change at the intersection of Doheny and Santa Monica, going south toward Wilshire. I asked Ellen to roll down the window, and yelled, "Hi Roman, remember me?"

"Oh hi," he responded. "How are you?"

"What are you doing in Los Angeles?" I asked.

"Making a picture."

"Where?"

"At Paramount," he continued as the light turned green.

"Good," I said. "I'll telephone you because I want you to meet a fantastic editor friend of mine."

He smiled and nodded goodbye as he sped off.

I had completed the music for a horror film entitled *Crypt Of The Living Dead* (also known in the United Kingdom as *Vampire Woman*) originally titled [get this], *Hannah: Queen Of The Vampires*, which was altogether saved by the brilliant reconstructive editing of David Rawlins. We worked on the post-production for this picture at M-G-M, where David had even changed the story line, making it more intriguing and suspenseful (which was an arduous task considering the innocuous script) by massive reorganization of the material, reshooting certain scenes and doing a variety of virtuoso tricks at the lab. In fact, during the final screening at M-G-M, the investor and his wife came up to me and said, "We want you to know how appreciative we are to you and David Rawlins. Without your brilliant score and his editing, we wouldn't have had a releasable picture."

During 1980, Scott Holton of Varese Srabande Records told me and others that my music to this picture was the most advanced and interesting soundtrack he had ever heard for any horror film. He wanted to put the recording out; however, union reuse payments (which neither of us could afford) prevented the commercial release of the album. At that time, David Rawlins was married to actress Brooke Mills (who was carrying their first and only child) and he was not getting the substantial assignments he should have been receiving and would be acquiring after his alert editing contributed to the success of *Saturday Night Fever* a few years hence. So I informed them both that I had accidentally encountered Roman Polanski, who told me that he was making a picture at Paramount, and I would be calling him to endeavor to arrange an introduction and see if he would hire David for whatever project he might be doing.

According to my calendar-log, I first telephoned Polanski the morning of Tuesday 19 February 1974. After his secretary announced who I was, he immediately picked up the receiver.

"Hi, how are you?" he asked.

"Fine," I responded, quickly adding, "Look, I know you must be extremely busy with your picture, but I really would like for you to meet David Rawlins, that wonderful editor I was telling you about."

"Listen," he went on, "I want to talk with you about something. I'm very busy now, but can you call me next week?"

"Sure," I said. "When?"

"Call me next Wednesday morning, a week from tomorrow."

"Fine," I ended, "I'll call you then." I marked my calendar-journal accordingly.

I phoned both David and Brooke to inform them that Polanski said he wanted to see me and that I had mentioned David quite strongly, so I asked them to be sure and give me a credit sheet (which they never did) in order that I might, perhaps, influence Polanski about employing David.

On the 27th of February I telephoned Polanski, who told me to come down to Paramount for lunch the day after, Friday 1 March 1974 at 12:45, but to call him first and confirm where.

Friday morning he said, "Do you know where that Mexican Restaurant, Lucy's is, on Melrose, not far from the studio?"

"I never go there, but I know where it is," I replied.

"Meet me there about 12:45. If I'm a little late, just wait for me."

I arrived a few minutes early at Lucy's El Adobe Cafe, with its faded blown-up portraits of then Governor Jerry Brown hanging in the foggy windows. I was shown to a rear booth and not too long afterward Polanski swaggered in.

"Sorry I'm late," he said in that remotely shy, fidgety monotone of his, nodding his head and hunching over the table. The dim daylight of the Cafe and the position of the table made me feel as if I were about to take part in some kind of organized crime effort.

"Roman," I said, breaking the silence, "When can you meet David Rawlins, my..."

"Who the hell is David Rawlins?" he interrupted raising his voice.

"You know, that sensational film editor I told you about."

"Film editor," he exclaimed. "Will you stop with this film editor shit? I already have a film editor; the picture is almost completed. I invite you down here to see if you would like to score my picture and all you talk about is a fucking film editor."

I was completely amazed. Even though I knew that Christopher Komeda had passed away, I never thought Polanski would ask me to do a score because, although I had written distinctive music for films, these motion pictures had never been critical or box office successes. Then too, a few of my soundtracks had been for documentaries and I knew in Hollywood that a film composer was almost never selected on the basis of the quality of his music, but by how fiscally prosperous, or pontifical the titles of his movie credits were.

"What's the name of your film?" I asked.

"*Chinatown*," he said, calming down.

"That's a great title," I said, "but wasn't there an old movie with the same name during the thirties or forties?"

"Was there? I don't know," Polanski shrugged, blinking his eyes and rubbing his thumb back and forth on the table. "Do you want to do this picture?"

"Who's the producer?"

"I'm producing the picture, but Bob Evans is the producer in name. It's his first picture as producer."

"Wait a minute," I smirked. "That guy has thrown out more scores as head of production at Paramount than in the entire history of Hollywood. I was told he even wanted to throw out Nino Rota's score for *Romeo And Juliet* because some pop record producer told him it wouldn't sell with the young audiences since it wasn't a rock'n-roll score, but Franco Zeffirelli miraculously kept it in. Can you imagine that? And that's only one incident out of dozens. Roman, I write distinctive music and I don't need to have my scores thrown out. I don't need that at all."

"Nobody's going to throw out your music. Bob Evans heard your music and he likes it, and besides, I'm in full control. Bob Evans won't even be around, I can guarantee it. It'll be just you and me. Bob Evans listens to me."

"What music?" I asked.

"I don't know, I think your agent sent me a classical recording of yours with some avant garde music on it, and I cut several scenes in the picture with your music. Everyone thinks it's great." Polanski started to smile.

Later I found out that Carl Forest of the Paul Kohner Agency had left my concert music recording, press reviews and credit sheet in Polanski's office some weeks earlier. This was the very same recording which (unbeknown to me a few years before) had been purchased in a New York City record store, along with other contemporary recordings by *The Exorcist* head editor, Jordan Leondopoulos, who used my *Structures for String Orchestra* as a guide-track in all the final work prints of *The Exorcist*.

My *Structures* ultimately became responsible for the eventual junking of Lalo Shifrin's *Exorcist* score. It seems Ted Ashley and the other Warner Bros. executives thought that the music on *The Exorcist* prints they were watching had been done by Lalo Shifrin. Ashley had telephoned then Music Department Head, Larry Marks (who later divulged the story to me) and said, "Congratulate Lalo Shifrin on a wonderful score."

To which Marks responded, "But Lalo Shifrin hasn't even seen the picture yet."

"Well, whose music is it?" asked Ted Ashley.

"You've got me," said Marks. "You'd better ask Friedkin."

Director William Friedkin hadn't seen that particular print, and when Ashley informed him about it he ran the work print and exclaimed, "That's exactly the type of music I want. Get Leondopoulos. Find out whose music this is." Leondopoulos had quit the picture and was off on a badly needed Caribbean vacation and I understood it took Friedkin's office two days to find out that it was my music.

Since my agent Paul Kohner had represented Max von Sydow (who played the elderly priest in *The Exorcist*) an alert secretary in Friedkin's cadre had recalled Paul Kohner recommending me to do the background score two years earlier, and they immediately contacted him. Unfortunately, we could never come to financial terms. I genuinely felt with such a powerful story (which I liked) that I could have composed a unique soundtrack. As everyone should know, Friedkin emulated Stanley Kubrick by eventually "tracking" the whole film's music from other existing commercially available phonograph recordings.

Briefly, I explained to Polanski what he had done with my music had also previously occurred in *The Exorcist* and he seemed mildly fascinated by the similitude.

"Come on," persuaded Polanski. "I think you have the right talent for this picture. We could do something good; that is, if you are interested in working with me."

"Roman," I said, "I've seen *Knife In The Water, Repulsion, Cul de Sac, Macbeth* (I purposely left out *Rosemary's Baby*, which I always had felt did not actually express his final cut and own intentions) and I would really love to collaborate with you. We could do something similar to what Eisenstein and Prokofiev did between director and composer."

Polanski nodded in agreement.

"But I know these Hollywood people like Evans. This isn't Europe. If you don't have legal control you don't have any control over a picture here, believe me."

"Will you stop?" he said agitatedly. "I told you I have complete control over this picture. You have nothing to worry about. The only person you have to please is me and yourself. You can write anything you want within the framework of what's needed."

"Okay," I went on. "If I'm responsible to you and only you, I'll do it. Now what about money? How much?"

Polanski ever so slightly hesitated, then reverting to that shy monotone of his said, "Twelve Thousand Dollars."

"Twelve Thousand Dollars," I exclaimed. "I'm a recognized concert composer. My music has been performed from The Philadelphia Orchestra to the Tivoli Gardens in Denmark. Twelve Thousand Dollars? I can stay at home and work on my symphonic music for just about as little as that. My score from Mineral King was chosen by the National Board of Review as best music in 1972," I said, endeavoring to get more money.

"Look," he continued in resignation, "it's not up to me. I want more money myself, but that's the budget. I don't control the money. What amount were you thing about?"

"Twenty Five Thousand Dollars," I shot back emphatically.

"They won't go for that."

"Wait a minute," I said, getting an idea. "You have a house in London, don't you?"

"Yes, a beautiful place, why?"

"I have to go to London in June for my concert music career and meetings with recording executives. I need a flat from which I can travel back and forth all over the Continent for a couple of months. If you let me use part of your home in London, and the kitchen, while I'm there, for free, and if I do an outstanding job on this picture and the executives like my score, and you arrange for them to give me a cash bonus, then I'll do your score."

Polanski liked the idea and asked me who my representative was. He then instructed me to telephone him at five o'clock that afternoon.

"We made a deal with your agent Kohner," said Polanski when I called. "Everything is all set. Call me Monday morning. I want you to see the film. We're still doing some editing, of course; little things. But anyway, I'm anxious to know what you think, because you've never seen the picture or read the script."

I met my then girlfriend, Madeline, that evening about 7:30. She was a young student of Zen Macrobiotics and my Sensei (teacher) Toyo Nakayama Furukawa, who owned the Zen Restaurant on Hollywood Boulevard near Gramercy (it's no longer there), along with her mother Miyoko, as usual, cooked a wonderfully balanced meal of noodles, grains and vegetables. Toyo and I had been working to improve Madeline's kidney condition, which was getting better through the intake of Hokkaido Kabocha Pumpkin, Adzuki Beans and Adzuki Bean Juice, together with natural Koda medium grain brown rice and the artful cooking of these Japanese Zen lady masters who, together with Georges Ohsawa, had survived World War II in Japan.

Madeline knew enough about Yin and Yang, visual diagnosis and Roman Polanski to become exceedingly fearful about my working with him. We both knew at the time that Polanski had Yang Sanpaku (three whites above the eye's iris), which often brings great harm and stress to those around people with this condition. Stalin and Charles Manson also had this condition and I could not refute that accurate Oriental Diagnosis because we know how much tragedy and stress had occurred to those around Polanski, Stalin and Charles Manson. The opposite to Yang Sanpaku is Yin Sanpaku (where the three whites of the eyes are below the iris) and people with this much more common condition have all lived and biologically attracted immense misfortune to themselves without exception: Lincoln, John F. Kennedy, Natalie Wood, John Belushi, John Lennon, Martin Luther King, Robert Kennedy, Marilyn Monroe, all had (Yin Sanpaku) large amounts of the white of their eyes showing under their iris. (For more information about Oriental Diagnosis read Michio Kushi's book on the subject, ISBN 0-87040-467-9).

The Yang Sanpaku which Polanski had is the result of the over consumption of extremely yang (contractive) foods and drink such as meat,

287

salty and highly spiced foods, which I witnessed him consume at Lucy's El Adobe Cafe. Yin Sanpaku is caused by excessive over consumption of Yin (expansive) food and drink, such as exotic fruits, sugars, acid vegetables, wines, drugs, alcohol and commercially packaged highly refined supermarket foods. The Yang Sanpaku of Polanski's type is an indication of aggressive behavior, uncontrollable passions and abnormal mentality.

"Phillip, I'm worried," Madeline said. "Look what happened to those around him; look what happened to his last composer."

Madeline was referring to the fact that Christopher Komeda had been drunk and slipped several times injuring his head. I understand that he remained in a coma for many months at a Los Angeles hospital until his wife got the bill in many thousands of dollars and aired Komeda to a less expensive communist hospital in Poland where he eventually died.

"I'm in pretty good balance now," I replied. "I've been a good Macrobiotic the last seven years and I should be able to harmonize with any adversity and Toyo and her mother will be cooking for me every day, so don't worry, I won't die. I'll survive Polanski's Yang Sanpaku."

Monday, 4 March 1974, I telephoned Polanski at 10:45 a.m. He informed me that he wanted me to see the film at 10:00 a.m. Wednesday March 6th in the Main Theater at Paramount. He said that the President of Paramount, Mr. Frank Yablans, would be there along with Thelma Roberts, who was Polanski's efficient secretary. I remember that we waited for Yablans for about an hour and were eventually informed around 11 o'clock that he wasn't going to attend, so Polanski ran *Chinatown* for just Thelma Roberts, himself and your humble court composer.

My first impression of the picture was (although there was a certain amount of vogue with Polanski's directing) that I knew immediately this movie was not going to be a commercial success: it lacked a well defined and potent story-line; it was neither an authentic drama nor a mystery; and the performances, although competent, could not have been any more than that with this machinated chronicle and dialogue.

Quite frankly, I was rather disappointed. I was expecting the mastery of the next logical upward progression from the director who had given us *Repulsion*. Instead, what I had witnessed was a number of talented people performing a script from which the only plausible asset seemed to be its powerful and intriguing one word title, *Chinatown*. Incidentally, it made as much sense to call this picture *Chinatown* as it would have been to call it Little Tokyo, or Korea Town; the film had absolutely nothing to do with Chinatown.

One thing which did please and astonish me was the fact that my good friend, actor Perry Lopez had a major role in it as Lt. Luis Escobar. I had only spoken with Perry a few times all year, but he never mentioned anything other than to say that he had been working on a film down at Paramount and just leave it at that. So it came as a complete surprise to me when I saw him enter a scene in the picture.

Polanski had sat alone in another part of the large theater and I had been sitting just a few seats away from Thelma Roberts. After the lights went on he came up to me and said, "Well what do you think?"

"It's very well directed," I said, "there's no question about that. But the story's a little off-beat, wouldn't you say?"

"There's still more editing to be done," Polanski said. "But what do you think about the scenes where I used your concert music?"

In *ROMAN by Polanski* on page 355 he writes, "For experimental purposes, I mixed one scene with some music by Philip (sic) Lambro, a young composer who had sent us a sample record. Evans was so impressed that we hired him." To set the record straight, I never sent Polanski anything because I did not even know he was in town until I saw him by chance several weeks earlier at the traffic intersection. As I previously said, Carl Forest of the Paul Kohner Agency told me (after I inquired) that he was the one who had given the Polanski office my recording, press notices and credit sheet because he felt I was the logical choice to do this film. Now, since Polanski ran *Chinatown* for me, and since I happen to know my own music fairly well, the recording Polanski is referring to was a recording I had conducted with the United States International Orchestra (Crystal S-861) on which I featured works by Cortes, Lombardo and my own *Music For Wind, Brass & Percussion* and my *Structures for String Orchestra*. Polanski mixed several scenes using both of my compositions in that work-print and not one scene as he erroneously maintains.

"Very interesting," I smiled. "But I don't think those concert works are appropriate for these scenes, do you?"

"Well, no, but that's the type of quality I want. I want something..." he groped.

"...with the same musical fabric," I injected, "but styled differently."

"Exactly," Polanski emphasized. "With the same musical fabric, but styled differently. Exactly," he added again. In fact, I would say that in the over two months I spent working almost every day with Roman Polanski (1 March 1974 through 5 May 1974) the words "exactly" and "absolutely" were to indicate to me his overwhelming approval.

The three of us ambled out of the giant theater into the alley-way with Polanski trying to elicit more of a response from me. All I could think of were those many faces with voices of friends and acquaintances who over the years had warned me against being truthful with "Hollywood Film People." "Keep your mouth shut," they used to tell me. "Don't tell them what you really think, unless what you really think will flatter their inflated egos," I heard echoing between my inner ear. I had never been able to do that because my talents as an artist had always demanded that I seek and speak the truth. Thomas Hardy's quote of St. Jerome reverberated simultaneously with the flashing face of Universal's Music Head, Joe Gershenson, Nick Cravat, Maximilian Schell and other motion picture people who had relayed their horrors to me for trying to be helpful with veracity. I had had several cinematic, social and professional scars myself for speaking candidly, in the form of banishments and blacklistings. "If an offense come out of the truth, better is it that the offense come than that the truth be concealed."

"Do you want a truthful response, artist-to-artist?" I asked politely. "Or do you want a Hollywood answer?"

"The truth," Polanski demanded. "You can tell me anything. I will never hold it against you."

"It's the story, Roman. The story's weak; but maybe with more editing..."

He turned and faced me, slowly walking backwards as Thelma Roberts and I walked ever so dilatorily forward.

"You think this piece of shit story is bad now?" Polanski exclaimed. "I'll show you the original script. Do you want to see it? It was the biggest pile of crap you ever saw. Thelma, make a note to remind me to give Mr. Lambro a copy of the original screenplay."

"That's not necessary," I responded, with Polanski still walking backwards.

On pages 346 and 347 of *ROMAN by Polanski* he states, concerning the script, "Unfortunately the character Gittes was overwhelmed by the intricate and almost incomprehensible plot. The screenplay required massive cuts, drastic simplification and the pruning of several subsidiary characters, all of them beautifully drawn but contributing nothing to the action. Bob Towne had worked on *Chinatown* two years and rightly regarded it as the best thing he'd ever done, but I knew him well enough not to pull any punches. I told him what I thought of his script over lunch at Nate 'n' Al's, the Beverly Hills delicatessen. He was naturally disappointed by my qualified enthusiasm."

Then on page 348 Polanski immediately contradicts himself by saying, "Bob Towne is a craftsman of exceptional power and talent. Every line of his screenplays testifies to his ear for dialogue and skill in conveying mood."

Then on page 355 Polanski goes even further: "The film picked up a clutch of Golden Globes and eleven Academy Award nominations and Bob Towne won a well-deserved Oscar for his screenplay," etc.

In reality, Polanski had an unquestionably low estimation of Robert Towne and his ability as a screen writer. On several occasions I heard him say so to associates while working on *Chinatown*, and the following Polanski quote from Films In Review (November 1974, page 561) I saw published in several newspapers and periodicals and is the one quote which I know actually reflected Polanski's true feeling toward Towne and his screenplay: "Asked how it felt to work from someone else's screenplay, Polanski said recently: 'It feels strange, because I've never done it before. I spent a good two months rewriting, although I take no credit for it. I molded it to my liking and somehow my style, but it felt uncomfortable because the film is written by someone who has no talent for the visual and I was somehow constantly bored with the material. I could not have enough interest in the visual side of the picture. Whenever I was trying to do something interesting, I realized that it was a vain effort and I was going against the grain."

"If you want," said Polanski again, "I'll show it to you. You won't believe it!"

"Who wrote it?" I asked.

"Robert Towne; but what you see here today on the screen, I actually wrote, but I'm not taking any credit for it. What do you say?" he asked, changing the mood with that faint smile of his. "Do you have any musical ideas?"

Thelma Roberts excused herself for lunch and I went on saying, "Look, if you really want, we could do a revolutionary type of cinematic music collaboration between director and composer that hasn't been done since Eisenstein and Prokofiev in 1945, but only on a more advanced level."

"Elaborate further," Polanski said.

"Great cinematic music must representationally put on the soundtrack aurally what is not on the screen," I continued. "In other words, most film-scorers today are not real composers and do not have the mechanical and technical amenities to add linear multi-contrapuntal dimensions through music to the scene which do not exist visually. For example," I went on, "this picture has a strong title, *Chinatown*; but outside of that one scene, which could be Los Angeles Street or Fairfax Avenue, there is hardly any visual representation alluding to the title; so we can make this possible through music." "Since I compose directly for orchestra, on orchestration paper, I can add at strategic points a certain contrapuntal Oriental flavor here and there to a few cues. This picture needs a lot of different kinds of music to hold it together. The aural representation, which at times would allude to the 1930's will help the audience through the complicated plot and give reference to the period."

"Exactly," Polanski said. "We need music which is original, but at the same time gives reference to the period. It should be contemporary, yet have overtones to the mood of what I have shot. You are absolutely right in thinking that I do not want the average Hollywood score. In those cues where we used your concert music, this is the type of fabric I wish, but of course you will change it to fit the style."

"I want you to feel secure," I went on, "and so there is no misunderstanding, I'll reduce my orchestration at the keyboard and play every cue for you so you'll know what I'm composing ahead of the sessions; similar to running a black and white work-print of a color movie. If you don't like anything, I can always change what you don't like before sending the full score to the copyists."

"Listen, you compose what you want," said Polanski. "I want you to feel free to do what you think is best for the picture. I know you're a good composer, or else I wouldn't have hired you. I don't like people telling me how to make my pictures and that is why I give all my people who work with me the greatest amount of freedom possible."

I thanked Polanski, but still insisted for the purpose of communication that I would like to play certain segments of my score for him on the piano, and he finally agreed.

Polanski instructed me to be at another screening the following day (Thursday 7 March 1974) at 4:30 p.m. and, of course, I wanted to do this because it would quickly give me another opportunity to study the film in more detail. Present were the editor, Sam O'Steen (to whom Polanski introduced me), Thelma Roberts, and Flo Williamson. After the second viewing I was totally convinced that this picture would not have any art-house or mass appeal. It was neither intellectually artistic, such as Alain Resnais' *Last Year At Marienbad*, nor was it commercial in the James Bond or action thriller sense. However, I felt with about twenty minutes cut from the film, the use of original effects with reverberation, some dialogue with echo in a stream-of-consciousness imprint in certain places, coupled with a unique score, which I knew I could give this film (and did), that the structural weaknesses could be shielded cosmetically.

Polanski (in the company of O'Steen) pressured me for my conviction as to where I felt the film moved too slowly. I mentioned two places in particular after which Polanski exclaimed to O'Steen, "You see? I told you we must shorten those segments."

On page 355 of *ROMAN by Polanski* he writes, "Editing proceeded swiftly and smoothly." This is altogether inaccurate, because Polanski was forever cutting and changing the film even after *Chinatown* had been edited down to its final form. I even had to change two music cues because his last-minute cuts had altered the length of the scenes, requiring your humble court composer to recompose my large orchestration (which was already in progress) to fit the timings of the new sequences. They were still making minute changes right down to the Preview (Friday 3 May 1974) and I heard that there had been modifications even after Polanski and I had left the production; so if this was "swiftly and smoothly," I would hate to be around when editing was not "swift and smooth."

Polanski took me into the cutting room along with Sam O'Steen. He wanted me to look at a few scenes on the editing machine with them, which I did. They made more cuts and revisions and finally I was excused, but told that there would be another screening tomorrow, Friday 8 March 1974 at 12:30 in the afternoon at the Executive Room.

Howard Koch Jr. (the fellow who had asked me to play ping-pong on the *Rosemary's Baby* set years before) was there now as assistant director, together with a couple of other people and Polanski. Also sitting next to me was John Hammell, an excellent music editor, along with his assistant, Pat Moore, who was a congenial gentleman with a kind face. It was at this screening that I thought of many interesting musical ways to help the film.

Monday, 11 March 1974 at 10:00 a.m., Windsor, right building. Polanski, along with myself, John Hammell and Pat Moore began spotting *Chinatown*: determining where and when music should go. We completed the first two reels and I even played some musical motifs on the tiny piano in the projection room the next day which Polanski "absolutely" liked.

One thing must be pointed out here: Roman Polanski, at that time, was a pure authoritarian. He did not care what anyone, or anybody thought. He wanted things done his way, and his way only. If he did not like something, or someone, he would tell you. So, when he said that he liked my music and encouraged my ideas (unless he was a complete schizophrenic) I, of course, believed him. After all, I was not a personal friend of his. I wasn't from Poland. I wasn't a movie star. He hired me because he enjoyed my music.

Monday, Tuesday, Wednesday and Thursday (four days!) were required by Polanski to spot the picture. John Hammell and I couldn't believe it. Polanski was uncommonly laggard with spotting, but he did have definite ideas as to where music should be and where it should not be; and most of the time (even though he was so painfully deliberate) I tended to agree with him.

An example of Polanski's autocratic behavior may be cited on one of the last days of spotting, where the scene of Jack Nicholson (Gittes) getting out of the seaplane at the so-called Albacore Club flashed on the screen, which caused Pat Moore to mention, "Oh, I know that place. It's over in Catalina. I spent a few days there with my wife last year."

"Who gives a fuck," barked Polanski.

Seeing that Pat Moore had been hurt by Polanski's cruel retort, I immediately stood up and said, "Come on, Roman...he didn't mean anything by that...apologize to Pat."

"Okay, I'm sorry," Polanski said. "This picture's got me up-tight."

Later, Pat Moore revealed to me that he had never seen anyone, in all his many years in the motion picture industry, ever stand up for a technician to a major director the way I had, and he thanked me. I told him that I thought Roman was wrong in the way he had acted and I was glad that he apologized.

Having now viewed *Chinatown* a number of times, I noticed that the cinematography in a few sequences did not match the rest of the picture. These scenes had the type of tasteful lighting and deep classic color which made you feel the thirties; in particular, the restaurant setting where Nicholson (Gittes) meets Faye Dunaway (Evelyn Mulwray). The script called for the interior of the Brown Derby; however, in reality, what had been shot was the inside of the Windsor Restaurant at 3190 West Seventh Street in Los Angeles.

I had mentioned to Polanski a number times how beautifully photographed and lit this section was. And since there are no credits on a work-print, he became uncomfortable each time I would rave about the photography of that particular scene, and then ask who the cinematographer was. He finally told me that John Alonzo was the cinematographer on the picture, but after citing these portions a few times to several of the technicians, I was informed that the visual segments I appreciated so much had indeed been shot by another cameraman: Stanley Cortez, who I was advised had been fired by both Robert Evans and Polanski.

On pages 349 and 350 of *ROMAN by Polanski* he has written, "Evans and I talked about this at great length. If we purposely imitated the look of, say *The Maltese Falcon*, I argued, *Chinatown*'s main characteristic would be its resemblance to a good old Hollywood thriller. I wanted Panavision and color--the works--but I also wanted a cameraman who could identify with the period. Still flushed with the success of *The Godfather*, Evans was all for using Gordon Willis, but he wasn't available--and anyway, I had a different look in mind. Stanley Cortez, I felt, would be a good choice; he'd worked with Orson Welles on *The Magnificent Ambersons*, that splendid evocation of a vanished world."

Then on page 350, "...our results left a lot to be desired. Cortez was full of old-fashioned charm, but he hadn't worked for several years. Completely out of touch with mainstream developments in the technology of film making, he began asking for equipment that was no longer in use. We watched his performance with growing dismay. He used an inordinate amount of light and was so excruciatingly slow that had we kept him on, we would never have completed the picture. Bob Evans passed the buck to me; it was my distasteful duty, on the tenth day of shooting to tell Cortez that he was being replaced. John Alonzo took over, which helped speed things up. *Chinatown* is the only other film I have ever brought in ahead of schedule--six days ahead, to be exact."

This is another example of Polanski's emotional and mental inconsistencies. His initial instincts were sound in hiring Stanley Cortez (who had also painted such wonderful images with his camera in *Three Faces Of Eve*, *Night Of The Hunter*, *Back Street*, and *Shock Corridor*), but to say Stanley Cortez was "completely out of touch with mainstream developments in the technology of film making" is simply and totally untrue. If that were the case, Cortez certainly would not have been capable of being involved with subsequent, and highly technical motion picture assignments at other major studios. What Polanski and Evans failed to understand was that Stanley Cortez was patiently ordering antiquated equipment in order to give *Chinatown* the 1930's character they were looking for and had requested from Stanley Cortez.

Stanley Cortez was responsible for Faye Dunaway not walking off *Chinatown* during the early days of shooting, after she emotionally exploded when Polanski during a close-up had noticed one of Dunaway's hairs protruding near her temple so he just pulled it out of her head causing her to scream, "Did you see what that motherfucker just did? I don't believe it. He pulled my hair out of my head!"

Afterward, Stanley Cortez told me that he was the happiest man in the world to have been relieved from having to continue his association with Robert Evans (whom he termed as "not a producer at all") and Roman Polanski about whom he said, "he's a person who often times does not know what is really going on as far as the camera is concerned."

Perry Lopez (Lt. Luis Escobar), who has acted in such classics as *Battle Cry* and *Hell On Frisco Bay*, relayed some interesting occurrences and remembrances as he was making *Chinatown*. During the major confrontation between Nicholson (Gittes) and Lopez (Escobar), the final draft screenplay of *Chinatown* had some dialogue which Lopez (who is as masculine as they come) felt was in bad taste and detracted from his scene with Nicholson. The lines came after Nicholson (Gittes) says to Lopez (Escobar), "I don't think I need a day or two--you're even dumber than you think I think you are. Not only that, I'd never extort a nickel out of my worst enemy, that's where I draw the line, Escobar." Then Lopez (Escobar) was supposed to say, "Yeah, I once knew a whore, who for enough money would piss in a customer's face--but she'd never shit on his chest. That's where she drew the line."

Lopez had questioned Polanski about those passages before the scene was to be shot.

"Roman, why should I be saying these lines? They really don't belong here. They're not part of the story; they're totally out of context."

"Say them anyway," Polanski said. "We can always cut them out."

"Hey, man," Nicholson injected, "I wrote those lines."

"Okay, Jack," snapped Lopez, "then why don't you say them?"

Nicholson did not respond and embarrassingly turned away.

Each time they enacted that scene everything was fine with the performances until Lopez arrived at that passage and would stop because, as he told me, "I just couldn't bring myself to say that dialogue, it was so out of place." After eleven takes, with nobody getting upset, the cast and crew broke for lunch. Outside, Lopez crossed paths with assistant director, Howard Koch Jr., who said, "Gee, don't you know your lines?"

"You don't even know what's happening," Lopez said as he turned away in disgust and walked in the opposite direction.

Three weeks later Lopez was summoned back on the set for the same sequence. He was trying to convince Polanski to delete those lines from the picture when two members of the crew came up and said, "Pardon me, Mr. Polanski, but we really don't need that kind of dialogue in this picture." Polanski immediately agreed with the seasoned union grips and omitted that passage. Lopez and Nicholson shot the revised scene in one take with a second take to cover.

Lopez also had some major scenes with Faye Dunaway, and unlike Polanski, Lopez found Dunaway to be "very cooperative and thoroughly professional; knew her lines and was a wonderful actress and a beautiful lady...I enjoyed working with her...I also liked working with Polanski," Lopez went on. "I did not appreciate the way John Alonzo was photographing me because I felt I came out flat. I've worked with some of the best cameramen in the business, but this guy didn't feel the actor knew where he should be going, which was an insult to me."

Friday, 15 March 1974 was my first real day of composing, since John Hammell had immediately furnished me with some cue-sheets. I had purchased an ample amount of large ozalid orchestration paper, and since I was capable of doing all my own work, I would not need the services of an arranger, orchestrator or ghost-writer (like many of the so-called "name" film-scorers) because, no matter what the deadline was, I was fertile enough and swift enough to do all of the tasks myself. Ideas came to me rapidly, as they always had, and I knew that this picture would not be any different from the others I had composed against the viewpoint of giving it its own special musical vogue.

One thing I had always abhorred in the film music community was that the majority of film-scorers (especially since 1964) repeated themselves and all their cues usually sounded the same because, in addition to having a limited musical vocabulary, they tended to use all the same band of orchestrators, arrangers and ghost-writers.

Studio musicians and other people would often approach me and ask how I managed to always get a unique quality to my soundtracks and I would invariably reply, "I guess it's because I do all of my own work."

I composed at good speed working seven days a week. I sometimes altered my work patterns by auditioning Oriental percussion instruments to be used at various places in the *Chinatown* soundtrack. Most of them I had already been acquainted with through my good colleague, percussionist Emil Richards, who had one of the foremost collections of exotic percussion instruments.

The Paramount executives asked me if I would like to have a limousine to either pick me up or a messenger service to secure my completed music, but I said that I'd prefer to drive myself and deliver my own work to the copyists who might have some questions.

The copyists once informed me of the annoyance that pop songwriter Marvin Hamlisch would cause them. It seems that Hamlisch when he delivered his music demanded that one of the copyists come out and meet him at the famous Paramount gate like Gloria Swanson (Norma Desmond) in *Sunset Boulevard*. I thought they were exaggerating until I personally witnessed one of those calls while at the Paramount music department. I must say, after examining several of his music cues, I could only come to the deduction that Marvin Hamlisch's effrontery was exceeded only by his lack of actual compositional ability.

Speaking of Hamlisch, Polanski sent me a memo from his office with a press clipping attached where a gossip columnist stated that Roman Polanski had been huddled with Marvin Hamlisch at a party given for Rudolf Nureyev discussing if Hamlisch would like to write the score for *Chinatown*. Polanski was quite disturbed by the item and said to me, "Don't pay any attention to what you might hear or read in the press. All I did was shake hands with the guy after someone introduced him to me. I would never hire that hack anyway; I can't stand his music." I said okay, but that I was actually too busy composing to read newspapers.

Monday, 18 March 1974: I was introduced to engineer John Norman and saw the sound stage where I was to record. My regular recording engineer (the brilliant former RCA sound engineer) Ivan Fisher, had introduced me a few days earlier to a new piece of equipment called DBX (and its inventor David Blackmer) which was infinitely superior to the Dolby System which I saw that Paramount was using. I had never really liked Dolby (at that time) because it had a tendency to cut off the high sounds in its attempt to reduce background noise. However, with DBX, it left all the highs true and clear while eliminating the remote hiss and fizz far better than Dolby. John Norman did not know anything about DBX since it was, literally, brand new, and he didn't seem too interested. I was eventually told to forget about it by Polanski (another faux pas in this saga) because few in the theaters would be able to distinguish the variance.

I maintained, for the future, if this film were to be made into video cassette or laser disc (nobody, including Polanski, knew what I was talking about in 1974 and they laughed at me about the then little known technology), if the quality was there, it could always be employed, but if the sound attributes were not there, it could never be applied.

John Norman just laughed and said nothing. Polanski finally ordered me to "shut up about DBX," but four months later I was the first to use DBX for any motion picture soundtrack in Marvin Chomsky's film *Murph The Surf*. For those of you who can still get the recording or tape on Motown Records (MG-830S1 mastered by RCA Red Seal), your ears will tell you how wrong those people were in not letting me use the DBX System for *Chinatown*.

Apropos *Murph The Surf* (or *Star of India, Blue Plus Two, Live A Little Steal A Lot* or *You Can't Steal Love*, some titles which were used for that one film), the talented actor, coach, director, producer, Tom Castronovo badgered its star, Robert Conrad, and director Marvin Chomsky into employing me for this interesting and well-made movie.

Eventually, I signed a contract through my representative, Walter Kohner, for eminently more money than I was being paid on *Chinatown*. Unlike *Chinatown, Murph The Surf* was a respectable motion picture with a poor title. Robert Conrad's performance was remarkable because, like Richard Burton in *Becket*, the stronger actor (Conrad) chose the emotionally weaker role which was more difficult to execute.

Performances by Paul Stewart, Luther Adler and Burt Young (who was also in *Chinatown*) were first-rate; however, the film suffered from the casting of Don Stroud as Murph and Donna Mills as his girlfriend. Had this picture been charted with Robert Redford as Murph and Jacqueline Bisset as his girlfriend, with the same balance of cast, then I believe you would have seen the production do well at the box office.

I was in contact with Polanski every day, either in the cutting room with Sam O'Steen or by himself, or in the main dubbing theater. I took him frequently into the Paramount recording studio where there was a large Steinway concert grand and played for him virtually every cue over the next several weeks. He liked everything and often smiled in amazement over how large my orchestration paper was, asking questions about how I achieved certain symphonic sounds, and how the musical creative process worked. In fact, during that time, Polanski was sneaking away taking piano lessons, in addition to his flying lessons, and all other kinds of private instruction for who knows what; Roman Polanski was forever enrolled in studies for something.

Monday, 1 April 1974. At 3:30 in the afternoon, I recorded two original cues which I actually composed utilizing mainly Oriental instruments, but which were to sound like Chinese music to be used as source fabric for additionally intercut montage sequences which I had finally convinced Polanski to shoot of Los Angeles' Chinatown in a vain attempt to, at least, give some visual and aural reference to the title. I had had a live rehearsal with the relatively small ensemble the preceding Thursday, 28 March 1974, at 2:30 in the afternoon. Unbeknown to me, Polanski and Paramount had hired an Oriental music expert by the name of Tak Shindo to see if what I had written and was now recording was indeed my own original music and not a copy of something else.

"Sound Chinese," said Tak Shindo, "but not Chinese...very clever. I never hear this music before."

I smiled at Polanski, John Hammell, Tak Shindo and all the other Paramount executives and politely said to Shindo, "Of course you have never heard this music before; I just composed it last week."

Tuesday, 2 April 1974, 9:30 a.m. Some Mariachi music was recorded which was casually improvised to match their on-screen background playing at the Noah Cross (John Huston) Ranch. At 12:00 noon of the same day, I left a pass at the front gate for my friend, Jean France Mercier, whom I wished to be at the main recording sessions; not only because he had always had an interest in my music, but because I knew that I could count on an honest opinion through him as to what the general reaction was since no one there, including Polanski, would have known that Jean France was a personal confidant of mine.

I began recording at 1:30 in the afternoon and finished at 5:00 p.m. I recorded the *Main Title, Finale, Roll-Up* and three other cues, including the difficult *Chase Sequence.* Polanski delighted in everything, as Jean France Mercier overheard him express to all those around him.

The *Main Title* was categorically the most musically advanced type of composition ever in a Hollywood motion picture production. I had an old-fashioned 1930's dance band playing simultaneously the Love Theme (from the only Dunaway-Nicholson romantic scene in the entire picture) within the symphony orchestra which was playing in counterpoint stream-of-conscious fragments from all the other important music cues from the film bleeding in and out. It was like having several independent pieces of music going on at the same time in sort of an auricular collage with the orchestra speaking in and out against the dance band. In other words, the dance band represented the musical protagonist while the symphony orchestra exemplified the antagonist. I was proud of it, because it satisfied my artistic standards of compositional and contrapuntal excellence and I also gave the film a potential love theme on which to promote the identification of *Chinatown* through a popular song.

In fact, the music contractor of Paramount (Phil Kahgan) made a little speech to the members of the orchestra at my last recording session Monday 15 April 1974: "Gentlemen," he said, "I think we owe this unique young artist a round of congratulations. Not only can he write very interesting contemporary avant garde music, but we have witnessed that he can also write a beautiful popular melody as well." The whole orchestra and Mr. Kahgan applauded my work for close to half a minute, and I thanked everyone genuinely for their cooperation and appreciation.

It was at the April 2nd recording session (after the first take) when

I turned around from my conductor's podium to get Polanski's approval that I recognized sitting next to him was none other than Robert Evans, looking very Gentleman's Quarterly in his blue striped shirt, dark cashmere sweater, navy blue gabardine slacks and gold embroidered black Pucci-Gucci loafers, with a beautiful leggy blonde who I found out later was a top New York model by the name of Lisa Taylor.

"That was wonderful; really great," said Polanski. "It's just what I want. Come here, Phillip; I want you to meet our producer, Bob Evans."

"I'm delighted to meet you," said Evans. "The music is very exciting and I'm very impressed, very impressed, indeed."

My mind flashed back seven years earlier to the Paramount commissary where Evans had virtually used the same four and nine letter words endeavoring to ventilate himself.

"Yes, we're all very, very impressed with your music," Evans continued as I tried not to smirk the way I recalled John Cassavetes had seven years heretofore.

Wednesday 3 April 1974: John Norman, the Paramount engineer, had persuaded me during the previous days recording, that the tin quality of the strings, which I had questioned during the initial playbacks, was not to be fretted about because he would mend that during the next day's dubbing. I informed John that if he needed to change microphones from one to another, to please stop me at anytime and do it. He assured me again that this was not necessary, but in the dubbing I kept saying, "John, the strings sound too metallic, too sharp; can't we get more of a natural string sound?"

John Norman continued to defend that in the theater system of movie house sound, nobody would hear what I was talking about, so it didn't matter. But it did matter to me, because the quality of tone did not capture what I was doing; it just sounded too tinny to me. I honestly wished that Ivan Fisher had been in the recording booth because he knew exactly what I meant after I played a copy of the dub-down for him. Ivan's first reaction was, "I can't understand this, John Norman is supposed to be a good engineer. He should know better than this. You're absolutely right, he used the wrong microphones."

Since I did not wish to "rock the boat" too much, I did the best I could in dubbing by instructing John Norman to add reverberation to the strings on certain channels and by pushing up weaker instruments such as the flutes and other winds. All in all, although John Norman did not like the way I was making him toil (I really didn't care), by the time the music tracks got to Polanski (whom, incidentally, I spared all of these issues) he never knew what I had to do to improve them and they did actually sound quite good.

Monday 15 April 1974. I recorded the balance of all the music which Polanski wanted. He liked everything; as Jean France Mercier again witnessed Polanski disclosing to those around him. There had been one short cue from the first session which Polanski said to me, "I'm not wild about this cue." To which I responded after a slight disagreement, "Okay, I'll write you another one," which I did and recorded at the second session. After hearing it Polanski said, "Yes, now I like this one much better for that scene." Everything else Polanski was pleased about. Believe me, if he hadn't, I would have been replaced immediately with as many financial and hidden political installments as were anchored to this production. If Polanski and Evans had supplanted a man of Stanley Cortez' stature the way that they had, you can imagine they would have gotten rid of me in less than two minutes had there been any dissatisfaction with my music.

Knowing how much Polanski wanted to enroll *Chinatown* within the upcoming Cannes Film Festival, and witnessing the daily vacillations and impediments caused me to remark sporadically, "Roman, you had better hurry up with this picture if you want to enter it in Cannes."

"Yeah, you're right," Polanski would respond; sometimes sighing dejectedly.

However, as April crept onward, it became quite apparent that Roman Polanski was losing his totalitarian grip on *Chinatown*.

One morning I made the fatal mistake of being too attentive during dubbing. I noticed that a medium shot of Jack Nicholson (as he walks into Ida Sessions apartment and discovers her murdered) showed an old time double-door-bell in the background which I had remembered from my childhood, but when Nicholson (a few moments earlier) had pressed the doorbell, a contemporary door buzzer sounded on the effects track. Then too, since a pane of glass from the front door had been shown broken, I observed that there had been no crumpled glass noises under Nicholson's feet as he entered the apartment. When I pointed out these minute, but rather glaring professional inconsistencies to Polanski, in the presence of all the celebrated Paramount technicians in the main dubbing theater, he flew into a rage against his effects staff. You would have thought Polanski was Adolf Hitler chewing the rug at Berchtesgarden after being informed of an attempt on his life.

"He's right!" Polanski screamed. "The fucking composer of this picture knows more than the effects department of Paramount Pictures.

Are we a major Hollywood production here, gentlemen, or are we a bunch of amateurs..? Will somebody please tell me, what the fuck am I doing here?"

You could have recorded the silence in the massive room, it was so loud.

"Lambro, I want you here everyday that we dub. You know more than the effects department of Paramount Pictures," Polanski said to me in a lower tone.

"Will I get more money?" I asked smiling.

"Don't worry," he continued. "I want you to tell me anything else you notice about anything. I've lost all judgment on this fucking picture; it's driving me crazy."

Just then the telephone rang. And as usual, when with Polanski, I was always instructed to answer it. "Mr. Yablans for Mr. Polanski," the secretary said.

"It's for you," I whispered loudly. "Frank Yablans."

"Hello...," said Polanski, dejectedly agitated. "Yeah...yeah..uh-huh... Yeah. Listen, Bob Evans is a nice guy, but he doesn't know fucking one about making a motion picture; so will you people please leave me alone? I'm trying to make a motion picture here. Yeah...okay...right. Why I don't grant an interview to Esquire Magazine? Because they ask personal questions, that's why. What personal questions? Like how many times I've had the clapp!" Polanski exclaimed. "Does that answer your question?"

It was all your humble court composer could do to refrain from laughing, but it seemed that I was the only one out of about eight muted technicians who found this scene amusing. "If they ask me civilized questions," Polanski went on with Yablans, "then I might grant them an interview; but no personal questions...Okay...yeah...yeah...goodbye," Polanski said, slamming the phone into the receiver.

Now, what had I gotten myself into? I thought. I had done all my work. I had pleased the Court, and even my professional peers in the orchestra, most of whom approached or telephoned me; so why couldn't I just close my lunch box and go home? Then, too, I had an agreement to score Marvin Chomsky's *Murph The Surf* and I wanted to leave for Europe and return to my contemporary concert music crusade as quickly as possible. However, with all the picayune machinations brewing on *Chinatown*, Chomsky reluctantly agreed (after Polanski had personally contacted him) to wait an extra four weeks for my services, so everything else on my schedule was disarranged.

A couple of days later (during the lunch break) I was relaxing stretched out on the sofa in front of the control panel of the main dubbing theater when Polanski ambled in with a Vassar-type of clean-cut attractive All-American girl who appeared to be on the sunny side of her late twenties and who was, supposedly, interviewing Polanski for one of the femme fatale magazines.

"This is our composer," said Polanski pointing to me still lying down. I did not get up, but I did acknowledge her; and although the young lady was one of those fair Anglo Saxon La-Dee-Da type of girls I had grown up with in Wellesley (even though I found her a bit attractive) her name completely escaped me. As usual, Polanski did most of the talking.

"That's a very interesting aspect with my films," Polanski went on with Miss La-Dee-Da from Mademoiselle Bazaar, or one of those New York fashion magazines where they teach a newborn woman how to dress and reach a sociological orgasm with an affluent man. I continued to lay there relaxed with my eyes closed. "None of my pictures have ever been straight-away critical or box office successes," Polanski said. "They usually have taken time, by word-of-mouth, to achieve whatever success they have achieved with the public and the critics. I have always had to struggle, in one way or another, with my productions."

Miss La-Dee-Da brought up the subject of *The Fearless Vampire Killers.*

"Now you're talking about a picture I really had problems with. They took that film away from me. It is now only my film in the version which is being shown with great success, I might add, in Germany. The version that was shown here in the United States and other areas is simply not my picture and never reflected my final intentions."

Just then, the Frenchman who was working on the *Chinatown* French subtitles came in and interrupted Polanski about his moving violation traffic ticket given to the translator for not stopping his car to acknowledge a pedestrian who had been in the crosswalk.

"Why must I go to court?" the translator asked. "I did not run over the woman. I missed her. I drove around her."

Polanski rattled off several sentences in French, then went back to his interview with Miss La-Dee-Da.

"This is California," I said to the translator, "not Paris. They put you in jail here for things like that. You must stop for all pedestrians within the entire crosswalk."

"I did not hit her. I did not kill her."

"No, for that in California they let you go free," I said jokingly, but sometimes not that far removed from the truth.

Polanski took the translator's citation away from him and told him that he would have the Studio take care of it, not to worry, and go back and work on the French subtitles.

Polanski itemized and continued to impress upon Miss La-Dee-Da about the many technical and cinematic firsts of his early films, such as putting the camera on the floor. And when he began running out of inaugural achievements, I surprised Polanski (as I lay there with my right forearm covering my eyes) by coming to his rescue with, "You were the first to put orgasm in a feature film." There was silence. "In *Repulsion*," I went on, "in that scene where the manicurist (Catherine Deneuve) is awakened by the sounds of her sister's sexual climaxes in the adjacent bedroom."

"Yes, he's right!" Polanski exclaimed. "I was the first to put orgasm on the screen; although the orgasm itself is not shown visually in *Repulsion*, I had it on the soundtrack and shot Catherine Deneuve's reactions in the next bedroom to her sister's sexual climaxes."

Miss La-Dee-Da seemed impressed in her efficient way as I heard her scribble some notes.

Not long after this (one evening about 10:00 p.m.) at my apartment, the telephone rang. "Hi, Phillip, this is Bob Evans. How are you?"

"Fine," I replied. "How are you?"

"Phillip, you'll be receiving a $1,000 bonus check for doing such a good job on the score. Everybody's very high on your work, and I want to show our appreciation by giving you this extra bonus; it's never been done before at Paramount."

"Thank you, very much," I said, attempting not to exhibit my disappointment at not securing, at least, a $5,000 bonus.

"I want you to promise me one thing, Phillip," Evans went on in his furtive tone. "Can you keep a secret?"

I did not respond.

"I want you to promise me that you won't tell Roman that I telephoned you. Everything now is just between you and me, all right?"

"Fine," I said. "What is it?"

"*Chinatown* needs more of your music, Phillip," said Evans, repeating my first name at every impossible opportunity. "Phillip, this picture just needs more of your music. Give me ten more minutes of music and I'll get you an Academy Award. Would you like an Academy Award?"

"Look," I replied, "Roman and I spent a week spotting the film and I just don't see how or where we can put anymore music without impairing the quality of the picture."

"Phillip, I've made a hundred and ninety seven pictures. Do you know what a hundred and ninety seven pictures are, Phillip?"

I wanted to say, I'm impressed, very impressed, indeed; but I didn't think, in Robert Evans' state of neurasthenia, he would have gotten the acerbic witticism of my mental retort.

"That's very interesting," I said instead.

"*Chinatown* needs more of your music, Phillip. Give me ten more minutes and I'll get you an Academy Award. Ten more minutes of music, Phillip. I'll bet you don't even know how many minutes of music you have in the picture right now, do you?"

"Well," I said, "I never took the time to add up all the cues, but I would say close to thirty minutes."

"Twenty-eight minutes of music, Phillip. I checked with John Hammell. Phillip, *Chinatown* needs more music...give it to me."

"You know as well as I do that Roman is quite explicit in what he wants," I went on. "He told me when and where he wanted music and I gave it to him."

"Phillip, I want you to tell Roman --do not, under any circumstances, tell him I told you-- that you want to write more music for *Chinatown*."

"Okay," I said, in resignation. "I'll see what I can do."

"Is there anything else I can get you, Phillip? Is there anything else you need?"

I felt like saying, how about a Steinway concert grand, or commissioning my next concert work, but I couldn't resist in finally asking, "Who was that attractive young lady you had in your company at the recording session when I first met you?"

"Oh, you like Lisa. That was Lisa Taylor; she's a model."

"She's very beautiful," I said.

"She's also very rich," Evans went on.

"Then she must be very rich and very beautiful," I said. "Is she your girlfriend?"

"We see each other; but she went back to New York."

Small wonder, I thought. My telepathic estimation of Lisa Taylor went up significantly.

During those days from 16 April 1974, through 3 May 1974, I was with Roman Polanski (when not composing) a majority of many days; either in the cutting room, the main dubbing theater, or a few times in his office. While waiting for Polanski on a number of occasions in the editing cubicle, I noticed a few of those sex newspapers which you could purchase from vending machines on the street in certain areas of Los Angeles, and I browsed through them from time-to-time, with their out-call ads and sex-for-sale come-on photographs.

At first, I thought they belonged to O'Steen, but in the personal ads column I saw one circled which read to the effect, "Sally in the Valley, fifteen years old, confidential, likes relationship with European man in forties." And on a handful of occurrences when I would answer the telephone in the editing room, particularly young girl voices would ask if Paul was in. Polanski was there once, and I said, "You must have the wrong extension, there's no Paul here." Then Polanski loudly whispered, "That's for me."

"Look Roman," I said, after he hung up. "It's none of my business, but this isn't France. Sally in the Valley is going to find out who you really are and hang you from the highest Sherman Oak. It's going to end up costing you a lot of money and some legal problems, too."

Perry Lopez distinctly recalls my informing him about the bona fide concerns I had over Roman's circled responses with under aged girls from those sex advertisements during this time.

Robert Evans continued calling me quite often and usually late at night, or at the Studio when Roman would go to the lavatory or step out of the dubbing theater for a few minutes. I began to wonder if Evans had had some sort of electronic surveillance system monitoring our moves because he would always contact me when Roman wasn't around.

The dialogue was perpetually the same and I began remembering my inaugural Hollywood motion picture score where I had been forced to "psyche" the producer in order to give the film the best possible music under adverse circumstances. My first agent had reminded me then that this was a low budget film and "Phillip, when you get to work on multi million dollar budgets in the future, these crazy things never happen." I had news for my initial William Morris Agency representative: here I was engaged on a 1974 multi million dollar major moving picture and even more disagreeable episodes were occurring.

I managed to stay Evans for awhile by advising him that I was discussing the situation with Roman. It worked for about a week because, in reality, the only reason Polanski tolerated Robert Evans was, in fact, that Polanski needed money; and big money to sustain his entourage and international life style. Polanski only communicated with Evans when he could not avoid it. Polanski did not respect Evans at all; and professionally, he was correct, because it was painfully clear that Robert Evans, at best, was only acting out the role of studio head and motion

307

picture producer. Truthfully, Evans was completely incapable of any valid creative or technical input into the making of a film as he was only superficially acquainted with the medium. Evans was like a shark on dry land, completely helpless, and in a sense, I felt rather sorry for him because it was tragic to see a man of his age so completely unskilled in the world of his obvious desires.

Two habits I acquired from Roman Polanski during my association with him were the constant chewing of sugarless gum in the dubbing theater, and profanity. I managed to break the former habit, but the latter on occasion creeps into my repertory of expressions.

One day in the dubbing theater while Polanski was sitting next to me (and I saw that he was in a reasonably good mood) I said, "Roman... can you keep a secret?"

"What kind of bullshit is this now?," he asked, putting two sticks of sugarless gum into his mouth.

"I'm serious," I said, smiling and putting a third stick of sugarless gum into my mouth.

"Do you know you're chewing three sticks of gum?" Polanski asked. "Are you crazy?"

"You and this fucking picture gave me the habit, but I'll stop as soon as I leave this dubbing room and you. Seriously, this is no joke. Can you keep a secret?"

"Of course, I can keep a secret. What is it?"

"Evans has been calling me. He told me not to tell you, but the guy is pestering me to write more music; especially the love theme. I tried to tell him what we have now is correct and what you want, but he keeps saying, 'Phillip, *Chinatown* needs more of your music; give me ten more minutes of music and I'll get you an Academy Award.' Who the hell wants an Academy Award? They've given them out to such non-talents lately, I wouldn't use one for a door stop. '*Chinatown* needs more of your music, Phillip.' Where the hell are we going to put more music, anyway? In the morgue scene?"

"Listen," Polanski went on, "you leave Evans to me. I'll handle him. You just be polite and pretend you are taking his suggestions seriously."

"I thought you promised that I wouldn't have to deal with him; that you were in complete control; and now he's calling me every day and night to convince you that we need more music like some sort of imbecilic infantile."

"Don't worry about a thing. The music we have now is correct and exactly what I want. I understand that you got a thousand dollar bonus."

308

"I was expecting, at least, five thousand. I was tempted to tell Evans to keep it."

"If you don't like the money," Polanski continued, "you can always give it to me. I'll show you what to do with it."

"Roman, why the hell don't you do controversial pictures the way you used to? Listen, I want you to read a book. *The Bell Jar*, written by my teenage friend from Wellesley, Sylvia Plath, the late poetess. It's an interesting story and perfect for you to direct."

"What's this *Bell Jar*? I never even heard of it. And Who's Sylvia Plath?"

"It's a brilliant feminine novel and you could make a fantastic picture out of it. I knew Sylvia; we were in the same painting class in school. I could help you with the casting and locations."

"Maybe...I'll read it if I have time; meanwhile, we have to finish this piece-of-shit picture. Don't worry about Evans. I'll take care of him."

Also, during this period of post-production, Bronislau Kaper, the film scorer and fellow Pole, telephoned fairly often. Polanski told me that he liked Kaper because Kaper was one of the few people who could make him laugh and whom he could speak Polish with. It must be noted here that Polanski once reminded me of his linguistic virtuosity: he declared that in addition to Polish, he was fluent in French, Russian, German, Italian and English. He does speak excellent English and when he would want to make a particularly sarcastic point with a couple of dubbing technicians, Polanski would invariably say, "Gentlemen, I know my English is not very good, but--," which was a lot of nonsense, because he had a better command of the English language than most Americans; so I am confident that Roman Polanski was quite articulate in all those other languages as well.

Since he was so intimate with Bronislau Kaper, I asked Polanski one day why he hadn't hired Kaper to score *Chinatown*. He told me, "For all intents and purposes, Bronik is too old and out of sync with motion picture music. And besides, the Studio executives would never hire him; he's not acceptable."

There were times when I answered the telephone and Polanski was occupied recording a take, or not in the dubbing theater, when Kaper would call and tell me how effective he thought I was as a composer, and other patronizing compliments which I just deflected and said thank you. He knew that I was a symphonic composer with major international performances, and I always had the feeling Bronislau Kaper was attempting to impress me with his concert music knowledge by sometimes making me listen over the telephone to his playing a few bars of a Mozart Sonata, or something else, since I'm sure he had to be calling directly from his piano bench. I was polite and respectful, but at the same time, I never sought to give Kaper an opportunity to extend his musical ego, which was considerable. I think Roman Polanski also relished Bronislau Kaper for the very same reasons conductor Zubin Mehta did: Kaper knew the telephone numbers of many of the comely aspiring starlets and actresses in Hollywood.

On 16 April 1974, Polanski had gone off to Canada for a few days of skiing, to repose and get away from *Chinatown*. But before he left, he said to both Sam O'Steen and myself in the dubbing theater, "Sam, you let Phillip dub the *Main Titles* while I'm gone since there is only music, and you dub the remaining reel since there is no music in it, okay?"

We both agreed and I dubbed the *Main Titles* with the collage of the symphony orchestra against the dance band in quite a revolutionary manner; even the usually stolid Paramount technicians were impressed.

I left the Studio because I now had to begin preparing *Murph The Surf* with its director Marvin Chomsky. That afternoon, at home, I received a telephone call from John Hammell who informed me to come down to the Studio at once because Sam O'Steen was redubbing my *Main Title* and had pushed the dance band tracks up into the foreground and buried the entire symphony orchestra collage to where it sounded as if it were coming out of Muzak speakers in a small elevator.

"Oh shit," I sighed. "Look John, Roman isn't here. I really don't want to get involved until he comes back in a few days."

"Don't say that I said so, but you come down right away and pretend to be just walking in then stay in the back and hear what he's doing to your *Main Title*. You've got to stick up for your rights in this business," John Hammell said.

"Roman isn't here," I repeated. "What can I do? I have no power over O'Steen. He's just playing Director."

"There's Bob Evans," John said. "But don't say that I said so, Phillip. Mum's the word."

"Don't worry, John." I sighed. "I won't tell. I'll be right down."

John Hammell was right. Sam O'Steen had completely ruined the balance of my *Main Title*. All you could hear was the dance band playing the romantic theme against what sounded to me like a fading symphony orchestra coming out of a two-inch broken car radio in a beehive.

"What are you doing to the *Main Title*?" I asked incredulously. "This is supposed to be a musical collage; you're ruining it."

"You had your say with it, now I'm having mine," said O'Steen, who had completely transformed into Mr. Hyde from his fashioned Dr. Jekyll. It was as if he had become drunk with directorial power in the dubbing theater now that Polanski was in Canada.

"But Roman said..."

"Roman's not here now," O'Steen sneered. "I'm in charge."

I walked out disenchanted and angry. What to do? I thought over what John Hammell had suggested and found myself doing the last thing I ever wanted: telephoning Robert Evans at his home.

"Oh Phillip, that's terrible," Robert Evans lamented as I revealed exactly what Sam O'Steen had done. "I cannot understand why Sam would do such a thing."

"Robert," I continued, "you have a great deal invested in this film, and I have a responsibility to do everything within my power to see that the music is the absolute best that it can possibly be."

"Absolutely, Phillip." Evans said, chewing gum as he talked. "I appreciate that very much."

"If I didn't care, I wouldn't be telephoning you now. If I didn't care, I wouldn't have confronted Sam O'Steen."

"Here's how we're going to handle this, Phillip. Tomorrow morning I'll be at the Studio early and I will ask Sam to have the projectionist run both versions of the *Main Titles*, and I personally will see what has been done and make my decision then."

"That's fine with me," I said. "Anyone with a pair of ears will know the difference immediately. Half the orchestra can't be heard in O'Steen's dub-down; it's a joke."

"You don't worry about a thing," consoled Evans. "Okay...?"

"Okay," I said.

John Hammell phoned the next morning to inform me that Evans, bright and early, was chauffeured to the dubbing theater in his limousine and asked the Paramount technicians (in the presence of O'Steen) which rendering was which; and when Evans became certain which one was mine, he said, "I like Phillip's version better, and I want it that way in the picture."

After hearing that, I began to have some hope for Robert Evans. Perhaps I had been too harsh on him. He did, at least, distinguish the difference; admittedly, not a hard task to do, but he did differentiate (or so I thought at the time) until a few weeks later, when I found out from a couple of Paramount executives who acquainted me with the fact that Robert Evans always predicated his current opinion and decision on the basis of the last person whom he had spoken with; and, of course, I had been the last individual before he went to the Studio.

The executives also warned that if O'Steen had telephoned Evans two minutes after I had, Evans would have conformed with O'Steen. That's how the Head of Production at Paramount Pictures Corporation, Ladies and Gentlemen of the Jury, made his daily determinations, believe it or not.

A few days later, I received a call from Robert Evans' secretary notifying me that my presence was required at his home the following Sunday, 28 April 1974, at 7:00 p.m. for dinner and a showing of *Chinatown* for a few selected guests in his private screening room. This would represent Polanski's final chronicle of *Chinatown* and, needless to say, I did not wish to be there for the ultimate rites.

It must be remembered that over the years the Paramount Board had been hearing conflicting accounts from Evans and the respective producers and directors of the proportionately few Paramount blockbusters such as *The Godfather, Love Story, Goodbye Columbus*, etc. as to who was actually responsible for their unqualified prosperity. Evans continually voiced that he was the propellant which spawned those flying colors and lamented over the fact that he was never allowed to financially share in the millions of dollars profit, as he was (poor boy) only on a contractual salary.

However, the producers and directors who actually nurtured those handful of timely Paramount successes would go into convulsions endeavoring to reveal to Board members that this was not so, and that Robert Evans could not make a successful motion picture if his life depended upon it.

In order to resolve this discord the Paramount hierarchy finally told Evans to pick a project, any production, from inception, and let us see you make a financially arrived film from which you can share in the profits. Of all the idiotic choices (when one considers that you have ninety-nine chances for failure) he decided upon *Chinatown*. His whole manufactured repute and years of vaunting responsibility for the infrequent Paramount megapictures hinged upon *Chinatown* and now the moment of truth was near. And even if Robert Evans could not sense that he was 30,000 feet in the air with a kite instead of a 747, your humble court composer knew, and I did not wish to be around for all the imminent retribution. After discussing the situation with my agent Paul Kohner, and the fact that Evans was still holding the balance of my fee, I recognized that I had to attend, inasmuch as I did not wish to.

I arrived shortly after 7:00 p.m. that Sunday at Evans' home on Woodland, north of Sunset in Beverly Hills. Evans' secretary had instructed me to use the rear entrance off Beverly Drive. I remember associating this with how Beethoven and other composers from the classical period were required to utilize posterior entries when they performed for their Court. I purposely drove my old white 1966 Chevrolet, which I knew would raise a few eyebrows and especially unsettle Polanski who had ridden in it on the Paramount lot a few times, and constantly admonished me for not driving a better looking car.

Actually, the rear entrance was just as pleasant as the front access, and there was ample parking for my Chevy amid the Rolls, Mercedes, and other exotic internal combustions including Polanski's new Corvette which he drove as if he were Jim Clark behind the wheel of a Ferrari Daytona. I was well dressed, in a casual style, as I alighted from my car and heard Polanski, in the company of two attractive females, begin to "grandstand" from the rear steps.

"Jesus Christ," he said. "When are you going to buy a decent car? Here we are paying you all this big money and all you drive is that terrible thing."

"What?" I retorted facetiously, "and drive a car like that plastic coffin you have? My car's great," I said, kicking the front left tire. "Good tires; gets me around. I don't need any false symbols. Why do you think a hundred thousand Mexicans drive this car around Los Angeles? They're no dummies; it's a good transportation vehicle. I was born in Wellesley," I continued. "I don't need to hide behind status symbols. I know who I am; I wasn't born in communist Poland."

The young ladies laughed with my humor directed at Polanski.

"You fucking Macrobiotic," he said, "you have an answer for everything, don't you?"

Once inside Evans' home, I was greeted by a distinguished butler, and then by Evans himself who toured me around the house and grounds. One could immediately perceive a disparity between the furnishings, which were rather well coordinated, and the tasteless framed wall posters and paintings. Later on, Evans informed me that he had had an interior designer do the entire house with the exception of the paintings and posters which he had selected himself. It reminded me of an elegant French provincial country home on too small a piece of land with a bunch of cheap reprints hanging on the walls.

Evans also puffed about how he achieved a lot of the gardening himself with, of course, the help of a professional gardener. "Oh, Phillip," he said, "I'm out there every weekend pulling the weeds right along side my gardener."

I'm sure, I thought, as I had visions of Evans pulling the flowers and cultivating the weeds, if his horticultural judgment was analogous to his motion picture assessments.

Evans did have a fascinating tree to the side of the yard which he claimed was reportedly over 400 years old. I was tempted to suggest that before he begin his next production, he first have a long chat with that tree; but I didn't think (in his obvious state of nervosa) that Evans would have appreciated such a remark, so I just smiled and said, "Very interesting."

Before he escorted me outside, Evans took a telephone call from Frank Yablans and asked me to sit down. It was pathetic to hear Evans whine about which theaters Yablans could or could not book *Chinatown* into. Although I could not hear what Yablans was saying, it was rather apparent that Yablans was the General as Evans was petulantly acting like some frightened Second Lieutenant about to go into his first real mission by way of a thirty-day crash course rather than four years at West Point.

In the yard, as I walked out with Evans, was Sam O'Steen conversing with Richard Sylbert near the pool. O'Steen smiled at me like one of those sinister James Bond characters, but I thought it best to ignore that and responded cordially. Sylbert acted as quietly arrogant as ever, but looked less like the Great White Hunter than in previous years, even though he was clad in his usual Banana Republic safari outfit. Evans introduced me to Jack Nicholson, and Polanski acquainted me with his British confidant, Andrew Braunsberg, co-producer of the Andy Warhol catastrophe *Frankenstein*. Braunsberg enjoys the distinction of being the most pompous superficially pedantic individual I have ever encountered. When he would address someone, you had the feeling he was vocalizing to them as if he were avoiding the stench of a foul odor.

Several other guests arrived and began chatting at the outdoor dining table near the 400 year old tree. I decided to keep my distance since, with O'Steen gazing at me with the eyes of a stalking King Cobra as he continued to converse with Sylbert, I began to feel like a downed pilot floating in shark infested waters hoping for a friendly school of dolphins to protect me. I went to the far side of the opposite yard where there was a small well-furnished projection room with large bi-folding windowed doors which had been opened allowing the entire outside to be adjacent with it.

Inside, I noticed a charming little boy who was quietly sitting in one of the large red leather chairs, and a Paramount projectionist who was patiently waiting next to the movie-house 35mm projector for the proceedings to begin. The youngster, who turned out to be Evans' son, was notably bright for his age having an ability to express himself with a vocabulary far greater than that of his father; which caused me to utter, half in jest to the projectionist, that the youngster, perhaps, should try and assist his Dad in running the Studio.

"Mr. Lambro, do you think you could suggest that we get started here?," asked the projectionist. "Because I have to go across the way and run a film for Miss Haber right after this."

"Joyce Haber of the Los Angeles Times?" I questioned, a little startled.

"Yes," replied the projectionist. "Mr. Evans has me run a lot of pictures for her and her husband, so I don't want to get over there too late."

I had wondered why, as I thumbed through my daily Los Angeles Times, I would read an inordinate amount of hyped Robert Evans particulars in Joyce Haber's column gooing over him as if he were Thalberg, Mayer and Goldwyn all rolled into one. Then, in her gossip pilasters, it was always "Handsome Bob Evans, the guiding light at Paramount, who is responsible for so many financial successes" this; or, "my spies at Paramount tell me that handsome Bob Evans, who is responsible for so many of Paramount's successes" that. It was enough (for those who knew) to make you ill reading all that assembled drivel, but now it was clear as to who Joyce Haber's spy at Paramount was; it was none other than her own back yard over-the-fence neighbor "handsome Bob" himself.

I went outside and informed Evans that his projectionist was ready and anxious to begin. Evans then quickly proposed that we all see *Chinatown* first and have dinner immediately afterward. Evans had his maid take his son into the main house, as I knew this kid was too rational to suffer through a film like *Chinatown*.

I seated myself all the way to the rear left corner and Jack Nicholson came in later and sat down right next to me. Before the film began, we talked and Nicholson revealed to me how he "fell into acting" while he had been working as a messenger boy for the cartoon department at M-G-M earlier in his life.

"I'm not a trained actor," Nicholson said. "I just sort of fell into it, doing bit parts for my friends who were making movies."

As Nicholson continued to verbalize about his career, I could see that his assessment was unequivocally precise. He was always Jack Nicholson. Whether or not he was in a sailor's uniform, a mental patient, or had a bandage on his nose, after listening to and pondering Nicholson that evening, I could sense that his screen characters always became Jack Nicholson rather than Jack Nicholson becoming those personages. He even admitted to me that he felt he had been awfully lucky with the career he had had in films. Even though I had liked him in a few pictures, I would now tend to agree with Nicholson's personal evaluation.

Robert Towne blew in from the wings like a nervously afflicted prima donna, explaining how maddeningly busy he had been and sat down in the front row as Robert Evans hastily expressed that he was sure everyone there had known Towne.

As it turned out, after seeing him, I remembered his face from about six years previously when a girlfriend of mine (as we were dining at The Aware Inn) casually introduced me to Towne, but I had forgotten his name.

Likewise, I was to discover from an outside source that much of Towne's inspiration and story material for *Chinatown*, actually developed from many meetings and conversations with his stepfather-in-law of that epoch, the distinguished screen writer Charles Lederer who passed away 10 March 1976. Robert Towne had been married to Julie Anne Payne the daughter of 1940's screen idol John Payne and actress Anne Shirley. Anne Shirley subsequently married Charles Lederer who, incidentally, is purported to have worked incognito on the script to the great Orson Welles American classic *Citizen Kane*; the loosely veiled controversial account of billionaire publisher William Randolph Hearst and his mistress Marion Davies. The fascinating entity about all of this is that Charles Lederer's mother just happened to be Marion Davies' sister.

As *Chinatown* played with all the credits from a clear fresh color print, one could sense the tenseness in the room. You could feel the particles of thought splitting like atoms. I just sat quietly, noting the entities, although I genuinely wished I could have been at home working on my score to *Murph The Surf* or composing concert music.

As the lights went up at the conclusion of the screening, the first remark was by Polanski who said, "Great music, huh?" It was rather embarrassing because everybody, save O'Steen and Sylbert, were raving about my score.

The uncomfortable thing about that is, if everyone is so delirious about the music, how good can the motion picture be? Robert Evans immediately came up to me and said, "You see, Phillip? We need more of your music...now don't give me an argument. I'll take care of Roman, but we need more of your music in this picture." "I hate music," Nicholson rejoined in that lazy sedated manner of his. "I hate music even more in films. None of my pictures ever have any music in them, so to speak, but this film needs more of your music."

"You see...?" Evans asked flatly.

"I wouldn't fuck with the first six reels," Nicholson went on, "they're okay, but the rest of *Chinatown* needs more of your music."

"Look, if you people and Roman want more music," I said, "I'll be happy to write more music, but exactly where do you propose that we put it?"

Just then Polanski exploded at Robert Towne so piercingly that everyone ceased chatting. "Will you please stop with your fucking suggestions? I'm tired of hearing them. I'm not changing anything anymore in this picture, so leave me alone. Next time, you direct your own lousy scripts."

I thought it rather cruel of Polanski to say that to Towne publicly, but since Towne was not a lowly technician, I wasn't about to intervene again and suggest that Polanski apologize.

Evans quickly ushered everyone out into the heated patio and, just as I was about to get up from my chair, Richard Sylbert came over to me and said (as if he were playing a role in a movie), "You know, everybody, including me, has been on the bottom of the barrel in this picture, except you. I just want you to know you're next," he smiled. "You're not getting away so easy."

I glanced at Nicholson then said smilingly to Sylbert, "I love you, too."

Robert Towne came up to me gushing with superlatives. "I can't tell you how thrilled I am that you gave the story such a unique score. I was so afraid that it would have been one of those stock Hollywood soundtracks which I hate."

I thanked Towne as Evans again summoned us for dinner.

Evans sat me next to Nicholson. Dinner, Ladies and Gentlemen of the Jury, was (if you can imagine) hot dogs and hamburgers with French-fries served with the finest linen, silverware and China by the formally attired butler and maid.

I whispered to the butler that I did not eat meat, but if he happened to have some steamed carrots and Chinese cabbage, I'd take that with a whole wheat bun.

"What's the matter?" Asked Nicholson, chomping on a cheeseburger with everything on it. "Aren't you hungry?"

"Don't you know," said Polanski, "he's one of those crazy Macrobiotics."

"Macrobiotics, huh...," Nicholson said, as if he were doing a take from *The King Of Marvin Gardens.* "What's that?"

The last thing I wanted to do was get into a Macrobiotic lecture, but with Jack Nicholson's obvious unbalanced condition (although he did have nice teeth), I enumerated briefly that what we eat and how we live in our environment can regulate the balance of our lives toward good or bad health, and I suggested that he read a book explaining the Oriental unique principles of diet and health by Georges Ohsawa. But having seen him in photographs and on television from time to time since 1974, Jack Nicholson (who needs Macrobiotics desperately) never paid heed to my suggestion.

After about fifteen minutes, Polanski, fidgeting as if he had become struck by some kind of bodily skin rash, excused himself and went home.

The gracious and apologizing butler did manage to fix me a plate of about four peas, two leafs of lettuce and three pieces of carrots with a hamburger bun. It seems that Evans' refrigerator didn't stock too many vegetables.

Incidentally, I did steal a delicious strawberry from Jack Nicholson's gigantic ice cream sundae when his head was turned, but I don't think he missed it because there were several more on top.

The rest of the evening I received pep talks from both Evans and Nicholson about writing additional music. When I informed them of what Polanski had wanted and what Polanski had not wanted, I could see that Roman Polanski's opinions and ideas did not count one iota with either Evans, or Nicholson.

"Listen," continued Nicholson, with the animation of a half-dead hospital patient as he and Evans huddled cross-armed on the table moving closer to me. "You don't have to defend Roman to us. We know what he is, and we know what you are. So you just don't worry about Roman. I'm telling you that *Chinatown* needs more of your music."

"Okay," I said, trying to survive this vice-like power play. "I'll do whatever you people decide."

"Wouldn't you like an Oscar, Phillip?" said Evans, as I consciously flashed upon the scene from The Exorcist where the possessed young girl, strapped to her bed, vomits jade green all over the priest. "Didn't you like the thousand dollar check I gave you last week?" Evans continued as I wished I could have disgorged jade green all over him, as I thought of how these Philistines had exploited and taken financial advantage of me.

It should be pointed out here that while Polanski never actually regarded Robert Evans as a true intimate (regardless of what he states in his automated biography), Polanski did, in fact, like Jack Nicholson and constantly referred to him as his very close friend. I know that Polanski would have been offended to have heard Nicholson refer to him in the manner which he had when Roman wasn't around. I witnessed this type of behavior at Evans' home when Roman was out of hearing range. To Polanski's credit, he usually wasn't that way at all. He would let you know what he thought and wasn't two-faced about it like Nicholson, Evans, Sylbert and O'Steen.

But the tragedy of the situation was that when I sought to inform Polanski about what was actually going on, he refused to accept the truth. He declined to believe that Nicholson, Sylbert and O'Steen were undermining him. Evans, he realized, had been seeking to do it all along and he was resigned to this condition; but after reading those portions of his autobiography, it is quite apparent Roman Polanski really did not know what his "friends" were doing to him at the end of *Chinatown*'s post-production, that's how deluded he was.

The next day Polanski telephoned me from his office. He sounded completely fatigued and dispirited. "Can you possibly write five or six more cues for the picture?" He sighed. "These people are driving me crazy over the score and they want more music, so I guess we have to give it to them. Okay?"

"If you want more music, I'll write whatever you want," I replied, knowing full well that Polanski was not in control of *Chinatown* anymore. Polanski was buckling under the pressures Evans had been slowly fastening upon him and these tensions were, in turn, instigated by those whispering into Evans' ear since, as the Paramount executives had said, "Bob Evans listens to the last person who has spoken with him." One thing I do know for certain is that Roman Polanski did not want anymore music than we already had.

I had received instructions to meet with Robert Evans 9:00 a.m. Tuesday 30 April 1974, in Dubbing H at Paramount. Polanski was there every minute as we went over where Evans felt more music should be. It was pathetic to hear Evans posture about music and respotting the picture. The man knew absolutely nothing about motion picture music. His suggestions were ludicrous as his behavior reminded me of utter desperation. In fact, Evans wanted one music cue redubbed because he

319

felt it was too loud, so I said alright; however, as we redid the take, I kept the music track on the control board at practically the same decibel, rather than proportionately softer.

"How's that, Bob?" I asked Evans who was sitting on the sofa in front of the control panel with his Pucci-Gucci loafers off in a quasi yoga lotus position.

"Much better, Phillip," Evans replied. "Much better. I think with the music softer, this scene plays better; don't you gentlemen?"

All the Paramount flesh-robots agreed with Evans as I rolled my eyes at the sound technician.

Friday 3 May 1974. A preview of *Chinatown* had been originally scheduled to be shown at a sophisticated theater in San Francisco; however, there had been a murder and the general public feared that the dormant San Francisco Zodiac Serial Killer had resurfaced again, so the preview was relocated to a suburb of Santa Barbara. Although I had been warned to go and protect my interests by a few of the Paramount executives, I fortunately had an excuse: I was composing more music and could not possibly leave. Even Polanski had asked me to go, but I said, "How can I go when I'm writing more music?"

I heard the preview had been a disaster and that the audience (which included a majority of teens and young people) did not like the picture at all.

Sunday morning, 5 May 1974, Polanski telephoned me and broke the news. "The preview was a disaster," Polanski said, "Several cards from the audience said that they didn't like your music and the Paramount executives now don't like or accept your score. I'm going to fight, but I think it's no use...I'm so tired. I don't know what I'll do."

I was only partially stunned because my original apprehension upon accepting this assignment had been justified. "Aren't you in control, anymore?" I asked, for nothing better to say.

"I've lost all judgment. I'm so tired, Phillip," Polanski sighed like a beaten man. "What can I say? They've cancelled your recording sessions." Then, after another pause, he continued. "Look, I'm going to try and fight them and I'll let you know what I can do."

"Who's them?," I asked.

"The Paramount executives," Polanski said.

"Which executives?"

"What the fuck difference does it make?" He erupted. "All the executives. Nobody likes your score."

I remained silent.

"I have to go now," Polanski calmed down, "but I'll call you tomorrow and let you know if anything develops."

Less than an hour later, Robert Evans telephoned me in a now precise official monotone. "Hello, Phillip, this is Bob Evans."

"How are you," I said, not asking.

"Not well, Phillip. Not well at all. The sneak preview was not very good, not very good at all, Phillip. Your music didn't play well with the audience. The audience just didn't like your score. I'm sorry, Phillip, but your music is coming out of *Chinatown*."

"Go ahead and take it out," I said. "You'll see how wrong you are."

"Phillip, I've made a hundred and ninety seven pictures. Do you know what a hundred and ninety seven pictures are?"

"Six hits in a hundred and ninety seven at bats," I said. "If you were playing for the Los Angeles Dodgers instead of Paramount Pictures, with stats like those, they would have scratched you a long time ago."

"Phillip," he continued with his furtive inflections, "your score is coming out."

"Fine," I said, "take it out."

An assistant to one of the Paramount executives told me that he had collected and reviewed all of the preview audience-cards and he said that he had not seen one card which mentioned my score in a negative way. However, he informed me that there had been numerous written comments generally stating that viewers did not particularly care for the story.

Thelma Roberts, Polanski's secretary, also revealed to me the following week that Polanski kept yelling in his office to Evans, "but this is the music I want for my picture. Why can't I have this music? It's what I want."

Even though Polanski probably does not know it to this day, it was Sam O'Steen (along with Polanski's other "friends") who put me, finally, into the bottom of the barrel as Richard Sylbert had prophesied. Had I not confronted Sam O'Steen and won out over the dubbing of the *Main Titles* with Robert Evans on my side that particular day, in all probability, my music would have remained in the film; but who really cares?

As I had said, (when people transmitted their condolences to me over the next few weeks) in this universe, the Earth is but a subatomic particle of an atom, so where does this leave *Chinatown*? In a year nobody would care in the movie-going public about this picture at all. They didn't make *Citizen Kane*, or *The Seven Samurai*. The only misfortune was that the public would not have had the opportunity to hear the score which was quite original and designed to the director's particular specifications.

Polanski called me a few times after this, and I reprimanded him by saying, "I told you it would happen, but you wouldn't believe me. Remember when you took me to that Mexican cafe where you asked me to do the music? You guaranteed me you were in complete control."

"Perhaps my next picture," Polanski lamented.

"You've got to be kidding," I said. "You know that title *Once Is Not Enough*?" I asked. "Well, once with you is more than enough."

Paramount did pay me what they owed me, but Polanski left for Spoleto to stage Alban Berg's opera *Lulu*, which I heard from Italy was another catastrophe.

My informants at Paramount advised me that Evans was in a quandary over whom to get to rescore *Chinatown*, until one of his girlfriends played him a recording of Jerry Goldsmith's score from the mid-sixties production of *A Patch Of Blue* and, true to form, since the girlfriend was the last person Evans had spoken with, he made the decision to hire Goldsmith on the total basis of *A Patch Of Blue*. Goldsmith, I was further informed, like me, didn't really wish initially to do the picture.

Another Paramount executive later revealed to me that, in addition to seconding Goldsmith's recommendation, that the executive also recommended Henry Mancini; however, Evans kept indicating that he didn't like Henry Mancini, and when pressed further for a reason Evans said, "I can't tell you why I don't like Henry Mancini, but I just don't, that's all."

I understood that before Polanski finally left for Spoleto that he did have some conversations with Goldsmith about the music he wanted. When I heard that, all I could do was nod and smile.

News travelled fast and now the producers of *Murph The Surf* were a little suspect about having me do their score even though director Marvin Chomsky (bless his heart) was the one who confidentially informed me of it, and said that he was battling on my behalf all the way.

I advised the Vice President in charge of Music at Paramount, William Stinson, that if I lost the score to *Murph The Surf* on the basis of Evans having thrown out an absolutely first rate soundtrack from Chinatown, that there would be the biggest law suit Evans and Paramount had ever seen.

It was common knowledge that Jimmy Webb had sued Paramount and won over Evans' junking of Webb's score to *Love Story*. So William Stinson contacted my Texas producers and said, "Look, Phillip Lambro did a fine score for *Chinatown*, but scores in Hollywood are replaced every day for one reason, or another. There isn't a major film composer who hasn't had at least one of his scores thrown out at one time, or another.

Phillip will do a good job for your picture, have no worry about that."

I did the music for *Murph The Surf* and everyone was exceedingly happy with it. That tough Tom Castronovo had tears in his eyes when I turned around to check with my engineer, Ivan Fisher, and looked in the glass-enclosed recording booth where a small audience was sitting after I had conducted the *Main Title*.

When the entire seven hour session was over, a stately white-haired gentleman (who was the father of producer Caruth C. Byrd) came up to me and said, "Young man, I want you to know that I have travelled all the way from Fort Worth, Texas especially to hear your music, and I must say that it was worth the trip." We both smiled and it was a touching moment for me as we shook hands.

Following the *Murph The Surf* recording sessions, I visited my good friend Antonio Carlos Jobim, the magnificent Brazilian songwriter who had composed such loving songs as *The Girl From Ipanema*, *Dreamer*, *One Note Samba* and dozens of other truly great popular songs which I had always adored.

Antonio (or Tom as we friends called him) came to the United States from time to time and was here for several months in an apartment on Kings Road and Willoughby sometimes with his then wife of many years, and teenage daughter. A few times while I was doing the *Chinatown* score, he came to my apartment and asked me to play some of my concert piano music which he liked, and then I would ask him to play something on the piano for me and he would extemporaneously compose an infectious Bossa Nova tune which he would sing about "Felippe Lambro, he's a good guy," etc. in Portuguese and we always had a good time with lots of laughs when we were together.

While visiting Jobim a few weeks later in his apartment, he felt saddened about my *Chinatown* experiences. He had always referred to these insensitive motion picture and music executives as "The Machine."

"Watch out, Felippe Lambro, for The Machine," he would warn me. "The Machine is in the black tower; watch out for it."

When he brought up *Chinatown* the last time I saw him in 1974 before departing for Europe, Jobim said, "Listen, Felippe Lambro...You remember that two hour symphony I composed for *The Adventurers*, well Paramount, before it was released, cut it down to a thirty minute suite; then they cut out my music further to an overture; last week I happened to see it on television and now my score is a commercial jingle!"

Both of us could not stop laughing for several minutes.

I was ready to leave for Europe and my concert music crusade on

Friday 21 June 1974. Polanski never kept his end of the bargain about letting me use his flat in London and that is a further significant insight into the word of this man. Another Paramount executive who was there at the time (and asked not to be quoted) told me, "Phillip, when you mention the names of Roman Polanski and Robert Evans, you are talking about the two biggest liars I have ever encountered in all my many years in the motion picture business. Those two will do anything and say anything to avoid blame for their own stupid blunders."

In spite of his character flaws, Roman Polanski was perhaps one of the most gifted cinematic talents of all time. But we must remember what Frank Lloyd Wright used to teach us about looking to nature for our answers.

There are flowers, like Polanski, which only bloom in the springtime then die. Then there are flowers, like Akira Kurosawa which bloom all year long. Mechanically and stylistically, Roman Polanski was masterful, but mechanics and style alone have never accounted for a good film. Polanski's initial instincts were (for the most part) sound, but when I witnessed his getting caught up in adversity after misfortune, we must deduce that his judgment was amiss.

I have always maintained that I would rather have an average person at my side with sound judgment than an intelligent person with faulty judgment. And that is exactly what Roman Polanski is as a film maker: an exceptionally intelligent person with defective final judgments. Polanski as a director has been finished since 1972. He is like a bottle of ginger ale that has been in the refrigerator too long. He has lost his sparkle. He can only direct with some modicum of success a film where the initial story is so powerful (e.g., *Macbeth* or *Tess Of The D'Urbervilles*), that if he is given any less of a story, he is at a complete loss about what to do with it.

Ladies and Gentlemen of the Jury, a Lelouche, a Kubrick, or a Kurosawa never would have begun shooting frame one on the basis of the final draft of *Chinatown* no matter if they were starving to death.

Not so with Roman Polanski. He has forfeited the creative skills of his early directorial exertions simply because he has no longer been making motion pictures. Since 1972, he has been struggling to make motion money.

As I suggested to him before we parted, "Roman, just think about what you did and how you lived when you were contributing to the cinema, and when you were happier and go back to that way of life. Avoid the course which brought you nothing but tragedy. Don't blame a person, place or thing for your problems; look into yourself for these solutions. If you don't and you just lust after base materialism, you'll be punished."

When Polanski notified me about *Pirates* I just laughed at the entire concept (which angered him) and suggested that he forget the whole idea; especially wanting to cast Jack Nicholson in the role of the main pirate and look for a more meaningful story such as Sylvia Plath's *The Bell Jar*, but Polanski never listened. I was with Polanski when he spoke with both Nicholson and Nicholson's agent over the telephone. Nicholson's fee was escalating with each discussion from about $500,000 to now well over one million dollars, to the frustration of Polanski. I understand Polanski got so exasperated with Nicholson that he finally confronted him and demanded to know how much money Nicholson actually wanted to star in *Pirates*; to which Nicholson responded like a wickedly possessed Oliver Twist, "I want more..."

If Roman Polanski is "a has-been," then Robert Evans must be termed "a never was," because, as Polanski himself said to Frank Yablans in a moment of acrimonious verity, "listen, Bob Evans is a nice guy, but he doesn't know fucking one about making a motion picture."

Had I not witnessed Robert Evans personally, I would not have believed what I have written about him myself. I did not mind Evans' equivocate about being responsible for the several successes while he was "there" at Paramount, if only he had told the truth about being responsible for the multitude of failures. Robert Evans could never express himself professionally in more than the few phrases he had picked up in the industry from others because he never knew the language of cinema; and when he was finally told that *Chinatown* was not going to be the unqualified success he phantasmed himself into believing it would be, he became like a drowning person in the ocean fighting the current and resisting those who were trying to save him.

When you have invested close to seven million 1973 and 1974 dollars into a film and it is completed, and it does not turn out to be what you have been finessed into expecting it to be, then you have only two alternatives before releasing that picture: you can reedit the film, and you can rescore the film.

As much as Robert Evans would have liked, he could not have thrown out Faye Dunaway from the picture (he had originally wanted Jane Fonda who rejected the role), to my mind Dunaway was the best casting in *Chinatown*; or anyone else without having to spend millions more in redoing the movie. He could not (which he should have done initially) rewrite or scrap the entire screenplay; so Evans did the least expensive and most illogical thing he could do, and that was to interrupt the inevitable by throwing out the score and blaming the perfectly balanced music as his scapegoat and placebo which he could take each evening (as he once told me) with his warm milk before retiring with his revolver and security blanket.

I did not appreciate having a worthwhile score cast out, but I knew who I was. And as I informed both Evans and Polanski, "My musicianship and compositional talents are not affected by this. My career in music goes on, even if I never score another motion picture in my life. My music making does not stop; it continues."

Following *Murph The Surf*, I returned to my concert music and conducted my compositions over Radio Italiana. The Rochester Philharmonic premiered my *Two Pictures for Solo Percussionist and Orchestra*, eliciting exceptional response from both the audience and press.

Herbert von Karajan, Gyorgy Sandor, Leopold Stokowski, Rudolf Firkusny, and many other internationally acclaimed concert artists lauded my music. I composed my *Night Pieces for Piano* which concert pianist Roman Rudnytsky premiered from Ohio to Paris, France. The sensational keyboard wizard, Santiago Rodriguez, performed my *Toccata for Piano* from The Kennedy Center to Tokyo, Japan. Aprile Millo of the Metropolitan Opera termed my *Four Songs for Soprano and Orchestra* "the finest songs I have encountered since Hugo Wolf." The Denver Symphony, New Orleans Symphony and other orchestras continued to perform my compositions.

Although I have never formally closed the door on scoring motion pictures, I have not accepted another assignment since *Murph The Surf* (although I have been asked over a dozen times) for reasons either in lack of merit, or financially it wasn't worth my time away from my concert music and humanitarian activities. Now that I hope to be able to do more guest conducting (unless the production is either intensely interesting, or I produce it myself) I doubt that I shall ever make any real effort to compose and conduct motion picture music again.

The medium is wonderful as both Maestro Stokowski and I used to discuss. However, more often than not, as Frank Lloyd Wright once said, "Mediocrity has a way of rising to prominence." And, although there have been prodigious technical and mechanical advances in the film medium, the quality of movies and motion picture music has regressed commensurate with the technical advancements because when we analyze the results, we find (for the most part) that the film medium is controlled like a medieval citadel and country club by people who, by virtue of

326

having made gigantic sums of money in other areas of commerce, have infiltrated and bought the industry like an extra toy and are, at best, only shallowly conversant with the artistry and technical aspects necessary to recognize talent. After all it takes talent to recognize talent, especially in the embryonic stages of growth.

And when, in any art form, you do not have rejuvenation of a concept, you will in the end always have regressive atrophy.

On page 355 of *ROMAN by Polanski*, he writes, "Unfortunately Lambro's score turned out to be a disappointment. Bronislau Kaper, whom I took to see the preview in Santa Barbara, loved the picture as a whole but felt the music badly impaired it. I knew he was right but hadn't dared say so because of our deadline; release dates and theater bookings are normally sacrosanct and can't be changed. Bob Evans, for whom only the best was good enough, carried enough clout to break this rule. He insisted on rescoring and bullied the studio into postponement. Jerry Goldsmith was hired to turn out a new score, which he did in record time."

Now, Ladies and Gentlemen of the Jury, I ask you if Polanski's Polish friend, film scorer Bronislau Kaper, who had written the scores for (but could never conduct them) *Two Faced Woman*; *Comrade X*; *Gas Light*; *Butterfield 8*; *Mutiny On The Bounty* (remake); *Lord Jim*; and in 1968, *A Flea In Her Ear*; was by Polanski's own admission to me, "for all intents and purposes, Bronik is too old and out of sync with motion picture music; and besides, the Studio executives would never hire him. He's not acceptable." Then, I ask you, how could Roman Polanski base any credence or opinion about my music score from a gentleman whom he admittedly deemed unfit musically to score that very same picture?

If Bronislau Kaper was "out of sync with motion picture music," and "the Studio executives would never hire him," then I should like to ask Mr. Polanski how is it possible that (if indeed what he states is true), in a matter of weeks, suddenly Bronislau Kaper is now eligible to professionally judge my music? The music Mr. Polanski overwhelmingly approved; that he raved about; the music he painstakingly dubbed and heard over and over and over again. The music which Robert Evans had given me a $1,000 bonus for; the music that Evans and Jack Nicholson had implored me to write more of; the music Evans had listened to over and over and over again.

Page Cook, the knowledgeable motion picture music critic for Films In Review, was one of the first to investigate the *Chinatown* soundtrack debacle and I did let him interview me in New York City a few times on my way to Europe during the last week of June 1974. I told him everything

I knew to be true, and he did some excellent investigating on his own, which resulted in quite an accurate account given in the November 1974 issue of Films In Review.

In Page Cook's article, he questioned one of the Paramount production manager's assistants who said, "Lambro's score was fine; it was clever, musically sound and moved with the film in subtle fashion. Everyone was high on it including Mr. Evans. But there was back-knifing and Lambro's enemies were important and mean enough. Actually, they weren't too thrilled with Goldsmith's score in the outcome, since they weren't able to get any 'exploitable' material. Also, Goldsmith's score was certainly, in no way, any better than Lambro's and, in some ways, a good deal inferior. At one point, Goldsmith's score was in jeopardy of going the same route as Lambro's---this time, replaced solely by source music."

During one of those interviews in New York City, Page Cook startled me by asking if I would like to go see *Chinatown* with Goldsmith's score in it. I thought he was joking at first because I had absolutely no interest in ever seeing that film again. But he said that it would help him with the research if I could tell him if Goldsmith's score embodied the features of Polanski's original intentions. From that point of view, I agreed and we immediately went to a theater in Times Square and saw *Chinatown*.

I have nothing against Jerry Goldsmith who has done some first-rate scores from time to time, but in all honesty, I found Goldsmith's background music, while functional, not anything more than that, and it was unquestionably the direct antithesis of everything Roman Polanski had informed me over a two month period that he wanted the music for Chinatown to be.

And further more (if you can believe this) I advised Page Cook that there seemed to me to be less than the 28 minutes of music which I had originally wrote and which, by Robert Evans' and Jack Nicholson's standards, was not enough. After Page Cook had investigated the timings, he found out that Jerry Goldsmith's score (under the purported guidance of Robert Evans) came to less than 20 minutes for the whole picture!

I understood from motion picture author Charles Higham (who the next February 1975 interviewed me for The New York Times) that "Evans fought bitterly with Goldsmith all through the scoring session." Page Cook said that Sam O'Steen had told him that O'Steen was never in favor of an original score at all for *Chinatown* and tried to convince Evans to replace Goldsmith's "unhappy" score with just source music this time.

Evans now wanted to scrap Goldsmith's soundtrack and use strictly source music, but the few powers over him said that that was "it" as far as music was concerned; you have two scores for *Chinatown*, take your pick.

Of course, Evans could not retrieve my score because that would be admitting Polanski's initial instincts had been correct; so Evans was obliged (as it were) finally, to stay with Goldsmith's undeniably short doleful score, which sounded to me like rejected cues from other Goldsmith film music never used.

Goldsmith was no fool. I could see that he had avoided as much work as possible in scoring Chinatown. He, naturally, circumvented all the difficult scenes, such as the Orchard Lanes sequence, which genuinely needed energetic chase music as Nicholson (Gittes) has a run-in with some "Red-faced Farmers." This section (which Polanski definitely wanted scored) required a lot of fast aggressive music, and that meant a multitude of notes per second and a tremendous amount of labor; even for someone like Goldsmith who never does his own orchestration, but works from a short non-transposing score which, in turn, is given to an orchestrator to translate into orchestral music score and parts.

Speaking of "source music," one of the really big faux pas in *Chinatown* stemmed from the portion where Nicholson (Gittes) is waiting to see Hollis Mulwray, the Department of Water & Power Chief Engineer. The script called for Nicholson to light up a cigarette at the DWP office and stroll along the wall looking at the photographs humming a few seconds of the Jerome Kern-Dorothy Fields 1936 tune *The Way You Look Tonight*. This song won the Academy Award in the Fred Astaire musical *Swing Time* and should have been cleared by contractual license before the scene was shot. However, they filmed the segment first and then went to the publisher who (knowing it was a key section) held up Robert Evans and Paramount for about $8,000 before granting the necessary authorization to let Nicholson just hum the melody for a few seconds on screen. When I heard that, I told the executive, "That's why you people couldn't pay me $25,000."

The day after I had seen *Chinatown* in New York City, I was in the Sol Hurok concert management offices making a few telephone calls when I began hearing fragments of my *Chinatown* score faintly in the background over the phone wires. I really could not understand it; but later that evening, I called Jean France and Lynda Mercier in Los Angeles, who were taking care of my Tabby Cat. Before I had the chance to ask how kitty was, Lynda exclaimed, "Oh, Phillip, they've put your music back in *Chinatown*! Jean France and I went to the movies last night and the coming attractions have all your music in it."

"You must be mistaken," I said. "I'm sure it's Goldsmith's, not mine."

"No, Phillip...wait a minute, here's Jean France."

Jean France knew every note of my score and declared that all the radio spots, TV advertisements and trailers (Coming Attractions) definitely had all of my music in them and no one else's. The next morning I spoke with the New York Paramount office and a few people disclosed that the decision to put my music back into all the trailers and promotional advertising had been made in New York after the department in charge heard Goldsmith's background score and decided that there was absolutely no exploitable music from which to track the trailers and promotional media.

William Stinson informed me several months later that it was the first time in the history of Paramount Pictures, he could recall, where the rejected score had been given a $1,000 bonus, discarded, then put back in to promote the very picture it had been thrown out of. I hadn't been hallucinating in the Hurok office; the radio spots with my music were even filtering into the telephone wires.

I was quite disenchanted, to say the least. If my music wasn't good enough for the film, then why were they using it to encourage the public into seeing the movie? Let them use Goldsmith's music. I telephoned Paul Kohner and he told me, "Phillip, please listen to me. Robert Evans' days are numbered at Paramount. *Chinatown* is not doing the business expected, so let us just wait and see what transpires, and we shall look into the matter when you return from Europe."

I had always trusted Paul and Walter Kohner. They were true gentlemen and the best representatives I had ever had, so I deferred to Paul's judgement. After all he had seen every deal there was in Hollywood and represented the likes of John Huston and Charles Bronson to Ingrid Bergman and Ingmar Bergman, so I agreed to wait before possibly confronting Paramount legally.

I stayed in Europe until the following September. I managed to lease a wonderful flat on Kings Road in the Chelsea area of London, from which I went all over the Continent on my contemporary music crusade. The only place *Chinatown* managed to follow me was in the London subway. There were these small posters of Dunaway and Nicholson staring at me from Charring Cross to Sloan Square which I really didn't appreciate.

I did fire off a hand-written letter to Polanski in Spoleto (my last communication to him) vilifying him for not keeping his word about letting me use his London flat, and adding that I had seen the Evans-Goldsmith version of *Chinatown* in New York and that it musically contained everything he had requested I avoid when he hired me.

I was informed by William Stinson, who was the epitome of the corporate man at Paramount, that if I would continue to grant Paramount the right to use my *Chinatown* music in all the trailers and spots, they would "Quit Claim" the entire ownership of the score back to me. I agreed because I wanted only the *Love Theme* which I might use someday in another picture, although I told Bill Stinson, "You know, I'm fertile enough a composer that I never repeat myself; so the *Chinatown* score is absolutely of no use to me outside of that picture. I might use the *Love Theme* someday, but then again, chances are I won't even do that."

But I wanted the option. After all, the famous *Godfather Theme* (which incidentally, Robert Evans also fought with Francis Coppola to have thrown out) was a melody which Nino Rota had previously written specifically for an Italian Sophia Loren picture many years ago which was totally rejected by the Italian producers and junked. So one never knows when a discarded piece of music might appropriately fit somewhere else and become as popular as the *Godfather Theme* eventually did. As for the rest of my thirty pounds of score, I destroyed my copies and recycled the paper which I hope ended up into something useful like a concrete block, a wicker chair, or even the paper for this book.

Polanski has written, on pages 355 and 356, "I wasn't around for the musical remixing, so the final chapter of the *Chinatown* story reached me in the form of press clippings. An immediate critical and box-office success, the film picked up a clutch of Golden Globes and eleven Academy Award nominations and Bob Towne won a well-deserved Oscar for his screenplay, so the clippings made pleasant reading--all except one. Staring at me from the midst of the bunch was a Hollywood journalist's interview with Bob Evans. According to Evans, I'd hired 'a rinkydink friend' to write the music, so he had to step in and get Goldsmith to repair the damage. I was 'brilliant if channeled properly,' he was quoted as saying, but my problem lay in being surrounded by sycophants who flattered my ego. 'And then his films turn out badly,' Evans went on. 'It takes guts to be a producer, and I have guts.' Now, after Chinatown's success, I'd acknowledge that he'd been right all along and we were 'going to make another picture together soon.' We never did team up again, and the excuse not to do so was always mine. It was the memory of that interview that made me say no. I'd considered Bob Evans more than a producer; he was a friend. Not for the first time, not for the last, a Hollywood experience had gone sour on me."

Well, Ladies and Gentlemen of the Jury, when I read that part in Polanski's automated biography, since I was obviously the "rinkydink friend," I did not know whether or not to send Polanski a handkerchief or a shovel. I did remember the article from the Los Angeles Times and, since I did not wish to keep such "scrap," as Maestro Stokowski used to warn me never to do, I faintly recall that the "Hollywood journalist" Polanski was referring to was none other than "handsome" Bob Evans' over-the-fence back yard neighbor, Joyce Haber herself.

To begin with, your humble court composer could have hardly been termed a "friend" of Roman Polanski's since I had never even been to his home once (although he did invite me several times to see his new giant TV and run the porno flick *Behind The Green Door* which I would have accepted had I not been so engaged composing *Chinatown*) and, other than meeting Polanski at Lucy's El Adobe Cafe that time he asked me to score *Chinatown*, I never so much as had lunch with him; so where Evans got "friend" I'll never know.

Actually, if anything, I was more Bob Evans' "friend" because I did, at least, go to his home once for a screening and ate four peas, two leafs of lettuce, three pieces of carrots and the strawberry I stole from Jack Nicholson's sundae; which, in Hollywood, has been known to represent intimate friendship. Now, "rinkydink" I do not know about because I have yet to find out what the word actually means even though I have asked several sources from the Random House Dictionary to one of Bob Evans' ex-girlfriends with whom I had had an affair with in 1975. "That's why I left that guy, even with all his money," she said. "He kept using such gross words as rinkydink and half the time I could never understand what he was saying."

Now, according to sources at Paramount, who specifically asked not to be identified, "Everybody in the industry knows that *Chinatown* was not a financial success." If *Chinatown* had made money, Robert Evans would have persisted another few years at Paramount and you would have seen *Chinatown II* go into immediate pre-production.

On Tuesday 11 February 1975, 10:00 a.m., Charles Higham came to interview me for The New York Times Sunday Edition 25 May 1975. He was a knowing and literate person who had a scholarly approach and understood the motion picture industry quite well.

"Why do you want to interview me?" I asked.

"You're held in high esteem as a composer and your colleagues who heard your score to *Chinatown* felt you got a raw deal."

"Well, that's past," I said. "Perhaps they're right; the picture, I understand, is making a lot of money."

"That's absolutely not true," Higham said. "I've seen the real figures and the film has not made money. *Chinatown* cost six-point-nine million to make, and with advertising, prints, cost of promotion, it will never make money."

"Yeah?" I replied, somewhat surprised. "I'm glad they took out my music because now they can't blame my score for *Chinatown* not making money. When I was in New York, it was the first time I had ever seen double full page ads in The New York Times for a motion picture. That must have been insanely expensive."

"Yes, it was." said Higham, in his precise English.

Higham took notes as he interviewed me, and asked interesting questions.

"If you were on a desert island, and you could only bring one film to see, what film would it be?"

"Akira Kurosawa's *The Seven Samurai*," I shot back. "It's the greatest piece of cinematic literature in the world today. I've seen it over twenty-five times. And the score is one of the best by Fumio Hayasaka."

I thought Charles Higham would fall off his chair. "As many years as I've been interviewing motion picture people in Hollywood, you are the first to ever select Akira Kurosawa's *The Seven Samurai*, and I'm in complete agreement with you. I believe it is one of the greatest films ever made."

"The greatest," I added. "Then, too, I'm not a motion picture person. I'm a concert composer who has composed film music, as distinguished from a film-scorer who has scored music for films, if you understand what I mean."

Higham did, and we talked about many other things relating to music and motion pictures. He was impressed at how simply I lived with my art, grand piano, drafting table for composing and my books. I served him some Japanese Mu Tea and informed him that it was the tea of supreme judgment; something I suggested that he take to both Evans and Polanski, and others in the industry. He mentioned that Evans had sent me his best regards; I just grinned.

"What do you say," Higham went on, "when Robert Evans maintains that his tenure as Head of Production at Paramount has lasted longer than all of his marriages combined?"

"All I can say to that is," I replied, "that his ex-wives are infinitely more intelligent than the Board of Directors at Paramount Pictures."

We had a good laugh, and Higham left after about another fifteen minutes of questions and answers. All-in-all, it had been a stimulating interview which had lasted close to an hour. His article was quite informative and he quoted me accurately.

Paul Kohner had been correct in all of his prognostications: *Chinatown* did not make money; Robert Evans lost his job as Head of Production; *Chinatown* won only one Academy Award out of eleven nominations; ironically, for a screenplay inspired and based upon original material from Charles Lederer, influenced in dialogue by Jack Nicholson, and which, according to Polanski, who spent two months rewriting it, bore little resemblance to what the Oscar recipient initially wrote. As Shakespeare scribed, "Cursed be he that moves my bones."

Even Joyce Haber was forcibly retired from the Los Angeles Times to her back yard. I was so delighted that I renewed my subscription to the Times now that the odds were excellent that I probably would not have to be subjected to another "Handsome Bob Evans, Paramount's 45-year-old Boy Wonder" article as I opened the Sunday Calendar section each weekend, and quite possibly be referred to once more as a "rinkydink friend" of Roman Polanski's.

The *Chinatown* storm had ceased. I had done my best to harmonize with the elements and not fight them; like a good Arab in the Sahara, I just sat as quietly as I could, wrapped in my shroud until the biting sand storm had wended.

Someday, I thought, it might make an interesting chapter in my autobiography; but who would believe the truth of this saga? It seemed so full of contradictions, like the *Chinatown* script itself, and like the final contradiction about my music as Polanski begins Chapter Twenty-Five [page 365] of *ROMAN by Polanski* where he admits, finally, that he did not agree with Robert Evans about replacing my score:

"It wasn't pique over Bob Evans' behavior or our differences over the score that prompted me to quit Hollywood before the final mixing of *Chinatown*. I had to leave for Italy to direct Alban Berg's *Lulu* at the Festival of Two Worlds in Spoleto."

Perhaps the truth within Roman Polanski is contradiction and distortion: like his autobiography; his films; his life. Akin to the changing of lens and focus, Polanski, perhaps, is so used to distortion that he is patently incapable of recognizing the verity of something even if he is standing on it.

On the basis of having worked with Roman Polanski, and having read those portions in *ROMAN by Polanski* which I personally experienced, and the events I was privy to, first hand as they were unfolding, in all honesty, his flagrant disrespect for the truth caused me not to bother with reading the rest of his book. This is a shame, because I'm sure there is a fascinating biography in Roman Polanski's real life, but I think it will take somebody else and an abundance of researchers to bring it to the surface.

I did not wish any Hell upon Polanski, Evans, Nicholson or any of the other persons who knifed my musical contributions to shreds like the tunic of Julius Caesar, because it was tragically evident, despite my warnings, that they were all headed in that direction anyway. Unfortunately for society, people like that (while whimsically inflicting unnecessary damage upon others) in the end punish only themselves. And in the time since my 1974 prophecy, we can see that Roman Polanski was arrested for having sex with a minor; sent to prison; tried and convicted on evidence furnished largely by Polanski's "friends" Jack Nicholson and Angelica Huston (in order to avoid prosecution for drugs found in Nicholson's home during the investigation) and causing Polanski to subsequently jump bail and return to the safety of France where he can never leave for fear of extradition.

Robert Evans went on a subsequent retrograding path with one motion picture disaster after another where along the way he was convicted of cocaine possession, and was investigated for murder in relationship to his desperate attempt to meet added production financing and repayments on his cinematic debacle *Cotton Club*. As one reliable source told me from Las Vegas where Evans reportedly received capitalizing for *Cotton Club*, "We'll give you the money. But we want it clearly understood that we get our money back. In other words, it's either the money, or your life." This is probably the main reason Robert Evans took out a multimillion dollar loan against his beautiful 1.43 acre home at 1032 North Beverly Drive in Beverly Hills with the 400 year old tree, 35 mm projection room, two bedrooms, three baths, pool and tennis court. Unfortunately, when Evans could no longer meet the timed payments, the bank eventually scheduled his property into foreclosure to be auctioned off 11 March 1993 for $1.342 million. Interestingly enough, reliable sources stated that Robert Evans influenced Jack Nicholson into purchasing the property for Evans in exchange for Nicholson not only to star in (which was a foregone conclusion), but also to direct Evans' catastrophic *Chinatown* sequel *The Two Jakes*. Evans had originally promised the directorial chores to Robert Towne (who presumably wrote the script) but reneged when Evans was confronted with the distinct possibility of becoming homeless in Beverly Hills. At that moment, parcel 4350010007 which was built in 1942 and valued 2 January 1990 at 2.5 million dollars was owned by Robert Evans and the Robert Evans Trust reportedly set up by Nicholson.

"Jack Nicholson," (to quote one of his associates on the financial and critical cataclysm *The Two Jakes*) "is so physically strung out on drugs, with his belly out to here, that he was completely unaware when green mucus was running from his nose during an important close-up."

However, Nicholson finally got his want when he inserted his beloved excised dialogue from *Chinatown* into *The Two Jakes* defeat: Nicholson (Gittes) says to a new police detective character "I'd never extort a nickel out of my worst enemy, that's where I draw the line." Then the additional detective responds, "Yeah, I once knew a whore, who for enough money would piss in a customer's face--but she'd never shit on his chest. That's where she drew the line."

Obviously, the actor desperately needed the job.

As I told both Paul and Walter Kohner in 1974, "I'd rather grow lettuce in Escondido than go through another turmoil like *Chinatown*.

Someone recently questioned me if, for enough money, would I ever work for Robert Evans again.

"While completing *Chinatown*," I replied, "I bumped into Francis Coppola who was driving his camper at about three miles an hour on the Paramount Lot when he stuck his head out of the window and asked what I was doing at the Studio. When I told him composing and conducting the music for *Chinatown*, Coppola rolled his eyes above his beard and said, 'Good luck with Evans...there isn't enough money in the world for me to ever work with that guy again." But obviously there was for Francis Coppola when *Cotton Club* furled around, but not for me; unless, of course, it's for 20 million dollars. For that amount of money, I wouldn't care if Evans re-recorded my music backwards.

During the fall of 1975, I was at the Old World Restaurant on Sunset Boulevard when I noticed Jack Nicholson all alone having somewhat of an arduous discussion about his afternoon order. It seems Nicholson had left all of his money and credit cards at home and didn't have a penny on him. I had heard from others that he was one of a few well-known personalities who sometimes made a habit out of indicating to the waiter that they had had so much on their mind recently that they inadvertently forgot to take any cash or credit cards with them. Usually, the maitre d' was so glad to have a major notable in his restaurant that he would tell the star not to worry and just mail in the remittance at their convenience; but these famous luminaries rarely did, and most of the time never returned to those particular eateries again.

The young girl at the Old World cash register wasn't impressed, and revealed to Nicholson (who already had ordered --what else?-- a hamburger) that he would have to go home and come back immediately with either a credit card or the money if he was going to eat. I grinned from the distance and Nicholson, noticing me, waved me over to his table.

"Hi, how are you," I asked. "Do you remember me?"

"I sure do," Nicholson replied, "Boy, you really got a bum deal on the score...say, listen, an embarrassing thing has happened to me," he went on as if he were doing a scene in a film. "I ordered lunch and I forgot to take some money with me; do you think you could loan me ten dollars?"

I smiled broadly. "Sure, Jack," I said, reaching into my pocket and giving him a ten from about my thirty-some dollars in ready cash.

"I'll pay you back," he said seriously, although I knew better, but really didn't care.

"If you get me a fifty thousand dollar film score," I continued still smiling, "you don't have to pay me back; we can call it even."

"Sit down, if you want," Nicholson said as his lunch arrived, and he ordered a milk shake to go with his hamburger. "Have you eaten?"

"I can only stay a minute because I have to meet someone."

"Geeze," he said, as I sat down watching him wrestle with the Ketchup bottle, "I bet you were mad as hell about what they did to your score in *Chinatown.*"

"Not really," I said. "It's their loss; they got what they deserved. My career in music goes on, it doesn't stop."

"Boy, I know I'd sure as hell be mad if that ever happened to me," he said, shaking his head side-to-side.

I attempted to be congenial as I had remembered how Nicholson used to be so effortless with Polanski when he was commiserating with him, then as soon as Polanski was out of habitat, undermine him in that sluggish manner of Nicholson's.

But who cared? I thought it rather amusing (regardless of whether or not Jack Nicholson had been one of the latent assassins of my background music) that here was your humble and unprosperous composer, Ladies and Gentlemen of the Jury, loaning super movie star, one Jack Nicholson, purportedly worth millions, the princely sum of ten dollars; which, incidentally, to this day, he has never repaid; not, as I said, that I had ever expected him to. He probably telephoned Polanski and Evans, (knowing

Nicholson) and possibly had a good laugh; which they most assuredly deserve when you consider that, out of those three, not one of them has a natural sense of humor.

"Why should I get mad?" I queried Nicholson. "Getting mad is unproductive and wastes energy. People like that always punish themselves in the end."

"You don't think I had anything to do with it, do you?" Nicholson asked, with his mouth overloaded to the brim with his burger.

"I don't think anything about *Chinatown*, Jack. I'm composing and conducting concert music, and proofing engraved compositions of mine which are about to be published, so *Chinatown*, as we say in Zen, was just a good bad-experience for me."

Just then my friend arrived and I excused myself from the table. Nicholson gave me his home address, and I gave him mine, as I offered to send him a copy of my newly released *Murph The Surf* soundtrack album; he might learn something I thought. As I left the Old World Restaurant, I briefly spoke with the cute teenage cashier who (to her credit) thought "Jack Nicholson had some nerve coming in here with no money," especially, she said, after he had done the very same thing once before and left her with an unpaid check which he never indemnified.

My good friend, Chinese acupuncturist Master Cheng Shen Wang, used to tell me in his limited English, "You do good, you get good...You do bad, you get bad." So the chases and confessions of both Robert Evans and Roman Polanski are rather tragic in their disparate ways: Polanski, who had an immense amount of faculty for the cinema; Evans who had none at all; but both who were driven to the point of desperation in their maniacal quest, not for cinematic excellence, but for the base materialism of hit box-office receipts; almost like the mirage behavior reminiscent in *Treasure Of The Sierra Madre*. Where has it gotten them? And what have they contributed to the motion picture medium and humanity? Even by their own mechanical monetary criteria of what they consider "success," what have been their achievements?

I recall informing Polanski that if he wanted to see an exceptionally good film to where you were entertained and you actually cared about the characters and situations, to view Claude Lelouche's *And Now My Love*. I told him it was one of the best love stories I had ever seen. That picture also disproves the idiotic theory which many film scorers have about not wanting a famous beautiful song on the same sound track with their score. The celebrated song, *And Now My Love*, did not prevent Francis Lai from composing another strong air for the *Main Theme*;

in fact, *And Now My Love* is a rare example of how two concentrated melodies can coexist within one moving picture.

When the master film genius Akira Kurosawa was asked what could help bring back slackening audiences into the movie theaters again, he responded that the matter was rather simple: a really good film with a really good story.

THE BOY FROM IPANEMA

I first met Antonio Carlos Jobim the end of January 1968 at Cyrano's Restaurant on Sunset Boulevard in West Hollywood, California. It was about 8:30 in the evening as I was driving home and although I had eaten much earlier in the day with my Japanese Zen Macrobiotic Restaurant cooks Toyo and Miyoko Nakayama, I was a trifle famished, but did not wish to have to prepare food in my kitchen during that dissolving hour. As I motored along Sunset Boulevard, I knew that the French chef at Cyrano's would assemble a quick pressed shrimp salad sandwich with garlic toast which would decidedly assuage my appetite.

My good friend Gio Casara from Milano was the maitre d' and since he was acquainted with my concert and symphonic credentials almost always addressed me in the Italian manner as Maestro, or Maestro Lambro as did most of the European waiters at Cyrano's.

Gio, along with his waiter brother-in-law Johnny, amid the flashing fanfares and echoes of Maestro sat me next to a table where two Latin looking men were eating their dinners.

After I had ordered, one of the gentlemen at the closely adjoining table gave me a friendly stare and with a slight accent said, "I am a Maestro, too."

"You are..?" I asked. "What is your instrument?"

"Piano. I'm a composer. Antonio Carlos Jobim. Do you know my music?"

"Oh, I love your songs," I said. "They're so unique. They are among my favorites. I'm very pleased to meet you."

Jobim then proceeded to ask my name; what type of music I composed; where I had studied (he was a great admirer of my last teacher concert pianist Gyorgy Sandor who had given many successful concerts and recitals in Brazil and had been Bartok's most celebrated pupil); and then he introduced me to his colleague a new Brazilian musician-arranger, Emir Deodato, who appeared to be around my age.

Jobim seemed impressed by the fact that I was a symphonic and concert composer and had the strength to live that arduous life. As we ate, I was rather astonished to discover that he was not actually a guitarist. "I only know a few chords on the guitar," he said. "I really do everything at the piano. I was forced to learn just the simple basics of the guitar as a result of the popularity of the guitar in relationship to the Bossa Nova."

Since I was a concert composer-conductor-pianist, Jobim inquired if I had ever heard of the Brazilian concert pianist Nelson Freire. When

I responded that I had listened to some of his recordings and enjoyed Freire's playing, Jobim told me that he and Freire had had the same piano teacher in Brazil. "But the life of a concert pianist was not for me," Jobim said. "Since I did not like to practice all day long, I went into popular music." We all laughed. "I usually went fishing when I should have been practicing the piano," Jobim went on.

Jobim also seemed fascinated by the actuality that I had been acquainted with his, as he condescendingly said, "these little simple songs I write" since I was firmly entrenched in the complex world of symphonic and concert music.

"Listen," I said. "Your songs are great. The ones I've heard are as good as the best of Cole Porter, George Gershwin or Franz Schubert."

"No, I don't think so," Jobim said.

Emir Deodato began to grin broadly as Jobim and I debated the virtues of Jobim's songs.

Jobim wondered how I had first encountered his music and I described to him how accidentally I had heard a little known imported Joao Gilberto recording around 1961 in New York City at the home of one of my Argentinean friends which featured a number of Jobim's most illustrious songs such as *Desafinado (Out Of Tune)*, *Chega De Saudade*, *One Note Samba*, *Insensatez*, *Corcovado*, *Meditation* and others.

"Ah yes," Jobim said. "Joao Gilberto was very important in my work. He was, as they say in Spanish, my verdugo."

"Verdugo..?" I asked.

"Yes, you know; verdugo."

"No, I don't know the word," I said.

"You mean to tell me, Felippe Lambro, that you live here in Southern California with the famous Verdugo Mountains all around you and you do not know verdugo?"

Suddenly Jobim and Deodato began conversing in Portuguese endeavoring to find the corresponding English meaning of verdugo.

"Executioner," Jobim softly exclaimed. "He was my executioner; the executioner of my songs."

During the course of our leisurely dinner we spoke about our performing rights societies: mine, ASCAP; his BMI. And his early struggles with Brazilian music publishers who eventually deposited his most prominent songs within BMI affiliated publishers here in the United States and world wide. I was rather appalled to learn that despite the immense international popularity of Jobim's songs that his BMI royalty checks were not enough then, at the height of his global prominence, to make him independently wealthy and that he still had to struggle within financial limits.

Jobim asked me if I had ever done work for the cinema and when I advised him of the motion pictures which I had scored, he informed me that earlier in the day Avco Embassy at Paramount Pictures had asked him if he would be interested in furnishing the soundtrack to the forthcoming motion picture The Adventurers.

"What kind of money do you think I should ask?" Jobim said to me.

"What kind of fee were you thinking about?" I countered.

"Well you know," Jobim went on, "In Brazil I've done only a few pictures and the prices are usually set. The industry in Brazil is not what it is here in the United States. I was thinking maybe to ask $15,000 dollars."

I exclaimed, "Are you crazy? You've struggled all your life and now that you're famous and in a position to demand big money, don't let them take advantage of you. Ask $50,000 dollars."

Jobim nearly choked on his food when he heard $50,000 dollars since the top salary at that time was $25,000 dollars and Deodato was equally astounded; but as I was to find out a few days later, Jobim heeded my advice and to his utter amazement, the producers agreed to pay him the $50,000 dollars after he had casually requested it.

Toward the end of dinner, I was considerably startled when Jobim asked me if I would be interested in orchestrating and arranging his music for *The Adventurers* provided he signed a contract to do it.

Even though it was not physically apparent, I could sense Emir Deodato's sinking disenchantment.

"Look," I said. "Even though I love and admire your work, I do not do anyone else's orchestration except my own. And besides," I went on, "what's wrong with him?" I nodded toward Deodato's direction to the revival of Deodato's confidence who I knew intensely wanted to acquire the assignment and at that period needed the money, as well as working with Antonio Carlos Jobim; "The Sacred Cow Of Brazil" as he was sometimes ascribed.

After dinner and more confabulation, we exchanged telephone numbers and walked toward Cyrano's foyer. An abrupt rain storm had just occurred and we could not believe how much water was pouring in torrents from the Los Angeles sky. I was surprised to learn that neither Jobim nor Deodato had an automobile, and the two had walked over a mile from their Sunset Marquis Hotel at 1200 Alta Loma Road off Sunset Boulevard to Cyrano's, so I recommended that it would be best if I take them home and to wait next to Cyrano's door while I ran to my car. I drove them to the Sunset Marquis where Deodato was in suite 334 and Jobim in suite 339.

A few days later I telephoned Jobim and we had the first of what were to be, on occasion, many lengthy and gratifying telephone conversations.

Jobim explained that he was in town to do a follow-up album with Frank Sinatra since their initial joint recording venture a few years previously (*Francis Albert Sinatra & Antonio Carlos Jobim*) had been so successful.

Jobim liked the charm of the Sunset Marquis residence hotel, but to our amusement he did not appreciate it while composing at his small spinet piano, playing softly, that his hotel neighbors would sometimes pound on the wall demanding that he stop. I found this rather incongruous because how loud can an Antonio Carlos Jobim Brazilian Samba Bossa Nova be?

I offered Jobim the use of my grand piano and apartment, but he enumerated that he wouldn't be staying in Los Angeles too long, and he would just have to put up with it until he returned to Rio.

A few evenings later at the Old World Restaurant on Sunset Boulevard I encountered Deodato and Jobim in the lobby. Even though Jobim threw his arms around me and gave me a warm embrace, I could sense that something was amiss.

"I thought you were recording with Sinatra tonight," I said as I also glanced at Deodato who gave me a rather abashed look.

"The sessions were cancelled," Jobim sighed lighting a cigarette.

"What do you mean the sessions were cancelled?" I asked. "What happened?"

"I told Frank he can't sing my songs," Jobim said.

"What do you mean Sinatra can't sing your songs," I replied. "I thought he was great on your last album. What the hell happened?"

"He wasn't singing the songs the way I wrote them. He was changing things, and when I tried to explain it to him matters became worse."

"Jesus Christ, Tom," I sighed to Jobim. "Popular singers are like that; they change things to fit their interpretation. I mean, after all, it's not as if you were recording the Rachmaninoff *Third Piano Concerto* with Sinatra. And even there, each pianist has a different approach and interpretation to the music."

"At least they play the right notes," Jobim went on as Deodato nodded and shrugged. "Frank wasn't singing the songs the way I composed them. He was sometimes changing the melody and especially the rhythm. I tried to teach him the correct rhythms, but he wouldn't listen. So we just cancelled the rest of the sessions.

"I can't believe this," I said. "Sinatra is a quality musician. Your last album was so good."

"Yes," Jobim said. "Frank did an excellent job on that one."

I tried to convince Jobim to endeavor to patch things up with Sinatra and at least finish the album with songs which perhaps were not as complicated, but Jobim told me that he really didn't care and wanted to get back to Brazil and go fishing.

The songs Sinatra and Jobim recorded that week were only enough to fill out one side of a 33 1/3 rpm long play record, so Sinatra went into the studio subsequently and saved his release by recording Irving Berlin's *Change Partners* and other tunes to finish out the additional side of the album by way of a Bossa Nova characteristic which would be compatible with the approved tracks Jobim and Sinatra had already recorded.

I know that Jobim liked and respected Sinatra, even though he perhaps did not openly display it. Jobim once described to me how much he had enjoyed staying several days at Sinatra's Palm Springs home. Jobim especially appreciated Sinatra's quality library of books and regretted to me that he could not have remained there longer to read more of them.

Before Jobim departed for Brazil, he gave me his home address and telephone number and suggested that I come and visit him someday. I told him that I had hoped to be invited to guest conduct in South America at some future date, and if this occurred, I would most definitely knock on his door.

With the vicissitudes of my career and life, I was not able to garner any guest conducting engagements in South America; although my Dutch concert manager of the time, Harry De Freese, did acquire several concerts for me to conduct the Symphony Orchestra in El Salvador which I finally had to cancel after several long distance telephone calls with the El Salvador management exposed the actualities that one of the key instrumentalists of the orchestra had died in revolutionary cross fire; and the harpist, and several other players, quite necessary for my programs of Miaskovsky, Ravel, Cortes and Lambro, had exited the orchestra. In fact, they said that they would guarantee my safety (with military escorts and tanks surrounding the concert hall) if I would change my mind and come and conduct concerts in music of the reduced orchestra of Mozart and the Baroque. I told them that if I came, I would in all probability invite the peasants and revolutionaries together with all the government militia to all of the concerts (provided that they discarded their weapons) and, perhaps, then after some live music, they would see how much a waste of time fighting each other was.

It wasn't until October of 1973 that I encountered Jobim again. He had taken a modest, but spacious apartment at 911 North Kings Road (south of Santa Monica Boulevard) on the corner of Willoughby. After he invited me to come by, he justified how he had chosen this particular rental building because it was within comfortable walking distance to the market and other basic utility stores since he did not have a car and did not like to drive.

It was during this time that Jobim and I got to know each other more elementally and that he suggested I call him by his diminutive name of Tom rather than Antonio, or Antonio Carlos. Jobim was a sensitive individual with an easy going phlegmatic personality; but, in spite of this, he possessed a notable sense of humor when ignited, and when we were together we always seemed to have an abundance of laughs no matter how much each of us were dispirited over the inhumane condition of world events, and the insanity of the entertainment and music industries.

When Jobim and I would bemoan the fate of quality art in the entertainment business, he invariably had a humorous way of collectively expressing the insensitivity of agents, and executives within the motion picture, television and recording companies by condescendingly referring to them as "The Machine."

"Watch out, Felippe Lambro, for The Machine," he would warn me. "The Machine is in the black tower; watch out for it." The black tower, of course, was the monolithic black steel and glass MCA Universal Pictures Studios executive building at Universal Plaza in North Hollywood where I had witnessed many career assassinations, including my own.

One afternoon sometime during November 1973, Jobim presented me with his recently released Aguas De Marco (Waters Of March) album which he warmly inscribed in Portuguese: "To Phillipe, Com um abraco, a amizade e a admiracao do Antonio, LA 73" which translated means, "To Phillipe, With a hug, with friendship and admiration from Antonio LA 73." The disc which had been recorded in New York City that previous December with orchestral accompaniments arranged and conducted by Claus Ogerman and issued by MCA earlier in 1973 was completely unknown to me.

"That's because MCA only sold twenty copies," Jobim said. "And I bought ten of them myself."

We laughed.

"Tom, come on," I said. "I can't believe MCA sold only twenty records."

"Well, it hasn't done very well, my friend," Jobim went on.

Since I only had a tape deck at home in my studio at that time, I asked Jobim to play the record on his turntable there in the apartment. I thought the principal song *Aguas De Marco (Waters Of March)* for which Jobim wrote both words and music and sang two versions on the recording (one in English and one in Portuguese) was absolutely unique. Jobim also gave me two copies of the sheet music folio which, although the song ran just five seconds under four minutes, was quite a lengthy avant garde Bossa Nova with a plethora of unsuspecting words and musical intervals. I was fascinated because I didn't know what word or note was coming next: "A stick, a stone, It's the end of the road, It's the rest of a stump, It's a little alone. It's a sliver of glass, It is life, it's the sun, It is night, it is death, It's a trap, it's a gun. The oak when it blooms, A fox in the brush, The knot in the wood, The song of a thrush. The wood of the wind, A cliff, a fall, A scratch, a lump, It is nothing at all. It's the wind blowing free, It's the end of the slope, It's a beam, it's a void, It's a hunch, it's a hope. And the riverbank talks Of the waters of March," etc.

I thought the song was matchless in its unimaginable charm and the beauty of how both the words and music meshed to form a whole additional dimension to the Bossa Nova.

The great difficulty I have always had with the majority of popular music is that it is quite uncommon to find tunes where you have an interestingly rare melody wedded to an equally unrivaled set of lyrics. Most of the songs one hears have such boring melodies attached to innocuously predictable words which you know are coming even before the artists chant them; it's enough to make one grieve. The aforementioned, in my opinion, (with or without words) may be equally applied to the majority of baroque, classical, romantic and contemporary concert music as well.

Jobim often appeared fatigued most of the time, which I concluded was from low blood sugar caused by smoking, drinking (although I never once saw him drunk), and a diet of coffee and animal products.

Shortly thereafter, Jobim's wife Tereza arrived for a visit from Brazil with her teenage daughter Elizabeth. I drove Tereza to the market on several occasions and helped her with the shopping. She was an attractively strong Brazilian woman whom Jobim had married against her father's wishes in 1949.

Tereza once told me, "My father who was rather German said to me, 'If you marry that broken down bar musician, you will starve to death

346

the rest of your life.' But we were in love and my father finally accepted it although he never approved."

What I concluded from the relatively few private conversations I had had with Tereza, and discerning the often apathetic personality of Jobim as I did, had it not been for the assertive promotion by Tereza of Jobim's early song writing efforts with Brazilian publishers, most of his wonderfully notable works of melody writing which I have never heard anyone surpass (not even Porter, Kern, or Gershwin who were among the very best) these songs would still be unknown and floating up the Amazon today as bait with some of Jobim's fishing partners.

Apropos Jobim's apparent love for fishing, I recall American singer Tony Bennett telephoning Jobim at his apartment one day extending Jobim an emphasized status on Bennett's forthcoming Television Special and Jobim responding, "I know Tony, I know. I appreciate your offering me to appear on your television show, and I could use the $25,000 dollars, but to tell you the truth, I'll be in Brazil fishing then." I nearly fell off my chair, but clearly that was the way Antonio Carlos Jobim was.

As I was about to leave Jobim's apartment once, and he walked me to the foyer, we found a note on his front door which read, "Dear Mr. Jobim, my wife and I buy all your records and we dig your songs, but could you not compose and play your music on the piano after ten p.m.? Thank you, your next door neighbors." We had another good laugh before I departed.

Once or twice during that period Jobim came to my apartment and asked me to play some of my concert piano music which he liked, and then I would ask him to play something on the piano for me and he would sometimes extemporaneously compose an infectious Bossa Nova tune which he would sing about "Felippe Lambro, he's a good guy," etc. in Portuguese and we always had a pleasant time with clusters of laughs when we were together.

On my apartment wall adjacent to the grand piano Jobim examined several framed musical mementos and photo inscriptions from my musical career given to me by such leading artists as Vladimir Horowitz and Leopold Stokowski. Jobim seemed impressed by the number of symphonic performances I had received including a framed program where Stokowski had performed my Miraflores for String Orchestra together with an autographed photo which the Maestro had sent me. Also his secretary had forwarded to me (presumably unbeknownst to Stokowski) a copy of a glowing letter of recommendation which the Maestro had sent to some foundation which also was included in the glass encased frame. Jobim wanted to know the type of person Stokowski was and became astounded to learn that with me as a twenty-one year old aspiring composer, he was quite a respectful and natural man in his singular way.

One day when Jobim had trouble remembering a couple of titles and names, I reminded him of the fact that Leopold Stokowski at that time, was sometimes quite forgetful of names. I relayed to Jobim how one day in New York City I had brought Stokowski some organic carrot juice which I thought would be good for the Maestro's health on a fairly warm day and what Stokowski had subsequently told me. "Oh, I have a juicer which this very famous conductor gave me," said Stokowski; who then took me into his kitchen and showed me this gigantic stainless steel vegetable and fruit juicer which did not actually look like a juicer. You could never have imagined the shape of this juicer as it supposedly had been constructed around 1945, with a futuristic design which resembled "R2-D2" in that space movie. It was a few feet high, and it had this tiny opening to put carrots in. A large carrot could never have fit into the entrance; you had to cut it up so that it would go into the relatively small hole.

"Yes," Stokowski went on, "this famous conductor, you know, gave me this. Oh what was his name?" Stokowski quietly thought for a long moment.

I rattled off a few names from that period; like Toscanini, Koussevitzky, and Szell endeavoring to help Stokowski recollect.

"No it wasn't him. It wasn't them." Stokowski said.

And then after a period of time Stokowski invariably would become slightly exasperated when he couldn't think of the person's name; then he would say, "Oh well, it doesn't matter anyway. It's not important."

Jobim loved the story and when either of us could not remember something, we had this running joke emulating Stokowski by saying, "Oh well, it doesn't matter anyway. It's not important." And then we would laugh.

Jobim revealed a wonderful story to me about the celebrated temperamental and phenomenal Italian concert pianist Arturo Benedetti Michelangeli whose public appearances were always distinctively infrequent. "Oh yes," said Jobim. "Michelangeli came to Rio and gave a great piano recital. And afterward, he seduced all the young women of Rio."

"Tom, what do you mean Michelangeli seduced all the young women of Rio?" I asked.

"Well," Jobim went on, "after the concert, there was a very large reception given for Michelangeli at the beautiful home of an important government official overlooking the Bay at Rio. The guests were eating and having refreshments, but Michelangeli was standing alone near the far corner of the large swimming pool with his arms folded staring intently into the bottom of the pool. Everyone was wondering what was wrong with Michelangeli because he looked so sad just staring in a fixed gaze into the bottom of the pool. And realizing how temperamental an artist he was (we were very fortunate in getting him to come and play) no one wanted to take on the responsibility of perhaps upsetting him which might cause him to leave this important social event. So a parade of beautiful women one by one went up to Michelangeli asking, 'Arturo, what is the matter? Why do you stare into the pool, looking so sad?"

Then Jobim told me, "Michelangeli at first said that nothing was wrong, then later when pressed by these lovely young Brazilian women pretended to be extremely lonely telling each of them that his was a life of practicing the piano all the time secluded in extreme isolation without romance and love. And over the next few days, Felippe Lambro, I tell you Michelangeli had all the women of Rio."

We were laughing so hard that tears came to our eyes.

Jobim was quite captured by the fact that I had met Brazilian composer conductor Heitor Villa Lobos who was one of Jobim's musical idols; and he asked me to tell him about my experiences with Villa Lobos, which I did. I encountered Villa Lobos a few years before his death while I was a student at the University of Miami in Florida. Villa Lobos came there to guest conduct the University of Miami Symphony Orchestra and I conveyed to Jobim how Villa Lobos was a short plump thickset man with long graying hair, a kindly face and a good sense of humor who liked to smoke Havana cigars. I was first introduced to Villa Lobos through Eugene Dubois, the violin professor and concertmaster of our orchestra, on the sidewalk in front of the University of Miami student center. Villa Lobos only spoke French and Portuguese, and he conversed with me in French through Eugene Dubois (who had been born in France) and gave me some good basic music career advice.

He said, "Young man, you have talent," but he continued, "Now make sure that you write the music of the earth you are standing on."

Eugene Dubois had been concertmaster with the renowned NBC Symphony under Arturo Toscanini until its ultimate demise and then came to the University of Miami Symphony Orchestra. Dubois was also quite an authority on fashioning perfumes which I discovered during the concourse with Villa Lobos. Dubois explained to both Villa Lobos and myself how he personally designed perfumes. Dubois was also violin soloist with the Orchestra and I remember his playing the Bruch

Concerto rather well.

One time as Jobim and I were about to leave his apartment to go somewhere, Tereza and Elizabeth had the television set going on even though no one was watching it, I suddenly heard Barbra Streisand militantly vocalizing Jobim's infectious *One Note Samba* which he had composed to words by Newton Mendoca.

"Tom, wait a minute," I said turning toward the TV. "Barbra Streisand is singing your song."

Jobim turned to watch and after about twenty seconds said to me, "What do you think?"

I did not wish to express my negative opinion of her gladiatorial rendition because I wanted to genuinely know what Jobim thought of Streisand's over-kill interpretation so I asked, "Well, what do you think?"

After another moment he said unemotionally, "I wish that woman would stop singing my songs. Let's go."

Toward the end of January 1974, Jobim asked if I would drive him to the ocean along with Tereza and Elizabeth (and Elizabeth's close girlfriend, Cristina, who had come all the way from Rio to vacation with her) since he said that he had never really had a chance to view Southern California beaches. I was rather amazed by the request as I would have certainly thought that Antonio Carlos Jobim (who had had a lifelong love affair with nature and the ocean) would have surely seen the Southern California Pacific long before this.

I agreed, but warned, "I hope you're not going to be too disappointed because as charming as Santa Monica and Malibu are, they're no match for your home town Rio de Janeiro beaches and ocean. And besides," I went on, "it's January and overcast today; the worst time of the year for the California coast."

"I know, I know," Jobim said. "I am not expecting the Copacabana. I just want to see some of the Southern California beaches and show them to Tereza and Elizabeth, and Cristina."

Well, there I was, Ladies and Gentlemen of the Jury, on that cloudy, eclipsed Wednesday afternoon 23 January 1974 driving my Brazilian friends via the more lengthy vegetation of Sunset Boulevard to Pacific Coast Highway (rather than the drab concrete and asphalt five-lane Santa Monica Freeway) in order to avoid what I imminently deemed would be the abruptness of disappointment.

To my surprise, they all did not seem bored by the drive. As soon as we reached the end of Sunset Boulevard we turned right and moved up Pacific Coast Highway and I did my best to keep Jobim and his family engaged by attempting to point out what few historic sites there were from the Getty Museum to the Mailbu Pier interspersed with recollections of notorious rock avalanches; former canyon fires and flooded mud slides; and the beach front homes of a few unpleasant motion picture producers whom I had been financially compelled to write music for.

As soon as we reached Webb Way, I turned left then right on Malibu Road and proceeded slowly along the Malibu Colony until we came to the end and Corral Beach; normally, a favored presentable shore. However, with the potent ravages of winter waves there had been a great deal of ocean floor debris from seaweed and driftwood to gigantic boulders which had washed up over the coastline punctuating the shadowed sky.

"Well, this is it," I said as I glanced at their courteously easy going expressions. "As I warned you, it's not Rio."

"No, it's nice. It's different," Elizabeth said.

"I imagine that it is quite beautiful in the summertime," Tereza added as Cristina affirmatively nodded.

"It has a rather stark beauty," Jobim said as he pulled up his overcoat collar.

"Would you like to get out and have a closer look?" I asked.

"No," Jobim said chuckling. He was obviously chilly; and the temperature was perhaps only in the mild mid 60's Fahrenheit.

I restarted the car and we returned to the Jobims' apartment.

After we arrived, I found out that Elizabeth's teenage intimate, Cristina, was the daughter of a fabulously wealthy white sugar cane manufacturer in Brazil. Of course being a good Macrobiotic humanitarian, over the path of the next several days (to the great amusement of Jobim) I managed to inform young Cristina of the prodigious physical detriment which processed white sugar has caused mankind throughout history; including the fact that there had never been any purported cases of leprosy in Africa until white man journeyed there to buy slaves in exchange for white sugar and chocolate. A few days later, youthful Cristina proudly revealed to me the scathing letter she had written her father demanding that he stop processing and distributing white sugar and instead produce and circulate the indigenous natural rice and barley malt sweeteners about which I had acquainted her with. One day several weeks later at the Jobims' apartment, after I had inconsequentially asked where Cristina was, I was advised that her father, subsequent to receiving Cristina's epistle, had demanded her immediate return home.

Jobim chuckling warned, "You had better watch out Felippe Lambro. Cristina's father is an important sugar industrialist. It's a good thing that he only sent his emissaries for Cristina after that letter and not you."

During one of our benign discussions on a solitary afternoon, I was startled to learn that the Military Junta in Brazil, for a time, had considered their politically ambivalent Bossa Nova Sacred Cow, Antonio Carlos Jobim, a subversive reactionary. And from what he incredulously told me, he was at one time under close military surveillance. I could not believe this, but apparently it was true.

We were wallowing in laughter when Jobim said, "Felippe Lambro, what kind of threat could I have ever been to the armed forces of Brazil with these little Bossa Nova songs I write? They thought I was going to overthrow the government with the guitar I can hardly play."

Jobim went on laughingly explaining, after one of his confidants from the secret police had privately informed him that his telephone conversations were being recorded, how when one of his musician friends would casually phone, Jobim would invariably and suddenly interject within the conversation, "Listen, I want you to order me one hundred tanks, two thousand rifles, twenty-five machine guns, and two atomic bombs. And tell the general everything will be ready tomorrow."

I could not understand how Jobim's BMI performance royalties, as he accounted to me on more than one occasion, were at that time never above $50,000 dollars a year. The plain truth of the matter was, that along with the Beatles, Jobim's songs were among the most played all over the world. Had his most popular songs been licensed through ASCAP, I'm sure that his annual royalties would have been close to $200,000 a year during the 1960's because ASCAP collected larger fees during that period. In fact, I suggested that he see what could be done about transferring his songs into ASCAP, but contractually it was not possible; although Jobim did inform me that he had become a member of ASCAP for a short time in 1967 to see what might happen.

"I wrote and recorded a few songs," Jobim told me. "But all I ever got from ASCAP were these massive royalty checks for two dollars and ninety-eight cents. So I went back to BMI."

For a moment I could not accept what he was telling me, but it was true as we both laughed at the tragic injustice of it all. To make Jobim feel a trifle better I acquainted him with my own first year's ASCAP royalties which were barely enough to cover my ten dollar annual membership dues.

The recording and ASCAP licensed songs Jobim was referring to were done in collaboration with lyricist Ray Gilbert during 1967 in New York City which produced one of the most undeservedly neglected and attractively romantic songs ever penned entitled *Photograph* which Jobim sang himself. Additionally, Jobim wrote the instrumental song *Surfboard* during that time as well.

Although I never met Joao Gilberto, Jobim revealed to me a hilarious story about him as Gilberto was struggling with a recording session in Rio. Jobim said that Gilberto (who has one of the most matchlessly euphonic soft voices in the world) was making a new album with a rather large orchestra and during the playbacks was a little bit disturbed by the brass instruments in the arrangements; so he requested to the arranger that the brass players be sent home. Thereafter, Gilberto thought the violins and other stringed instruments interfered with his sensitive guitar accompaniment; so the entire string section was later dismissed. Then he felt some of the woodwinds, such as the oboe and flute were too weighty. By the end of the day, the orchestra had been reduced to just one bassist, one rhythm player on percussion, and Joao Gilberto's voice and guitar. After listening to more of the recorded takes, Gilberto decided to terminate the bass and rhythm players and record the whole album with just his own guitar accompaniment.

February 1974 through the middle of June 1974 I was so wholly occupied with not only composing, arranging, orchestrating, and conducting the film music for *Chinatown* and *Murph The Surf*, with all the impetuous political machinations those two on-and-off-screen motion pictures entailed, and an abundance of other things, that I was unable to telephone Jobim more than two or three times. However, he recognized what I was going through and forewarned me about "The Machine". Following the *Murph The Surf* recording sessions, I went to call upon Jobim at his lodgings. He felt saddened about my *Chinatown* experiences at Paramount.

"Well, "The Machine" finally caught up with me, Tom," I said laughingly.

"Listen, Felippe Lambro...You remember that two hour symphony I composed for *The Adventurers*, well Paramount, before it was released, cut it down to a thirty minute suite; then they cut out my music further to an overture; last week I happened to see it on television and now my score is a commercial jingle!"

Both of us could not stop laughing for many minutes.

"Can you imagine what they did to my music?" Jobim laughed. "It's now a TV jingle like in a soap commercial."

We had another hour of pleasant conversation and giggles before saying goodbye. I was ready to leave for Europe and my concert music crusade on Friday 21 June 1974. I told Jobim that I would contact him upon my return in the autumn.

After I disembarked in Los Angeles September 1974, I went to see Jobim again, but the building manager told me that he had gone back to Brazil.

"Your friend, Mr. Jobim, is a nice man," said the building manager, "but he nearly scared the daylights out of me."

"How come?" I asked.

"There was big smoke comin' out of the kitchen window one day last summer, and somebody called the Fire Department. Seems he was all alone and had a few pieces of bread in his toaster which jammed and he forgot about it 'cause he was sitting at his piano workin' on a song until the firemen nearly broke down his door."

"That's the way he is," I smiled. "Perhaps we'll have another great Brazilian song called *Burnt Toast.*"

At that time Jobim lived at Rua Codajas 108 in the Leblon area of Rio de Janeiro and every once in a great while I would write him a comical letter or send him a program or recording of one of my concert performances.

Where the years fared, I have no idea. Except that it was not until 23 June 1986 that I noticed in the Los Angeles newspaper that Antonio Carlos Jobim would be appearing at the open air Greek Theater in a concert with his small Brazilian chamber ensemble that evening. I put on my suit; went to the Greek Theater; bought a ticket; and listened to the concert which was attended by a capacity audience of adoring fans and sprinkled with some Hollywood notables all of whom were not disappointed by the liberal renditions of Jobim's most favored songs. Jobim was always a distinguished interpreter of his own music even though he was not a performer in the show business sense. He genuinely did not like to operate in public and actually was never what the popular music industry considered as a working singer, pianist or guitarist. But what Jobim did with his limited dulcet masculine voice, the sparse chords and simple one note piano lines he injected into his sensuous arrangements and whatever few rhythmic Bossa Nova chords he knew on his foreign guitar were something to particularly marvel.

At the end of the concert I made my way to the artists entrance of the stage door where there must have been over two hundred friends, former acquaintances, industry executives, studio musicians, and admirers with their programs and recordings awaiting an autograph.

"I'm an old friend of Mr. Jobim's," I said to the young security guard who was wearing a business suit at the artists entrance.

"Mr. Jobim gave strict orders that he did not wish to see anyone after the concert," the security guard said.

"I have not seen him in twelve years," I said. "I'd hate to have come all the way here and go home without surprising him by at least saying hello."

The security guard sighed. "Look," he said. "Do you have a business card? All I can do is take your business card with these hundred others I'm holding in my hand here and give them to him."

"I don't have a business card," I said. "I'm a composer. Do you have a piece of paper and a pen I can write a note on?" I asked.

The security guard had neither a pen nor a piece of paper.

"Here," I said looking through my credit cards and pulling out my ASCAP (American Society Of Composers Authors & Publishers) plastic membership card. "Give him this."

The security guard went inside and locked the door behind him. While he was absent I spoke with a few young girls who were disappointed at the prospect of not having their Jobim record albums autographed. I was agreeably astonished to learn during this height of the rock 'n roll era that some of the more youthful generation treasured Jobim's sophisticatedly romantic songs as well.

Ten minutes later the security guard returned and told the crowd, "Mr. Jobim will not see anyone with the exception of this gentleman here," as he pointed my ASCAP membership card toward my hand.

I was relieved, but as the laments rang out as I went through the artists entrance of the stage door, I felt a little regretful for the fans, but less remorseful for the rest; many of whom were well known socialites, lyricists, record producers and recording executives ("The Machine") who had either been familiar with Jobim or had exploited him in the past.

I was directed to Jobim's suite of dressing rooms. The large outer reception living room was totally empty.

"Tom..?"

"I'm back in here, Felippe Lambro," I heard Jobim's rather wearied voice echoing from about two rooms away. "Back in here, Felippe Lambro. You are the only one, my friend. The only one I want to see. Back in here, Felippe..."

Finally, in the third room there he was slouched in his chair with a white towel around his neck. As I approached, he quickly got up, cast the towel on the table, and we affectionately embraced each other.

"How are you, my friend?" Jobim asked as he escorted me to the outer large reception room in front of his dressing room. "You look

355

very healthy."

"I'm still a Macrobiotic I said." Years before I had tried to influence Jobim into changing his diet and was amazed when he informed me that his parents in Brazil had adopted the Macrobiotic way of life; but he himself never did.

"Did you get my letters and my concert recording which I sent you?" I asked.

"Yes, thank you. I got everything, my friend."

"I was a little apprehensive because I did not hear from you and I've been reading in the newspaper how the mail is being stolen in Brazil."

"I have not been feeling too well, and my Doctor made me give up smoking," Jobim went on. "But I did receive everything. Don't worry. In Rio, I went to see the head of the post office; a very important government official who likes me and he personally guaranteed that all a person has to do is write Antonio Carlos Jobim, not even Rio, just Brazil and he said that I would get every piece of mail that is addressed to me."

"Gee," I said. "That's rather impressive."

"This guy is like the head Mafioso in the Brazilian post office, so everything you mail to me I will definitely get." Jobim said.

"I was so surprised to learn in the paper today about your concert," I said, "because I know how much you don't like to give concerts and tour."

"You are right," Jobim said motioning me to sit down as he returned to an easy chair. "But what can I do? My friends and family members in the orchestra need money and they pressure me every once in a while into touring so they can make enough money to live a few years without having to come to me for financial support. That's the only reason I'm giving these concerts. I have to help them."

Just then, one of Jobim's musicians came into the room and proceeded to dispute in Portuguese about the fact that Jobim should allow some of the people backstage to meet him. I agreed and mentioned the melancholy young girls who were patiently waiting for the possibility of seeing him and getting his autograph on their Jobim albums. Just then Jobim's second younger wife, Ana, whom he married in 1978, came in shouting at him in Portuguese about what I assumed was the same subject. Jobim introduced me to her, but even though she calmed down and smiled at me for an instant, she did not seem too lighthearted with Jobim and abruptly left.

I slightly rolled my eyes at Jobim and we laughed for a moment. I could see why Jobim had not wished to see anyone, because it was obvious that he was physically and mentally jaded and the additional matrimonial and professional nagging he was catching backstage just made him all the more reticent.

After a few minutes an onslaught of people filled the reception room. Lyricist, Norman Gimbel, who had rephrased the Portuguese words into English for a few of Jobim's early hits traversed his way to the front. Jobim stood up and was politely affable with Gimbel even though I had remembered in 1974 how Jobim could not comprehend why Norman Gimbel who had paraphrased the Portuguese words of Jobim's songs into English was receiving more performance royalties than Jobim was; especially, when Jobim revealed to me how much Norman Gimbel's English words did not suit him. This is probably why Jobim mentioned to Gimbel that the Japanese had recently paid Jobim $150,000 dollars for the commercial use of one of Jobim's tunes and $75,000 dollars for a license to use another. I was glad to hear that Tom Jobim's finances were coming up in the world because he certainly deserved it.

Another woman and I brought the young girls to the forehead of the crowd and presented them to Jobim who was absolutely charming and gave each of them warm inscriptions on their album covers.

Jobim introduced me to Ferde Grofe Jr. (the son of the prominent 1931 Grand Canyon Suite composer) and his South American wife Constanza who had met Jobim through mutual friends in Rio. I happened to inquire as to how Elizabeth was and Jobim said, "There she is right over there." We both looked at one another and I did not recognize her since in twelve years Elizabeth had lost all of her teen age baby fat and was a slender, taller, rather solidified young lady who had forgotten me. Elizabeth was one of the several back-up singers in the Jobim ensemble who also shook some maracas and other Latin percussion instruments to the Bossa Nova rhythms of her father's tunes.

A female member of the Brazilian Consulate approached Jobim after which he grabbed my arm and said, "Follow me, because we have to go to a reception the Brazilian Consulate is giving for me across the way in the next building."

Jobim with the help of security guards dragged me through the dense applauding crowd outside of the artists entrance and into an adjacent building where there was a far less crush of people with ample Brazilian food and drink.

There was an attractive Brazilian girl I met at the punch bowl whom I was trying to passively interest. And even though Jobim was immersed in a contrapuntal dialogue between the Brazilian Consulate and the

Consulate's attendants he absorbed the whole incident and later satirized it by telling the girl in my presence, "You had better watch out for this Italian Latin lover composer Felippe Lambro. He has broken the hearts of many women."

"Tom, how can you say that?" I moaned. "Don't you believe a word of what he's saying," I said to the Brazilian girl. "It's absolutely not true."

About thirty minutes later Jobim informed me that he had to go to the Brazilian Consulate's home for an hour or so and asked that I go with his son Paulo (Elizabeth's brother) and the Ferde Grofes and a few other people to the lounge of the Hotel Le Mondrian at 8440 Sunset Boulevard where Jobim and his troupe were staying and he would meet us there later.

We all arrived at Le Mondrian in several cars around eleven p.m. I had engaging conversations with Ferde and Constanza Grofe and Paulo Jobim. Ferde Grofe Jr. in addition to administering his late father's royalties, was president of his own documentary film company which, as I recall, specialized in aviation films. Paulo Jobim had the awkward task of trying to decide what it was he wanted to do in life as the son of perhaps Brazil's greatest musical treasure. I understand that Paulo had studied both architecture and art in Brazil working with famed architect Oscar Nemier who conceived the dazzling synchronous construction of capital Brasilia. Paulo Jobim had also furnished the art work to Jobim's Waters Of March album, and was studying music since he enumerated that he had had offers from Brazilian record companies to make some albums. He was a handsome and intelligent young gentleman and I hope that he has found his own identity other than that of being the stripling of Brazil's most sacred white cow.

As it was now approaching two a.m. I informed everyone that I was going home to sleep and to tell Tom Jobim that Felippe Lambro would not even wait up for Beethoven past two o'clock in the morning, even if Beethoven could be cloned and resurrected.

Realizing that Jobim, in all probability, did not get back to the hotel and to bed before five a.m. I waited until the following afternoon before telephoning him where we were able to have a confidential chat.

"How's Tereza?" I asked. "Give her my best."

"She's fine," Jobim replied. "We're still friends and speak practically every day on the telephone to the consternation of Ana who is very jealous."

"Jealousy is not good in any relationship," I said. "It's a sickness. Why the hell did you get married again, anyway?" I asked.

358

"Yes, you are right," Jobim said. "I should have torn up the contract."

We both laughed.

Jobim was a bit agitated over the fact that the major record stores in Los Angeles were not stocking his recordings.

"I went to Tower Records the other day," Jobim said. "And most of the clerks did not even know who I was until one young boy said, 'But Mr. Jobim why an important person such as yourself has to come in here to promote your recordings? The record company should be doing this.' Can you imagine Felippe? Tower Records hardly had any of my albums which people write me about and can't get."

"What can I say?" I said. "The same thing happened to Mozart and Chopin with their printed music. And Tower Records stopped carrying my two albums which are about to be cut from the catalog. So what can you do?"

Jobim was infinitely pleased over the fact that his music had been gaining a resurgence in Japan where the Japanese recording companies were remastering and reissuing many of his discontinued classic albums, and endeavoring to promote these sonically improved discs in other countries as well.

Jobim informed me of his new address which was Rua Sara Vilela 50, Rio de Janeiro and his new telephone numbers. He also gave me his address in New York City where he had taken an apartment at 30 East 85th Street for the purpose of having a little home there when he came to New York to make recordings and so that his two new children by Ana (Jose Francisco and Maria Luiza) could benefit from special schools in New York.

He also suggested again that I come and visit him in Rio and I told him that I would as soon as there was an opportunity in the insane activity of my endeavoring concert music career.

Jobim continued to admire the fact that I was still devoted to my craft as a symphonic and concert composer and although he never openly admitted it, I believe he wanted to have had a career similar to mine. "Felippe Lambro, you are a very brave man to function in the difficult field of classical music," he remarked to me several times over the years. "I wish I could write symphonies the way you do, but all I can write are these simple little songs."

"Will you stop saying that?" I would declare. "Your songs are art songs; masterpieces; little gems. They're as good as any of the songs Schubert or Gershwin ever wrote."

"You think so?" He would respond.

"I know so." I would say.

We spoke about how we had both missed our old dialogues, and the laughs we used to have here in Los Angeles and that I was hoping my concert manager of the time would secure some guest conducting engagements for me with some of the Brazilian symphony orchestras, so that I could have an immediate justification to go to Brazil and also call upon him.

When I asked what the symphonic musicians were like in Brazil Jobim replied, "They are the same all over the world with their little gold watches and protecting their instruments."

We talked about another project which I had been actively involved with since 1974; namely, the non-toxic natural cancer therapeutic Amitosin which had been discovered by an associate of mine, Dr. Wilburn Henry Ferguson, during the early 1950's as the result of Dr. Ferguson's plant extract research with the dreaded Jivaro Indians in the Amazon region of Ecuador. I was endeavoring to bring Amitosin and Dr. Ferguson to the general public by way of a book and then through a motion picture. At adequate dosage levels, Amitosin had on every occasion proven to totally prevent cancer cell proliferation. Not only were there no side effects with the therapy, but other substances within Amitosin so stimulated the immune system that normal growth quickly replaced the area of cancer destruction.

It wasn't until a few days after the first of January 1991, that I telephoned Jobim in Rio only to find out that he was at his apartment in New York City. We had our usual electronic visitation during which I discovered that in about eight weeks when I was scheduled to be in New York, Jobim would be back in Rio. "Who can fight The Machine?" I remarked to him.

Amid this conversation (during which Jobim proudly described the two new grand pianos he had recently purchased) I could tell that Jobim was not too enthusiastic about staying in New York City because he asked me to investigate the present environment in the California sections of Ojai, Santa Barbara and San Diego, and suggest to him which of those three cities I thought he would like best since he had been seriously contemplating about moving to one of them.

Several days later, I wrote Jobim a letter suggesting that he personally go to each of these towns and see for himself what they were like and then make his own decision. However, I informed him that personally I had always been partial to Santa Barbara because when I was twenty years

360

old, that is where I had had a scholarship to The Music Academy Of The West studying with Gyorgy Sandor. I also enclosed a recent article about the crime, poverty, and juvenile oppression in Rio de Janeiro from the Los Angeles Times which I knew would interest him. I encouraged Jobim to keep on composing and that I was expecting some good avant garde Bossa Nova songs from him with a lot of polyatonality and ninths.

Around December 1992, I telephoned Jobim in Rio and we had an extended colloquy during which I proposed that he become personally involved with my lifelong crusade against overpopulation. I indicated that in my opinion, all the infirmities of our society were related to, or stemmed directly from, overpopulation; and that if we had a mandatory worldwide govermental birth control policy of two people not permitted to have more than two children then the birth rate would come into balance with the death rate and this most assuredly would extinguish a large part of human suffering while saving the destruction of the Amazon; not to mention that two being equal to two, we then would be able to completely eliminate money and the profit motive thereby replacing it with optimum scientific excellence where everyone would be able to have the best of everything.

"Look, Tom," I said. "All these famous rock groups which go and give concerts in Brazil and raise millions of dollars to prevent the destruction of the Amazon Rain Forest just isn't working and will never work because it does not approach the core of the problem. These peasants who have in excess of three children and have an opportunity of making four dollars a day instead of one dollar if they cut down the Amazon trees, really don't know these rock groups and could care less about the Amazon."

"Yes," Jobim said. "They continue to cut the trees down in the Amazon so that Americans can have more briquettes to barbecue their steaks on."

I told Jobim that he was right. We Americans use over sixty percent of the earth's resources and that out of the developing countries, we are the fastest procreating nation in the world; and the third most populated behind China and India. This is the main reason for the environmental, sociological, and monetary breakdowns within our society.

I could tell that Jobim really enjoyed this talk because he again invited me to come to Brazil offering to pay for my whole trip. However, since I was knee deep in depositions in a law suit which I had filed over the film *Medicine Man* which was an obvious misappropriation of my literary and film property *Tsanza* based upon Dr. Wilburn Henry Ferguson's life (which was to be resolved October 1994) I apprised Jobim that as soon as my legal battles with "The Machine" were over, that I would definitely and specifically fly down to Rio and see him.

During April 1993, it seemed our laughable prophetic fantasy scenarios which we used to concoct during the 1970's regarding the MCA Tower ("The Machine") had become a reality. I wrote Jobim enclosing an article from the Los Angeles Times which explained how a disgruntled terminated ex-employee of MCA casually with a high powered rifle took up a position across the street and ambivalently fired 35 to 40 rounds of ammunition into the MCA Tower shattering the black tinted glass windows and causing pandemonium among the executives and secretaries who were crawling around on the floors before mighty mogul Lew Wasserman walked to each floor notifying everyone to get up because the assault was over. Fortunately, nobody was injured.

Early November 1994 I began to think about Tom Jobim quite often. He was in my thoughts practically four or five times each week and especially toward the beginning of December every day. I promised myself that either a few days before Christmas or a few days after the New Year, I would telephone him in Rio or New York City and advise him that I would be taking two weeks out of the automatic pilot in my treadmill and finally would be flying down to Brazil to see him after all these years.

At the beginning of December 1994 I was having dinner with a young University student named Mary at my apartment and she was admiring some framed musical mementos on the wall next to my concert grand piano of the major career performances which I had had, encompassing autographed photos from renowned musicians which included Jobim's assembled album inscription to me from 1973. Mary was not familiar with Jobim's music so before dinner I introduced her to a few of his recorded songs including *Photograph* which Jobim sang himself and which she highly enjoyed. At dinner I said to Mary, "I must telephone my friend Tom Jobim and finally go down to Rio and visit with him."

The next day, Mary called me saying, "Oh, Phillip, I heard on the radio that your friend Antonio Carlos Jobim has just died."

In a way, I was not ambushed by the news; but I was terribly disappointed with Jobim's passing. I found out that Jobim had been journeying back and forth from Rio to New York City mainly to visit doctors and hospitals. After being against performing a By-pass heart operation, doctors finally did an angio-plast after which Jobim died of heart failure at Mount Sinai Medical Center Thursday 8 December 1994. I understand that Jobim also was afflicted with cancer.

362

As I reflected over our last conversation December 1992, and the way he passively implored that I come and stay with him (even offering to pay for my trip which I told him was not necessary) I could sense now that Jobim (although he never disclosed this to me) as sensitive a person as he was, perhaps, inwardly savored the biological reality that within the not too distant future he would be faring off into the next dimension.

Although Jobim smoked cigarettes, and finally cigars; drank alcohol; and ate too many animal products; and whatever other minor faults he may have retained; because of his tremendously unique artistic musical contribution to the siring of Brazil's infectious Bossa Nova and Jazz Samba which gave so many people all over the world so much pleasure, including this concert and symphonic composer, I am hoping that my friends The Elohim Extraterrestrials (whom I have been in contact with since I was five years old and whom Jobim knew about because I gave him their Messages in both English and Portuguese) took his DNA cell just before his death and scientifically recreated Jobim on The Planet Of Eternals (as only they can with the relatively few people they have taken in 13,377 years from this primitive and unenlightened earth society) in a new third stage cloned perpetually young body where quite possibly he is now having a swinging time with six sexy biologically programmed females under a favorite fruit tree.